Ovid and Adaptation in Early Modern English Theatre

Ovid and Adaptation in Early Modern English Theatre

Edited by Lisa S. Starks

EDINBURGH
University Press

Edinburgh University Press is one of the leading university presses in the UK. We publish academic books and journals in our selected subject areas across the humanities and social sciences, combining cutting-edge scholarship with high editorial and production values to produce academic works of lasting importance. For more information visit our website: edinburghuniversitypress.com

Edinburgh University Press Ltd
The Tun—Holyrood Road
12(2f) Jackson's Entry
Edinburgh EH8 8PJ

Typeset in 11/13 Adobe Sabon by
IDSUK (DataConnection) Ltd, and
printed and bound in Great Britain

A CIP record for this book is available from the British Library

ISBN 978 1 4744 3006 7 (hardback)
ISBN 978 1 4744 3008 1 (webready PDF)
ISBN 978 1 4744 3009 8 (epub)

Contents

III. Affect, Rhetoric, and Ovidian Appropriation

IV. Ovid Remixed: Transmedial, Rhizomatic, and Hyperreal Adaptations

Permissions

Permission for the illustration *La Métamorphose d'Ovide figure*, A Lyon: Par Ian De Tournes, 1564, is courtesy of Rauner Special Collections Library, Dartmouth College Library. Permission for the image of *P. Ovidii Nasonis*, Antwerp, 1591, is courtesy of the Getty Research Institute, Los Angeles (92-B20688), via HathiTrust.

Acknowledgments

I would like to express my most sincere thanks to the contributors of this collection and my deepest gratitude to Jay Looney, my graduate research assistant, without whom I would never have been able to complete this volume in a timely manner. I would also like to thank the participants of my 2016 Shakespeare Association of America Seminar, Representing Ovid on the Early Modern Stage, especially M. L. Stapleton and Heather James; the supportive Shakespeare and adaptation community, particularly Christy Desmet (in loving memory) and Douglas M. Lanier; my English Program colleagues at University of South Florida St. Petersburg; the librarians of the Folger Shakespeare Library; and Michelle Houston, along with the editorial staff at Edinburgh University Press, for their guidance and assistance.

For My Father

Notes on Contributors

Jim Casey is Associate Professor at Arcadia University in Philadelphia. Although primarily a Shakespearean, he has published on such diverse topics as fantasy, monstrosity, early modern poetry, medieval poetry, textual theory, performance theory, postmodern theory, adaptation theory, old age, comics, anime, masculinity, Shakespeare, Chaucer, and *Battlestar Galactica*. He is the recipient of a National Endowment for the Humanities Grant, a Fulbright Grant, and coedited the critical collection *Shakespeare / Not Shakespeare* (Palgrave Macmillan, 2017) with Christy Desmet and Natalie Loper.

Simone Chess is Associate Professor of English and affiliate of Gender, Sexuality, and Women's Studies at Wayne State University in Detroit. She is the author of *Male-to-Female Crossdressing in Early Modern English Literature: Gender, Performance, and Queer Relations* (Routledge, 2016). With Will Fisher and Colby Gordon, she is coediting a special issue on "Early Modern Trans Studies" forthcoming from the *Journal for Early Modern Cultural Studies* (JEMCS). She is currently at work on a book about disability, queerness, and adaptation in the early modern period.

Jennifer Feather is Associate Professor of English and Women's and Gender Studies at the University of North Carolina Greensboro. She is the author of *Writing Combat and the Self in Early Modern English Literature: The Pen and the Sword* (Palgrave, 2011). She has also coedited a collection, *Violent Masculinities* (Palgrave, 2013), with Catherine E. Thomas. She is currently working on a monograph about the premodern roots of modern human rights discourse.

John S. Garrison is Associate Professor of English at Grinnell College, where he teaches courses on early modern literature and culture. He is the author of *Friendship and Queer Theory in the Renaissance* (Routledge, 2014), *Glass* (Bloomsbury, 2015), *Shakespeare at Peace* (cowritten with Kyle Pivetti, Routledge, 2018), and *Shakespeare and the Afterlife* (Oxford University Press, 2019). He is currently at work on a monograph about Shakespeare's sonnets.

Louise Geddes is Associate Professor of English at Adelphi University. She has published essays on Shakespeare in performance and adaptation. Her book publications include *Appropriating Shakespeare: A Cultural History of Pyramus and Thisbe* (Fairleigh Dickinson University Press, 2017) and *The Shakespeare User: Creative and Critical Appropriations in a Networked Culture* (coedited with Valerie Fazel, Palgrave, 2018). She is currently working on a monograph, *The Shakespeare Multiverse: Fandom as Literary Praxis*.

Ed Gieskes is Associate Professor of English at the University of South Carolina. He has published on Shakespeare, Greene, Jonson, Marlowe, Middleton, Kyd, and other playwrights. He coedited (with Kirk Melnikoff) *Writing Robert Greene: New Essays on England's First Notorious Professional Writer* (Ashgate, 2008), and is the author of *Representing the Professions: Administration, Law and Theatre in Early Modern England* (University of Delaware Press, 2006). He is completing a monograph on generic change in the sixteenth and seventeenth centuries.

Shannon Kelley is Associate Professor at Fairfield University, where she specializes in ecocriticism, Women's Studies, and English Renaissance literature. She recently received a Renaissance Society of America – Huntington Short Term Fellowship and a National Endowment for the Humanities Summer Seminar Fellowship in support of her current manuscript, *Wounded Trees and the Poetics of Trauma in the English Renaissance*, which investigates stories of women who become trees in early modern lyric.

Daniel G. Lauby is a Ph.D. student at the University of New Hampshire where he studies Shakespeare adaptation. His paper, "Sadomasochistic Cyclicality: Appropriations of Shakespeare's 'Dark Lady' Sonnets in Dickens's *Great Expectations*," was awarded the Rick Smith Memorial Prize for best graduate student essay and was published in the 2016 issue of *Selected Papers of the Ohio Valley Shakespeare Conference*. His current work explores appropriations of Shakespearean liminal spaces and the queering of early American nationalism.

Liz Oakley-Brown is Senior Lecturer in Premodern Writing and Culture at Lancaster University, UK. Her publications include *Ovid and the Cultural Politics of Translation in Early Modern England* (Ashgate, 2006) and the edited collection *Shakespeare and the Translation of Identity in Early Modern England* (Continuum, 2011). She is currently working on two book-length projects: premodern surfaces and Elizabethan life-writing and emotion.

John D. Staines is Associate Professor of English at John Jay College of the City University of New York. He has published essays on Spenser, Milton, Shakespeare, and the early modern passions, and has forthcoming work on Aphra Behn. He has published *The Tragic Histories of Mary Queen of Scots 1560–1690: Rhetoric, Passions, and Political Literature* (Ashgate, 2009). He is currently working on a project on sublime rapture in sixteenth and seventeenth-century literature.

Goran Stanivukovic is Professor of English at Saint Mary's University, Halifax, Canada. His books include *Knights in Arms: Prose Romance, Masculinity, and Eastern Mediterranean Trade in Early Modern England, 1565–1655* (University of Toronto Press, 2016); *Tragedies of the English Renaissance* (with J. Cameron, Edinburgh University Press, 2017); and two edited volumes of essays, *Queer Shakespeare: Desire and Sexuality* (Bloomsbury, 2017 hb. and 2019 pb.) and *Timely Voices: Romance Writing in English Literature* (McGill-Queen's University Press, 2017).

Lisa S. Starks is Professor of English at University of South Florida St. Petersburg. She has published essays and edited special issues on Shakespeare, cinema, Ovid, and related topics. Her books include *Spectacular Shakespeare: Critical Theory and Popular Cinema* and *The Reel Shakespeare: Alternative Cinema and Theory* (coedited with Courtney Lehmann, Fairleigh Dickinson University Press, 2002); and *Violence, Trauma, and* Virtus *in Shakespeare's Roman Poems and Plays: Transforming Ovid* (Palgrave, 2014). She is currently working on a monograph, *Shakespeare, Levinas, and Adaptation*.

Deborah Uman is Professor of English at St. John Fisher College. She has published numerous essays on women translators, and her book publications include *Women Translators in Early Modern England* (University of Delaware Press, 2011) and *Staging the Blazon in Early Modern Theatre* (coedited with Sara Morrison, Ashgate, 2013). Currently, she is focusing on radical adaptations of Shakespeare as well as the role of the humanities within institutions of higher education.

Catherine Winiarski is Lecturer in the Department of English at the University of California, Irvine. She has published on the religious and political significance of marriage and adultery in biblical texts, early modern religious tracts, and Shakespearean drama; she also researches and teaches animal studies and ecocriticism. Her current work concerns spousal and neighborly relations in the Hebrew Bible, the epistles of St. Paul, and Shakespeare's *Othello*.

Introduction: Representing "Ovids" on the Early Modern English Stage

Lisa S. Starks

When the clock strikes eleven and Faustus's moment of reckoning swiftly approaches, he feverishly calls out to halt the passing of time, conjuring the ghost of Ovid in a line appropriated from *Amores*: "*O lente, lente currite noctis equi!*" (xiii, 70).[1] This quotation, which Faustus utters frantically at this climactic moment in Christopher Marlowe's tragedy, generates multiple, disparate meanings in its old and new contexts: in Ovid's poem, the lines refer to the wish for lingering sexual intimacy; in Marlowe's play, the desperate plea for survival. The trace meanings from Ovid thus haunt the last hour of Faustus's miserable existence, characterized as it has been by his empty pursuit of unattainable desires. More generally, the quotation further tags Marlowe as the preeminent Ovidian poet-playwright of his age; and, seen in light of the multifarious, layered Ovidian appropriations throughout his writings, Marlowe's citation from *Amores* points to the rich complexity of textual and theatrical metamorphoses in this play and others. These Ovidian strategies of adaptation and appropriation[2] that Marlowe, Shakespeare, Jonson, and many other early modern playwrights employed shaped the early modern English theatre, which thrived at the height of the Ovid craze in the 1590s.

Following Marlowe's death, Ben Jonson resurrected him on stage by portraying him as the character Ovid in *Poetaster* (1601), which Ed Gieskes and I discuss in our chapters, and by lampooning him as an Ovidian poet in his satiric city comedy *Bartholomew Fair* (1614), both of which comment on the earlier Ovidian theatre now preserved in later theatrical memory. In the latter comedy, a dolt from the country named Bartholomew Cokes attends the fair bearing his name, where he is mesmerized by Lanthorne Leatherhead's puppet show – a sendup of Christopher Marlowe's *Hero and Leander* – even though he has no understanding of the poem or myth it parodies. In the show, Marlowe's *epyllion* (itself an adaptation of Musaeus with appropriations of Ovid) is remediated into a puppet show, in which the mythological characters and places are adapted to the everyday world: Leander a dyer's son, Hero a wench, Cupid a drawer, and the waterway separating the lovers the Thames rather than the Helles-pont. Jonson highlights the processes of adaptation in this parody by revealing how and why the characters appropriated this poem for the puppet stage. Earlier, Leatherhead had asked the incompetent play-wright, John Littlewit, to compose a play that would be accessible for his lowbrow audience, one that is "a little easy" and "modern for the times" (V, iii, 115–17, 120–21).[3] The result is the silly puppet show that transfixes audience members like Bartholomew Cokes.[4]

This puppet show, a meta-dramatic moment presented in the climax of this city comedy, functions in multiple ways: it satirizes Jonson's world and audiences, conjures the ghost of Marlowe's Ovid, and parodies the Ovidian practices of appropriation and adaptation on the early modern English stage. Inseparable from earlier Ovidian theatre, Marlowe, by this time, served as a stand-in for or representative of Ovid. And the puppet show itself, a bur-lesque of Marlowe's poem, humorously foregrounds the processes of textual and theatrical metamorphosis that had been associated with Ovid in the Renaissance – his poetry, tales, and characters – as well as numerous adaptations and appropriations of them, both on stage and off.

To explore these textual and theatrical metamorphoses, the chap-ters in *Ovid and Adaptation in Early Modern English Theatre* apply Shakespeare and adaptation/appropriation studies, in consort with other contemporary literary perspectives and cultural studies, to examine the multidimensional, ubiquitous role that Ovid and Ovid-ian transformations played on the early modern stage in England. They make interconnections to other contemporary theoretical approaches while building on previous studies of Ovid in Renais-sance drama – not to supplant earlier work or undermine previous methods, but rather to offer some fresh, alternative points of view on the plethora of adaptations and appropriations of Ovid in early modern English theatre.

1. Ovid and the Early Modern English Stage

As the poet of creative transformation, Ovid profoundly influenced the art, literature, and theatrical practices of the early modern period, leading to his widespread influence and his long, rich afterlife. Writers and artists adapted the subject matter of his poetry and appropriated his notion of metamorphosis in the invention of their own written and visual art. Ovid offered unconventional structures, methods, and perspectives – all of which enabled the stage to explore multifarious Ovidian transformations of mythological characters, tales, and themes that had permeated Renaissance literature in England and abroad.

In part, the prevalence of Ovid on the early modern English stage can be traced to the role of Ovid in humanist education in grammar schools, where students were immersed in studies of rhetoric and oratory, a close cousin of acting on the stage, and in acting at university.[5] John Lyly's court dramas and the university plays appropriated Ovid, as in the Cambridge play *The Second Part of the Return from Parnassus*, in which the character of Will Kempe complains that "Few of the University men pen plays, well, they smell too much of that writer Ovid, & that *writer* Metamorphoses."[6] Here, the university dramatist ridicules Kempe in this satiric jab at the public theatre as lowbrow entertainment. But, despite Kempe's protest, the public theatre – not just university plays – did greatly "smell" of that "writer Ovid" and *Metamorphoses*.

Indeed, the public theatre was immersed in Ovidian models. Writers like Marlowe and Shakespeare employed them to merge classical and native British dramatic conventions and preoccupations. Marlowe's *Doctor Faustus* is a perfect example of this fusion, in which the medieval morality play structure is incorporated into an early modern tragedy that is fully invested in probing and questioning Reformation theology and Renaissance humanist culture. Appropriating Ovid's *Metamorphoses*, playwrights like Marlowe and Shakespeare experimented with strategies of adaptation to blend elements, embed circular narrative structures, and construct temporal/spatial hybrids that flagrantly deny the strictures of time and place.

2. Ovid, *Imitatio*, and Adaptation

Ovid's innovative approach to appropriations, adaptations, and translations of inherited Greek and Roman material inspired Renaissance artists, for it spoke to their shared vision and the nature of mythology itself.[7] As Julie Sanders points out, "Mythical literature depends upon, incites even, perpetual acts of reinterpretation in new contexts, a process that embodies the very idea of appropriation."[8] Ovid himself fully developed these possibilities in transforming and appropriating earlier Greek and Roman mythology and legend. Of course, many classical authors besides Ovid, particularly Virgil, provided models for emulation and strategies for revisions of Greek myths. However, Ovid was different. His methods of remediating myths provided alternative strategies for Renaissance writers to employ in their own translations and adaptations of his poems.[9] In contrast to other ancient writers, the counter-classical Ovid offered more inventive choices of generic models and structures; more range in making the past present, the foreign domestic; more daring in his depiction of violence and grim humor, often reversing the roles of predator and prey; more freedom in attacking authority and mocking the gods; and less reverence for past heroes – amounting to a rejection of the dominant, heroic masculine values underpinning the Virgilian epic.[10]

In the early modern era, Ovidian metamorphosis propelled intertextual exchange, the translation and transmediation of texts across cultures and centuries, as realized through the extremely malleable yet common thread of myth. Ovid became virtually synonymous with this exchange, for authors "described the processes of translation and the adoption of figurative language as metamorphosis," as Miriam Jacobson has explained.[11] These writers also depended on a sophisticated understanding of the embedded, interconnected web of adaptations that Ovid himself fashioned from textual variations of those myths. They perceived a complex textual interplay between contemporary writing and that of antiquity, one that emphasized tension and discontinuity as well as tradition and continuity.[12]

Renaissance authors emulated Ovid and struggled to equal – or surpass – his Latin verse with their own vernacular. They drew from previous texts but revised them into completely new works through the process of *imitatio* – the deliberate emulation of identifiable stylistic characteristics and/or subject matter of a canonical author's texts in order to situate one's own literary texts alongside those of the past.[13] Tied to pedagogical practice and rhetorical study, *imitatio* involved a deep respect for the work of literary predecessors, but not a complete submission to it. A similar concept, *translatio* referred to the adaptation of texts to one's own contemporary world. A prime example of the latter is Ovid's own practice of revising past Greek myths to his own time and place, which Arthur Golding continued in his incredibly popular and influential "Englished" translation of *Metamorphoses* in 1567.[14] Moreover, early modern writers often grafted together pieces of myths, remediating and shifting genres, and constructing new myths in a process called *transvestitio*.[15]

Ovid was especially influential in the Renaissance practices of *imitatio* and *translatio* because of his unique uses of them as a poet. Ovid often rebelled against the texts he appropriated, undercutting the perceived sanctity of revered works by deliberately overturning their established form and content. In his *Metamorphoses*, Ovid critiques Virgil's *Aeneid* and Augustinian patriarchal values through the poem's circular structure, multiple narrative perspectives, and shifts from the epic hero to minor characters (often victims). In so doing, Ovid in this poem employs *imitatio* to undermine and challenge the idea of *imitatio* itself – taking the rivalry aspect of emulation so far that he defies the concept by its own use. Ovid thus overhauled *imitatio* for future generations by questioning its goals, practices, and underlying ideology – making him an audacious and daring choice for an early modern writer's own experimental appropriations. Ovid's rebellious strategies for textual transformations enabled Renaissance writers to go further in their own: to adapt more loosely and creatively; to undercut an earlier text and/or its values even while refreshing it in a new context; and to appropriate models in which the origin (the author's "original" to be imitated) virtually disappears. Significantly, Ovid gave writers the license to defy the work of a canonical author, even if that author was Ovid himself. In the Renaissance, it became very Ovidian to mess with Ovid.

In their own use of this classical terminology, early modern writers demonstrated and often self-consciously focused on processes that now fall under the rubric of contemporary adaptation or appropriation studies, as well as classical reception studies (described below). Pointing out the similarities between adaptation and classical *imitatio*, Linda Hutcheon explains that both processes are creative, for "[l]ike classical imitation, adaptation also is not slavish copying. It is a process of making the adapted material one's own. In both, the novelty is in what one *does with* the other text."[16] Similarly, outlining the processes and goals of classical reception studies, Lorna Hardwick points out that the "reception of classical texts" is nothing new, not "just a modern phenomenon," for it existed in antiquity. As she notes, classical writers and artists "were also engaged in this type of activity – refiguration of myth, meta-theatrical allusion, creation of dialogue with and critique of entrenched cultural practices and assumptions, selection and refashioning in the context of current concerns."[17]

Nevertheless, the past and present terms "adaptation" or "appropriation" and "*imitatio*" or "*translatio*" are not synonymous. *Imitatio* and *translatio* both denote a writer's conscious textual strategies;

whereas, contemporary concepts of appropriation and adaptation may include either conscious or, importantly, unconscious textual borrowing. There are contrasting definitions of the terms "appropriation" and "adaptation" in this field.[18] Julie Sanders argues that with appropriation, the new text is further distanced from its source than with an adaptation, for instance.[19] I am following Christy Desmet and Sujata Iyengar, who see the two terms working along the same spectrum, with a "difference in degree rather than kind."[20] In my usage, "adaptation" refers to a larger scale intertextual engagement, whereas "appropriation" suggests smaller scale or more obscure intertextual engagement. The two can and do occur simultaneously. Therefore, like reception studies, adaptation or appropriation studies – when employed alongside classical rhetoric used by Renaissance writers, with a clear distinction between when classical and modern concepts are employed – can enable a rich analysis of intertextual relationships that both fall within and exceed the definitions of *imitatio* or *translatio*. Moreover, contemporary theory makes it possible to discuss intertextual transformations that may be both directly or indirectly attributed to "Ovid" – his poetry and adaptations or appropriations of it, as well as his complex afterlife.

3. Classical Reception Studies and Adaptation/ Appropriation Studies

Drawing from similar critical backgrounds, both classical reception and adaptation studies have addressed the necessity of using contemporary lenses to view premodern textual exchanges and transformations, analyzing them in their own original contexts as well as subsequent ones in which revised versions of these texts resurfaced. Both fields emerged out of poststructuralist theories, which challenged previous notions that a work (literature or other) has a fixed, monolithic meaning and that a canon, tradition, or legacy follows a clear, linear, path that should be examined in isolation from cultural contexts. Both have also developed along parallel trajectories. Breaking new ground, Charles Martindale initiated classical reception studies in *Redeeming the Text* (1993);[21] Christy Desmet and Robert Sawyer introduced appropriation to Shakespeare studies in *Shakespeare and Appropriation* (1999); Hardwick set the parameters and identified the goals of classical reception studies further in *Reception Studies* (2003); Linda Hutcheon theorized the framework for future adaptation studies in *A Theory of Adaptation* (first published in 2006); Julie Sanders examined the distinctions and interrelated meanings of "appropriation" and "adaptation" in *Adaptation and Appropriation* (2006); and Hardwick and Christopher Stray revisited the term "tradition" in light of contemporary classical reception studies in *A Companion to Classical Receptions* (2008).[22]

As such, both classical reception and adaptation/appropriation studies overlap on some of their concepts and theoretical underpinnings, even though they function as separate fields that have not necessarily been in direct dialogue with each other. They share poststructuralist notions of the text, as mentioned above, both stressing the nuanced distinctions in meaning that texts generate within various contexts and for disparate uses; they both concentrate on the transformation of texts, the intertextual relationships between them, and the remediation of them into newly generated texts; and they share some terminology (such as "adaptation" and "appropriation"), although sometimes with slightly different stipulated definitions for particular terms.[23]

Nevertheless, there are some important dissimilarities between them, so much so that, in my view, each field could benefit from a mutual exchange with the other. As Douglas M. Lanier has pointed out, Shakespeare and adaptation/appropriation studies has been conflicted over issues of fidelity in past years, often bogged down with analyses of the adaptation versus the "original," rather than the multiple variances of the adaptation in its own right, or in reference to other adaptations. He praises current work that focuses more on the adaption's attention to "the cultural politics of reception."[24] Although he does not make a connection to classical reception studies in this description, Lanier seems to be using it in a similar sense. In classical reception studies, the term refers to "the ways in which Greek and Roman material has been transmitted, translated, excerpted, interpreted, rewritten, re-imaged and represented," according to Hardwick and Stray.[25] Despite this conception of intertextual transformations and fluid textual meanings, however, classical reception studies still tend to insist on an identifiable source – tangible material being "received" – even if that source's meanings are transformed by its various receptions in its own time and future cultural moments. The necessity of a clear source in classical reception studies becomes evident in analyses of drama, since theatrical performance slips away from any sense of an "established 'text'" per se, as Hardwick has pointed out.[26] Although performances are still examined from the perspective of classical reception studies, the focus of this field remains on the reception of a discernible text in its own or later contexts.

Conversely, contemporary adaptation/appropriation theory, particularly in Shakespeare studies, stresses the elusive nature of any kind of "original" text or source, as often new texts are not necessarily generated from that source but also later variations on it. Moreover, as Margaret Jane Kidnie has argued, variations shape or, in a sense, create what is then later considered to be the "original" source material. She explains that "no *a priori* category that texts and stagings are a production *of*"[27] exists, for "[t]he work, far from functioning as an objective yardstick against which to measure the supposed accuracy of editions and stagings, whether current or historical, continually take shape as a *consequence* of production."[28] Classical reception studies also examine how the source material is refashioned by subsequent receptions, which are consequences of later productions, but that source material itself tends to be conceived of as more tangible to begin with.

4. Ovid and Shakespeare Adaptation/ Appropriation Studies

Although Shakespeare and adaptation or appropriation theory shares much in common with classical reception studies and the larger field of adaptation studies, it differs in some crucial respects, mainly in its approach to the pervasive and manifold nature of its particular subject. It is important to note, however, that the field is by no means monolithic. On the contrary, it encompasses several approaches, some with shared underlying theoretical foundations, others with contrasting ones. In his broad overview of Shakespeare and adaptation or appropriation studies, Lanier breaks down the field into these general models:

> Foucault's discursive model, which stresses the interconnection between particular discursive modes of truth-making and legitimation, and the institutional agents of those modes; the arboreal model, in which "the Shakespearean text" serves as originary root and all other works are derivative offshoots; the rhizomatic model in which "Shakespeare" is a network of adaptations through a series of decentered relationships or relays, a network with nodes but no originary center (Lanier, "Shakespearean Rhizomatics"); the actor-network model, which places stress upon the aggregated agency of individual producers within the network but remains agnostic on the question of a textual center.[29]

Depending on the model used, most current Shakespeare and adaptation/appropriation studies tend to fall in line with Lanier, whose own use of Gilles Deleuze and Félix Guattari's theory of the rhizome from *A Thousand Plateaus* challenges the arboreal model.

Recent theory sees Shakespearean adaptations and appropriations, as well as the playtexts (quartos and folios) themselves, as plural, connected in a kind of network or web of interconnections without a fixed sense of origin or a discernible, linear intertextual chain or line of influence. Seen from these perspectives, Shakespeare becomes "Shakespeare," a term that encompasses not only writings attributed to William Shakespeare, their performances, and receptions of them, but also everything connected to or stemming from Shakespeare or Shakespearean adaptations that are marked as "Shakespeare" or not.[30] Indeed, adaptations or appropriations may be unconsciously made because of the ubiquitous, spectral presence of Shakespeare on so many cultural levels of culture now and at previous historical moments. Recent Shakespeare and adaptation/appropriation studies have underscored the need for further inquiry into the question of what does or does not constitute "Shakespeare," which is now an important matter of debate in the field.[31]

So, why use Shakespeare and adaptation/appropriation studies to examine Ovid on the early modern English stage? Similar in many ways to Shakespeare since the eighteenth century to the present, Ovid – and Ovidian methods, themes, characters, tales, and so on – permeated Renaissance culture and art, as explained above, and consequently became a pervasive, underlying force in the creation of theatre in early modern England. As in Maurizio Calbi's description of Shakespearean spectrality, phantom Ovids haunted the early modern stage, with a spectral presence that flickered in and out of plays and helped to shape conceptions of the theatrical experience.[32] Just as there is a "Shakespeare," as noted above, there is an "Ovid," with multifarious, interconnected appropriations and adaptations throughout the early modern era. Although most criticism on Ovid in the Renaissance has stemmed either from traditional scholarship or from classical reception studies,[33] the chapters in this volume employ and adapt Shakespeare and adaptation/appropriation theory to explore these multilayered Ovidian transformations that proliferated on the early modern English stage – both the marked and unmarked. The goal is not to replace classical reception studies with that of Shakespeare and adaptation/appropriation, but rather to provide readings that complement or stand alongside others, to offer additional points of view – some of which may overlap in some ways, others not.

5. Ovid and Adaptation in Early Modern English Theatre

Using Shakespeare and adaptation/appropriation studies, these chapters explore "Ovid" in early modern English theatre while making new connections between this field and other contemporary perspectives. The book is divided into four parts according to the critical approaches employed in each: "Gender/Queer/Trans Studies and Ovidian Rhizomes," "Ovidian Specters and Remnants," "Affect, Rhetoric, and Ovidian Appropriation," and "Ovid Remixed: Transmedial, Rhizomatic, and Hyperreal Adaptations." There are theoretical and thematic interconnections between chapters within each section and also across sections. They deal with Shakespeare to a large extent, given the full and diverse range of his Ovidian appropriations – and, of course, Marlowe – along with Ben Jonson, Thomas Heywood, John Lyly, Mary Sidney Herbert, and Edvardus Fuscus (most likely a pseudonym, author of an obscure closet drama).

Part I, "Gender/Queer/Trans Studies and Ovidian Rhizomes," features chapters that examine intersections between Lanier's use of Deleuze and Guattari's theory of the rhizome and gender, queer, and trans studies in early modern Ovidian adaptations and appropriations. In "Queer Gender Informants in Ovid and Shakespeare," Simone Chess uses a combination of gender/queer/trans and disability studies with Lanier's rhizomatic theory to explore the "queer gain" generated by characters that serve as "queer informants" in plays such as *Antony and Cleopatra*. Chess argues that Shakespeare uses these characters to "work through . . . his own early modern gender issues" and, in so doing, he "anticipates our modern trans and gender theories." For Chess, the trans codeswitching that occurs in Shakespeare's appropriations of Ovid's most non-normative characters is similar to that of rhizomatic adaptation, characterized by "underground, disorderly connections," which "creat[e] a web of recognition, identification, and resource-sharing across genres, iterations, and generations." Like Chess, Shannon Kelley likens the rhizome to ways that Ovid was adapted for the early modern stage. In "Women in Trees: Adapting Ovid for John Lyly's *Love's Metamorphosis* (1589)," she maps this theory onto ecofeminist and history of the book perspectives. For Kelley, Lyly strengthens Ovid's feminism by presenting "different ways of deploying Ovid [that] reject the literary trope of a mute, tree-locked Daphne and challenge mainstream understanding of the arboreal model of textual adaptation" that Lanier's rhizomatic theory contests.

Daniel G. Lauby also employs this theory of rhizomatic adaptation, grafting queer theory onto Lanier's notion of projection in relation to questions of fidelity. In "Queer Fidelity: Marlowe's Ovid and the Staging of Desire in *Dido, Queen of Carthage*," Lauby uses Lanier's theory to argue that "Marlowe reconstructs the classical Ovid through a 'projection,'" the refashioning of a "precedent through appropriative selection."[34] For Lauby, Marlowe uses strategies of appropriation to transform the queer elements of Ovid's poetry into his play. Lauby contends that in *Dido*, "the play's staging of desire utilizes visibility and remembrance through homoeroticism, gender reversal, and bodily dissonance to demonstrate fidelity to the queer ideologies of Ovid's texts." Dissonance, coupled with rhizomatic "becoming," factors in Deborah Uman's chapter on early modern appropriations of Ovid's Salmacis and Hermaphroditus as well. For Uman, Hermaphroditus becomes the "figure . . . for practices of appropriation," following Lanier's and Desmet's conceptions of adaptation as "potentiality" and "virtuality." In "'Let Rome in Tiber melt': Hermaphroditic Transformation in *Antonius* and *Antony and Cleopatra*," Uman sees the oscillating senses of "becoming" and "difference" at play in Ovid's tale and its appropriations in Shakespeare's tragedy and Mary Sidney Herbert's translation of Robert Garnier's closet drama. Through these appropriations, Uman examines the "theme of gender fluidity and the practice of literary transformations," with both plays denouncing "masculine rigidity" in favor of "a more flexible view of gender and artistic creativity."

Part II, "Ovidian Specters and Remnants," shifts the focus from rhizomatic theory to those dealing with specters, afterlives, and remnants. In "Ovid's Ghosts: Lovesickness, Theatricality, and Ovidian Spectrality on the Early Modern English Stage," I adapt Maurizio Calbi's concept of Shakespeare's contemporary spectrality, based on Derridean "hauntology," to Ovid in the early modern era. I explore Ovid as an icon of lovesickness and theatricality, with interconnections between these terms, in early modern representations of and debates on the theatrical experience itself. My analysis moves from the height of Ovidian theatre to its shadowy afterlife – focusing primarily on Shakespeare's *Romeo and Juliet*, Jonson's *Poetaster*, and the obscure interregnum closet drama *Ovids Ghost* – to explore the uncanny returns of spectral Ovids in related discourses concerning metamorphic illusion and the "self-shattering effects of painful love." John S. Garrison also employs Derridean hauntology to analyze the "undead," or what is "neither living nor dead," in "Medea's Afterlife: Encountering Ovid in *The Tempest*." Garrison likens

Shakespeare and Prospero to Ovid and Medea, arguing that, for Prospero, "the spectralization of older elements in Prospero's speech bolsters his power and instantiates how 'appropriation is intrinsic to building a self.'"[35] He suggests that Shakespeare's play and later film adaptations are made richer when one "trace[s] . . . the phantom presence of Ovid." Catherine Winiarski continues this sense of Ovidian afterlives, but through a different theoretical lens and metaphor. In "Remnants of Virgil, Ovid, and Paul in *Titus Andronicus*," she uses Hutcheon and Gary R. Bortolotti's "On the Origin" to theorize the relationship between "ancestor" and "descendant" texts, in which "narratives [function as] as 'replicators' that seek to adapt to various cultural environments through concrete 'vehicles.'"[36] She adds competition among narratives to this theory in addressing the "survivor" or "remnant" in Shakespeare's play and in Renaissance practices of adaptation. In addition, she analyzes how the remnants of earlier, pre-Christian Roman culture is adapted to "a Protestant Christian environment rooted in the texts of St. Paul."

In Part III, "Affect, Rhetoric, and Ovidian Appropriation," the chapters consider appropriations of Ovid that engage emotion through language in plays that are both unmarked and marked as Ovidian adaptations. Jennifer Feather treats the former in "Power, Emotion, and Appropriation in Ovid's *Tristia* and Shakespeare's *Henry V*," employing work by Desmet, Elizabeth Rivlin, and Alexa Huang in addressing questions of ethics, appropriation, and authority in rhetorical strategies that buttress political power. Focusing on two texts – Ovid's *Tristia* and Shakespeare's *Henry V* – she analyzes "the role of affect in the operation of imperial power . . . in two contexts on the cusp between shifting forms of government." In "Appropriating Ovid's Tyrannical Raptures in *Macbeth*," John D. Staines addresses language and emotion as well, but in terms of *raptus*, which he sees as "as a figure for appropriation." Staines explores "words" that "share with desire the terrifying power to carry the mind and body to extremes of feeling." Like Feather, Staines here investigates an unmarked Ovidian play through rhizomatic theory (as well as hauntology), exploring how Shakespeare appropriates Ovid through words that strive to "speak the unspeakable." Goran Stanivukovic discusses language and emotion in "Ovid and the Styles of Adaptation in *The Two Gentlemen of Verona*" as well, but in relation to amatory discourse rather than political or violent rhetoric and in a play more clearly marked as "Ovidian." Stanivukovic examines the "complex and often complicated relationship between adaptation, appropriation, and imitation" in early modern drama, arguing that Shakespeare appropriates strategies from Ovid's Heroidean verse-epistle to fashion the "emotional interiority" of his characters, to endow "affective immediacy to the lover as a speaking subject" in *Two Gentlemen of Verona*. Thus, for Stanivukovic, Shakespeare adapted Ovid to form his own "poetic discourse of love within a culture of literary appropriation."

Part IV, "Ovid Remixed: Transmedial, Rhizomatic, and Hyperreal Adaptations," includes chapters that examine strategies of adaptation, various ways in which Ovid was appropriated and transmediated in early modern theatre. In "'Truly, and very notably discharg'd': The Metamorphosis of Pyramus and Thisbe and the Place of Appropriation of the Early Modern Stage," Louise Geddes addresses the multifaceted network of Ovidian adaptations and transmediations by focusing on Shakespeare's appropriation of Ovid's Pyramus and Thisbe in *A Midsummer Night's Dream* as a focal "transmedial remix," one through which Shakespeare provides a model for "treat[ing] remixed material." She uses Lanier and fandom theory to explore the "rich network" of Ovid's tale, which demonstrates the playwright's own adaptive strategies and "displace[s] the notion of a core canonical text, instead imagining a de-territorialized text that allows practitioners the liberty of tapping into the 'spirit' of Shakespeare or Ovid, through a complex, and often abstract network of associations."[37] Liz Oakley-Brown analyzes this complex rhizomatic interplay in "The Golden Age Rescored?: Ovid's *Metamorphoses* and Thomas Heywood's *The Ages*," describing Elizabethan and Stuart England as "a kind of Ovidian plateau," in Lanier's words, a "space where particular meanings or energies temporarily intensify and 'territorialize.'"[38] Oakley-Brown argues that Heywood's *Ages* become a "self-vibrating region"[39] of concentrated "Ovids." Written before the binary of original/copy was solidified, *Ages* create an "adaptation before-the-letter," one that "chime[s] with (rather than cite[s]) Ovid's *Metamorphoses*." The *Ages* depend on the interplay within the dualities of "classical / not classical" and "Ovid / not Ovid" – similar to Shakespeare / not Shakespeare in Desmet, Loper, and Casey's work – and decenter the binary of "original / copy" in a constant state of rhizomatic becoming.

The final two chapters switch from rhizomatic theory to alternative approaches drawn from Hutcheon and Jean Baudrillard. Focusing on issues of adaptation and translation, Ed Gieskes employs Hutcheon's definition of translation as a "recoding of a communication act into a new set of conventions"[40] to examine early modern playwrights' translation as adaptation. In "'*Materia conveniente modis*': Early

Modern Dramatic Adaptations of Ovid," Gieskes demonstrates how Ovid's *materia* – in terms of "technique" or "structure" as well as subject matter – is adapted and appropriated in the works of Jonson, Shakespeare, and Marlowe. For Gieskes, these dramatists "move between adaptation and appropriation as they translate classical work, model their new productions on those works, and deploy the representational resources of the varied traditions that they draw on and work with." In the closing chapter, "Worse than Philomel, Worse than Actaeon: Hyperreal Ovid in Shakespeare's *Titus Andronicus*," Jim Casey comments on the state of adaptation theory and its use in examining ways Shakespeare appropriates Ovid, particularly in representing "'unspeakable,' 'obscene,' and 'irreligious acts'" while "consider[ing] the very act of adaptation itself." In so doing, Casey questions Lanier's rhizomatic theory, claiming that it erases the agent who appropriates, and instead draws from Jean Baudrillard's notion of the *simulacra* to analyze adaptation as "hyperreal." For Casey, adaptors do not actually draw from the "real" text or writer like Shakespeare, but rather from what they imagine "the indispensable *qualia*" of it to be. Casey uses his theory to analyze the way that Shakespeare employs "hyperreal Ovids" to explore traumatic "unspeakable" acts in *Titus Androncius*.

Taken all together, these chapters offer different, often complementary angles from which one may approach the rich, multifarious adaptations and appropriations of Ovid in early modern English theatre. As the icon of transformation itself, Ovid provided the subject matter and model for adaptations that, in part, created the remarkable theatrical events that characterized the experience of playgoing in Elizabethan and Jacobean England. The phantom of Ovid that haunted the Renaissance stage celebrated, critiqued – and, above all, appropriated – the power of metamorphic illusion that was inextricably bound up in the idea of "Ovid."

Notes

1. Marlowe, *Doctor Faustus*. The line translates as "Oh, run slowly, slowly, horses of the night." It is somewhat altered from Ovid's *Amores*: "'*lente currite, noctis equi!*'" (I, xiii, 40), which in context refers to the lover's request that a night of lovemaking never end. Ovid, *Delphi Complete Works of Ovid*. Marlowe translated *Amores* as *All Ouid's Elegies*.
2. For a definition of these terms, see below.
3. Jonson, *Bartholomew Fair*.

4. I am indebted to Sarah K. Scott for reminding me of Jonson's parody as an example of adaptation in her unpublished essay, "'Modern for the Times': Barry, Marlowe, and Ovid."

5. See Cartwright, *Theater and Humanism*, and Enterline, *Shakespeare's Schoolroom*.

6. Anon., *Return from Parnassus*, p. 337.

7. Some portions of the following section are adapted and revised from my essay, "Ovidian Appropriations."

8. Sanders, *Adaptation and Appropriation*, p. 63.

9. See Burrow, "Re-embodying Ovid," p. 302.

10. See Starks-Estes, *Violence, Trauma, and* Virtus, pp. 3–18.

11. Jacobson, *Barbarous Antiquity*, p. 11.

12. Bate, *Shakespeare and Ovid*, pp. 84–7.

13. Ibid. p. 131.

14. On Golding's "Englishing" of Ovid, see Lyne, *Ovid's Changing Worlds*, p. 19.

15. See Lafont, "Introduction," p. 2, and Starks-Estes, *Violence, Trauma, and* Virtus, p. 10.

16. Hutcheon, *A Theory of Adaptation*, p. 20.

17. See Hardwick, *Reception Studies*, p. 4.

18. For an overview of these definitions, see Desmet and Iyengar, "Adaptation, Appropriation, or What You Will."

19. Sanders, *Adaptation and Appropriation*, pp. 17–41.

20. Desmet and Iyengar, "Adaptation, Appropriation, or What You Will," p. 7.

21. On the impact of this text in Renaissance studies, see Hardie, "*Redeeming the Text*"; on the field of classical reception studies, see especially Martindale, "Introduction," and Hardwick, *Reception Studies*, pp. 1–11; for an overview of the field, see De Pourcq, "Classical Reception Studies."

22. Desmet and Iyengar provide an excellent, brief overview of Shakespeare and adaptation/appropriation studies in "Adaptation, Appropriation, or What You Will"; and Douglas M. Lanier examines the past and current state of the field, especially in relation to fidelity issues, in "Afterword." For a general overview of adaptation studies, see Cutchins, Krebs, and Voigts, *The Routledge Companion to Adaptation*.

23. On terminology in classical reception studies, see Hardwick, *Reception Studies*, p. 9.

24. Lanier, "Afterword," p. 303.

25. Hardwick and Stray, *A Companion*, p. 1.

26. Hardwick, *Reception Studies*, p. 51.

27. Kidnie, *Shakespeare and the Problem*, p. 9.

28. Ibid. p. 7.

29. Lanier, "Afterword," p. 295.

30. On "unmarked adaptations," see Lanier, "Afterword," p. 300.

31. See Desmet, Loper, and Casey, *Shakespeare / Not Shakespeare*, pp. 1–22.
32. See Calbi, *Spectral Shakespeares*, pp. 1–20. In our chapters, both John Garrison and I adapt the Derridean concept of hauntology and Calbi's Shakespearean spectrality to Ovid in early modern theatre.
33. A recent notable exception is Badir, McCracken, and Traub, *Ovidian Transversions*. See especially the Introduction (pp. 1–14), which employs Lanier's theory in examining Ovidian transformations.
34. Lanier, "Afterword," p. 299.
35. Garrison, p. 113 in this volume, quoting Desmet and Iyengar, "Adaptation, Appropriation, or What You Will," p. 5.
36. Winiarski, p. 129 in this volume, quoting Hutcheon and Bortolotti, "On the Origin," p. 447.
37. Geddes, p. 204 in this volume, quoting Lanier, "Afterword," p. 299.
38. Oakley-Brown, p. 226 in this volume, quoting Lanier, "Shakespearean Rhizomatics," p. 29.
39. Lanier, "Shakespearean Rhizomatics," p. 29.
40. Hutcheon, "From Page to Stage," pp. 40–1.

Bibliography

Anon., *Return from Parnassus*, in J. B. Leishman (ed.), *The Three Parnassus Plays, 1598–1601* (London: Nicholson & Watson, [1601] 1949).

Badir, Patsy, Peggy McCracken, and Valerie Traub (eds), *Ovidian Transversions 1350–1650* (Edinburgh: Edinburgh University Press, 2019).

Bate, Jonathan, *Shakespeare and Ovid* (Oxford: Clarendon Press, 1993).

Burrow, Colin, "Re-embodying Ovid: Renaissance Afterlives," in Philip Hardie (ed.), *The Cambridge Companion to Ovid* (Cambridge: Cambridge University Press, 2002), pp. 301–19.

Calbi, Maurizio, *Spectral Shakespeares: Media Adaptations in the Twenty-First Century* (New York: Palgrave Macmillan, 2013).

Cartwright, Kent, *Theater and Humanism: English Drama in the Sixteenth Century* (New York and Cambridge: Cambridge University Press, 1999).

Cutchins, Dennis, Katja Krebs, and Eckart Voigts (eds), *The Routledge Companion to Adaptation* (New York and London: Routledge, 2018).

De Pourcq, Maarten, "Classical Reception Studies: Reconceptualizing the Study of the Classical Tradition," *The International Journal of the Humanities* 9.4, 2012, pp. 219–25.

Desmet, Christy, Natalie Loper, and Jim Casey (eds), *Shakespeare / Not Shakespeare* (New York: Palgrave Macmillan, 2017).

Desmet, Christy and Sujata Iyengar, "Adaptation, Appropriation, or What You Will," *Shakespeare* 11.1, 2015, 1–10.

Desmet, Christy and Robert Sawyer (eds), *Shakespeare and Appropriation* (New York and London: Routledge, 1999).

Enterline, Lynn, *Shakespeare's Schoolroom: Rhetoric, Discipline, Emotion* (Philadelphia: University of Pennsylvania Press, 2012).

Hardie, Philip, "*Redeeming the Text*, Reception Studies, and the Renaissance," *Classical Receptions Journal* 5.2, 2013, pp. 190–8.

Hardwick, Lorna, *Reception Studies* (Oxford: Oxford University Press, 2003).

Hardwick, Lorna and Christopher Stray, *A Companion to Classical Receptions* (Malden, MA and Oxford: Blackwell, 2008).

Hutcheon, Linda, "From Page to Stage to Screen: The Age of Adaptation," in Michael Goldberg (ed.), *The University Professor Lecture Series* (Toronto: University of Toronto Press, 2003).

Hutcheon, Linda and Gary R. Bortolotti, "On the Origin of Adaptations: Rethinking Fidelity Discourse and 'Success'—Biologically," *New Literary History* 38.3, 2007, pp. 443–58.

Hutcheon, Linda with Siobhan O'Flynn, *A Theory of Adaptation*, 2nd edn (New York: Routledge, 2013).

Jacobson, Miriam, *Barbarous Antiquity: Reorienting the Past in the Poetry of Early Modern England* (Philadelphia: University of Pennsylvania Press, 2014).

Jonson, Ben, *Bartholomew Fair*, E. A. Horsman (ed.), Revels Plays edn (New York and Cambridge, MA: Methuen and Harvard University Press, 1960).

Kidnie, Margaret Jane, *Shakespeare and the Problem of Adaptation* (London and New York: Routledge, 2009).

Lafont, Agnès, "Introduction," in Agnès Lafont (ed.), *Shakespeare's Erotic Mythology and Ovidian Renaissance Culture* (Farnham and Burlington: Ashgate, 2013).

Lanier, Douglas M., "Shakespeare / Not Shakespeare: Afterword," in Christy Desmet, Natalie Loper, and Jim Casey (eds), *Shakespeare / Not Shakespeare* (New York: Palgrave Macmillan, 2017), pp. 293–306.

Lanier, Douglas, "Shakespearean Rhizomatics: Adaptation, Ethics, Value," in Alexa Huang and Elizabeth Rivlin (eds), *Shakespeare and the Ethics of Appropriation* (New York: Palgrave Macmillan, 2014), pp. 21–40.

Lyne, Raphael, *Ovid's Changing Worlds: English Metamorphoses, 1567–1632* (Oxford: Oxford University Press, 2001).

Marlowe, Christopher, *Doctor Faustus*, in Roma Gill (ed.), *The Complete Works of Christopher Marlowe*, vol. II (Oxford: Clarendon Press, 1990).

Marlowe, Christopher, *Hero and Leander*, in Roma Gill (ed.), *The Complete Works of Christopher Marlowe*, vol. 1 (Oxford: Clarendon Press, 1987).

Martindale, Charles, "Introduction: Thinking through Reception," in Charles Martindale and Richard F. Thomas (eds), *Classics and the Uses of Reception* (Malden, MA and Oxford, Victoria: Blackwell, 2006), pp. 1–13.

Martindale, Charles, *Redeeming the Text: Latin Poetry and the Hermeneutics of Reception* (Cambridge: Cambridge University Press, 1993).

Ovid, *Delphi Complete Works of Ovid*, Delphi Classics, Kindle edn (Kindle Location 32713).

Sanders, Julie, *Adaptation and Appropriation* (London and New York: Routledge, 2006).

Starks, Lisa S., "Ovidian Appropriations, Metamorphic Illusion, and Theatrical Practice on the Shakespearean Stage," in Christy Desmet, Sujata Iyengar, and Miriam Jacobson (eds), *The Routledge Handbook of Shakespeare and Global Appropriation* (New York and London: Routledge, forthcoming).

Starks-Estes, Lisa S., *Violence, Trauma, and* Virtus *in Shakespeare's Roman Poems and Plays: Transforming Ovid* (Basingstoke: Palgrave Macmillan, 2014).

Part I

Gender/Queer/Trans Studies and Ovidian Rhizomes

Chapter 1

Queer Gender Informants in Ovid and Shakespeare

Simone Chess[1]

In Ovid's *Metamorphoses*, Jupiter and Juno call on Tiresias, who has lived both as a man and a woman, to adjudicate their argument about male and female pleasure in sex; in Shakespeare's *Antony and Cleopatra*, Cleopatra interrogates the eunuch Mardian about the nature of his affections, and Mardian later speaks as an authority on Cleopatra's feelings after her supposed death. In both cases, genderqueer – even possibly transgender – characters are seen to be experts on sex, gender, and romance because of their boundary-crossing bodies and lived experience. Shakespeare adapts characteristics and strategies from Ovid's most non-normative characters (Tiresias, Caenis/Caenus, Iphis) in creating some of his own queerest roles (Mardian, Portia/Balthazar, Viola/Cesario), designing them to serve as valuable gender informants. Inspired by Ovid and other classical traditions, Shakespeare positions his eunuchs and crossdressers as codeswitchers who are especially poised to make crucial judgments and give critical insights. Following Ovid's use of queer figures as gender informants in the *Metamorphoses*, these characters' representation reveals a kind of "queer gain" for the plays, where the informant's knowledge and experience are often beneficial cruxes in the development of other characters and plots.

In these instances of queer adaptation, then, Shakespeare generates what Douglas Lanier calls "rhizomatic networks" between his influences, himself, and his readers.[2] Shakespeare appropriates from Ovid an understanding of queerness as a benefit and a strategy; he echoes Ovid by making his queer characters informants and agents of action and knowledge; he adapts less the story of any one character than that character's type or feeling; he adapts their queerest elements, still recognizable in their essence, for his own use. Further, as gender informants, the characters themselves enact a kind of adaptative translation, crossing between genders and reporting their insights. In adapting Ovid in a rhizomatic way, Shakespeare not only imitates Ovid's work, but also imitates the queerest elements of Ovid's methodologies, the act of *transvestio*, which Lisa S. Starks-Estes describes as a "method of collecting, reassembling, and revising sources gathered from a broad spectrum of texts and traditions."[3] The characters, too, experience a kind of trans codeswitching, either literal or figurative, as they disassemble and reconfigure their genders, reporting to their audiences as they go. In borrowing the Ovidian attitudes towards non-normative gender and sexuality and, with them, a model of queer gain through trans/cross gender experience, Shakespeare works through his own early modern gender issues and also anticipates our modern trans and gender theories, in which nonbinary and trans gender informants allow for a richer, more complex, queerer view of gender in general. Shakespeare's use of Ovid's queer models is an adaptation without strict fidelity.[4] But the rhizomatic, underground, disorderly connections are there, creating a web of recognition, identification, and resource-sharing across genres, iterations, and generations.

To understand Shakespeare's adaptation of Ovidian queer gain, I am borrowing from two critical discourses in queer and disability studies. First, the idea of "gender informants" emerges from a common discourse about trans and gender nonbinary individuals: the expectation that, since they have experienced social and cultural norms from the position and perspective of being read as male *and* female, they have special insight or knowledge about the machine of gender and sexuality in society. While this concept has been discussed in academic sources,[5] it is especially striking and pervasive in popular culture. Take, for example, the provocative heading of a 2016 *Time Magazine* article about trans men:[6] "Cultural sexism in the world is very real when you've lived on both sides of the coin."[7] In a different online article from 2015, James St. James confirms the trope of the trans gender informant: "Having been treated as both a man and a woman, these privileges are glaringly obvious to me. And there are far, far too many to count."[8] Articles like these see trans perspectives as special, more insider, and they suggest that, because transmasculine individuals have experienced sexism as women and as men, they are uniquely situated to do the gender informant work of confirming misogyny and male privilege.[9]

I draw the language of queerness, and genderqueerness specifically, as *gain* from the emerging Deaf Studies concept of "Deaf Gain," which has since been expanded to "disability gain" more broadly. By theorizing deafness as a gain rather than a loss, H-Dirksen L. Bauman and Joseph M. Murray have argued that deafness can be a benefit not only for deaf individuals (intrinsic value), but can also potentially "contribute to the general good of humanity" (extrinsic value).[10] For many queer and genderqueer people, the language of intrinsic and extrinsic deaf gain articulates a familiar feeling. Andrew Solomon describes the common ground of gain:

> I am well-placed to recognize Deaf Gain, because I am gay. Most straight people wouldn't wish to be gay, just as most hearing people wouldn't wish to be deaf, yet both gay culture and Deaf culture are cherished by those who participate in them.[11]

The synergy between queer, trans, and disability cultures, in terms of struggle and exclusion but also gain and social benefit, has generated a rich and growing range of queer and disability theory and analysis motivated by recognition and dual identification.[12]

The queer gain in Shakespeare's plays grows out of his rhizomatic adaptation of Ovidian gender informants, who model this exact ethos of utopian possibility and capaciousness. Some of the most memorable episodes in the *Metamorphoses* center on genderqueer or trans or nonbinary characters whose genders embolden and enrich episodes celebrating their insights and authority. In these cases, Shakespeare has only a queer fidelity to Ovid. Instead of strict adaptation, he is in conversation with Ovid's themes and tropes, revisiting and revising the meanings and manifestations of queer practice in the worlds of both texts. Following Ovid, Shakespeare experiments with staging three genderqueer types: the omniscient bigender truth-teller, the genderqueer adjudicator and avenger, and the alluringly androgynous youth. The reiterative effect of adaptation amplifies the importance of characters such as these, whose queerness not only makes the text more fabulous but also enables and enhances the plot.

Ovid provides the archetypal demonstration of queer gain in his description of Tiresias, who, having struck a pair of mating snakes, was "made a woman straight" and "seven winter lived so" (III, 409).[13] Though Tiresias finds and strikes the mating snakes again in his eighth year as a woman and is then "straight return'd his former shape in which he first was borne" (III, 414), the rest of the episode makes it clear that there is not much that is "straight" about the situation. Even if Tiresias looks the same externally when he returns to his former shape, he has obviously been transformed by his experience of living as a woman. And so, famously, when Jove and Venus disagree about whether men or women better enjoy sexual pleasure, "To trie the truth, they both of them agree / The wise Tyresias in this case indifferent judge to bee, / Who both the man and womans joyes by tryall understood" (III, 403–5). This passage, as it is translated by Golding, is striking in two queer ways: first, rather than assuming that Tiresias is suspect because of his trans-gender experience, the gods take it as a given that his experience makes him an optimal and impartial "indifferent" judge.[14] Second, the gods make the glorious assumption that Tiresias's gender-informing knowledge will come from first hand sexual experience as a man *and* a woman; the poem celebrates his queer gender and the queer sex acts that it enabled (all the while normalizing queer sex in the first place), and then it further recognizes that gendered knowledge to be a valuable and much-needed asset.

Serving as gender informant, Tiresias reveals that, based on his "tryall," he thinks that women enjoy the most pleasure in sex; though he is punished by Venus with blindness, he earns from Jove "sight in things to come" to make up for it. The gods gain from his experience and adjudication, and he benefits from the psychic gift for the rest of his life. If Tiresias's queerness informs and serves the gods, then the queerness of Mardian, Cleopatra's eunuch in *Antony and Cleopatra*, offers the same to his queen. A minor queer character with major impact, Mardian distinguishes himself as a special confidant with unique access to Cleopatra's thoughts and plans.[15] Though Mardian is male, because he is a eunuch he is frequently staged among Cleopatra's intimate circle of maids.

At ease in this situation and able to codeswitch between flirting with the queen and being one of the girls, Mardian's most notable scene is in Act one, scene five where Cleopatra asks him to talk with her about sex, in an erotically charged dialogue that Oriana Palusci refers to as "spicy."[16] When Mardian asks, "What is your highness' pleasure?" (I, v, 8),[17] Cleopatra responds, "Not now to hear thee sing; I take no pleasure / In aught an eunuch has: 'tis well for thee, / That, being unseminar'd, thy freer thoughts / May not fly forth of Egypt. Hast thou affections?" (I, v, 9–12). Like Jove and Venus before her, Cleopatra is curious about what a genderqueer informant can tell her about love, sex, and desire.[18] In his answer, Mardian not only responds to Cleopatra's question – he does, indeed, have affections – but also, like Tiresias, undercuts the idea that a queer body is deprived of robust sexuality. If Tiresias, when he was a woman, went right ahead with "tryalls" to understand female sexuality and sexual pleasure, so too does Mardian, after his castration, continue to think and feel sexually, even lasciviously. And he's proud to report on it, to a fascinated (and possibly aroused) queen.

Distinguishing between sex act and sex thoughts and informing the queen about eunuch affections, Mardian reports, "Not in deed, madam; for I can do nothing / But what indeed is honest to be done: / Yet have I fierce affections, and think / What Venus did with Mars" (I, v, 15–18). The fact the Mardian's erotic thoughts focus on classical gods, and on Venus in particular, seems an overt nod from Shakespeare to the influence of classical queers in this gender informing role – while Mardian is not a faithful adaptation of Tiresias, he enacts Tiresias's function. While Mardian isn't called upon to adjudicate the nature of male and female desire and attraction on Cleopatra's behalf, her discussions with him do help her to think through her own complex relationship with Antony. Enslaved and castrated, Mardian is restricted even as he is granted respect and access. Yet, despite being able to "do nothing," he finds freedom and autonomy in his fantasy life; he is, as Ellis Hanson puts it, "at once freed and imprisoned by his castration."[19] In this way, Cleopatra's questions to Mardian thus are more than teasing or flirtation; as a queer figure he can inform her own position, in which she simultaneously has great power and freedom *and* is tremendously restricted by her gender and race, by logistics, by the law, and by Antony's whims. What Mardian offers in this scene, perhaps, is a solution grounded in queer gain: at this moment, Cleopatra cannot act on her desires, at least not to the extent that she wants; but she can, potentially, use the substitute of fantasy to meet her needs temporarily.

Cleopatra takes up Mardian's offer. Immediately after he confesses his erotic classical fantasy, even stychomythically sharing the line where he describes his fantasy, Cleopatra tries her own hand at fantasy, asking Charmain to help her imagine where Antony is at that moment, what he is doing, and how he looks:

> Oh Charmain,
> Where think'st thou he is now? Stands he or sits he?
> Or does he walk? Or is he on his horse?
> O happy horse, to bear the weight of Antony!
> Do bravely, horse, for wo'tst thou whom thou mov'st?—
> The demi-Atlas of this earth, the arm
> And burgonet of men. He is speaking now,
> Or murmuring "Where's my serpent of old Nile?"—
> For so he calls me. Now I feed myself
> With most delicious poison. (I, v, 18–27)

From her interview with Mardian, Cleopatra gains the practice of imaginative erotics, which she puts to work in creating and recreating her vision of Antony – standing, sitting, walking and riding. Through the imagined horse, she meditates on the weight of Antony, on the sensation of being ridden by him. She amplifies his form, thinking of his body and comparing him to classical centerfold-muscle-man Atlas. And she imagines him, not speaking, but murmuring his sweet talk to her. Learned from Mardian, her fantasy is a "delicious poison" that elevates her affections even when she can't act on them. In this scene, like Mardian, she is "chaste and honest indeed, but he is obscene by virtue of his [and, I'd add, her own!] imagination."[20]

Mardian's final scene comes in Act four, scene fourteen, when Cleopatra has been rejected by Antony and makes her panicked plan to fake suicide. Addressing Mardian by name, she commands him, "Mardian, go tell him I have slain myself; / Say, that the last I spoke was 'Antony,' / And word it, prithee, piteously. Hence, Mardian, / And bring me how he takes my death" (IV, xiv, 7–10). That Cleopatra selects Mardian to be her messenger is another sign of Shakespeare's use and adaptation of Ovidian queer gain. As a eunuch, Mardian is masculine enough to approach Antony, but not so masculine as to be a threat; he is feminine enough to speak for Cleopatra and to channel her "piteous" tone, but not so feminine as to be overlooked or put at risk. Indeed, though Antony calls Mardian a "saucy eunich" (IV, xv, 25), he listens to his speech and believes him. Though Mardian is lying, he delivers his speech poetically and dramatically; he channels something of Tiresias's prophetic vision, and, like Tiresias, his bigender status gives him authority. After conveying Cleopatra's message, Mardian does not speak again in the play; as Anston Bosman reports,

> in the final scene he stands silent and unmentioned. Most modern editors, in fact, alter the folio entry direction and remove Mardian from Act five, scene two entirely. The joke is irresistible: How does a queen (or an editor) treat a eunuch? By cutting him off.[21]

But Mardian's role in *Antony and Cleopatra* is more than a joke, whether or not he is on stage at its conclusion, because Mardian isn't simply presented as a man who has been castrated, cut. Like Tiresias, he speaks for both masculinity and femininity, with the ability to understand and adjudicate the affairs of powerful lovers. Mardian is lying when he piteously describes Cleopatra's suicide. But, at least according to the Folio, he is on stage when he sees his prophetic vision manifest, when Cleopatra kills herself with Antony's name on her lips, just as the eunuch promised.

Mardian is, to my knowledge, the only eunuch with a speaking role in Shakespeare. In place of the castrated male gender informant, Shakespeare further practices abstract adaptation of Ovidian queer gain in other plays through the figures of female-to-male (FTM)/transmasculine crossdressers, Shakespeare's most noted strategy for drawing attention to queer gender.[22] Among Shakespeare's male-presenting crossdressers, Portia is an outlier. Keith Geary, for example, claims that "Portia's disguise, unlike those of the other heroines, reveals no interest in exploring the psychological consequences of a sexual disguise,"[23] while Jean E. Howard calls Portia's crossdressing "more disruptive" than Viola's because "Portia is not so stereotypically feminine a subjectivity."[24] It is true that, when Portia crossdresses as the Doctor of Law Balthazar, there is a notable dearth of sexual punning, an unusual attention to her actual work, and, though she is motivated by her relationship with Bassanio and his with Antonio, little flirtation or sexual play. Only the ring scenes in the play's conclusion come close to approximating the overt queer play of crossdressing episodes like Viola's in *Twelfth Night* or Rosalind's in *As You Like It*, and even there Portia's and Nerissa's easily fooled husbands are the butt of the joke rather than Portia and Nerissa themselves, the crossdressing wives.[25]

The very aspects that make Portia different from Shakespeare's other crossdressers offer another rhizomatic connection to Ovid and queer gain. Her cross-gender presentation is motivated by her desire to right a wrong: she hatches her plan after confirming with Bassanio the exact nature of his debts and the exact risks faced by Antonio in court. Despite telling Lorenzo that she plans to "live in prayer and contemplation" (III, ii, 28), Portia immediately begins her plan to pass as male and take care of the problem herself as Balthazar. Describing her intended transformation, Portia tells Nerissa that they will be "in such a habit / That they shall think we are accomplished / With what we lack" (III, ii, 61–3). While the line suggests that the "lack" they will be hiding is phallic, more emphasis should be placed on the idea of crossdressing to overcome a lack of "accomplishments," including credentials and authority. Thomas C. Bilello argues that, by converting herself into a man, "Portia converts the law into an instrumentality of her will."[26] Portia is confident in her ability to steer her own fate (as she does in the casket game), but without cross-gender expression, she can't prove her credentials or authority beyond her own domestic sphere.

Portia's actual judgments have dubious merit, but no one doubts her authority and intelligence in the courtroom as Balthazar, however misdirected or unethical. I want to hold open the possibility, then, that Shakespeare designs the plot to include crossdressing not only because it allows Portia access to the all-male courtroom but also because queering her character, having her appear to the audience as both female and male with both masculine and feminine rhetorical and ideological attitudes, operationalizes the Ovidian mode of queer gain. In taking action and authority over the outcomes in the play in order to seek her own brand of justice, enabled by crossdressing, Portia's trial scene follows the logic of Ovid's Caenis/Caenus episode in Book 12 of *Metamorphoses*. Like Portia, Caenis (Ceny in Golding's translation) is introduced as a beautiful daughter whose father's plan to marry her off is failing. She has had a "store of wooers who in vayne / In hope to win her love did take great travail, suit and payne. / . . . But Ceny matcht with none" (XII, 215–19). Caenis doesn't find a Bassanio to resolve her marriage problem, though; instead, when she is walking alone, Caenis is raped by Neptune. Offered retribution, she demands that he transform her into a man:

> The wrong heere doone to mee
> (Quoth Ceny) makes mee wish great things. And therfore to th' entent
> I may no more constreyned bee to such a thing, consent
> I may no more a woman bee. And if thou graunt thereto,
> It is even all that I desyre, or wish thee for to doo.
> In bacer tune theis latter woordes were uttred, and her voyce
> Did seeme a mannes voyce as it was in deede. For to her choyce
> The God of sea had given consent. (XII, 224–31)

Caenis is transformed to Caenus before she completes her wish, her voice deepening even as she speaks. In fact, Golding's Ovid grammatizes the transformation, using feminine pronouns in line 230 ("for to *her* choyce") and masculine pronouns in the next line, where "he [Neptune] graunted *him* [Caunus] beside," with the additional superpower of being impervious to steel.

Where Portia disguises herself to gain the authority necessary to address a wrong perpetuated against Bassanio, Caenis' gender transformation is more like the personal defense system adopted by more-typical-for-Shakespeare Rosalind and Viola. Still, there is a rhizomatic connection between the two characters. Both understand being female to be limiting their safety and control over their choices. And so both make use of their transformations to effect serious judgments with serious consequences, setting to right problems that they understood but couldn't correct before. They bring the biases and opinions from their female experience into their decisions as men, decisions that they make when they are no longer "constrayned" by the limitations of being female. Transformed into men who are informed by having been women, both Portia/Balthazar and Caenis/Caenus seek extreme reparations from men. In these instances, Ovidian queer gain looks less like transgender omniscience and wisdom and more like gender-queer vigilantism, in which queer and trans context informs the ways wrongs are corrected in cis-masculine social spheres.

Portia-as-Balthazar manipulates the legal system toward literal benefits for her new husband and his friend; in doing so, she also makes a grand gesture that proves to Bassanio that she will always have the upper hand in their marriage. Her cold mercy may not be traditionally feminine, but it's a perversion of the exclusively male space of the court; her approach to legal analysis is as queer as her gender as she sits on the bench, a boy pretending to be a woman pretending to be a man pretending to be a judge. Though almost no modern readers or audiences are satisfied by Portia's judgment, the character claims to be; she tells Bassanio, "I, delivering you, am satisfied, / And therein do account myself well paid" (IV, i, 410–11).

As for Caenis's revenge, in this case Ovid is less direct than Shakespeare. At the end of Caenis/Caenus's story, Caenus risks his life – and, ultimately, loses it – in the Battle of Lapiths and the Centaurs. Though it isn't explicit, the scene can be understood as linked to Caenus's queer-gender origin story, in that he dies in part because he is interrupting a potential rape. In this part of Book 12, just as he is building up to the epic battle in which Caenus is a star, Ovid interrupts Nestor's battle narrative for a digression about a pair of centaur lovers, Hylomene and Cyllarus. Beautiful, monogamous, and truly devoted to one another, these lovers set an example for loving, consensual, mutual love. Though they are heterosexual, the fact that they are centaurs queers the erotic description of their love; as Jeri Blair DeBrohun describes it, the Hylomene/Cyllarus digression looks closely "both at these hybrid creatures and at hybridity itself."[27] The hybridity, then, draws a connection between the centaur lovers, whose very embodiment is both human and animal, and Ceanus, who had experienced both female and male embodiment and experience.

When the fight resumes following Nestor's lush ekphrastic descriptions of these lovers, Cyllarus suddenly falls, killed by a dart to his heart; immediately Hylomene is moved to suicide. But at the same time as she is moving to kill herself in an act of love, the battle around her is becoming violent and holds the threat of sexual violence; for example, Nestor reports that "Cymelius threw a dart / Which lyghted full in Nesseyes flank about his privie part" (XII, 498–9). Among the many fighters mentioned, Hylemone is the only beautiful female. In this context, Ceanus emerges as the strongest fighter in the battle, at one point singlehandedly killing five men. His intensity here functions as a kind of judgment against those who might have harmed Hylemone, had she not killed herself, and also against those whose violence interrupted her consensual love and replaced it with violence. In the end, Caenus's victory is short-lived; the angered Latreus kills him by burial in a heap of timber. Still, before his execution, Ceanus defends his own honor and, at least in theory, tries to protect Hylomene or seek vengeance on her behalf. In doing so, he defends both Hylomene's feminine chastity and her hybrid animal–human body, judging both worthy of protection. In the end, Nestor eulogizes Ceanus as "a valeant knight" (XII, 587). Born a woman, possibly motivated in battle by his female experience and priorities, he dies a man. As Nestor puts it, "The straungenesse of the cace made all amazed that it sawe" (XII, 550).

If, in the rhizomatic network of connections between Ovid and Shakespeare's queer characters, Tiresias and Mardian demonstrate queer gain as truth tellers, and if Portia/Balthazar and Caenus/Caenis show it through magnified powers of judgment and vengeance, then a final pairing, Iphis and Viola/Cesario, displays the potential for queer gender experiences to inform and explode love and romance. In these episodes within *Metamorphoses* and *Twelfth Night*, queerness generates, rather than limits, desire and romantic empathy. Iphis's transition from female to male is perhaps the most captivating of the many transformations in the *Metamorphoses*. Because Iphis's father has threatened to kill his newborn child if it is not a son, when Iphis is born female, her mother, Teluthusa, lets her husband "beleeve it was a boay" (IX, 833). Keeping Iphis's sex a secret, the mother raises the child "unperceyved" and in garments that "were a boayes" (IX, 839). As a teen, Iphis falls in love with Ianthee, "a wench of looke demure" (IX, 842), and they plan to wed. Iphis meditates at length on the situation:

Herself a Mayden with a Mayd (ryght straunge) in love became.
Shee scarce could stay her teares. What end remaynes for mee (quoth shee)
How straunge a love? how uncoth? how prodigious reygnes in mee?

If that the Gods did favor mee, they should destroy mee quyght.
Or if they would not mee destroy, at least wyse yit they myght
Have given mee such a maladie as myght with nature stond,
Or nature were acquainted with. (IX, 853–8)

And yet, rather than dwelling on the seeming impossibility of her situation, Iphis's first impulse is to add a second apparent impossibility to the first, proposing a trans solution to a queer problem. She wonders whether Daedalus, "with all his conning crafts" could "now make a boay of mee?," and further asks, "Or could he, O Ianthee, change the native shape of thee?" (IX, 873–4). Iphis ultimately believes that this sex change solution cannot happen, setting it aside and replacing with the unhappy resolution to follow her father's will by marrying Ianthe with the caveat that their marriage will be chaste, and therefore torture. Still, when Ovid concludes the episode by enacting the very sex change that Iphis imagined, the fact that the trans solution is, apparently, possible, has the further queer effect of undermining the pat assumption that the same-sex marriage would have been impossible in the first place.[28]

Finally, on the day of the wedding, in response to Teluthusa's most desperate prayer for her child, the gods act. Ovid itemizes Iphis's transformation, which is surprisingly general:

And Iphys followed after her [Teluthusa] with larger pace than ay
She was accustomed. And her face continued not so white.
Her strength increased, and her looke more sharper was to sight.
Her hair grew shorter, and she had a much more lively sprite,
Than when she was a wench. (IX, 923–7)

Though we are to understand that Iphis experiences a bodily, anatomical change, what Ovid gives us is not so different than any one of Shakespeare's descriptions of female characters crossdressing as male. Iphis adjusts his gait, becomes less fair, feels stronger, sees more clearly, and feels more spirited; as for his hair, its magical shortening is no less wondrous than the fact that he hadn't had it cut in a masculine fashion while he was passing for male. Just as his father never inspected his body at birth, we readers are prevented from examining it now. Our gaze is limited to less-than-secondary sex characteristics, more aspects of gender presentation or disguise than actual indicators of sex. At the same time, the poem leaves no doubt that Iphis's transformation is real, and no indication that sex change should be anything other than miraculous and beneficial for everyone involved.

In a memorial plaque commemorating Iphis's miracle at the end of Book 9, we read:

> The vows that Iphys vowd a wench he hath performd a Lad.
> Next morrow over all the world did shine with lightsome flame,
> When Juno, and Dame Venus, and Sir Hymen joyntly came
> To Iphys mariage, who as then transformed to a boy
> Did take Ianthee to his wyfe, and so her love enjoy. (IX, 933–7)

At the end of his queer narrative, Iphis celebrates his trans-gender experience as one that heightens his love and commitment. His vows and their performance are doubled in meaning because of his two forms. Their queer wedding is witnessed by gods. Ovid celebrates the queerness of Iphis's union, and gives every indication that Iphis's disguise and transformation, rather than perverting her marriage, will make it special, sexy, and sacred.

Shakespeare adapts elements of these attitudes toward queer impossibilities without fidelity to the Iphis plot, in *Twelfth Night* through Viola's crossdressing as Cesario. Of Shakespeare's crossdressers, Viola is perhaps the queerest. Jeffrey Masten has demonstrated that, even when she takes on her disguise, Viola/Cesario evades gendered categorizations:

> I want to remind us that Cesario – this boy played by a woman played by a boy – is indicated in this play through a range of categories, from "boy" to "man" (including "youth"), categories whose relationships with each other is neither mutually exclusive nor always logically developmental (boy *to* man), nor entirely systemic.[29]

In a similar vein, Cristina Malcomson has discussed Viola/Cesario's multiple and overlapping relationship dynamics, which similarly evade simple categorization, suggesting that "Viola's relationship to Orsino includes both that of woman to man and that of servant to master."[30] In sum, Jean Howard calls Viola "the woman who can sing both high and low, and who is loved by a woman *and* by a man, . . . a figure who can be read as putting in question the notion of fixed sexual difference."[31] Viola/Cesario is queer protagonist who resists and complicates binary distinctions, showing knowledge and expertise about both and bringing that knowledge to bear on the plot. For the audience watching her seamless transition from boy actor to eligible woman to androgynous youth and almost back to eligible woman again, Viola/Cesario is a gender informant, who (not unlike Iphis) puts perspectival knowledge to work toward gain and satisfaction.

When Viola first takes up her disguise she is described as a eunuch, and Orsino describes Cesario's "small pipe," a descriptor of both a small penis and feminine vocal range, both of which are "semblative of a woman's part" (I, iv, 31, 33). This description forces a recognition that the results of Viola's crossdressing are never seamless masculinity, but instead marked by ambiguous characteristics and anatomical incongruities. Though Orsino appears to be mocking Cesario's appearance and masculinity here, in fact, he finds great merit in the page's androgyny, which makes him the ideal surrogate suitor to Olivia. Orsino sees Cesario as a gender informant, and he aspires to queer gain through his messenger's success. Shakespeare is copious in showing off Viola/Cesario's skill as a gender informant who decodes and interprets masculine and feminine rules and norms. With Orsino, s/he engages in heady discussions on age differences in marriage and whether men or women feel love most deeply (II, iv). In this discussion, Viola/Cesario easily switches back and forth between her male and female voices ("we men say more," II, iv, 115; "I am all the daughters of my father's house," II, iv, 119), reminding herself, Orsino, and the audience of her queer perspectives in matters of gender and love.

At the end of *Twelfth Night*, in a betrothal that echoes Iphis and Ianthe's queer wedding, Orsino pledges to marry Viola by speaking to her as Cesario: "Cesario, come— / For so you shall be while you are a man; / But when in other habits you are seen, / Orsino's mistress, and his fancy's queen (V, i, 372–5). Like Iphis for Ianthe, Viola's queerness is a benefit, a gain, rather than a loss for Orsino. Her disguise and her ensuing trials deepen the veracity of her love and elevate their connection.

The trouble with queer adaptation, rhizomatic and unfaithful, is that there's no clear path of attribution, no acknowledgment of influence. But Tiresias and Mardian, Caenus and Portia, and Iphis and Viola are nevertheless interconnected, in conversation. They are marvels, mechanisms for exploration and information, sources of unabashed desire. When Shakespeare looks to Ovid to find and lend legitimacy to these queer gender informants, he also participates in codifying Ovid's gender informants, multiplying their presence and rendering their capacity for queer gain visible and familiar to his audiences. Adapting less the details than the essence, Shakespeare uses the authority of Ovid to animate queer and trans tropes in his texts, even when the adaptation is abstract; in turn, we do the same to Shakespeare, reading his plays and poems with an eye for recognition of those same queer and trans types.

Notes

1. Many thanks to Lisa Starks, for including me in this collection, for her good editorial feedback, and for teaching me everything I know about adaptation studies; I am grateful to John Garrison for introducing us and for convincing me that I had something to say about Ovid. At home in Michigan, Valerie Traub has been a generous and insightful reader.
2. Lanier, "Shakespearean Rhizomatics," pp. 21–40.
3. Starks-Estes, *Violence, Trauma, and* Virtus, p. 10. See also Lafont, "Introduction," p. 2.
4. The adaptation-studies term "fidelity" is especially rich in the context of queer approaches to adaptation, because queer culture and communities have often unsettled definitions of fidelity by validating and including polyamory and other types of nonmonogamy alongside other models for relationships. For more on Shakespeare and (in)fidelity, see Lanier, "Afterword," pp. 293–306.
5. To offer just a small sample of academic discussions that engage, at least in part, with the idea of trans subjectivity and the perspectives it enables, see Enke, *Transfeminist Perspectives*; Nadal et al., "Emotional, Behavioral, and Cognitive Reactions"; Whitley, "Trans-kin Undoing and Redoing Gender"; and Hines, *Transforming Gender*.
6. While transmale and transmasculine perspectives on gender and feminism have often been praised and fetishized, for transwomen and transfeminine individuals, the idea of being a queer gender informant has more frequently been discussed in negative ways; for more on transfeminist responses to trans exclusion from feminism, see Serano, *Whipping Girl*, and Koyama, "The Transfeminist Manifesto," pp. 244–62.
7. Tiq Milan, quoted in Alter, "Seeing Sexism from Both Sides."
8. St. James, "These 25 Examples of Male Privilege."
9. For complex discussion around the potential traumas of being an unwilling gender informant, see Hari Zayad's article about their nonbinary experiences while being perceived as male; Zayad importantly draws out the intersections of their nonbinary identity with race: Zayad, "What I Learned from Being Non-Binary."
10. Bauman and Murray, "Reframing: From Hearing Loss to Deaf Gain," pp. 3–4.
11. Solomon, "Foreword," p. x.
12. For some examples of queer/crip/disability/sexuality work, see Shildrick, *Dangerous Discourses of Disability, Subjectivity, and Sexuality*; McRuer and Wilkerson, "Desiring Disability"; McRuer, *Crip Theory;* McRuer and Mollow, *Sex and Disability*; and Kafer, *Feminist, Queer, Crip*.
13. Ovid, *Shakespeare's Ovid*. Citations in parentheses are to this edition.
14. Is Golding making a grammar gender joke here, referring to Tireius as having an "indifferent case," in a mode similar to the title-jokes of *Hic Mulier* and *Haec Vir*? If so, the obsession with cases and pronouns for

nonbinary individuals is still at the forefront today, especially since the rise of "singular they."

15. The more discussed site of queer gender in *Antony and Cleopatra* is usually not the eunuch Mardian but the (speculated) crossdressing of Antony in the opening scene of the play (and then, later, the confusion where Enobarus thinks Cleopatra is Antony in drag in I, ii). This instance has been the subject of some debate and is not explicit in the play's text. See Jones, "The 'Strumpet's Fool' in *Antony and Cleopatra*." In contrast to Antony, Cleopatra has been seen to be masculinized in the play, especially when she recalls wearing Antony's phallic sword in II, v or plans to go to battle and "Appear there for a man" (III, vii, 17). See Singh, "Renaissance Antitheatricality, Antifeminism," pp. 99–121.

16. Palusci, "'When Boys or Women,'" p. 612.

17. Shakespeare, *Antony and Cleopatra*. Citations for all Shakespeare plays in parentheses are to this edition.

18. For a discussion of Mardian's queer desirability through a disability framework, see Crawford, "Desiring Castrates," pp. 59–90.

19. Hanson, "Aught an Eunuch Has," p. 50.

20. Ibid. p. 49.

21. Bosman, "'Best play with Mardian,'" p. 138.

22. I have written elsewhere about early modern male-to-female crossdressing, and about the *lack* of transfeminine or male femininity in Shakespeare's work: Chess, *Male-to-Female Crossdressing in Early Modern English Literature*.

23. Geary, "The Nature of Portia's Victory," p. 58.

24. Howard, "Crossdressing, the Theatre," p. 433.

25. For more discussion of the ring exchanges in *Merchant*, see Newman, "Portia's Ring," on the gendered aspects of power demonstrated by ring exchange in the play; and Boose, "The Comic Contract and Portia's Golden Ring," on the ring as a contract.

26. Bilello, "Accomplished with What She Lacks," p. 110.

27. DeBrohun, "Centaurs in Love and War," pp. 417–52.

28. On the fiction of queer impossibility in the Renaissance, see (of course) Traub, *The Renaissance of Lesbianism in Early Modern England*.

29. Masten, "Editing Boys," p. 116.

30. Malcomson, "What You Will," p. 29.

31. Howard, "Crossdressing, the Theatre," p. 433.

Bibliography

Alter, Charlotte, "Seeing Sexism from Both Sides: What Trans Men Experience," *Time Magazine*, 27 June 2016, <http://time.com/transgender-men-sexism> (last accessed 14 December 2016).

Bauman, H-Dirksen L. and Joseph M. Murray (eds), "Reframing: From Hearing Loss to Deaf Gain," *Deaf Studies Digital Journal* 1, Fall 2009, pp. 1–10, <http://dsdj.gallaudet.edu> (last accessed 15 November 2016).

Bilello, Thomas C., "Accomplished with What She Lacks: Law, Equity, and Portia's Con," in Constance Jordan and Karen Cunningham (eds), *The Law in Shakespeare* (New York: Palgrave Macmillan, 2007), pp. 109–26.

Boose, Lynda E., "The Comic Contract and Portia's Golden Ring," *Shakespeare Studies* 20, 1988, p. 241.

Bosman, Anston, "'Best play with Mardian': Eunuch and Blackamoor as Imperial Culturegram," *Shakespeare Studies* 34, 2006, pp. 123–58.

Chess, Simone, *Male-to-Female Crossdressing in Early Modern English Literature: Gender, Performance, and Queer Relations* (New York: Routledge, 2016).

Cohen, Jeffrey Jerome, "Queer Crip Sex and Critical Mattering," *GLQ: A Journal of Lesbian and Gay Studies* 21.1, January 2015, pp. 153–62.

Crawford, Katherine, "Desiring Castrates, or How to Create Disabled Social Subjects," *Journal for Early Modern Cultural Studies* 16.2, 2016, pp. 59–90.

DeBrohun, Jeri Blair, "Centaurs in Love and War: Cyllarus and Hylonome in Ovid *Metamorphoses*," *The American Journal of Philology* 125.3, Autumn 2004, pp. 417–52.

Enke, Anne (ed.), *Transfeminist Perspectives In and Beyond Transgender and Gender Studies* (Philadelphia: Temple University Press, 2012).

Geary, Keith, "The Nature of Portia's Victory: Turning to Men in *The Merchant of Venice*," *Shakespeare Survey* 37, 1984, pp. 55–68.

Hanson, Ellis, "Aught an Eunuch Has," in Madhavi Menon (ed.), *ShakesQueer: A Queer Companion to the Works of Shakespeare* (Durham, NC: Duke University Press, 2011), pp. 48–54.

Hines, Sally, *Transforming Gender: Transgender Practices of Identity, Intimacy and Care* (Bristol: Policy Press, 2007).

Howard, Jean E., "Crossdressing, the Theatre, and Gender Struggle in Early Modern England," *Shakespeare Survey* 37, 1984, pp. 418–40.

Jones, Gordon P., "The 'Strumpet's Fool' in *Antony and Cleopatra*," *Shakespeare Quarterly* 34.1, 1983, pp. 62–8.

Kafer, Alison, *Feminist, Queer, Crip* (Bloomington: Indiana University Press, 2013).

Koyama, Emi, "The Transfeminist Manifesto," in Rory Dicker and Alison Piepmeier (eds), *Catching a Wave: Reclaiming Feminism for the Twenty-First Century* (Lebanon, OH: Northeastern University Press, 2003), pp. 244–62.

Lafont, Agnès, "Introduction," in Agnès Lafont (ed.), *Shakespeare's Erotic Mythology and Ovidian Renaissance Culture* (Farnham and Burlington: Ashgate, 2013).

Lanier, Douglas M., "Shakespeare / Not Shakespeare: Afterword," in Christy Desmet, Natalie Loper, and Jim Casey (eds), *Shakespeare / Not Shakespeare* (New York: Palgrave Macmillan, 2017), pp. 293–306.

Lanier, Douglas, "Shakespearean Rhizomatics: Adaptation, Ethics, Value," in Alexa Huang and Elizabeth Rivlin (eds), *Shakespeare and the Ethics of Appropriation* (New York: Palgrave Macmillan, 2014), pp. 21–40.

McRuer, Robert, *Crip Theory: Cultural Signs of Queerness and Disability* (New York: New York University Press, 2006).

McRuer, Robert and Ana Mollow (eds), *Sex and Disability* (Durham, NC: Duke University Press, 2011).

McRuer, Robert and Abby L. Wilkerson, "Desiring Disability: Queer Theory Meets Disability Studies," *GLQ: A Journal of Lesbian and Gay Studies* 9.1–2, 2003, pp. 1–24.

Malcomson, Cristina, "'What You Will': Social Mobility and Gender in *Twelfth Night*," in Valerie Wayne (ed.), *The Matter of Difference: Materialist Feminist Criticism of Shakespeare* (Ithaca: Cornell University Press, 1991), pp. 29–57.

Masten, Jeffrey, "Editing Boys: The Performance of Genders in Print," in Peter Holland and Stephen Orgel (eds), *From Performance to Print in Shakespeare's England* (New York: Palgrave Macmillan, 2006), pp. 13–134.

Nadal, Kevin L., Kristin C. Davidoff, Lindsey S. Davis, and Yinglee Wong, "Emotional, Behavioral, and Cognitive Reactions to Microaggressions: Transgender Perspectives," *Psychology of Sexual Orientation and Gender Diversity* 1.1, 2014, pp. 72–81.

Newman, Karen, "Portia's Ring: Unruly Women and Structures of Exchange in *The Merchant of Venice*," *Shakespeare Quarterly* 38.1, 1987, pp. 19–33.

Ovid, *Shakespeare's Ovid: Being Arthur Golding's Translation of the Metamorphoses*, W. H. D. Rouse (ed.) (London: De La More Press, [1567] 1904).

Palusci, Oriana, "'When Boys or Women Tell Their Dreams': Cleopatra and the Boy Actor," *Textus* 20.3, 2007, pp. 603–16.

Serano, Julia, *Whipping Girl: A Transsexual Woman on Sexism and the Scapegoating of Femininity*, 2nd edn (New York: Seal Press, 2016).

Shakespeare, William, *Antony and Cleopatra*, in Stephen Greenblatt, Walter Cohen, Suzanne Gossett, Jean E. Howard, Katharine Eisaman Maus, and Gordon McMullan (eds), *The Norton Shakespeare*, 3rd edn (London: W. W. Norton, 2015).

Shakespeare, William, *Merchant of Venice*, in Stephen Greenblatt, Walter Cohen, Suzanne Gossett, Jean E. Howard, Katharine Eisaman Maus, and Gordon McMullan (eds), *The Norton Shakespeare*, 3rd edn (London: W. W. Norton, 2015).

Shakespeare, William, *Twelfth Night*, in Stephen Greenblatt, Walter Cohen, Suzanne Gossett, Jean E. Howard, Katharine Eisaman Maus, and Gordon McMullan (eds), *The Norton Shakespeare*, 3rd edn (London: W. W. Norton, 2015).

Shildrick, Margrit, *Dangerous Discourses of Disability, Subjectivity, and Sexuality* (Basingstoke: Palgrave Macmillan, 2009).

Singh, Jyotsna, "Renaissance Antitheatricality, Antifeminism, and Shakespeare's *Antony and Cleopatra*," *Renaissance Drama* 20, 1989, pp. 99–121.

Solomon, Andrew, "Foreword," in H-Dirksen L. Bauman and Joseph M. Murray (eds), *Deaf Gain: Raising the Stakes for Human Diversity* (Minneapolis: University of Minnesota Press, 2014), pp. ix–xii.

St. James, James, "These 25 Examples of Male Privilege from a Trans Guy's Perspective Really Prove the Point," *Everyday Feminism Magazine*, 30 May 2015, <http://everydayfeminism.com/2015/05/male-privilege-trans-men> (last accessed 13 December 2016).

Starks-Estes, Lisa S., *Violence, Trauma, and* Virtus *in Shakespeare's Roman Poems and Plays: Transforming Ovid* (Basingstoke: Palgrave Macmillan, 2014).

Traub, Valerie, *The Renaissance of Lesbianism in Early Modern England* (Cambridge: Cambridge University Press, 2002).

Whitley, Cameron T., "Trans-kin Undoing and Redoing Gender: Negotiating Relational Identity among Friends and Family of Transgender Persons," *Sociological Perspectives* 56.4, 2013, pp. 597–621.

Zayad, Hari, "What I Learned from Being Non-Binary While Still Being Perceived as a Man," *Everyday Feminism Magazine*, 6 February 2016, <https://everydayfeminism.com/2016/02/genderqueer-amab-experience> (last accessed 29 August 2018).

Chapter 2

Women in Trees: Adapting Ovid for John Lyly's *Love's Metamorphosis* (1589)

Shannon Kelley

In the world of Ovidian myth, tree metamorphosis is usually permanent. Daphne, Myrrha, Leucothoë, Dryope, and the Heliades per-
severe as arborified women without the capacity to speak for the
remainder of their lives. The silence of these female trees is particularly compelling when we consider the fate of Daphne, who transforms into a laurel tree to escape Apollo's attempted rape. In the
Western tradition, this celebrated event reinforces the gendered roots
of authorship, wherein male poets create verse and attain literary
fame based on lost or dead women. Even today, some modernist
female poets who inherit this tradition and adapt Ovid identify with
Daphne, who is hunted, silenced, and trapped in a tree:

> Any moment I can be
> Nothing but a laurel-tree
>
> > (Edna St. Vincent Millay)

> I live in my wooden legs and O
> My green green hands.
>
> > (Anne Sexton)

> I will grow myself quiet leaves
> in the difficult silence of chastity.
>
> > (Nina Kossman)

> The trees reached out to me.
> I silvered and
> I quivered. I shook out
> My foil of quick leaves.
>
> > (Eavan Boland)[1]

For these female writers, authorship and literacy seem impossible, since they contradict how patriarchy structures lived existence, qualifies resistance, and strives to categorize women as the mute beloved. Apollo's power endures, creating "wooden subjects" torn between objectification and voice well into the twenty-first century.[2] The structure used to emblematize both female silence and literary adaptation is a tree, a mute plant that is incapable of reaching the level of creative expression required by the poet laureate.

Given this context, it is significant to recover an example from Ovid that notably deviates from Daphne's pattern of tree metamorphosis by presenting a sacred female tree whose branches support literacy, adaptation, and verse in her community, and who finds the courage to speak back to her oppressor before she dies. This moment is buried within a longer episode in Book 8 of Ovid's *Metamorphoses* concerning Erisichthon, an impious man who fells a sacred tree and is punished with insatiable hunger. Because the tree speaks in protest before she dies, she transcends Daphne's fate and gets revenge: Famine (gendered female) curses Erisichthon, who dies after ruining his life and consuming his property.

John Lyly's gritty, late-Elizabethan adaptation of this story, *Love's Metamorphosis* (1589), significantly deepens Ovid's latent feminism and expands his implied vision of women as writers by showing us women who copy, memorize, and write Ovidian verse as they engage in courtship and pastoral repose underneath the sacred tree, which Lyly names "Fidelia," a gesture toward his own tendency to borrow more or less faithfully from Ovid. Lyly's experimental court comedy adapts Ovid in multiple ways: it translates, directly quotes, and expands lines from the Erisichthon episode; its poet-lovers recite memorized verse from the *Amores*; and its opening scene exposes the material processes of adapting as outdoor composition near a tree without any books at all. In combination, these different ways of deploying Ovid reject the literary trope of a mute, tree-locked Daphne and challenge mainstream understanding of the arboreal model of textual adaptation, wherein a source text is the first "originary root and all other works are derivative offshoots."[3] When we consider the Fidelia's victorious afterlife, and the tale's overarching revisionist image of literary composition and adaptation, we find a strong feminist intervention in adaptation studies, for in a number of moments in Lyly's play women write, speak, and adapt verse. Equally importantly, a courageous female-tree speaks in her own defense, breaking a longstanding tradition and demonstrating how women read, interpreted, and consequently adapted Ovid differently in early modern England.

1. Tables, Garlands, Escutcheons: Adapting in the Rhizome

In *Love's Metamorphosis*'s most radical challenge to adaptation theory, Lyly expands what it means to become a tree and subverts the arboreal model of literary production. By doing so, he antici-pates Gilles Deleuze and Félix Guattari's frustration with trees in *A Thousand Plateaus: Capitalism and Schizophrenia* (1987): "we are tired of trees," they write, since structuralism, linguistics, and related fields deploy a root-tree model to analogize the "most classical and well reflected, oldest, and weariest kind of thought."[4] In this model, a pivotal taproot (the "strong principal unity" of the first, original idea or text) supports secondary roots or tree branches (successive ideas or texts). For Deleuze, a better analogy for how knowledge exists over time appears in another way to conceptualize plant life: as a dynamic colony, or rhizome, a subterranean root system that produces shoots across and through space rather than the single erect tree that grows toward maturity. Rhizomatic thought understands all phenomena as existing within temporary, more or less stable, non-linear and decentralized, collectives. To "think rhizomatically" about the text has become a fundamental part of adaptation theory since Douglas Lanier's 2014 essay, "Shakespearean Rhizomatics: Adapta-tion, Ethics, Value," which identifies Deleuze and Guattari's theory of rhizomatic literary production as a better way to "reconceptualize Shakespearean adaptation post-fidelity."[5]

Predictably, trees figure importantly in poststructuralist models of literary adaptation as false or misrepresentative analogies of how texts and associated textual documents circulate, grow, change, and reproduce over time since the tree model presupposes that one static text exists as a definitive center, or concrete origin, from which other texts branch off. These branches, according to critics of the tree model, are seen as simply duplicating a newer, less pure version of the first idea, a process that does not fully account for the many nuances of literary adaptation in practice, nor for the problems in identifying a definitive version of any text. While criticism of the arboreal model is understandable, it has become apparent through critical plant studies that trees are not obvious, clear-cut structures with which to visualize the transmission of ideas or books in the first place, nor should we speak about trees in a way that is unreflectively transhistorical. Even Deleuze distinguishes between the root-book "aroborescent" model of representation and the radicle-system, or "fascicular root," which acknowledges representation as "an immediate, indefinite multiplicity of secondary roots" grafted onto an aborted "principal root." Soon after, he suggests that "a new rhizome may form in the heart of a tree, the hollow of a root, the crook of a branch."[6]

Fortunately, the Renaissance features different, now-obsolete ways of seeing and experiencing trees and books that resemble post-structuralist thought, and that are relevant to feminist adaptation theory. First, grafting complicates a straightforward (needless to say, non-specialist's) understanding of plants that grow by duplicating branches and producing fruit from a centralized root-tree. Grafted material results from non-hierarchical, nonlinear convergences of one plant's stem (source text) and a separate plant's branch (adapted text). A grafted union's fruit is considered equally fascinating and suspicious during the early modern period: in *The Winter's Tale*, Perdita banishes grafted gillyflowers from her garden since they are "Nature's bastards,"[7] and Andrew Marvell's Mower criticizes "forbidden mixtures" dealt between "bark and tree," which produce "uncertain and adulterate fruit" in "The Mower against Gardens."[8] Of particular note in Lyly's 1589 homage to Ovid is not the reification of a single source text-as-tree (the symbol of which is destroyed in the second scene), but an exploration of how to graft poetic devices – escutcheons, garlands or crowns, and wax writing tablets – onto a flexible, non-linear Anglo-Ovidian tradition that is explicitly sacred to a female deity. That this literary tradition signifies the actual body of a woman who associates her existence with Daphne (Fidelia becomes a tree to escape being raped by a satyr) serves at least one additional function: the scene requires a revisionist myth of poetic voice centered on a woman whose self-chosen exile into the tree signifies agency, allows her to keep both voice and chastity, and operates as a valuable message board for Arcadia's poets. After discussing how grafting complicates the arboreal model for adaptation, I turn to history of the book scholarship to explore what exactly (table, garland, crown) wedges into the crevice of Ovid's early modern bark, and how Deleuze's assumptions about material books fall short of the variety of texts and composition practices that comprise early modern literacy.

Lyly opens *Love's Metamorphosis* by visualizing literary adaptation as grafting: foresters inscribe Ovid's verse onto wax tablets which they hang on a leafy stage tree. After adding garlands to the tree, three nymphs edit, erase, or amend the wax tablets by completing or changing the forester's Latin quotations, reinforcing an early modern sense of authorship as collaborative *imitatio*. In the world of the play, Ceres's sacred tree (soon revealed to be

Fidelia) has a long history of hosting these games and courtship rituals, for she is the site of worship, fellowship, song, composition, and dance. Importantly, the foresters who hang green-tinged tables inscribed with Ovid's verse on the tree's branches refer to them as "scutcheons." An "escutcheon" (which George Puttenham classifies as a "device" in his discussion of poetic ornament) is the blank shield on which a coat of arms is painted, but, in arboriculture, an "escutcheon" is also "a shield-shaped portion of a branch, containing a bud, cut for use as a graft."[9] The term was not uncommon; William Lawson's 1618 guidebook for gardening, *A New Orchard and Garden*, includes a small image of the letter "H" in a section that describes the procedure known as "Graffing in the Scutcheon."[10] As Lawson explains, "grafting" was curious but easily shown: the "reforming of the fruite of one tree with the fruit of another, by an artificial transplacing or transposing of a twigge, bud, or leafe" from a separate tree.[11] When Lyly places Ovidian fruit in a scutcheon on Fidelia's branches, he shows how grafting is adapting, and how both produce new fruit.

In two widely available illustrated versions of Ovid from the sixteenth century we see three distinct plates devoted to this story in Book 8 – the tree felling, Famine's approach, and Erisichthon's death. In the first plate (Figure 2.1), the tree bears floral garlands and writing tables, as in Johann Spreng's illustrated *P. Ovidii Nasonis Metamorphoses*.

In the foreground, two garlands hang on the left and two tablets hang on the right to visualize Ovid's "fillets, crownes, and tables, many one, / the vowes of such as had obteynd theyr hearts desyre" and in Sandys, "wreathes, ribands, grateful tables, deckt with boughs / and sacred stem."[12] One sees a similar display of writing materials and poesy (three wax tablets, two garlands) in Bernard Salomon's work, as seen in *La Métamorphose d'Ovide Figurée* (Figure 2.2).

If we use these visuals – which were likely available to Lyly – as sources for Lyly to stage the same episode in his play, we see authorship and literary adaption as book-free, outdoor activities involving tree, garlands, and tablets. It is worthwhile asking how Deleuze would interpret these two illustrations as they pertain to his longstanding disappointment with the arboreal model of adaptation. The grafted tables and garlands signify the early modern fruits of *imitatio* that in Deleuze's theory should belong to the category of the branch/book, but since they are not permanent, stable, or even – in the case of the garlands – language-bearing, they are simply too different to

ERISICHT. QVERCVM EXSCINDIT. XIII. 2ɪɪ

Figure 2.1 *P. Ovidii Nasonis*, Antwerp, 1591. Getty Research Institute, Los Angeles (92-B20688).

qualify as reproduced copies or definitive outgrowths of a single master author or source text. Moreover, the single vertical stem that supports these texts is wounded and clearly about to collapse. This Renaissance composition scene – and Lyly's stage adaptation of the same episode, which I discuss below – offers a radically different explanation for how texts exist, multiply, or change over time by emphasizing textual vulnerability, lines of flight, and the unwieldly processes of becoming described by Deleuze as rhizomatic: "perpetually in construction or collapsing."[13]

As composing tools, writing tables are strongly associated with literary adaptation (or, in the idiom of the period, *imitatio*), for students learned to write by copying another person's words. Of particular importance in this scene of authorship is the fact that

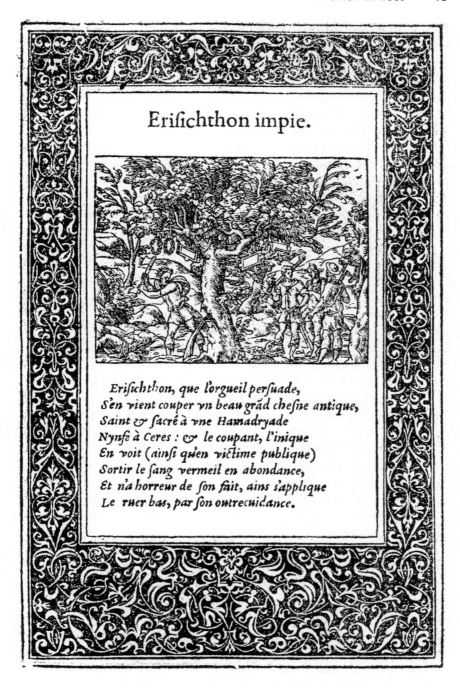

Figure 2.2 *La Métamorphose d'Ovide Figurée*, A Lyon: Par Ian De Tournes, 1564. Courtesy of Dartmouth College Library.

Lyly's Arcadians graft Ovid's letters – not their own – onto their sacred tree. Lyly's foresters lift all three quotations ("Penelope will yield, continue and conquer," "Fair faces lose their favours if they admit no lovers," and "Endure a rival patiently") directly from *Ars amatoria*, a popular collection of Ovid's love poetry. The nymphs in turn deploy commonplaces from Ovid's *Heroides, Ars amatoria,* the *Metamorphoses,* and *Remedia amoris*: Niobe actually completes Silvestris's inscription, indicating that she can identify his line; she had already decided to memorize it; and she is capable of completing it for a different cause. Lyly's onstage composition reveals shared reading practices across the sexes, but also the shared ability to select adages judiciously. A 1632 gloss of this specific episode in George Sandys's translation of the *Metamorphoses* strengthens the argument that garlands and inscriptions include writing tablets: according to Sandys, Ceres's sacred oak tree "gave Oracles like that of *Dodoni,* being garnished with tables, hung up by such as there had payed theire vows either for their recovery of health, or delivery from dangers; wherein the manner of both were painted."[14] That one could "garnish" a tree with tables was an important detail for Sandys's readers to know when they read this episode. Later, when Silvestris presents a multicolored floral garland to Cupid, he refers to it as a "garland of flowers" (a term we might find repetitive), to distinguish material and figurative fruits of poetry (IV, i, 29). A "garland" is both a wreath used for decorative purposes or worn as a crown by a person, and a "collection of short literary pieces, usually poems and ballads; an anthology, a miscellany."[15] The crowns Ovid mentions suggest both floral garlands, but also poems – a "crown" or "corona" is a form of verse wherein the first line of each stanza repeats the last line of the last stanza (but usually in a new context), or more generally a "sequence of related poems" with this structure.[16]

Even wooden tablets have rich connections to plant life. As Richard H. and Mary A. Rouse explain, the wood-backed tablet "had a longer uninterrupted association with literate Western civilization than either parchment or paper, and a more intimate relationship with literary creation."[17] The English word "book" has etymological roots with two trees – boxwood (Latin *buxum*) and beech (Anglo-Saxon *boc*) – that happened to be the standard backing for writing tablets; boxwood and beech were long "associated with writing, in two different cultures that nurtured the English language."[18] In Lyly's adaptation, tablets also solve a common problem associated with staging scenes of early modern writing, for the play opens with a need to stage three men who recall appropriate Latin tags, write them without inkhorn, desk, or lantern, and somehow hang them on the tree. The presence of tables solves this dramaturgical dilemma, for tables are small enough to be portable (thus also capable of hanging on a tree), easily held while standing, and erasable.

Tables carved with Ovidian tags – what I suggest are Lyly's rhizomatic adaptations – differ from printed editions of his works in their expression of textual durability and memory. On the one hand, since a tablet is erasable, its contents are more ephemeral than the book. On the other hand, a tablet signifies language important enough to memorize and redeploy as one's own, arguably making its contents more enduring. In his influential essay on *Hamlet*, Peter Stallybrass observes that Renaissance tables "were part of a pedagogical system that emphasized the gathering of commonplaces, their organization under topical headings, and their redeployment as the materials of one's own writing."[19] From the Middle Ages through the Renaissance, "erasable tables were used by every literate social class" for a variety of purposes, from bookkeeping and composing verse to teaching children to write.[20] Lyly's onstage writing scenes emphasize a more complex approach to formal adaptation and literary allusion: a playwright does not need to display a physical book onstage to evoke another author's importance. Since students commit Ovid to memory by copying verse on tables, Lyly's presentation of Ovidian tags advertises the ephemeral process by which writing becomes another person's over time. For Stallybrass, and later Margreta de Grazia, a pressing discussion of consciousness emerges from Shakespeare's table book scene in *Hamlet*. As de Grazia asks, "what relation can commonplaces have to Hamlet's own thoughts? Are they *his*, if they originate in the words of others?"[21] To adapt in this way is to memorize, recall, and find occasion to use a line of verse at the moment when you know the lines so well that you may not remember that they once belonged to someone else, precisely what transpires in Lyly's Arcadia.

If memorizing and deploying verse with erasable boxwood tablets comprise the baseline material practices in literary adaptation, the arboreal model that so exhausts and frustrates Deleuze matters little since adaptation occurs in early modernity without anyone dutifully or always consciously replicating a master author or a classic text to produce a new material book, with pages, spine, and text, meant to outlast time. At least this sense of textual lineage does not appear in the commonplace, graffiti, or tablet tradition, the last of which is evoked in *Love's Metamorphosis*. To graft these very different kinds of signifiers (tablet, garland, scutcheon) into a very different kind of tree gives the arboreal model of adaptation and authorship post-structuralist implications, which Lyly intensifies in his feminist revision, explored in the next section.

2. Speaking Trees: Women Who Adapt Ovid

Even if we concede to Deleuze and Guattari that, at some level, trees signify in the same way across time and space, it matters that this particular symbol of writing and reading Ovid begins to talk on stage. The tree that I previously discussed as the space of grafting turns out to be an arborified woman (Fidelia) who speaks in her defense, experiences grief, feels pain, remembers the past, finds comfort among her fellow trees, and bleeds to death on stage. As I have argued, trees appear in two narratives related to literacy: the hierarchical theory of how we adapt classic books and writers, and the myth of Daphne and Apollo, which silences women and elevates men as authors. When, if ever, do these two ways of deploying trees as structures intentionally intersect?

In *Love's Metamorphosis*, Lyly demonstrates his poststructuralist or rhizomatic vision of adaptation-as-grafting, and he challenges the mute-tree tradition by creating proto-feminist characters who loosely adapt Ovid (sometimes with tablets). At the same time, Lyly transforms his Ovidian source text himself. As a speaking tree covered in verse and composition materials, Fidelia personifies adaptation in multiple ways, yet her adapting is far from precise. Rather than replicate her source text, she models adaptation as grafting from an ecofeminist perspective: she combines stories out of order, adding examples from Books 3 and 7; she invents a soaring manifesto on chastity and consent; she describes herself as "knitting garlands," which we know signifies poetic composition; and she calls on her fellow nymphs to witness her death. These female poets and adapters of Ovid in turn report to the female deity Ceres, who summons Famine, who is gendered female, and who completely dominates Erisichthon. As Emily Detmer-Goebel notes, unlike Lavinia in *Titus Andronicus*, Fidelia is not denied a tongue to talk about rape, nor does patriarchal culture silence any of the many women in this play.[22] The task for the modern reader is to learn to see Fidelia and her nymph's ability to knit garlands or read *floreligium* as writing and adapting practices that secure poetic identities. Indeed, Juliet Fleming suggests that the linearity required in the arboreal model maligned by Deleuze is at odds with forms of reading and writing featured in devices such as garlands and escutcheons. "The early modern nosegay," Fleming notes, "was a writing practice that had at its disposal a choice of somatic registers through which to display that special indistinction between natural objects and rhetorical figures that was its particular mode of compliment."[23] Engraved jewelry, posies written in rings, hair bracelets entwined with slips of paper, and decorated crockery propose "a mode of knowledge that simultaneously thinks through matter and accords it a sensibility of its own."[24]

As Fidelia tells her story, she describes her status as a tree as a form of juridical sanctuary by recourse to two Ovidian precedents, Daphne and Myrrha:

> Divine *Phoebus*, that pursued
> *Daphne* till she was turned to a Bay tree, ceased then to
> Trouble her. Ay, the gods are pittiful. And *Cinyras*, that
> With furie followed his daughter *Mirrha*, till shee was
> Changed to a Mirre tree, left then to prosecute her. Yea,
> Parents are natural. Phoebus lamented the loss of his
> Friend, Cinyras of his child; but both gods and men either
> Forget or neglect the change of Fidelia – nay, follow her
> After her change, to make her more miserable. So that
> There is nothing more hateful than to be chaste,
> Whose bodies are followed in the world with lust. (*Love's Metamorphosis* I, i, 99–109)

Here, Fidelia transforms the arborified woman literary trope into a feminist tradition, equating tree metamorphosis with refusal to consent and successful evasion of sexual violence. What's further remarkable about Fidelia's adaptation at this moment is its gaping error: Myrrha is infamous for seducing her biological father, not for being chaste. Fidelia creates a unified Ovidian narrative about sexual consent and arborified women where there is no unified narrative, which we could argue allows her to summon political strength through her practice of adaptation as intentional misreading. During this moment of crisis, with an ax hanging over her, she founds a legacy of sisterhood trees, inserts herself inside, and testifies for forty-seven (rather than Ovid's four) lines about her innocence, which includes naming the satyr who tried to rape her. She resists her attacker at the moment of death, when she commands her friends – "Go, ladies, tell Ceres I am that Fidelia that so long knit garlands in her honour" – reiterating that she too is a poet (I, ii, 138–9). For Victoria Bladen, a woman who becomes a tree enters a "static and passive state . . . unable to defend herself," but Fidelia (albeit, while immobile) sends the nymphs on a revenge quest, a resolute act of agency.[25] Lyly intervenes once again in Ovid's tale by insisting that the three witnesses to Fidelia's speech are "impudent" (immodest, disrespectful) women, not male foresters. It is these nymphs' celebration that torments Erisichthon, who attacks the tree to silence their creative expression and to better locate the forest's game, only to hear the tree emit a fourth female voice of opposition. In Lyly's play, one of these women – Nisa – courageously tries to stop the attack by pleading, "the tree poureth out blood, and I hear a voice" (I, ii, 103). Lyly's version floods the scene with female adapters, auditors, and readers of Ovid (one imagines women in the audience may have been equally Ovid-literate) who witness male violence and take action. In short, Lyly recognizes and intensifies Ovid's latent feminism, transforming the episode from the *Metamorphoses* into something both familiar and new. I suspect Lyly recognized the power and appeal of this episode for Queen Elizabeth, for the story challenges the women in trees tradition and its tragic consequences for the female voice in literary history.

The moment is extraordinary on its own, but Lyly also reflexively addresses his own process of adapting Ovid in his other innovations: the tree's name, "Fidelia," especially when we consider the play's second heroine, "Protea." Recently, Douglas M. Lanier and Christy Desmet have explored fidelity as a core principle of adaptation. For Lanier, adaptations ought to be weighed based on their fidelity to a network rather than a text, while Desmet seeks a broader understanding of fidelity as closer to "fealty," "responsibility to and for another, either text or person."[26] In the *Oxford English Dictionary*, "fidelity" refers to both loyalty to a "person, party, bond" and to "strict conformity to truth or fact" of either a person or a translation.[27] As it pertains to translation, "fidelity" gauges the "exactness" of the new version as it compares to the original. Exactness does not reflect the spirit of Lyly's adaptation of Ovid, since a tree by the name of Fidelia undercuts the concept of adaptation as strict, word-by-word fidelity to a source text. At the same time, Lyly's second heroine is "Protea," a spirited woman whose name suggests a more promiscuous approach to textual reproduction and adaptation. Protea inhabits the world of romance, oceans, and exchange, for even when Erisichton (her father) forces her to marry a merchant against her will, she soon escapes by changing shape and sex: "Chop and change me," she proclaims, "I am ready," knowing that her former lover Neptune gave her the gift of self-metamorphosis (III, ii, 21).

Protea signifies a sustainable resource, a tree that Erisichthon can consume, chop, or sell without cessation to stave off famine's curse. Protea provides wry, worldly commentary on Arcadia's lovers, gamely challenges a Siren, and attains her heart's desire, a loyal shepherd named Petulius, whose affection she receives with open arms. As much as we mourn Fidelia's death, Protea (probably performed by and recognized as the same boy actor who played Fidelia inside the chopped stage tree) serves as a reminder that adapting Ovid for the stage presents a second level of fluid intertextuality, for no two performances are ever the same.

With "chop and change me," Protea provides meta-theatrical commentary on the transient life of Lyly's stage tree, an important prop he showcases in two other plays inspired by Ovid's *Metamorphoses* – *Gallathea* (1588) and *Endymion* (1588). A different tree is felled onstage in *A Warning for Fair Women* (anon. 1599), and Thomas Kyd's *c.*1588 *The Spanish Tragedy*, where Hieronimo's grief-stricken wife, Isabella, hews a tree and then commits suicide. Vin Nardizzi argues that the play's "iconic 'star' is a stage prop – a tree" that "the play's human characters . . . destroy in the final act."[28] At this point, the Elizabethan court knew much of stage trees: unlike ordinary trees, theatrical companies assemble and dismember them routinely, even altering their appearance with different species of branches and leaves. As the play's second female talking (stage) tree, Protea adapts to life through a protective shield of becoming, calls upon the mutations of theatre, and inevitably participates in the constructing/ collapsing cycle of performances.

Despite their differences, both talking trees emerge victorious to further exemplify the play's feminist overtones. During her negotiations with Cupid for Erisichthon's release, Ceres commands that, from now on, "all Ceres' grove shall [Erisichthon] deck with garlands, and / account every tree holy. A stately monument shall he erect in remembrance of Fidelia, and offer yearly / sacrifice" (V, i, 45–8). The humbled forester now must decorate an entire forest of untouchable female trees with verse (floral and written garlands) in honor of the woman he killed. Thus, while Theodora A. Jankowski decries the "rape-murder of Fidelia," her reading of the play as "steeped in extraordinary amounts of violence directed against women, specifically virgins" seems to me an exaggeration, in part because Fidelia's three nymphs are treated with equal dignity and never forced to marry the foresters, who mourn Fidelia throughout the entire play.[29] One of these men, Ramis, equates the loss of the sacred tree with the loss of voice, mistress, and fortune,

> I fear our fortunes cannot thrive, for Erisichthon hath felled down the holy tree of Ceres, which will increase in her choler, and in her nymphs cruelty. Let us see whether our garlands be there which we hanged on that tree, and let us hang ourselves upon another. (III, i, 162–5)

With these lines and others, Lyly emphasizes that his lovestruck foresters will be good husbands: they recoil from Erisichthon's cruelty, return to the felled tree to find their verse, and then even suggest using the garlands to hang themselves. In Act five, scene four, the play's final scene, Montanus feels no obligation to apologize for abandoning his starving master, whose reproach falls on deaf ears,

> Erisichthon: But you foresters were unkind, that in all my maladies would not visit me.
> Montanus: Thou knowest, Erisichthon, that lovers visit none but their mistresses. (V, iv, 192–5)

Leah Scragg's edition glosses Montanus's reply as an "inadequate excuse," which Erisichthon readily accepts to demonstrate his new-found humility, as though a new brotherhood constituted by submission to women has emerged.

Finally, Silvestris still desires his mistress, but he stands by Fidelia's position on consent. When he resists forcing the nymphs (through his or Ceres's commandment) to wed, he articulates his position by combining lines from Ovid's *Ars amatoria* and *Remedia amoris*: "For what joy can there be in our lives . . . [if] every kind word proceed of fear, not affection? Enforcement is worse than enchantment" (V, iii, 15–19). By releasing the women from Cupid's spell of sea-rock, bird, and flower, he frees them to self-determine. In turn, their newly restored identities and voices create heightened awareness of this freedom. Astonishingly, one claims she will "nor fear again to be changed to stone"; one delighted in the view of heaven as a bird; and the third enjoyed her time as a sweet flower. With Ceres's encouragement they consent to wed, but without defeat, for their metamorphoses change, improve, and empower them as they begin to face their future roles as wives: Nisa retains the stubborn spirit of the rock, Niobe quotes Ovid's *Ars amatoria* to explain that she still has wings to fly – "*Non custodiri, ni velit ulla potest*" ["No watch can be set over a woman's will"] – and Celia retains thorns and the rose's prickly nature (V, iv, 167). All three journey into types of voiceless nonhuman objects against their will, only to return stronger than before, equally able to voice their experiences by adapting

Ovid's verse to the occasion. What has changed, I believe, are the four men in the play, who learn how to respect and acknowledge women's consent.

3. Conclusion

Poststructuralist thinkers such as Deleuze consider trees to be false or misrepresentative analogies of literary adaptation while simultaneously ignoring a longstanding tradition of women trapped in trees as the defining moment of Apollo's laureate ambition. However, critical plant studies complicate our understanding of trees through grafting, which resembles the decentered, non-hierarchical Deleuzian rhizome by creating new fruit from more than one stem. At the same time, scholarship on the history of the book produces convincing evidence – from wax tablets, escutcheons, and floral garlands, to outdoor composition on a variety of inscription surfaces – that early modern adaptation may not involve books or writing practices as we know them at all.

If we must modify the arboreal model of adaptation to account for these differences, and I agree that we must, we must also come to terms with how the recurring story of silent female victims of sexual assault not coincidentally involves a tree as an iconic sign of oppression. Daphne's fate captures the titanic forces by which patriarchy silences women across time, but it also signifies the difficult process by which women do speak in spite of the ordinary and sometimes violent restrictions against doing so. Simply put: women may at any moment become trees, for they may feel literally or figuratively robbed of self-identity and safety enough to become temporarily or forever without voice. Because of this phenomenon, women surely learn to speak, read, adapt, and compose differently, especially in the presence of men who seek to force their consent. With Fidelia, Lyly acknowledges this difference, and suggests that for women adaptation promotes but does not guarantee survival.

Notes

1. "Daphne," Edna St. Vincent Millay; "Where I Live in This Honorable House of the Laurel Tree," Anne Sexton; "Daphne Herself," Nina Kossman; and "Daphne with Her Thighs in Bark," Eavan Boland; in Kossman, *Gods and Mortals*, pp. 38–41.

2. Zamir, "Wooden Subjects," p. 277.
3. Lanier, "Afterword," p. 295.
4. Deleuze and Guattari, *A Thousand Plateaus*, pp. 15, 5.
5. Lanier, "Shakespearean Rhizomatics," p. 29.
6. Deleuze and Guattari, *A Thousand Plateaus*, p. 6.
7. Shakespeare, *The Winter's Tale*, IV, iv, 83.
8. Marvell, "The Mower Against Gardens," lines 22, 23, 25.
9. "Escutcheon," *n.*1.d. *Oxford English Dictionary.*
10. I am grateful to Vin Nardizzi and Miriam Jacobson's essay, "The Secrets of Grafting in Wroth's *Urania*," especially p. 179.
11. Lawson, *A New Orchard*, p. 33.
12. Sandys, *Ovid's Metamorphosis Englished*, p. 374.
13. Deleuze and Guattari, *A Thousand Plateaus*, p. 20.
14. Sandys, *Ovid's Metamorphosis Englished*, p. 396.
15. "Garland," *n.*4.fig. *Oxford English Dictionary.*
16. "Crown," *n.*25.a and b. *Oxford English Dictionary.*
17. Rouse and Rouse, "The Vocabulary of Wax Tablets," p. 220.
18. Ibid. p. 222.
19. Stallybrass et al., "Hamlet's Tables and the Technologies," pp. 410–11. In Peter Stallybrass's discussion of scenes that involve writing on the Renaissance stage, he notes that for writing that involved paper, inkhorn, and pen, two things were necessary: a stool or desk for the writer to use for support and as a place to dip the pen in ink, and servants, who supplied aid to the person writing. Wax tables are sometimes named in the scene, or a scene might explicitly call for tables, or we might deduce their presence from the playtext.
20. Ibid. p. 403.
21. De Grazia, "Soliloquies and Wages," p. 77.
22. Detmer-Goebel, "The Need for Lavinia's Voice," p. 75.
23. Fleming, *Graffiti and the Writing Arts*, p. 135.
24. Ibid. p. 164.
25. Bladen, "Pruning the Tree of Virtue," p. 43.
26. Lanier, "Afterword," p. 297; Desmet, "Recognizing Shakespeare, Rethinking Fidelity," p. 41.
27. "Fidelity," 1.a, 2.b, *Oxford English Dictionary.*
28. Nardizzi, "'No Wood, No Kingdom,'" p. 205.
29. Jankowski, "'The scorne of Savage people,'" pp. 124, 123.

Bibliography

Bladen, Victoria, "Pruning the Tree of Virtue in Shakespeare's *Titus Andronicus*," in Brett D. Hirsch and Christopher Wortham (eds), *"This earthly stage": World and Stage in Late Medieval and Early Modern England* (Turnhout, Belgium: Brepols, 2010), pp. 39–61.

de Grazia, Margreta, "Soliloquies and Wages in the Age of Emergent Consciousness," *Textual Practice* 9, 1995, pp. 67–92.

Deleuze, Gilles and Félix Guattari, *A Thousand Plateaus: Capitalism and Schizophrenia*, Brian Massumi (trans.) (Minneapolis and London: University of Minnesota Press, 1987).

Desmet, Christy, "Recognizing Shakespeare, Rethinking Fidelity: A Rhetoric and Ethics of Appropriation," in Alexa Huang and Elizabeth Rivlin (eds), *Shakespeare and the Ethics of Appropriation* (New York: Palgrave Macmillan, 2014), pp. 41–57.

Detmer-Goebel, Emily, "The Need for Lavinia's Voice: *Titus Andronicus* and the Telling of Rape," *Shakespeare Studies* 29, 2001, pp. 75–92.

Fleming, Juliet, *Graffiti and the Writing Arts of Early Modern England* (London: Reaktion, 2001).

Jankowski, Theodora A., "'The scorne of Savage people': Virginity as 'Forbidden Sexuality' in John Lyly's *Love's Metamorphosis*," *Renaissance Drama* 24, 1993, pp. 123–53.

Kossman, Nina, *Gods and Mortals: Modern Poems on Classical Myths* (Oxford: Oxford University Press, 2001).

Lanier, Douglas M., "Shakespeare / Not Shakespeare: Afterword," in Christy Desmet, Natalie Loper, and Jim Casey (eds), *Shakespeare / Not Shakespeare* (New York: Palgrave Macmillan, 2017), pp. 293–306.

Lanier, Douglas M., "Shakespearean Rhizomatics: Adaptation, Ethics, Value," in Alexa Huang and Elizabeth Rivlin (eds), *Shakespeare and the Ethics of Appropriation* (New York: Palgrave Macmillan, 2014), pp. 21–40.

Lawson, William, *A New Orchard and Garden* (London: 1618).

Lyly, John, *Love's Metamorphosis*, Leah Scragg (ed.) (Manchester: Manchester University Press, 2008).

Marvell, Andrew, "The Mower against Gardens," in Nigel Smith (ed.), *The Poems of Andrew Marvell* (Harlow: Pearson Longman, [1681] 2007), pp. 133–4.

Nardizzi, Vin, "'No Wood, No Kingdom': Planting Genealogy, Felling Trees, and the Additions to *The Spanish Tragedy*," *Modern Philology* 110.2, 2012, pp. 202–25.

Nardizzi, Vin and Jacobson, Miriam, "The Secrets of Grafting in Wroth's *Urania*," in Jennifer Munroe and Rebecca Laroche (eds), *Ecofeminist Approaches to Early Modernity* (New York: Palgrave Macmillan, 2011), pp. 175–94.

Ovid, *Ovid's Metamorphoses: The Arthur Golding Translation of 1567*, John Frederick Nims (ed.) (Philadelphia: Paul Dry Books, 2000).

Rouse, Richard H. and Mary A. Rouse, *The Vocabulary of Wax Tablets* (Turnhout, Belgium: Brepols, 1989), pp. 220–30.

Sandys, George, *Ovid's Metamorphosis Englished, Mythologized, and Represented in Figures* (Lincoln: University of Nebraska Press, 1970).

Shakespeare, William, *The Winter's Tale*, Mario DiGangi (ed.) (Boston: Bedford/St. Martin's, 2008).

Stallybrass, Peter, Roger Chartier, John Franklin Mowery, and Heather Wolfe, "Hamlet's Tables and the Technologies of Writing in Renaissance England," *Shakespeare Quarterly* 55.4, 2004, pp. 379–419.

Zamir, Tzachi, "Wooden Subjects," *New Literary History* 39.2, 2008, pp. 277–300.

Chapter 3

Queer Fidelity: Marlowe's Ovid and the Staging of Desire in *Dido, Queen of Carthage*

Daniel G. Lauby[1]

At first glance, Christopher Marlowe and Thomas Nashe's[2] *Dido, Queen of Carthage* seems to reify heteronormative paradigms. It is overtly Virgilian and reinforces the epic mythos of Aeneas as the heroic forefather of Western civilization while also adhering to gender stereotypes that associate femininity with overwhelming passion and masculinity with measured reason. But the staging and rhetoric of desire immediately fracture the play's conservative framework and undermine its normative facade through queer reversals, inconsistencies, and erotic encounters largely appropriated[3] from Ovid's *Metamorphoses*, *Amores*, and *Heroides*. By doing so, Marlowe reconstructs the classical Ovid through a "projection" that Douglas M. Lanier describes as the refashioning of a precedent through appropriative selection.[4] However, *Dido*'s Ovidian mode also filters through an inherited Ovidian landscape, complicating the play's allegiance to the Ovid of antiquity. The consequence is a pervasive tension between the Virgilian and Ovidian, the heteronormative and the queer. Though the distinctions frequently seem to collapse into one another, I argue that the play's staging of desire utilizes visibility and remembrance through homoeroticism, gender reversal, and bodily dissonance to demonstrate fidelity to the queer ideologies of Ovid's texts.

By discussing Marlowe's queer fidelity – his faithfulness to Ovid's subversive rhetoric – I use early modern queer theory that addresses the embodiment of power and identity beyond heteronormative borders. These queer hinterlands are not merely bound by sexuality but include *loci* of social, economic, and political disruptions, often through the destabilization of dyadic male and female or dominant and subordinate roles. Even though "heteronormativity" seems to

speak to modern sensibilities about gender and sexuality, I take my
cue from Alan Sinfield,[5] Theodora A. Jankowski, and others who
use this term to describe early modern passion and social order as
constructed along gendered binary lines. In her discussion of queer
virginity in early modern English drama, for example, Jankowski
contrasts medieval Catholic and early modern Protestant England,
claiming that the latter "organized gender in terms of bodily differences and an actively heterosexual gender paradigm."[6]

Notably, I do not refer to homosexuality since early modern passion
operated outside the scope of sexual identity. Therefore, I acknowledge Madhavi Menon's assertion that "queer" can and should look
beyond gender or desire,[7] and I incorporate David Halperin's expansive definition, "whatever is at odds with the normal, the legitimate,
the dominant."[8] Queering in this sense describes the subversive influence of classical texts like Ovid's *Metamorphoses* or *Amores* and early
modern plays like Marlowe and Nashe's *Dido, Queen of Carthage*. In
these cases, heteronormative constructions are inverted, disrupted, or
otherwise subordinated to taboo expressions of power.

Though co-written with Nashe, Marlowe's *Dido* incorporates
appropriations that adhere to a queer Ovidian mode that extends
throughout Marlowe's plays and poems as he interrogates sexual,
political, religious, and class boundaries.[9] *Dido* accomplishes such
queering through complicated intertextualities that weave together
the Ovidian and Virgilian. In doing so, Marlowe draws from a complex web of precedents, both explicitly and implicitly, from Augustine of Hippo to Edmund Spenser. By drawing on the "False Aeneas"
tradition, for example, Marlowe not only reconnects with Ovid's
Heroides and Dido's complaint of Aeneas's deceit, but he also recalls
intermediary precedents that Sara Munson Deats argues reflect a
revival of the false Aeneas in fourteenth- and fifteenth-century works
like Geoffrey Chaucer's *The House of Fame* and John Lydgate's
Troybook.[10] But in reclaiming the classical, queer Ovid, Marlowe
and others also implicitly recall its antithesis – the allegorical, early
Christian moralizing of Ovid through works such as Prudentius's
Contra Symmachum, which Jonathan Bate claims, "drew together
the transformation of Lot's wife into a pillar of salt and the metamorphosis of Niobe into stone, thus foreshadowing a strategy that
would become common a thousand years later."[11] Bate further argues
that these later texts, like the anonymously written *Ovide Moralisé*,
reimagined a "morally elevated" rather than an "erotically charged"
Ovid that eventually became secularized through various mythological texts during the early modern period.[12] As a result, *Dido*'s

complex adaptation network emerges through a rhizomatic model Lanier describes as constituted by a multiplicity of precedents in a "process of endless becoming."[13] Even before Marlowe's own projection, the early modern Ovid is filtered through contemporary translations, authorial selectivity, Petrarchan appropriations, resistant discourses, cultural memory, and contemporary iconography, forces unbound to a single poet, politician, or devotee.

Nevertheless, lines can be drawn, particularly since Marlowe and many of his contemporaries conscientiously attempt to reclaim the classical precedent. Despite operating within the rhizome, therefore, Marlowe's plays and poems settle into clear Ovidian traces of influence, so *Dido* necessarily recalls the unresolved epistolic complaints and mnemonic gaps in *Heroides*, the cyclicality of *Metamorphoses*, and the reversals of *Amores*. In doing so, Marlowe selectively chooses appropriations that refashion the precedent into a Marlovian Ovid that preserves queer ideology by undermining the very cultural boundaries it sometimes pretends to endorse. Among the intersections embedded within Ovid's narratives, conservative and queer ideologies uncomfortably collide, such as in occasions throughout *Metamorphoses* and *Heroides* when epic narratives and Caesar Augustus's traditional moral codes, or *mos maiorum*, establish the framework for reversals, eroticisms, and inversions. Lisa S. Starks-Estes describes Ovid as "collecting, reassembling, and revising sources gathered from a broad spectrum of texts and traditions," practices that inspired early modern writers "to appropriate his work in innovative ways, often grafting together pieces of myths and crossing from one genre to another through a method known as *transvestitio*."[14] Marlowe similarly utilizes a variety of intertexts, including conservative precedents and heteronormative constructions that serve as the textual landscape for queer interventions, intersecting the masculine epic with *epyllionic* femininity, for example, and interrogating those sites of textual and ideological intersections through language and staging practices that powerfully assert an Ovidian queer fidelity that upsets social and political norms.

Intercepting an eventual Virgilian frame, the staging of *Dido*'s opening scene projects a particularly Ovidian moment through the display of homoerotic and politically disruptive bodies. The result is a queer occasion that echoes throughout the play as its staging is reenacted. When the curtains draw, Jupiter sits "dandling" Ganymede on his knee while Hermes sleeps, and other scenes later mirror the prologue's eroticism with different sexual and political implications, as when Dido holds the flirtatious "Cupid as Ascanius" in her lap (III, i, 25)[15] and later "dandlest" Cupid in her arms (V, i, 45). In either case, the staging of Dido's encounters with Cupid glance backward to the pederasty of the first scene and an Ovidian reversal in which the subordinate love object gains influence over a lover in the dominant subject position. In its homoeroticism, the prologue queers normative power relations while also parodying the sexual commerce that underlies the Children of Her Majesty's Chapel and similar boy acting companies.

Though it is unknown whether *Dido* was ever performed, the title page of the 1594 Woodcocke manuscript designates "the Children of her Maiesties Chappell" as the acting company. Elizabethan boy-actors in such troupes would range generally from six to fourteen years old, according to Shehzana Mamujee,[16] and the varied physicality, as well as the context for those bodies' presence on stage, offers dramatic opportunities for emphasizing homoeroticism while queering normative gender and sexual hierarchies. Jackson I. Cope argues, for example, that a teenaged Jupiter "dandling" a pre-pubescent Ganymede exposes the "boys' imposed predicament"[17] of Elizabethan child-actor predation. Cope notes that Masters of the Chapel were given free rein to seize young boys throughout England,[18] so with Queen Elizabeth's support, captured child actors found themselves thrust into a sexual and theatrical marketplace where they fell prey to desiring gazes.[19]

Despite the prologue's implications, pederasty was neither unusual nor taboo during the sixteenth century as long as it reified certain normative constructs. Stephen Orgel argues that pederastic relationships were commonplace and rarely punished, largely because boys and women were similar both physically and socially.[20] Yet desiring a "Ganymede" was not the same as desiring a woman, since pederasty particularly required the maintenance of a strict sexual hierarchy that Joyce Green MacDonald describes as "categories of social status and experience."[21] Within the pederastic relationship, then, the older man must maintain influence over the subordinate child,[22] so one expects Jupiter to dominate Ganymede due to several imbalances in Jupiter's favor, not the least of which is linked to mortality and metaphysical hierarchy.

However, Jupiter seems entirely in Ganymede's control throughout the prologue, creating a queer power imbalance that rhizomatically incorporates the kind of masochistic Petrarchan desire found throughout the sonnet tradition, including Sir Philip Sidney's *Astrophel and Stella*. Petrarch's *Rime Sparse* incorporates a rich Ovidian intertextuality within which the speaker pines for an unobtainable love object, and this desire generally threatens to effeminize the speaker.[23] Sidney and others adopt Petrarch's use of Ovidian images as they similarly portray forlorn lovers who suffer "Love's" arrows, apostrophize various gods, and allude to mythological scenes, developing an Ovidian landscape projected through the Petrarchan style. So when Jupiter complains that he "should deny thy youth" when asked to punish Juno for insulting Ganymede and is unable to resist his young lover, he invokes a Petrarchan tradition rooted in rich Ovidian precedents. In *Dido*, such connections are often rather clear, such as when Jupiter admits that he has "oft driven back the horses of the night" just to continue gazing upon Ganymede's feminine body. In this appropriation of *Amores*, Jupiter places himself in the position of Ovid's speaker who pleads, "*lente currite noctis equi*," run slowly horses of the night (*Amores* I, xiii, 40), as he lies in the arms of his lover Corinna.[24] Marlowe projects the eroticism of *Amores*.

The projection is an Ovid filtered through Petrarchan sonnets that in themselves also rely upon Ovidian precedents rooted in the pursuits of *Metamorphoses*. Jupiter's subordination becomes obvious when he offers to "pluck her [Juno's] spotted pride," the peacock, to "make thee fans wherewith to cool thy face" (I, i, 34–5).[25] Jupiter even goes so far as promising to rip off the sleeping Hermes' wings before finally surrendering Juno's wedding jewels to Ganymede in a ceremoniously staged act of infidelity. On one level, Jupiter's gift makes visible the pederastic exchange implicated in child company performances where men pay for erotically charged visual encounters with young boys, yet it inverts normative influence since the usually preyed upon male child holds sway over the mature, influential desirer, leading MacDonald to argue, "Ganymede is Ovid's pretty boy with a vengeance, wickedly aware of his own attractiveness and of Jupiter's enslavement by his charms," so "there is no doubt that Marlowe's Ganymede is an active and self-conscious seducer."[26] Like Gaveston in Marlowe's *Edward II*, Ganymede belongs to a subordinate class in relation to his lover, yet Gaveston and Ganymede both wield a queer femininity that, rather than stripping them of masculine privilege, empowers them in a sexual economy where erotic utterance and sensuous touch is exchanged for political influence. Therefore, the staging of the petted boy and the doting god queer normative sexual hierarchies.

Yet the prologue may prove all the more powerful for what goes unstaged, since the image of Jupiter sitting with Ganymede on his knee is not the scene most inscribed in cultural memory during the medieval and early modern period. When spectators watch erotic reversals embedded in the prologue, they are meant to recall iconic projections of Ganymede's abduction. The homoerotic relationship is either described or alluded to in contemporary artwork as well as translations of Virgil's *Aeneid* and Ovid's *Metamorphoses, Heroides*, and *Tristia*.[27] Leonard Barkan traces the myth as it moves from a purely Christian allegory of the middle ages to portrayals such as Michelangelo's *Ganymede* in which a passive male figure ascends in the clutches of an eagle, erotic mainly because the illustration invokes a narrative in which Ganymede willfully surrenders his body to the eagle. But it is also paired with another drawing, *Tityus*, which depicts the agony of torture at the hands of a similar bird that tears into Tityus's flesh. Together, Barkan argues that these drawings communicate a psychological connection between the "ecstasy and torment of passion,"[28] projecting the central paradox of Petrarchan love poetry that Spenser also appropriates during the Busrayne episode of *The Faerie Queene*.[29] Spenser's Ganymede is "faire," "bare," and delighted in the face of a real threat identified by shepherds whose warnings of falling and whose admonishments to "take surer hould" suggest both practical and moral implications (*The Faerie Queene* III, xi, 34). At its core, Barkan argues that Spenser's use of Ovidian contradiction "emphasizes visual deception as he retells the stories,"[30] and the same is true for *Dido*. But instead of crafting the story after the *moralisé* tradition, the subterfuge unveils and unravels heteronormative expectations.

Through a projection that discards, recalls, and invents certain aspects of the Ganymede story, *Dido* offers a complicated interrogation of a pederastic relationship through the staging of mythology, eroticism, reversal, and meta-theatrics. Collectively, Marlowe relies on the invocation of memory within a remembrance environment. Building on the work of Eviatar Zerubavel, Evelyn B. Tribble argues that memory is biological and social, individual and shared;[31] and Lina Perkins Wilder describes the application of memory in a theatrical environment that utilizes props, utterances, and staging that is both present and absent.[32] As spectators watch the boy actors perform seduction on stage, they cannot help but recall Ganymede's abduction by the eagle, an experience fraught with a kind of traumatic eroticism that mirrors the early modern abductions of children for the sake of public entertainment and men's erotic pleasure. As is the case in many of Marlowe's plays, the interrogation turns back on itself as the performance queers subject and object positions: Ganymede as both subject and object, Jupiter's carnal prey and adept seducer, destabilizing Jupiter's position within the dyad of sexual politics.

However, staging related to Dido and Cupid-as-Ascanius also evokes the memory of Jupiter and Ganymede's pederasty within the play. Such instances complicate the initial prologue's Ovidian reversal by pairing two equally queer characters within an erotic frame that resists patriarchal subversion. Cupid sits on Dido's lap at the beginning of Act three in order to pierce her with his arrow, but in doing so, he reenacts the prologue's staging of Jupiter and Ganymede's affair. The discourse between them even takes on an erotic flavor as Cupid hangs about Dido's neck and gives her kisses while once again requiring a material exchange for his affection. Cupid asks, "What will you give me? I'll take this fan" (III, i, 32), reflecting Jupiter's earlier promise to pluck the feathers from Juno's peacock "To make thee fans to cool thy face" (I, i, 135). But this time, the child's "lover" is no doting man, but a woman who conflates maternal, heteroerotic, and homoerotic affection. The potential for an actor doubling as both Ganymede and Cupid emphasizes the link between the similarly queer Ovidian moments of gender and power that Jane Kingsley-Smith argues is already established "through gestures, visual imagery, and terms of endearment."[33] Therefore, Jupiter's and Dido's roles as heads of heaven and state, respectively, reflect each other despite being – on their face – contradictory homoerotic and heteroerotic constructions. Dido and Cupid also occupy similar positions within the sexual hierarchy, for Dido wields political power, but she still does not escape the identification as a "medium of exchange" that Orgel argues links boys and women as sexual objects within the patriarchal structure.[34] The relative similitude is further expressed by the two performing male bodies on stage. The result is a deeply queer scene in which gender positions tumble over and over. Dido is masculinized through her political influence and the male player's body underneath her costume, which promotes a tension between maternal and homoerotic desire in the flirtatious dialogue and repetition that pairs this scene with the prologue.

Later, Cupid-as-Ascanius's request for the nurse to hold him mimics the staging of both the prologue and Dido's interaction with the boy. After agreeing to carry Cupid, she claims the title of "mother," leading the god to conclude, "So you'll love me, I care not if I do" (IV, v, 17). Yet the nurse is not satisfied with maternal affection and begins imagining the man "Ascanius" will become. The nurse's assertion that "I am young, / I'll have a husband, or else a lover" (IV, v, 22–3) fails to convince, and Cupid comically protests, "A husband, and no teeth!" (IV, v, 24). Though her desire eventually transfers to the memory of a spurned ex-lover, the transition nonetheless conflates the two, especially since the nurse does not reveal the object of her fantasy until the final line of the scene. The nurse's imagination merges child and adult, staging an intergenerational eroticism associated with the prologue's pederasty and Dido's female desire. Yet the scenario is fundamentally unstable as the nurse's self-assessment and her valuation of love. This staging of imaginative uncertainty exposes the spectator's own predicament in association with the child actors, one in which desire and gender identity are layered and in flux.

Intersections between boyhood and womanhood on and off stage mean that heteroeroticism in *Dido* is always a site of both Ovidian desire and danger. The crossdressed male body not only suggests homoerotic subtexts, but it also evokes early modern anxieties about gender instability. Simone Chess refers to Thomas Laqueur's *Making Sex: Body and Gender from the Greeks to Freud* when she describes the contemporary Galenic belief that male and female bodies were "homologous and, therefore, changeable," so a female to male crossdresser could transform biologically into a male as a result or vice versa.[35] Such a Protean threat medically theorizes an Ovidian metamorphosis brought about by external influences. However, the eroticism evoked on stage was also thought to pose a threat to male spectators who were in the position of not only desiring the woman but the boy underneath, leading Phillip Stubbes to promote a fear of accidental same-sex unions where "in their secret conclaues (couertly) they play the Sodomits, or worse."[36] Yet while Stubbes seems primarily concerned about the confusion derived from what Cope calls the "doubleness" of child actors, Alisa Solomon argues that early modern spectators acknowledged and accepted those differences and subsequently found pleasure in the pretense.[37] As Christine Woodworth points out, "If the boys were objects of sexual attraction in everyday society, why would that attraction be subverted on the stage?"[38] Thus, the relationship between male spectator and boy actor was an expected one since it reified a pederastic dynamic that Orgel claims "is both explicit and for the most part surprisingly unproblematic" in the "Elizabethan erotic imagination."[39] As inhabiting this staged female body, the boy actor embodies a potential that destabilizes political and sexual politics.

Costuming, then, becomes the primary vehicle for transformation in *Dido* since it enables "doubling" and signifies normative hierarchies that are then queered. On one hand, clothes allow boys to change into women who are desired by a largely male audience due to a recollection of the female body induced by the boy's feminine traits and costume. In her discussion of the early modern remembrance environment,

Wilder identifies the female body as a "not-quite-empty space" where it is "remembered first, desired second,"[40] and such remembrance is deployed because of the male actor's attire, making the "absent object a source of danger but also of theatrical elaboration" as the spectator is erotically influenced by the "fiction of a female presence."[41] This kind of objectification projects the male-oriented desire and blazoned female objects of Petrarchan sonnets, yet *Dido* resists such familiar heteronormative roles, instead positioning Dido as the desiring subject and Aeneas as the sexual object.

Because Dido is such a powerful centerpiece of the play, she avoids many of the sonnet conventions that would usually be attributed to a desirable woman in Petrarchan poetry of the late sixteenth century in which an unattainable lover is blazoned amongst Ovidian imagery and landscapes. There is no mention of Dido's beauty throughout the play, not to mention any blazon that dismantles it. Dido escapes Aeneas's desirous gaze, even when Ilioneus tells him to "view her well" (II, i, 72). Though Aeneas sees Dido, he does not linger on her body and, instead, inverts the look back onto himself when he complains, "she sees not me" (II, i, 73). Such reversal makes sense since the play privileges the female perspective, like Ovid's *Heroides*, yet Dido's position as the Petrarchan lover and Aeneas's role as the Petrarchan love object queers normative dynamics.

The only mention of the queen's beauty is when Dido herself asks, "Am I yet fair than when thou sawest me first?" (V, i, 114–15). Even in answer to the question, Aeneas is elusive, defining Dido's beauty by what she is not by declaring, "O Queen of Carthage, wert thou ugly-black, / Aeneas could not choose but hold thee dear" (V, i, 125). It is as if Aeneas cannot perceive Dido's body, for her appearance rejects any semblance of the blazon.

Iarbas is hardly better at seeing Dido than Aeneas, even though he actively pursues the queen. He merely hints at the value of seeing her body after Dido forbids him to look on her, and he begs, "Then pull out both mine eyes, or let me die" (III, i, 54). Otherwise, Iarbas is more concerned about his rivalry with Aeneas and a masochistic desire associated with unrequited love rather than Dido's physical beauty. Iarbas's infatuation leads to many of the play's comic moments, but his relationship with Anna also doubles Dido's pursuit of Aeneas. In the midst of a staged sacrifice and Iarbas's "plaining prayers" (IV, ii, 8), Anna pleas for Iarbas to let "Anna be thy song" (IV, ii, 45). But Iarbas's response, "I will fly from these alluring eyes" (IV, ii, 50), calls attention to Anna's gaze. In its doubling of Dido's pursuit of Aeneas, it replicates a queer scenario throughout the play in which the gaze is directed away from female bodies in order to emphasize homoerotic and female desire.

The reversal in which Dido lusts after Aeneas and objectifies him not only conveys her centrality in the play, but it also associates gender reversal with early modern conceptions of lovesickness. Dido certainly perceives Aeneas's body after having been touched on the breast by Cupid's arrow. Cupid-as-Ascanius sits in Dido's lap, and the arrow's effect seems to take its course as she grows nonsensical while speaking to Iarbas, calling him forth, sending him away, and comically continuing to frustrate and confuse the suitor. Finally, Aeneas approaches, and Dido orders Anna to "tell them none shall gaze on him but I, / Lest their gross eye-beams taint my lover's cheeks" (III, i, 72–3). Though she is already under Cupid's spell, Dido anticipates the power of Aeneas's "gross eye-beams," a reference to Marsilio Ficino's Neoplatonic version of love-sickness called "fascination" that Lesel Dawson describes as love entering "through the eyes, infecting the body and initiating the pathological sequence of erotic melancholy."[42] Dawson explains that the consequence of lovesickness, aside from associations with fire and burning, are that "[l]overs are blind to the imperfections of their beloved, transforming any physical flaw into a distinguishing asset."[43] Lovers lack control of their own desire and, in *Dido*, fascination results in queer gender expression.

Within the play, men are feminized and women masculinized in ways that similarly project Ovidian gender reversals that render women burning with desire in pursuit of men. Dido cannot help but blazon Aeneas's face and body. In Ovidian extravagance, she dismantles Aeneas when she proclaims,

> I'll make me bracelets of his golden hair;
> His glistering eyes shall be my looking-glass,
> His lips an altar, where I'll offer up
> As many kisses as the sea hath sands.
> Instead of music I will hear him speak,
> His looks shall be my only library
> And thou, Aeneas, Dido's treasury,
> In whose fair bosom I will lock more wealth
> Than twenty thousand Indias can afford. (III, i, 84–95)

Dido's anticipation of breaking Aeneas into "bracelets," a "looking-glass," an "altar," a "library," and a "treasury" reflects the material and civic interests of a monarch. Marlowe effectively turns the Ovidian blazon on its head, using it to reassert female power and influence in the face of compromising infatuation. Starks-Estes notes that the Petrarchan deployment of the blazon misogynistically fragments the female body as a method of reasserting manhood in response to the masochism of lovesickness,[44] and Dido succumbs to the same debilitating desire; yet the stage direction when Dido confesses, "I am free from all, / [aside] And yet, God knows, entangled unto one" (III, i, 152–3) also suggests that her desire extends beyond the Petrarchan mode. Marlowe's use of "entangled" serves as a mnemonic cue that aligns Dido's desire with the sexual aggression and seizure characteristic of *Metamorphoses*, particularly that of Salmacis, who rather violently entangles Hermaphroditus. As such, Dido's blazon serves as a signifier of female power as it relates to governance and sexuality.

Marlowe further deploys Ovidian reversals after Dido and Aeneas enter the cave and consummate Dido's desire, yet the scene also emphasizes the comical naivety and inexperience of *Amores*'s speaker in order to undermine the masculinity of what ought to be a perfect example of male virility in the epic hero. In the cave, Dido seduces Aeneas by describing his eyes that "do pierce" (III, iv, 11), his "amorous face" that "sparkles fire" (III, iv, 18) and his "burning arms" (III, iv, 21), but Aeneas completely ignores Dido's body and misrecognizes her desire, asking, "What ails my queen? Is she fall'n sick of late?" (III, iv, 23) and "What means fair Dido by this doubtful speech?" (III, iv, 30). The blazon continues the Petrarchan objectification of Aeneas in Ovidian language that is unfamiliar to the naive, male love object, leaving Dido to concoct strategies for managing his behavior. As Aeneas admits in his embedded narrative, "Manhood would not serve" (II, i, 272). From these multiple reversals, normative power constructions are inverted, and the masculinity of an epic tradition – as well as that of early modern heteronormativity – are queered.

Such reversals abound in *Metamorphoses*, *Heroides*, and *Amores* through queer gender roles and political subversion. *Heroides* appropriates episodes from epic narratives and feminizes them through female-authored letters of complaint against male lovers; and Marlowe's own *All Ovid's Elegies* incorporates what M. L. Stapleton refers to as Ovid's "psychology of desire in their narratives so marked by fissures and gaps"[45] associated with an inconsistent and unreliable speaker who denies being a "circus rider of love," or "*desultor amoris*" (*Amores* I, iii, 15), even though he proves to be exactly that. In *Metamorphoses*, reversals occur when desiring women pursue beautifully feminized men: Salmacis's snakelike embrace imprisons the unwilling Hermaphroditus (*Metamorphoses* IV, 449); Venus seduces the beautiful Adonis (X, 839); Aurora abducts Cephalas (VII, 905), and Myrrah lusts after and seduces her father, Cinyras (X, 500–34). At first glance, many of these examples of Ovidian queerness may seem to reify normative politics disagreeably. But while Salmacis, Venus, and Aurora do express womanly desire in ways that subvert Roman *virtus*, or manliness, they perform their desire within a sexual hierarchy that asserts Olympian dominance and mortal servitude.

As illustrated by the *desultor*, Ovidian reversal is characterized not by pure inversion but by problematic disruption, paradox, and inconsistency. By reifying one construct, another is dismantled. Myrrah endorses a powerful heteronormative order that privileges a mature, paternal partner, yet the same construct shatters when desire pushes too far toward paternal incest. Similarly, pursuing goddesses disrupts normativity through the performance and consequence of the masculine sexuality and seizure they mimic. In asserting one norm, they subvert another, producing a precedent of complicated queering that Marlowe then projects into his plays and poems through the kind of dialogue and staging that appears in *Dido*'s homoerotic scenes. In yet another intratextual reference to the prologue, for example, Dido crowns Aeneas king in Act four and declares,

> Now looks Aeneas like immortal Jove:
> O where is Ganymede, to hold his cup,
> and Mercury to fly for what he calls?
> Ten thousand Cupids hover in the air
> and fan it in Aeneas' lovely face! (IV, iv, 45–9)

Dido has just given Aeneas a "diadem" and "golden scepter," pointing to the splendor of his royal attire and, by extension, Jupiter's elegant costume. Dido's words are multipurpose in that they appear to reconfigure the prologue's eroticism along heteronormative lines. Previously, Dido is situated as Jupiter through the repeated language and imagery of the first scene. This time, Ganymede, Cupid, and Mercury are all evoked along with the emblematic fan while Dido performs the role of lovesick ruler, but she compensates for Aeneas's disinterest by foisting monarchal power upon him. Despite her attempt to place Aeneas in the role of the desiring Jupiter, Dido only succeeds in yet another complex Ovidian reversal where reifying heteronormative gender roles only leads to more queering because, despite his crown, Aeneas continues as the Ganymede to Dido's Jupiter. So when Dido asks "where is Ganymede," the answer points toward Aeneas.

Aeneas's association with Ganymede is staged through clothing and physicality. When Dido first meets Aeneas, he is clad in "base robes" and seeks her affirmation that "Aeneas is Aeneas" (II, i, 84). In doing so, Dido asserts the right to define Aeneas and establish herself as the stable influence on a character whose identity as the epic or traitorous "hero" remains in flux throughout the play, a direct appropriation of Dido's lament in *Heroides* aimed at the "false Aeneas." Therefore, Aeneas occupies a clearly subordinate position in regards to Dido, emphasizing the social disparity associated with the cup-bearing Ganymede (*Metamorphoses* X, 166). Before Cupid infects Dido with his arrow, she exerts powerful control over Aeneas by managing his appearance and diverting the spectator's gaze. When Ilioneus reveals to Aeneas that "here Queen Dido wears th'imperial crown, / Who for Troy's sake hath entertained us all / And clad us in these wealthy robes we wear" (II, i, 63–5), he establishes Dido as a woman who rules through artifice, exerting her power by reducing men to portraits. A move that may have extended far beyond costuming, since Mary E. Smith suggests that large portraits of Dido's suitors were likely draped over a "mansion" representing the palace walls,[46] though Andrew Duxfield argues in favor of a largely "empty" stage for the sake of spatial fluidity.[47] As a result, the Trojan men become a collective homage to Dido's wealth and influence because without the Carthaginian costume linking them directly to her, they are reduced to rag-wearing vagabonds. Therefore, Dido's use of Aeneas's and his men's attire to demonstrate her power would simply reaffirm her use of visual rhetoric.

Though Dido repeatedly defines her rule through an iconography that projects Ovidian female power, the actors' bodies link Dido and Aeneas to the prologue's queer dynamics. Considering that Dido carries Cupid in her arms, Cope reasons that the character is intended for an older boy capable of holding an eight-year-old child.[48] Therefore, Dido is at least as big as Aeneas, and it is possible that Dido may even loom over Aeneas, further replicating the dynamic between Jupiter and Ganymede. Drawing the comparison between Ganymede and Aeneas allows spectators to realize that Dido's gift of the crown and scepter to Aeneas is not unlike Jupiter's gift of the marriage jewels to Ganymede. Both exchanges are motivated by a disempowering desire that unsettles the monarchal status quo. By surrendering Juno's marriage jewels, Jupiter differentiates between the infidelity linked to his pederasty and his heteronormative trysts, since the gift not only fractures matrimonial faithfulness but also dynastic integrity. Therefore, Dido's presentation of the diadem and scepter to Aeneas – though normative in appearance – encourages the same recognition of institutional fracture. The staging that links Aeneas to Ganymede is important because it cleverly interrogates political instability through queer subject positions. In her discussion of class and duty in *Dido*'s prologue, MacDonald argues, "Jove's offering of Juno's wedding jewels to Ganymede outrages the heterosexual and patriarchal order which underscores Aeneas's epic quest toward lordship and dynastic marriage"; and she claims that "Marlowe uses his Ganymede as a weapon against heterosexual and familial, as well as generational, hierarchies."[49] Jupiter's gift to Ganymede undermines epic constructions of masculinity and marriage. Rather than marriage serving as a device for *virtus* through the possession and control of female bodies, the jewels carry with them connotations of heteronormative erosion, as Ganymede trespasses filial and matrimonial boundaries.

By reshaping a largely Virgilian narrative through Ovidian appropriations, Marlowe makes possible the interrogation of hierarchies and identities as well as the intersections between public and private life. Though *Dido* often seems to reify normative sexuality and power, it ultimately queers through transformations that make the very production possible. Bodies merge and identities destabilize in multiple ways throughout the play as it evokes the protean instability of gender and power through staging and rhetoric that emphasize the reversals, fissures, and eroticism that reconstructs Ovid's queer ideologies through a complex rhizomatic network. Ovidian appropriations are projected and filtered through Petrarchan desire as well as its antecedents and antitheses, and in doing so, the play demonstrates an Ovidian mode that reverberates throughout the rest of Marlowe's plays and poems.

Notes

1. A special thanks to Lisa S. Starks for her helpful feedback and continual support.
2. The degree of Nashe's involvement is contested; however, it appears evident that some partnership occurred. See Murphy, *The Marlowe-Shakespeare Continuum*, as well as Wiggins, "When Did Marlowe Write *Dido*?," pp. 521–41.
3. When using the term "appropriation," I refer to Jean I. Marsden's description in *The Appropriation of Shakespeare*, p. 1 as "seizure for one's own uses," and I distinguish between appropriation and adaptation through Christy Desmet and Sujata Iyengar's explanation as a "difference of degree rather than kind" in their article "Adaptation, Appropriation, or What You Will," p. 7.

4. Lanier, "Afterword," p. 299.
5. Refer to Sinfield, *Shakespeare, Authority, Sexuality*, pp. 89–90 for further discussion about early modern heteronormativity. In reference to gender, Sinfield notes the expectation of a dominant, masculine role and the subordinate, effeminate roles of women and male children.
6. Jankowski, *Pure Resistance*, p. 11.
7. Menon, "Introduction," pp. 6–7.
8. Halperin, *Saint Foucault*, p. 62.
9. Sara Munson Deats describes interrogative drama as being constructed "from a series of statements and counterstatements, both of which are often equally valid" related to questions about a variety of topics including "love, justice, sovereignty, nature, imagination . . . sex, gender, and desire." Deats, *Sex, Gender, and Desire*, p. 89.
10. Ibid. p. 106.
11. Bate, *Shakespeare and Ovid*, p. 25.
12. Ibid. pp. 26–7.
13. Lanier, "Shakespearean Rhizomatics," p. 27.
14. Starks-Estes, *Violence, Trauma, and* Virtus, p. 10. Also see Lafont, "Introduction," p. 2.
15. Textual references to *Dido, Queen of Carthage* are taken from the *Revels Plays* (1968), edited by H. J. Oliver.
16. Mamujee, "Performing Boys," pp. 715–16.
17. Cope, "Marlowe's *Dido*," p. 319.
18. Ibid. p. 318.
19. Lisa Jardine claims that early modern theatrical performances were largely aimed toward male spectators and eliciting arousal through the homoeroticism underlying staged crossdressing. See Jardine, *Still Harping on Daughters*, pp. 16–31.
20. Orgel, *Impersonations*, pp. 70, 71, 103.
21. MacDonald, "Marlowe's Ganymede," p. 100.
22. Such differentiation contrasts sexual dyads from homosocial pairings that imagine "*the friend as another self*," a relationship that John S. Garrison explains was built on equitable dyads versus imbalanced, carnal oppositions. See Garrison, *Friendship and Queer Theory*, p. 13.
23. See Starks-Estes's *Violence, Trauma, and* Virtus for a discussion of sadomasochism and the sonnet tradition.
24. References to Ovid's *Amores* refer to *Heroides and Amores*, translated by Grant Showerman.
25. Arthur Golding's 1567 translation of *Metamorphoses* is used throughout.
26. MacDonald, "Marlowe's Ganymede," p. 106.
27. Thomas Churchyard's 1572 translation of *Tristia* includes Ganymede in the Second Book during a recounting of love's tragic victims.
28. Barkan, *The Gods Made Flesh*, p. 205.
29. I refer to the 1590 edition printed by John Wolfe for William Ponsombie. Archived at the Folger Shakespeare Library.

30. Barkan, *The Gods Made Flesh*, p. 235.
31. Tribble, "'The Dark Backward and Abysm of Time,'" p. 154.
32. Wilder, *Shakespeare's Memory Theatre*, p. 2.
33. Kingsley-Smith, "Cupid, Infantilism and Maternal Desire," p. 129.
34. Orgel, *Impersonations*, p. 103.
35. Chess, *Male-to-Female Crossdressing*, p. 6.
36. Stubbes, *Anatomie of Abuses*, pp. 144–5.
37. Solomon, *Re-Dressing the Canon*, p. 37.
38. Woodworth, "Boys in Dresses," p. 53.
39. Orgel, *Impersonations*, p. 70.
40. Wilder, *Shakespeare's Memory Theatre*, pp. 2–3.
41. Ibid. p. 3.
42. Dawson, *Lovesickness*, p. 26.
43. Ibid. p. 18.
44. Starks-Estes, *Violence, Trauma, and* Virtus, p. 49.
45. Stapleton, *Marlowe's Ovid*, p. 33.
46. Smith, "Staging Marlowe's Dido," p. 180.
47. Duxfield, "'Where Am I Now?,'" pp. 82–4.
48. Cope, "Marlowe's *Dido*," p. 322.
49. Macdonald, "Marlowe's Ganymede," p. 107.

Bibliography

Barkan, Leonard, *The Gods Made Flesh: Metamorphosis and the Pursuit of Paganism* (New Haven: Yale University Press, 1986).

Bate, Jonathan, *Shakespeare and Ovid* (New York: Oxford University Press, 1993).

Chess, Simone, *Male-to-Female Crossdressing in Early Modern English Literature: Gender, Performance, and Queer Relations* (New York: Routledge, 2016).

Cope, Jackson I., "Marlowe's *Dido* and the Titillating Children," *English Literary Renaissance* 4.3, September 1974, pp. 315–25.

Dawson, Lesel, *Lovesickness and Gender in Early Modern English Literature* (Oxford and New York: Oxford University Press, 2008).

Deats, Sara Munson, *Sex, Gender, and Desire in the Plays of Christopher Marlowe* (Newark, DE: University of Delaware Press, 1997).

Desmet, Christy and Sujata Iyengar, "Adaptation, Appropriation, or What You Will," *Shakespeare* 11.1, 2015, pp. 10–19.

Duxfield, Andrew, "'Where Am I Now?': The Articulation of Space in Shakespeare's *King Lear* and Marlowe's *Dido, Queen of Carthage*," *Cahiers Élisabéthains: A Journal of English Renaissance Studies* 88.1, October 2015, pp. 81–93.

Garrison, John S., *Friendship and Queer Theory in the Renaissance: Gender and Sexuality in Early Modern England* (New York: Routledge, 2014).

Halperin, David, *Saint Foucault: Towards a Gay Hagiography* (New York: Oxford University Press, 1995).

Jankowski, Theodora A., *Pure Resistance: Queer Virginity in Early Modern English Drama* (Philadelphia: University of Pennsylvania Press, 2000).

Jardine, Lisa, *Still Harping on Daughters: Women and Drama in the Age of Shakespeare* (Sussex, England: Harvester Press and Totowa, NJ: Barnes & Noble, 1983).

Kingsley-Smith, Jane, "Cupid, Infantilism and Maternal Desire on the Early Stage," in Agnès Lafont (ed.), *Shakespeare's Erotic Mythology and Ovidian Renaissance Culture* (Farnham and Burlington: Ashgate, 2013).

Lafont, Agnès, "Introduction," in Agnès Lafont (ed.), *Shakespeare's Erotic Mythology and Ovidian Renaissance Culture* (Farnham and Burlington: Ashgate, 2013).

Lanier, Douglas M., "Shakespeare / Not Shakespeare: Afterword," in Christy Desmet, Natalie Loper, and Jim Casey (eds), *Shakespeare / Not Shakespeare* (New York: Palgrave Macmillan, 2017), pp. 293–306.

Lanier, Douglas, "Shakespearean Rhizomatics: Adaptation, Ethics, Value," in Alexa Huang and Elizabeth Rivlin (eds), *Shakespeare and the Ethics of Appropriation* (New York: Palgrave Macmillan, 2014), pp. 21–40.

Laqueur, Thomas, *Making Sex: Body and Gender from the Greeks to Freud* (Cambridge, MA: Harvard University Press, 1992).

MacDonald, Joyce Green, "Marlowe's Ganymede," in Viviana Comensoli and Anne Russell (eds), *Enacting Gender on the English Renaissance Stage* (Urbana: University of Illinois Press, 1999).

Mamujee, Shehzana, "'To Serve Us in That Behalf When Our Pleasure Is to Call for Them': Performing Boys in Renaissance England," *Renaissance Studies*, 28.5, November 2014, pp. 714–30.

Marlowe, Christopher, *Dido, Queen of Carthage*, in H. J. Oliver (ed.), *The Revels Plays* (London: Methuen, 1968).

Marlowe, Christopher, *The Tragedie of Dido Queene of Carthage Played by the Children of Her Maiesties Chappell* (At London: Printed, by the widdowe Orwin, for Thomas Woodcocke, 1594). Reproduction.

Marsden, Jean I. (ed.), *The Appropriation of Shakespeare: Post-Renaissance Reconstructions of The Works and the Myth* (New York: St. Martin's Press, 1991).

Menon, Madhavi, "Introduction," in Madhavi Menon (ed.), *ShakesQueer: A Queer Companion to the Complete Works of Shakespeare* (Durham, NC: Duke University Press, 2011).

Murphy, Donna N., *The Marlowe-Shakespeare Continuum: Christopher Marlowe, Thomas Nashe, and the Authorship of Early Shakespeare and Anonymous Plays* (Newcastle upon Tyne: Cambridge Scholars Publishing, 2013).

Orgel, Stephen, *Impersonations: The Performance of Gender in Shakespeare's England* (Cambridge and New York: Cambridge University Press, 1996).

Ovid, *Heroides. Amores.*, Grant Showerman (trans.) (Cambridge, MA: Harvard University Press, 1977), pp. 318–511.

Ovid, *Ovid's Metamorphoses: The Arthur Golding Translation of 1567,* John Frederick Nims (ed.) (Philadelphia: Paul Dry Books, 2000).

Sinfield, Alan, *Shakespeare, Authority, Sexuality: Unfinished Business in Cultural Materialism* (New York: Routledge, 2006).

Smith, Mary E., "Staging Marlowe's Dido Queene of Carthage," *Studies in English Literature, 1500–1900* 17.2, 1977, pp. 177–90.

Solomon, Alisa, *Re-Dressing the Canon: Essays on Theater and Gender* (London: Routledge, 1997).

Spenser, Edmund, *The Faerie Queene Disposed into Twelue Books, Fashioning XII. Morall Vertues* (London: Printed [by John Wolfe] for William Ponsonbie, 1590).

Stapleton, M. L., *Marlowe's Ovid: The Elegies in the Marlowe Canon* (New York: Routledge, 2014).

Starks-Estes, Lisa S., *Violence, Trauma, and* Virtus *in Shakespeare's Roman Poems and Plays: Transforming Ovid* (Basingstoke: Palgrave Macmillan, 2014).

Stubbes, Phillip, *Anatomie of Abuses* (London: The New Shakespeare Society, [1583] 1877), pp. 144–5.

Tribble, Evelyn B., "'The Dark Backward and Abysm of Time': The Tempest and Memory," *College Literature* 1, 2006, p. 154.

Wiggins, Martin, "When Did Marlowe Write *Dido, Queen of Carthage*?," *The Review of English Studies* 59.241, September 2008, pp. 521–41.

Wilder, Lina Perkins, *Shakespeare's Memory Theatre: Recollection, Properties, and Character* (Cambridge: Cambridge University Press, 2010).

Woodworth, Christine, "Boys in Dresses: The Sexualization of Renaissance Child Actors," *Text & Presentation: Journal of the Comparative Drama Conference* 24, April 2003, p. 53.

Chapter 4

"Let Rome in Tiber melt":
Hermaphroditic Transformation in
Antonius and *Antony and Cleopatra*
Deborah Uman

Ovid's gender-bending tale of Hermaphroditus and Salmacis captured the attention of early modern writers and readers. In addition
to Golding's and Sandys's translations of the entire *Metamorphoses*,
poetic versions and commentaries on this tale alone were penned
by Thomas Peends (1565), Francis Beaumont (1602), and Edward
Sherburne (1651), with the figure of the hermaphrodite appear-
ing in numerous texts ranging from medical treatises to Spenser's
Faerie Queene.[1] Predictably, critical attention centers on a variety
of gender-focused questions, although Jonathan Bate examines the
hermaphrodite as a metaphor for art, which brings two opposite
things together, and particularly for the hybrid practice of translation. Focusing on writers including Shakespeare and Montaigne,
who are drawn to Ovid's work, Bate sees what he calls the "aesthetics of hermaphroditism" everywhere he looks: Ovid's compositional
methods, the susceptibility of the Hermaphroditus and Salmacis tale
to opposite interpretations, and the sexual ambivalence of erotic
Ovidian poetry. In Shakespeare's work, Bate identifies a penchant
for hermaphroditic hybridity in the combination of Shakespeare's
mind "of supreme originality" and his commitment "to an art of
translation."[2]

Hermaphroditism can work equally well as a figure for the more
expansive practices of appropriation, particularly when we consider
Ovid's multivalent story of Hermaphroditus's creation, which can
be understood as both an act of sexual aggression that focuses on
difference and a harmonious comingling of souls. As Christy Desmet explains, recent definitions of appropriation fluctuate similarly,

depicting the practice as a kind of theft, where one party gains at the other's expense, and as a form of donation that recognizes a practice of exchange and mutuality.[3] In his exploration of Gilles Deluze and Félix Guattari's idea of the rhizome as a model for appropriation, Douglas Lanier could almost be describing the metamorphosis of Hermaphroditus, noting that Deluze and Guattari "stress the potentiality and virtuality – what a thing might become through the inexorability of difference of desire."[4] Both the emphasis on becoming and difference as well as the recognition of competing desires speak to the complex and gendered narrative of desire, struggle, and transformation, which in turn resonates with the persistent, and at times pernicious, gendered views that surface when discussing concepts of originality, imitation, translation, and appropriation.

In this chapter I will use the tale of Salmacis and Hermaphroditus as a vehicle for considering the connections between the theme of gender fluidity and the practice of literary transformations in Shakespeare's *Antony and Cleopatra* and Mary Sidney Herbert's earlier translation of Robert Garnier's closet drama *Antonius*. The two works, both clearly in debt to Plutarch's *Lives of the Noble Grecians and Romanes*, also include numerous appropriations of Ovid's *Metamorphoses*. Although never referred to directly in either play, Hermaphroditus's story provides a useful Ovidian model for the plays' shifting concerns. Indeed, Ruth Gilbert, in her extensive study of early modern hermaphrodites, reads Antony as a paradigm of the often dreaded figure – a hyper-masculine man "ungendered by his devotion to a powerful queen."[5] Although Gilbert focuses on Shakespeare's Antony, we can define him thusly in Sidney Herbert's play as well. Additionally, *Antony and Cleopatra* includes remnants of Hermaphroditus's tale of watery violation/consummation in its many references not just to gender reversals but also to rivers that overflow their boundaries and threaten to undo even the simplest of distinctions. The characters in both versions of Antony and Cleopatra's story demonstrate the simultaneous desire for and resistance to transformation, presenting a world view that parallels Hermaphroditus's own contradictory hatred of his disempowering metamorphosis and his prayer for anyone who bathes in Salmacis's fountain to be similarly changed. As mentioned above, the story often allows for seemingly contradictory interpretations of this union of opposites, and as such serves as a useful lens through which to understand Sidney Herbert's and Shakespeare's plays, which fluctuate between anxieties over female power and recognition of the loss of clear markers distinguishing men and women, Rome and Egypt, conqueror and conquered, original and imitation. Despite such anxieties, the two plays finally reject notions of masculine rigidity in favor of a more flexible view of gender and artistic creativity.

As the editors of the complete works of Mary Sidney Herbert have pointed out, her translation of *Antonius* was the first English dramatization of this otherwise well-known story and is an early demonstration of Sidney Herbert's artistic talents and ambitions. Although Garnier's original was performed in France, his Senecan drama, with its focus on rhetoric instead of action, would look noticeably different on stage from Shakespeare's retelling of the story.[6] In completing her brother's translation of the *Psalms*, Sidney Herbert would later establish her reputation as a poet through her experimentation with form and meter as well as her commitment to developing a characteristically English poetic style.[7] In this earlier work, despite a close adherence to the meaning of the original, Sidney Herbert already reveals her adaptive skills through her conversion of Garnier's alexandrine couplets into iambic pentameter with a variety of stanza lengths and rhyme schemes. In a detailed explanation of the various forms used throughout *Antonius*, Victor Skretkowicz describes her process as translating "from one textured style into another," with the result of creating a "parallel but pre-eminently personal poetic and language register."[8] This combination of fidelity and experimentation provides an example of translation as a hybrid – or hermaphroditic – art form. In so doing, Sidney Herbert, like many women who used translation as an acceptable vehicle to enter into the male sphere of literary creation, challenged longstanding views of faithful translations as derivative and servile.[9] Skretkowicz suggests that Sidney Herbert chose to translate Garnier's play, at least in part, for its feminist depiction of Cleopatra "as an unwavering and loyal wife, alienated by an Antony who misunderstands her motives."[10] By shifting our attention to Antony, we can locate a more complicated view of gender, suggesting that the play does more than exonerate one famous woman. It is also interested in the possibility of collapsing gender binaries and challenging the dichotomy between original and translation, and thus expanding the possibilities for women dedicated to beauty and poetry.

Sidney Herbert's translation process exhibits hermaphroditic ideas about gender and transformation, which is particularly visible in the Ovidian citations throughout the play. When Cleopatra elaborates on her overpowering grief when Antony rejects her, and again after his death, she speaks in Ovidian terms. Antonius does the same when he condemns his beloved queen for his loss at Actium, comparing his defeat to Actaeon's dismemberment. In one such attack – the play's opening lines – Antonius reveals that underneath his anger lie anxieties of feminization. He begins the play searching for places to lay blame, finally landing on Cleopatra who pursued him and caught him "in her allurements" (I, 12). His fluctuation between the subjective and objective case of the first person reflects his shifting view of his own role in his downfall, acknowledging, for instance, that he "[d]isdain'd my freends, and of statelye Rome / Despoilde the Empire of her best attires" (I, 14–15). Antonius's depiction of his actions against Rome as a kind of undressing provides an early example of his focus on the body, and he quickly reveals his own fear of being stripped, describing his military loss as a figurative undressing: "am me unarm'de / Yeelded to *Caesar* naked of defense" (I, 26–7). Antonius uncomfortably links the spheres of fashion and war and imagines himself becoming a visible and feminized symbol of Caesar's military conquest.

The vulnerability and feminization associated with nakedness is an important motif in Ovid's "Salmacis and Hermaphroditus." After he has rejected her initial overtures, Salmacis hides in the bushes and watches Hermaphroditus as he strips off his clothes before jumping in the pool. While already enamored, Salmacis becomes inflamed only upon seeing Hermaphroditus's "naked beautie"; and she feels assured of her victory once she sees her beloved swimming in the water "through which his bodie faire and white doth glistringly appeare" (IV, 437). Spying on the naked Hermaphroditus, Salmacis resembles Ovid's Actaeon, spying on the naked Diana, though her voyeurism results in a desired union rather than dismemberment. Antonius's description also offers a complex reconfiguration of the Actaeon myth.[11] In his version, Antonius plays both the naked goddess and the unfortunate hunter, while he is conquered, not just by Caesar, but also by Cleopatra, who "has me vanquisht: not by force . . . but by sweete baites / Of thy eyes graces" (I, 34–6). Another subtle reference to Actaeon surfaces as Antonius imagines resisting Caesar until death:

But when that Death, my glad refuge, shall have
Bounded the course of my unstedfast life,
And frozen corps under a marble colde
Within tombes bosome widdowe of my soule:
Then at his will let him it subject make:
Then what he will let *Caesar* doo with me:
Make me limme after limme be rent. (I, 44–50)

As he envisions himself removed from his tomb and dismembered by Caesar, Antonius predicts a loss of control over his own representation. Although he imagines himself torn apart, his vision is not a straightforward reversal of a blazonic gendered equation.[12] Antonius is both the agent and the object of dismembering; and when he describes being conquered by his love for Cleopatra, he adopts the subject position of a typical Petrarchan lover who creates his own poetic memorial.[13] Noting that Ovid frames the Hermaphroditus and Salmacis myth by the Actaeon story of Book 3, Bate suggests that Ovid takes pleasure both in the reversal of literary convention that occurs when Salmacis watches Hermaphroditus undress and in "imagining the metamorphosis of a male body into an artwork."[14] In contemplating a noble death, Sidney Herbert's Antonius is able to think of himself as artist and artwork.

In a later reference to clothing, Antonius's companion tries to comfort the demoralized soldier by reminding him that even the great Hercules was undone by love for a woman. Here the fear of being feminized by love for a woman is made explicit in Lucilius's rhetorical questioning:

> Great Hercules, Hercules once that was
> Wonder of earth and heav'n, matchles in might,
> . . .
> Did he not under Pleasures burthen bow?
> Did he not Captive to his passion yelde,
> When by his Captive, so he was enflam'de,
> As no your selfe in Cleopatra burne?
> Slept in hir lapp, hir bosome kist and kiste,
> With base unsemelie service bought her love,
> Spinning at distaff, and with sinewy hand
> Winding on spindles threde, in maides attire?
> His conqu'ring clubbe at rest on wal did hang:
> His bow unstringd he bent not as he us'de"
> Upon his shafts the weaving spiders spunne:
> And his hard cloake the freating mothes did pierce. (III, 1221–38)

Given that Plutarch's Antony claims Hercules as his ancestor, the reference to the hero's dressing as a woman at the behest of his lover Omphale is apt. This passage also shows Sidney Herbert's hand in shaping the allusion. As Skretkowicz explains, by omitting Garnier's explicit reference to Omphale as Hercules's captor (*Quand d'Omphale captif*), Sidney Herbert "builds on Hercules's paradoxical submission to his prisoner,"[15] thus offering a vivid picture of what Lisa S.

Starks-Estes refers to as the masochistic scenario in which the heroic male both longs for and dreads being dominated by his mistress.[16] Additionally, the conclusion of this passage offers an unusual image of encasement and atrophy. Focusing now on the manly apparel that Hercules is not wearing, Lucilius imagines the great hero's shafts and cape being attacked by bugs. That Hercules's hyper-masculine attire is attacked both by the piercing moths and the weaving spiders demonstrates Lucilius's unease in imagining his leader completely conquered by a woman but also acknowledges a link between the memorializing process and a specifically feminine form of artistic creation.

Antonius's response to Lucilius's attempts at comfort demonstrates his desire to regain some form of masculinity by taking over the memorializing process. Initially he acknowledges being like his ancestor only because he has fallen captive to a woman; and because of this admission, Antonius turns to thoughts of suicide as his only recourse. Characterizing such an end as "brave," "noble," "glorious," and "courageous," Antonius sounds desperate to pick up his sword and reclaim his manhood. He tells Lucilius, "I must deface the shame of time abus'd, / I must adorne the wanton loves I us'de / With some couragiouse act: that my last daie / By mine owne hand my spots may wash away" (III, 1251–4). His repetition of the first-person pronoun (now only in the nominative case) coupled with active verbs demonstrate his insistence on erasing any feminizing influence through manly action. But speaking within a genre that values language over action, Antonius cannot fully escape the pull of aesthetics, and his promise to adorn his love with a courageous act provides a stark contrast to his insistence on defacing his shame.

Even during his earlier attack on Cleopatra, Antonius acknowledges this pull, pointing to the allure of "the lookes, the grace, the woords" of his Queen (I, 102). Unable to prioritize among her "virtues," he directly acknowledges Cleopatra's verbal powers as well as the pull of her appearance and bearing; as a result, he momentarily gives up the emotional struggle with his love just as he gave up the military battle with Caesar. In so doing, his thoughts turn away from the battlefield and towards aesthetics:

Thy only care is sight of *Nilus* streames,
Sight of that face whose gilefull semblant doth
(Wandring in thee) infect thy tainted hart.
. . .
Enough of conquest, praise thou deem'st enough,

If soone enough the bristled fields thou see
Of fruitfull *Ægipt*, and the stranger floud
Thy Queenese faire eyes (another *Pharos*) lights. (I, 111–19)

Antonius's emphasis on sight and eyes leads him to thoughts of praise, the work of poetry. Although he quickly returns to attacking Cleopatra and women in general, this moment again reveals his recognition of the value of physical and literary beauty, a recognition that Cleopatra shares along with her playwright and translator.

In its association of the seductive queen and the powers of the Nile, these lines also provide a link to the story of Hermaphroditus and Salmacis, in which the desirous nymph spends her time bathing, combing her hair, and consulting the pool to ponder her increasing beauty. In Ovid's version, Salmacis actively pursues an unwilling Hermaphroditus.[17] The gender reversal of Ovid's typical narrative is evident, as is the tenor of violation in his description of the nymph's underwater embrace and conquest of the resistant youth:

The price is won (cride Salmacis aloud) he is mine wone.
And therewithal in all post hast she having lightly throwne
His garments off, flew to the Poole and cast hir thereinto,
And caught him fast between hir armes for ought that he could doe.
Yea maugre all his wrestling and his struggling to and fro,
She held him still, and kissed him a hundred times and mo.
And willed he nillde he with hir hands she toucht his naked brest:
And now on this side now on that (for all he did resist
And strive to wrest him from hir gripes) she clung unto him fast,
And wound about him like a Snake, which snatched up in hast
And being by the Prince of Birdes borne lightly up aloft,
Doth writhe hir selfe about his necke and griping talants oft,
And cast hir taile about his wings displayed in the winde:
Or like as Ivie runnes on trees about the utter rinde:
Or as the Crabfish having caught his enmy in the Seas,
Doth claspe him in on every side with all his crooked cleas.
   (IV, 440–55)

Golding's translation emphasizes Salmacis's dominance of Hermaphroditus, although the similes in this passage reflect the shifting sense of power and strength that marks this tale of metamorphosis.[18] In the first comparison, in which Salmacis is the snake and Hermaphroditus the eagle, she is figured as the captive who is able to manipulate its body and overcome its captor. The phallic symbolism of the snake, along with the serpent's prominence in Christian-gendered iconography, only further complicates this unstable image, which is similarly destabilized in both plays' dramatizations of Cleopatra's suicide.[19] The image of ivy and trees deviates from any language of predator and prey, but still suggests a kind of reversal as the thin, fragile vine strangles its much stronger counterparts. By the last example, Salmacis is compared to a crabfish (Ovid writes *polypus*) capturing its enemy. The visual image matches the other two, but the narrative of the underdog's victory is less clear, forecasting the granting of Salmacis's wish to be joined with Hermaphroditus forever, such that "yet could not say it was a perfect boy, / Nor perfect wench: it seemed both and none of both to beene" (469–70). Here the dissolution of gender binaries undoes the possibility of anyone's victory, even as Salmacis's name and presence disappear.[20]

The ending of this tale is nothing if not paradoxical, as the metamorphosed Hermaphroditus rails against his "weakened" condition and calls for anyone else who jumps in this pool to be similarly made "halfe a man." While Sidney Herbert's Antonius also hates himself for being unmanned and victimized by a powerful woman, I would argue that the play's acknowledgement of the power of language and female beauty and the translator's dedication to poetic transformation offer a counterbalancing outlook that is mirrored by the early modern view of the hermaphrodite as "an elevated ideal, the perfect union of opposites, a philosophical and spiritual fantasy of harmonious plentitude."[21] Shakespeare's play appropriates this theme of plentitude as a central motif in his *Antony and Cleopatra*, and its frequent references to water and crossdressing amplify the links to the Hermaphroditus myth and Ovid's retelling of it. In an analysis of "Venus and Adonis," which he reads as the joyful fulfillment of the potential in the Hermaphroditus and Salmacis story and a demonstration of Shakespeare's fascination with the myth, Bate argues that Shakespeare, like Beaumont in his more straightforward translation of Ovid's tale, recognizes the "enduring reminder of the creative potential of sexuality" evident in the dissolution of sexual identity occurring in both unions.[22] Bate sees a similar dissolution of identity in Shakespeare's *Antony and Cleopatra*, which he employs to support his conception of Shakespeare's use of Ovid less as a source than as a precedent that facilitates an investigation of internal and emotional transformation.[23] Relatedly, I have argued that Shakespeare's fascination with the idea of metaphorical translation is part of his larger ruminations on the power of theatre and art.[24] While Sidney Herbert may not have had the privilege of treating translation so liberally, her emphasis on beauty and her attention to poetics suggest a comparable interest that Shakespeare is able to magnify in his sprawling Ovidian tragedy, even as he moves generically further from the unadulterated poetry of Ovid's epic.

Numerous critics have pointed to the gradual deconstruction of binary oppositions, particularly gendered oppositions, in *Antony and Cleopatra*. A few have linked this indeterminacy to Ovidian citations and themes.[25] Focusing on different aspects of the *Metamorphoses*, Jonathan Gil Harris and Joyce Green MacDonald both suggest that reading *Antony and Cleopatra* within an Ovidian context reveals a play that does not simply banish Cleopatra to the realm of the exotic femme fatale, but rather offers a radical view of politics that relies on an eroticized and fluid understanding of gender and power. For Harris, this means seeing the relationship between Rome and Egypt as one not of opposition but of "specularity," in which Cleopatra inhabits the role of Narcissus's watery image, reflecting the male gaze as the "self-same." [26] MacDonald argues that the play, like Ovid, blurs myth and history and rewrites Virgilian epic with the goal of claiming "the imperial for the erotic."[27] She focuses specifically on moments when "Antony sheds the dictates of Roman masculinity" and suggests that his "desire for Cleopatra threatens to breach, even to dissolve his body's boundaries."[28]

The theme of fluidity that MacDonald sees as particularly Ovidian is exemplified in the story of Hermaphroditus and Salmacis. Ovid's own revision of this tale points to its ambiguity and multivalency. Pointing out that in earlier depictions Hermaphroditus was shown as a female figure born with male genitals, Matthew Robinson explains that Ovid transforms the tradition by adding "overtones of effeminacy."[29] He also sees inconsistencies in the story, which finally presents "the result of the metamorphosis not as a seamless combination of Hermaphroditus and Salmacis . . . but rather as just Hermaphroditus alone, angry at the loss of his masculinity."[30] Lauren Silberman also notes Ovid's revision of the myth when comparing early modern versions, which vacillate among an "abhorrence of physical androgyny," an association of "civic harmony," and a "tempering of barbaric violence."[31] I understand *Antony and Cleopatra* as offering similarly contradictory attitudes that often surface in what Walter Cohen calls the play's "language of liquification."[32] This language, which frequently suggests the transgression of boundaries, gender or otherwise, is not necessarily joyful. Antony's rejection of Caesar, "let Rome in Tiber melt" (I, i, 35), is meant to glorify his embrace of Cleopatra and rejection of national boundaries, but it is tinged with a sense of guilt and regret, as Cleopatra's subsequent echo, "Melt

Egypt into Nile" (II, v, 78), signals her despair at losing Antony to Octavia. But as represented by the fertile Nile, this liquification is also the substance of life and love. In describing the river to his Roman compatriots, Antony tells both of the Egyptians' understanding of its ebb and flow and of the mysterious "slime and ooze" that helps to produce a bountiful harvest.

Fittingly it is on another river, the Cydnus, that Antony first sees Cleopatra. Again this scene is narrated to the Romans, this time by Enobarbus, whose language highlights Cleopatra's regal status, the decadence of her boat, and her apparent ability to bring about paradoxical impossibilities. Her male attendants stand and "[w]ith divers-coloured fans whose wind did seem / To glow the delicate cheeks which they did cool, / and what they undid did" (II, ii, 209–11). Likewise, Enobarbus recalls Antony whistling in the air, "which but for vacancy / Had gone to gaze on Cleopatra too, / And made a gap in nature" (II, ii, 222–4). These passages closely mirror Plutarch's description of Antony's first sight of Cleopatra: both compare her to Venus and her female attendants to Nereides, which can bring us back to Hermaphroditus, whose mother Aphrodite is the Greek version of Venus, and to Salmacis, a Naiad or water nymph who can be understood as a cousin of the goddesses of the sea.[33] These connections underscore the myth's and play's explorations of female power, both erotic and political, and the helplessness of men under such women's spells.

Evoking Hermaphroditus and Salmacis's underwater battle, *Antony and Cleopatra* similarly locates water as the site of multiple power struggles in which it is often difficult to extricate clear gendered and hierarchical divisions. After Antony has left for Rome, Cleopatra looks for diversions and calls for her fishing rod. In imagining herself as a fisherwoman catching Antony, Cleopatra offers an analogous play on the predator/prey metaphors of the Hermaphroditus myth. But by describing the fish as "tawny" (II, v, 12), using the same adjective used to characterize her own color, she again complicates any notion of simple role reversal, as does Charmian's reminiscence of her mistress tricking Antony into believing that he won a wager by having her servant hang a preserved fish on Antony's hook. As both winner of the bet and victim of a practical joke, Antony occupies paradoxical positions vis-à-vis his queen, who constructs a comical memorial of him in his absence partly to delay the messenger's perhaps more accurate report of Antony's status in Rome.

The domestic and perhaps trivial nature of these fishing stories contrasts with the far-reaching implications of the play's central, yet unstaged struggle, the battle at Actium. In this case, Antony's insistence on fighting by water is inextricably linked to his submission to Cleopatra, whom he calls Thetis, Achilles's mother and one of the fifty Nereides alluded to earlier. This decision absolutely undoes him. Enobarbus's warning that "your ships are not well manned" (III, vii, 34) foreshadows Antony's emasculating retreat. Similarly, Camidius's comment, "So our leader's led, / And we are women's men" (III, vii, 69–70) underscores the social upheaval created by Antony's decision. Antony's loss to Caesar also demonstrates the contrast between the two men. James W. Stone reads Caesar's victory as a demonstration of Caesarean fullness, which "melts, inundates [and] floods all opposition" and Antony's defeat as a loss of himself.[34] If taken alone, this scene might confirm a reading of the play that sees only harm in female power and gender fluidity; but the back and forth of Antony's military status, his relationship with Cleopatra, and his view of Roman masculinity undermine such an interpretation.

The play foreshadows Antony's unmanning at Actium from the opening lines of the play as well as in his act of drunken crossdressing in which he put on Cleopatra's "tires and mantles" while she wore his "sword Philippan" (II, v, 22–3).[35] This oft-remarked upon episode brings to mind the reference to crossdressing in which Sidney Herbert's Antonius is compared to Hercules spinning while dressed in women's attire.[36] Shakespeare's play also includes explicit allusions to Antony's mythic ancestor, including the Ovidian evocation, in which Antony claims to feel "the shirt of Nessus" (IV, xiii, 43) upon him and cries out to harness the rage that led Hercules to hurl the unassuming Lichas into the sea, for use against himself and his treacherous queen. Although Shakespeare's Antony does not bring up Hercules' crossdressing here, his references still highlight his wavering sense of identity, not only in terms of his masculinity but also in terms of his nationality, which itself has a gendered significance. Clayton Mackenzie notes that while Hercules is often depicted as the epitome of Romaness and military prowess, the play offers a contrary view producing a love myth "that is unprecedented and free of the shackles of Classical mythology."[37] For John Michael Archer, who points out that Herodotus claims that Hercules came from Egypt, such references highlight Antony's anxiety about his origins and his "Roman masculinism."[38]

In contrast to the ambiguity of Hercules and Antony stands Caesar, the indisputable representative of Rome and masculinity, whom Stone describes as "univocal" and "solid," despite his victory at sea.[39] In her discussion of the Antony/Caesar dichotomy, Laura

Levine demonstrates how Caesar's adherence to traditional gender definitions contributes to her interpretation of him as a stand-in for the antitheatricalist fear that acting can change one's identity; despite his final victory, she reads the play as repudiating this sentiment and revealing antitheatricality "as a posture, a front, for all the things that anti-theatricality itself expressly repudiates."[40] In this way, we can read Caesar like Salmacis. Both are victorious in water, but both ultimately disappear from the text. Salmacis is absorbed body and name into Hermaphroditus. Caesar's attempt to control the narrative fails before the poetic memorial constructed by Cleopatra. For Levine, the play's embrace of gender fluidity runs parallel to its view of theatricality, which she calls "the constitutive condition of existence itself." I would add that Shakespeare's theory of drama and art are deeply Ovidian. Transformation is required for theatre to work and is perhaps the primary focus in Shakespeare's plays and poetry. And good art should transport the audience as well, to another time and place certainly, and perhaps, if only momentarily, to another way of being.

Both Antony and Cleopatra understand language and performance as potentially transformative, and as such their attempts to memorialize each other match the view of the hermaphrodite that sees the union of opposites as a "metaphysical transcendence of dualism."[41] In the first example, Antony is flushed with his land victory over Caesar; and he rushes to embrace her, proclaiming, "O thou day o'th' world, / Chain mine armed neck; leap thou, attire and all, / Through proof of harness to my heart, and there / Ride on the pants triumphing" (IV, ix, 13–16). Despite this shift from fluid water to solid ground, Antony's language suggests an embrace of transcendent unity. He asks to be both ensnared and pierced by Cleopatra even as he points to the strength of his protective armor (the armor that Cleopatra earlier dressed him in). Instead of a resistant Hermaphroditus, Antony seeks Cleopatra's embrace and he sees no loss of self in this moment of coalescence.

After Antony's death, Cleopatra uses similarly triumphant language, describing him to Caesar's officer, Dolabella. In her imaginings, Antony unites opposites. He is "a sun and moon" (V, ii, 79). His bounty, "that grew the more by reaping" (87) resembles the fertile Nile. Though her narrative touches on numerous elements, the references to water are prominent and memorable: "his legs bestrid the ocean"; "his delights / Were dolphin-like" (81, 87–8). Cleopatra gives the play its final Antony, and it is not the Antony who curses his queen and adheres to limits. In her imagination at least, it is an

Antony who transgresses boundaries and embraces the transformative potential of human nature. The Cleopatra of Sidney Herbert's *Antonius* offers her own extended tribute to the fallen Antony, casting herself in the role of Niobe, though one whose tears have not yet turned her to stone. After blazoning herself in her grief, she creates another for Antony, "[o] neck, o armes, o hands, o breast where death / (Oh mischief) comes to choake up vitall breath" (V, 17–18), before uttering this final couplet, "That in this office weake my limes may growe, / Fainting on you, and fourth my soule may flowe" (V, 2021–2). Although not the triumphant imagining spoken by Shakespeare's Cleopatra, Sidney Herbert's queen still spends her last breaths constructing a memorial that is fluid and suggests the possibility of her final union with her beloved. The moving words of both Cleopatras present us with perhaps the ultimate revision of the Hermaphroditus myth, the version narrated by Salmacis who rejoices in her transformation and allows the potential for her story to be interpreted as showcasing the artistic and human potential for translation and the union of opposites.

Notes

1. Two valuable examples of scholarship on early modern views of Hermaphroditus are Gilbert, *Early Modern Hermaphrodites*, and Jones and Stallybrass, "Fetishizing Gender."
2. Bate, "Elizabethan Translation," pp. 34–6.
3. Desmet, "Recognizing Shakespeare," pp. 41–2.
4. Lanier, "Shakespearean Rhizomatics," p. 27.
5. Gilbert, *Early Modern Hermaphrodites*, p. 62.
6. See Hannay et al., "Antonius: Literary Context," pp. 139–41. For more on the conventions of Senecan or closet drama, see Straznicky, *Privacy, Playreading*.
7. See for example Fisken, "Mary Sidney's *Psalms*," pp. 166–83.
8. Skretkowicz, "Mary Sidney Herbert's *Antonius*," pp. 18–19.
9. Recently, theorists have called for rethinking of textual fidelity. As Lanier rightly points out, some level of fidelity is required for any adaptation to function, since there must be some resemblance to its source for an adaptation to be understood as such, see Lanier, "Afterword," pp. 293–306; much of this conversation has focused on the work of women translators. The number of books and articles on the topic of early modern translation is too large to include in a footnote, though I reference many of them in *Women as Translators in Early Modern England*, in which I develop my argument about translation and the access to authorship it provided for women.

10. Skretkowicz, "Mary Sidney Herbert's *Antonius*," p. 7.
11. Sarah Carter sees the myth of Actaeon emphasized in Peend's translation, in which he expands his description of Salmacis with a hunting metaphor and compares Salmacis to Actaeon. For Carter, this provides further evidence of Peend's distaste for the hermaphroditic state, compared with Sandys's more accepting view, in Carter, *Ovidian Myth and Sexual Deviance*, p. 205.
12. For a discussion of the Actaeon myth in relation to Shakespeare's Antony, see Starks, "'Immortal Longings,'" pp. 247–9.
13. In linking the blazonic tradition with depictions of Actaeon, I draw heavily from Vickers, "Diana Described," pp. 265–79.
14. Bate, "Elizabethan Translation," p. 42.
15. Skretkowicz also speculates that Sidney Herbert left Omphale unnamed in order to avoid the frequent conflation of Omphale and Iole in Renaissance versions of the story, see Skretkowicz, "Mary Sidney Herbert's *Antonius*," pp. 19–20.
16. Starks-Estes sees a similar pattern in Shakespeare's Antony, as discussed in her chapter on the play in Starks-Estes, *Violence, Trauma, and Virtus*, p. 103.
17. In his discussion of Ovid's revision of the myth, Robinson points out how atypical Salmacis is. While most nymphs in the *Metamorphoses* are virgin huntresses in danger of being violated, Salmacis wants nothing to do with hunting and Diana, and instead plays "the part of the lustful deity, lusting after what we suspect now to be a male-looking Hermaphroditus," see Robinson, "Salmacis and Hermaphroditus," pp. 217–19.
18. Several critics, including Gilbert, compare the various early modern translations of the Salmacis and Hermaphroditus tale. Maslen suggests that it is likely Shakespeare knew and used more than just the Golding translation, and he points out that Peend's earlier version expands on Ovid's fable to heighten the anti-feminist message that women's bodies are "outwardly feeble" but can also "conceal immense reserves of strength capable of overwhelming unguarded adolescent males" in Maslen, "Myths Exploited," p. 23.
19. A note in the Norton edition of *Antony and Cleopatra* reminds us that in calling the snake a "worm," the Clown suggests its similarity to a penis, fn V, ii, 238. By applying the worm to her breast, Cleopatra stages a death that can be read as a merging of the masculine and the feminine.
20. Pinkus reads the conclusion of Ovid's story as the transformation of Hermaphrodite into a half-man, because the woman disappears, see Pinkus, "Hermaphrodite Poetics," p. 106.
21. Gilbert, *Early Modern Hermaphrodites*, p. 9.
22. Bate, *Shakespeare and Ovid*, p. 65.
23. Ibid. pp. 83, 181.

24. See Uman, "Translation, Transformation," pp. 66–91. While I focus on the Ovidian tale of Philomel present in the *Dream*, Darlena Ciraulo has recently pointed to echoes of the Hermaphroditus tale in Ciraulo, "Ovid's Myth of Salmacis," A95–A108.

25. For example, Paul Dean sees the allusions to Ovid's *Metamorphoses*, *Ars Amatoria*, and *Amores* as evidence of the play's rejection of the "militaristic and moralistic values promulgated by the Augustan regime," in Dean, "*Antony and Cleopatra*," p. 75; MacKenzie similarly links mythological references to a movement away "from a dour Roman perspective of the world and towards a fresh and vibrant world view," see MacKenzie, "*Antony and Cleopatra*," p. 309.

26. Harris, "'Narcissus in thy face,'" pp. 410–11. The thematic links between the Narcissus story and that of Hermaphroditus have been highlighted in early modern translations of Ovid as well as in critical assessment of these works. See, for example, Bate, "Elizabethan Translation," p. 42, and Maslen, "Myths Exploited," p. 23.

27. MacDonald, "Antony's Body."

28. Ibid. para. 12.

29. Robinson, "Salmacis and Hermaphroditus," p. 216.

30. Ibid. p. 220.

31. Silberman, "Mythographic Transformations," p. 643.

32. Cohen, "Introduction to *Antony*," p. 2638.

33. Robinson points out that Hermaphroditus's parentage recalls the recently recounted tale of Aphrodite's "adultery with Ares (IV, 171–89) and the reaction of her jealous husband, who binds the two together," see Robinson, "Salmacis and Hermaphroditus," pp. 222–3. The frequent references to Antony and Cleopatra as Mars and Venus again suggests indirect connections to the Hermaphroditus myth.

34. Stone, *Crossing Gender*, p. 100.

35. In a wonderful reading of the opening lines of the play, Levine points out that Philo's description of Antony's heart as a "fan / To cool a gypsy's heart" is followed immediately by Cleopatra's entrance with a train of eunuchs fanning her, in Levine, *Men in Women's Clothing*, p. 45.

36. Barroll reads this scene as part of the "allusive tissue" of the play, linking Hercules to Plutarch's Hercules, in Barroll, "The Allusive Tissue," pp. 283–4.

37. MacKenzie, "*Antony and Cleopatra*," p. 326.

38. Archer, "Antiquity and Degeneration," p. 12.

39. Stone, *Crossing Gender*, p. 99.

40. Levine, *Men in Women's Clothing*, p. 45.

41. Silberman points to this view in the writings of the fourteenth-century moralist Bersuire, who reads the tale of Hermaphroditus and Salmacis as an "allegory of the incarnation," see Silberman, "Mythographic Transformations," p. 647.

Bibliography

Archer, John Michael, "Antiquity and Degeneration: The Representation of Egypt and Shakespeare's *Antony and Cleopatra*," *Genre: Forms of Discourse and Culture* 27.2, 1994, pp. 1–27.

Barroll, Leads, "The Allusive Tissue of Antony and Cleopatra," in Sara Munson Deats (ed.), *Antony and Cleopatra: New Critical Essays* (New York: Routledge, 2004), pp. 275–90.

Bate, Jonathan, "Elizabethan Translation: The Art of the Hermaphrodite," in Shirley Chew and Alistair Stead (eds), *Translating Life: Studies in Transpositional Aesthetics* (Liverpool: Liverpool University Press, 1999), pp. 33–51.

Bate, Jonathan, *Shakespeare and Ovid* (Oxford: Oxford University Press, 1993).

Carter, Sarah, *Ovidian Myth and Sexual Deviance in Early Modern English Literature* (New York: Palgrave Macmillan, 2011).

Ciraulo, Darlena, "Ovid's Myth of Salmacis and Hermaphroditus in Shakespeare's *A Midsummer Night's Dream*," *Philosophy and Literature* 41.1, 2017, pp. A95–A108.

Cohen, Walter, "Introduction to *Antony and Cleopatra*," in Stephen Greenblatt, Walter Cohen, Jean E. Howard, and Katharine Eisaman Maus (eds), *The Norton Shakespeare, Based on the Oxford Edition*, 2nd edn (New York: W. W. Norton, 2008).

Dean, Paul, "*Antony and Cleopatra*: An Ovidian Tragedy?" *Cahiers Élisabéthains* 40, 1991, pp. 73–7.

Desmet, Christy, "Recognizing Shakespeare, Rethinking Fidelity: A Rhetoric and Ethics of Appropriation," in Alexa Huang and Elizabeth Rivlin (eds), *Shakespeare and the Ethics of Appropriation* (New York: Palgrave Macmillan, 2014), pp. 41–57.

Fisken, Beth Wynne, "Mary Sidney's *Psalms*: Education and Wisdom," in Margaret Hannay (ed.), *Silent But for the Word: Tudor Women as Patrons, Translators, and Writers of Religious Works* (Kent: Kent State University Press, 1985), pp. 166–83.

Gilbert, Ruth, *Early Modern Hermaphrodites: Sex and Other Stories* (New York: Palgrave, 2002).

Hannay, Margaret, Noel J. Kinnamon, and Michael G. Brennan, "Antonius: Literary Context," in Margaret Hannay, Noel J. Kinnamon, and Michael G. Brennan (eds), *The Collected Works of Mary Sidney Herbert Countess of Pembroke* (Oxford: Clarendon Press, 1998), pp. 139–46.

Harris, Jonathan Gil, "'Narcissus in thy face': Roman Desire and the Difference it Fakes in *Antony and Cleopatra*," *Shakespeare Quarterly* 45.4, 1994, pp. 408–25.

Herbert, Mary Sidney, *The Collected Works of Mary Sidney Herbert Countess of Pembroke*, Margaret Hannay, Noel J. Kinnamon, and Michael G. Brennan (eds) (Oxford: Clarendon Press, 1998).

Jones, Ann Rosalind, and Peter Stallybrass, "Fetishizing Gender: Constructing the Hermaphrodite in Renaissance England," in Julia Epstien and Kristina Straub (eds), *Bodyguards: The Cultural Contexts of Gender Ambiguity* (New York: Routledge, 1991), pp. 80–111.

Lanier, Douglas M., "Shakespeare / Not Shakespeare: Afterword," in Christy Desmet, Natalie Loper, and Jim Casey (eds), *Shakespeare / Not Shakespeare* (New York: Palgrave Macmillan, 2017), pp. 293–306.

Lanier, Douglas, "Shakespearean Rhizomatics: Adaptation, Ethics, Value," in Alexa Huang and Elizabeth Rivlin (eds), *Shakespeare and the Ethics of Appropriation* (New York: Palgrave Macmillan, 2014), pp. 21–40.

Levine, Laura, *Men in Women's Clothing: Anti-theatricality and Effeminization, 1579–1642* (Cambridge: Cambridge University Press, 1994).

MacDonald, Joyce Green, "Antony's Body," *Early Modern Literature Studies* Special Issue 19, 2009, paras 1–23, <https://extra.shu.ac.uk/emls/si-19/macdanto.html> (last accessed 30 November 2016).

MacKenzie, Clayton, "*Antony and Cleopatra*: A Mythological Perspective," *Orbis Litterarum* 45, 1990, pp. 309–29.

Maslen, R. W., "Myths Exploited: The *Metamorphoses* of Ovid in Early Elizabethan England," in A. B. Taylor (ed.), *Shakespeare's Ovid: The Metamorphoses in the Plays and Poems* (Cambridge: Cambridge University Press, 2000), pp. 15–30.

Ovid, *Shakespeare's Ovid: Being Arthur Golding's Translation of the* Metamorphoses, W. H. D. Rouse (ed.) (London: De La More Press, [1567] 1904).

Pinkus, Karen, "Hermaphrodite Poetics," *Arcadia* 41.1, 2006, pp. 91–111.

Robinson, Matthew, "Salmacis and Hermaphroditus: When Two Become One: (Ovid, Met. 4.285–388)," *The Classical Quarterly* 49.1, 1999, pp. 212–23.

Shakespeare, William, *The Norton Shakespeare, Based on the Oxford Edition*, 2nd edn, Stephen Greenblatt, Walter Cohen, Jean E. Howard, and Katharine Eisaman Maus (eds) (New York: W. W. Norton, 2008).

Silberman, Lauren, "Mythographic Transformations of Ovid's Hermaphrodite," *The Sixteenth Century Journal* 19.4, 1988, pp. 643–52.

Skretkowicz, Victor, "Mary Sidney Herbert's *Antonius*, English Philhellenism and the Protestant Cause," *Women's Writing* 6.1, 1999, pp. 7–25.

Starks, Lisa S., "'Immortal Longings': The Erotics of Death in *Antony and Cleopatra*," in Sara Munson Deats (ed.), *Antony and Cleopatra: New Critical Essays* (New York: Routledge, 2004), pp. 243–58.

Starks-Estes, Lisa S., *Violence, Trauma, and* Virtus *in Shakespeare's Roman Poems and Plays: Transforming Ovid* (Basingstoke: Palgrave Macmillan, 2014).

Stone, James W., *Crossing Gender in Shakespeare: Feminist Psychoanalysis and the Difference Within* (New York: Routledge, 2010).

Straznicky, Marta, *Privacy, Playreading and Women's Closet Drama, 1550–1700* (Cambridge: Cambridge University Press, 2009).

Uman, Deborah, "Translation, Transformation and Ravishment in *A Midsummer Night's Dream*," *Allegorica* 22, 2001, pp. 66–91.

Uman, Deborah, *Women as Translators in Early Modern England* (Newark, DE: University of Delaware Press, 2012).

Vickers, Nancy J., "Diana Described: Scattered Woman and Scattered Rhyme," *Critical Inquiry* 8.2, 1981, pp. 265–79.

Part II

Ovidian Specters and Remnants

Ovid's Ghosts: Lovesickness, Theatricality, and Ovidian Spectrality on the Early Modern English Stage

Lisa S. Starks[1]

During the English Civil Wars, after the last of the Jacobean playhouses had been closed, there remained a nostalgic yet often ambivalent memory of the pre-Civil Wars' theatre, particularly its Ovidian heyday with the plays of Marlowe and Shakespeare. At the end of the previous century, Marlowe adapted and popularized the Roman poet for the public stage; Shakespeare then continued to appropriate Ovid as the icon of metamorphosis, theatricality, and lovesickness – often playing on interconnections between these associations, as in Q2 of *Romeo and Juliet* (1599). Ultimately, Ben Jonson, in *Poetaster* (1601), followed by Shakespeare, in *The Tempest* (1610–11), closed out the era with farewells to Ovid. Later that century, just prior to the Restoration, Ovid made an uncanny return in the short closet-drama attributed to Edvardus Fuscus (most likely a pseudonym), entitled *Ovids Ghost, or Venus overthrown by the Nasonian politician* (1657),[2] which makes the haunting of Ovid – and the Ovidian theatre now long past – literal. In this interregnum closet-drama, the Roman poet appears as a specter who renders advice for lovesickness – a disease that had become inextricably linked with Ovid as an icon of love maladies and the transformational, metamorphic experience of theatre. This satirical play uses Ovid's image to criticize the Puritan ideology of the interregnum, in particular the antitheatricality that silenced the stage.

1. Spectral Ovids

Ovid's ubiquitous traces permeate early modern English theatre in a way that is both omnipresent and transient – a phantom lurking throughout the plays, their reception in playhouses, and the theatrical discourses that framed them. In this way, Ovidian appropriations on the early modern stage resemble the kind of spectrality that Maurizio Calbi attributes to Shakespeare in the contemporary mediascape.[3] Calbi applies Jacques Derrida's description of the "hauntological" nature of Shakespeare, which becomes a "Thing" that "inhabits without properly residing" – disappearing and uncannily reappearing over and over again.[4] Speaking of the initial appearance of the Ghost in Shakespeare's *Hamlet*, Derrida describes the haunting as "[a] question of repetition: a specter is always a *revenant*. One cannot control its comings and goings because it *begins by coming back*."[5] In theorizing Shakespearean appropriations and adaptations in twenty-first-century global, digitized media, Calbi argues that "'Shakespeare' is a 'Thing' that keeps on coming back, an uncanny, multilayered mediatized body that is repeatedly on the point of vanishing only to reappear elsewhere and in different (media) format."[6]

Mindful of the complex differences between Shakespeare's spectrality in twenty-first-century media and Ovid's in early modern English theatre, I contend that Calbi's use of Derrida's theory to explain contemporary Shakespearean appropriations may be fruitful when applied to Ovid on the early modern English stage. Before the Elizabethans appropriated and "Englished" Ovid in the sixteenth century, variations of his poetry had already undergone centuries of imitations, transformations, or adaptations, circulating images and meanings that accumulated to create "Ovid" as a "Thing" in the way that Derrida and Calbi describe the phenomenon of "Shakespeare." Meditations on the spectral afterlives of Ovid uncannily appear and reappear throughout the era, both onstage and off, suggesting and sometimes directly relating his status as "undead poet" to the idea of reincarnation or Pythagoras's theory of the transmigration of souls, which Ovid expounds on at length in Book 15 of *Metamorphoses*. During the sixteenth century, Ovid's focus on Pythagoras was given great weight of importance; Arthur Golding, for instance, points to it in his Epistle to his translation as a central theme in the poem that joins pagan and Christian beliefs about life after death.[7] Notably, Francis Meres makes an explicit link between Pythagoras, Ovid, and Shakespeare in the famous comment that "[a]s the soule of *Euphorbus* was thought to live in *Pythagoras*: so the sweete wittie soule of Ovid lives in mellifluous & honytongued *Shakespeare*."[8] For Meres, one of the "spectral Ovids" was channelled through Shakespeare himself.

As a cultural phenomenon or spectral idea, "Ovid" – like "Shakespeare" in later centuries – inspired global Renaissance artists and poets in general, providing a model for creatively adapting and appropriating texts. Renaissance verbal and visual artists directly and indirectly adapted and appropriated myths, characters, and quotations from Ovid in Latin and in numerous vernacular translations and adaptations. On the early modern English stage specifically, "Ovid" – his image, poetry, and characters – enjoyed rich, multilayered afterlives. Playwrights like Shakespeare frequently appropriated tales and key, iconic figures from Ovid's poetry to embody and comment on concepts and issues surrounding theatricality metadramatically on the stage. Specific Ovidian characters – Hecuba, Niobe, Philomela, Daphne, Actaeon, Venus, Medea, Ganymede, Pygmalion, and so on – garnered broader significations beyond the context of their own tales, taking on multifarious spectral resonances. Therefore, when actors portrayed these figures on stage, or even just cited them, they suggested rich intertextual associations and made immediate, yet significant, lasting effects on their audiences. Moreover, Ovid sometimes appeared as a spectral entity fused with a character appropriated from his poetry: Shakespeare's Romeo and Juliet in *Romeo and Juliet*, Proteus in *The Two Gentlemen of Verona*, or Prospero (as Medea) in *The Tempest*; and as a character himself in Jonson's *Poetaster*; or a Ghost of himself in Fuscus's *Ovids Ghost*.

2. Ovidian (Anti)Theatricality, Personation, and Lovesickness

"Ovid" made uncanny returns beyond the playtexts as well, circulating in/outside discourses concerning performances, performing spaces, and audiences. Ovid came to represent the theatrical experience itself and its interconnections with lovesickness, providing a venue for exploring the metamorphic illusion and its relationship to the sometimes comic, other times self-shattering effects of painful love. Besides inspiring the rich potential of intertextual transformations, Ovid was appropriated to conceptualize, explore, articulate, and debate the nature of theatre and theatrical practices in early modern England, as I have explained elsewhere.[9] Both the enemies and the friends of the stage appropriated Ovid to take sides on the political divide on theatricality. A wide range of writers – such as Stephen Gosson, William Prynne, and Thomas Heywood – indirectly and directly cite or quote Ovid when attacking or defending the stage in their treatises. The debate on theatricality centered on the effects of plays on audiences and also the players themselves and the early modern concept of acting as "personation," the act of taking on the form and emotions of another onstage. The antitheatricalists regarded acting as fiendishly deceptive metamorphosis, in contrast to the pro-theatricalists, who viewed the player's transformative art as an inspired, godlike, creative act. Importantly, polemicists on both sides of the debate cited Ovid and agreed that the player's metamorphosis triggered powerful effects on audiences, differing only on whether or not they deemed these effects to be morally corrupting or edifying.[10]

In the English public theatre, Ovid was also appropriated to revolutionize the theatrical medium in the conception of personation (the actor's embodiment of a role) as metamorphic illusion, which was created and embodied by the actors' internalization of emotion. As embodiments of metamorphic illusion, players often referred to themselves as specters – insubstantial essences or shadows. Through the transformative power of personation, actors thus became "the Ghosts of our ancient Heroes" to have "walk't againe," in Thomas Gainsford's words;[11] or the specter of a hero such as Talbot, "rais[ed] from dead — bones newe embalmed with the teares of 10,000 spectators" in Thomas Nashe's.[12]

The transfigurative effects of personation were thought to induce physiological changes in the actor's own face and body and then, in turn, engender psychophysiological affective responses in audience members. Joseph R. Roach claims that "[t]he predilection of the age for Ovidian alterations of bodily state further emphasized the actor's capacity to assume the 'perfect shape,' as Heywood called it, 'to which he had fashioned all his active spirits.'"[13] Furthermore, as Roach explains, early modern descriptions of acting indicate the belief in the actor's ability to change his exterior shape, to undergo an "instantaneous" psychophysiological transfiguration that was scripted by playwrights, who ordered that players "depict the passions and sudden and violent metamorphoses."[14] The actor's personation was thought to then "irradiat[e] the bodies of spectators through their eyes and ears, . . . literally transform[ing] the contents of his heart to theirs, altering their moral natures," his emotion affecting the audience and playing space.[15]

Playwrights often showcased this metamorphic potential of human identity by way of Ovid's Proteus.[16] Although it was often considered to liberate creative energies, Protean metamorphic illusion also posed a potential hazard – the vulnerability to emotion and the risk of the imagination breaching the brain's faculties and taking control over the self, thereby causing severe melancholy and the dissolution of identity. In his *Anatomy of Melancholy*, Robert Burton points to the dangers of becoming another "Proteus, or a chameleon [who] can take all shapes," for it has the force to "work upon others as well as ourselves."[17] With the imagination defenseless, the self was thought to be too susceptible to penetration by harmful agents, both external and internal. Protean metamorphosis posed the most dangerous threat for the actor, whose entire identity was at risk in taking on a role, as it left him vulnerable to attack from the imagination, which could invade the self and entirely damage one's emotional and physical well-being.[18]

As a type of melancholy, lovesickness (or love-melancholy) was thought to be caused in much the same way and to produce similarly alarming psychophysiological symptoms. Those writing about the experience of theatre made this connection between the dangers of lovesickness and theatre, for both were thought to leave the actor or audience members vulnerable to the grips of emotional excess, leading to the self-shattering effects of melancholy, as with love-melancholy. Unsurprisingly, antitheatricalists harped on the erotic titillation of the theatre, which they saw as a kind of siren luring unsuspecting spectators into sin and degradation, especially males in danger of becoming the love slaves of women. As Lesel Dawson has argued, lovesickness was described as a malady that caused great distress and, depending on the sufferer's gender, also carried with it value-charged assumptions that complicated and shaped the experience.[19] Described in rhetoric of disgust and shame, male love-melancholy greatly challenged ideals of masculinity. The male lover flouted societal expectations, deriving pleasure in submission and reveling in his own masochistic pleasure of endless longing and unrequited love. As such, Dawson claims, lovesickness may have allowed for some freedom from dominant notions of gender identity and sexual norms.

Although early modern lovesickness afflicting either gender was sometimes thought to be produced either by a humoral imbalance or need for sexual copulation, it was also thought to be caused by the penetration of the imagination by the beloved's image in two other prominent discourses. In both of these two theories, the perceived image (in this case, of beauty) was thought to be carried from the senses through the ventricles of the brain via spirit or *pneuma*, which translated it into a *phantasm* and carried it to the soul. Along the way, writers assumed, the lover's pleasure of incorporating the image itself caused the faculty of judgment to falter, so that it became idealized and exaggerated in the lover's mind.[20] Once under the spell of lovesickness, the sufferer overestimated the beauty, grace, or overall greatness of the beloved in an internalized fantasy completely divorced from reality, causing deep inner anguish and illness. This description of the onset of lovesickness mirrored the same psychophysiological metamorphosis that was thought to afflict susceptible actors and spectators.

As the icon of both theatricality and lovesickness, Ovid thus came to represent the interconnections between these experiences. Notably, when condemning male effeminacy, an assumed effect of playgoing, Gosson appropriates Ovid's description of Roman audiences from *Ars Amatoria*:

> In Rome, when Plaies or Pageants are showne: Ovid chargeth
> his Pilgrims to creep close to the Saintes whom they serve and
> shew their double diligence to lifte the gentlewomens roabes
> from the grounde for rolling in the duste.[21]

Moralists like Gosson and defenders of theatre like Heywood both evoke Ovid in their writings when pointing out the elicit dangers of lovesickness, particularly to the masculinity of male spectators at plays. Similarly, Prynne uses the term "metamorphosing" itself when describing personation, which he saw as a damnable art.[22] As a phantom inhabiting the stage, Ovid characterized the fears and underscored the depth of the emotional power of both love and theatre.

3. Spectral Ovids and Lovesickness in *Romeo and Juliet* and *As You Like It*

Exploiting this connection, Shakespeare appropriates Pyramus and Thisbe from *Metamorphoses* in *Romeo and Juliet*, which he parodies in *A Midsummer Night's Dream*, infusing it with spectral Ovids that haunt this tragedy of lovesickness.[23] Pyramus and Thisbe itself had a complex intertextual legacy, as did Arthur Brooke's *Tragicall Historye of Romeus and Juliet* (1562), which provided Shakespeare the rough outline of the story and characters for his tragedy.[24] In *Romeo and Juliet*, Shakespeare radically adapts Brooke's poem into a play, infusing it with complex, nuanced "Ovids" through characters that stand in for the Roman poet himself and his character, Myrrha. The intertext of Myrrha's tale provides a more transgressive and disturbing instance of lovesickness than that of Pyramus and Thisbe.

Shadowy apparitions of Ovid, often fused with ultimate-Ovidian poet-playwright Christopher Marlowe (who translated Ovid's *Amores* in 1595), uncannily surface in *Romeo and Juliet*, further linking his spectral image to that of lovesickness, with its torment and exquisite joys. In their first meeting, when Romeo and Juliet touch hands as if in prayer, "palm to palm" (*Romeo and Juliet* I, v, 100),[25] and speak dialogue in sonnet form, they resemble the lovers in Marlowe's *Hero and Leander*, who "parled by the touch of hands," shot through with "Loves holy fire," or lovesickness (*Hero and Leander*, 184, 193).[26] As in this Marlovian-tinged meeting, Romeo and Juliet both embody the specter of Ovid as an icon for love-melancholy. Romeo appears as the Ovidian figure, via Petrarch, of the melancholy lover. Shakespeare both gently mocks and examines male lovesickness in his portrayal of Romeo as the one who exhibits its most typical symptoms from the Latin elegiac and later Petrarchan sonnet traditions. Romeo describes in conventional terms the love that he suffers for Rosaline as "a smoke made with the fume of sighs," and "[a] madness most discreet, / A choking gall and a preserving sweet" (I, i, 190, 198). When he bewails his tormented passion for Rosaline to Mercutio and Benvolio as they head to the Capulet ball, he describes himself as "too sore empiercèd with his shaft / To soar with his light feathers, and so bound / I cannot bound a pitch above dull woe. / Under love's heavy burden do I sink" (I, iv, 19–22). Romeo's expression of lovesickness, of course, prompts bawdy puns and obscene banter from his comrades. Romeo is chided to "man up" and "get over it" by both his peers and the Friar. Mercutio teases his friend relentlessly, often with fanciful insults. The Friar also criticizes Romeo's surrender to his emotions, lecturing against the dangers of "doting," or excessive passion in love, and warning that lovesickness may weaken or effeminize him, for "[w]omen may fall when there is no strength in men" (II, iii, 78, 76). Interestingly, however, Shakespeare's play does not necessarily completely endorse the Friar's point of view nor entirely condemn Romeo for his "unmanly" loving. In part through Romeo as the lovesick "Ovid," Shakespeare critiques conventional masculinity, hinging it from cultural expectations of gender identity.

Ovidian lovesickness also provides the character of Juliet the chance to exceed social boundaries of gender in her expanded role in Q2 of the play. According to Heather James, Juliet's speech as enacted by the boy player serves Q2's overall project of "reconceiv[ing] Ovid's place in the late Elizabethan theater."[27] James explains that Juliet takes on the roles of the *docta puella*, or intelligent ingénue of the

Roman elegy, the Petrarchan Laura, and the voice of the Roman poet of erotic elegies, as evidenced in her monologues and soliloquies, as in the "balcony scene" and the eve of her wedding night (II, ii; III, ii, 1–31).[28] I would add that, as Romeo does in his role as Ovidian melancholy lover, Juliet becomes a character that serves as a stand-in for Ovid-as-lovesickness himself – as well as Marlowe.[29] Juliet in Q2 not only evokes "Ovid" through her role as elegist, but also through her connection to other Ovidian characters – Thisbe, in terms of the dominant plot, and Myrrha, on more spectral levels.[30]

In particular, I see the uncanny, spectral appearances of Myrrha most fully associating this play with traumatic lovesickness and transgressive longing. In Ovid's *Metamorphoses*, the tale of Myrrha forms the centerpiece of Book 10, which is composed of myths that revolve around the conflation of love and loss, told as the song of Orpheus lamenting the death of his wife, Eurydice. Myrrha, wounded not by Cupid but apparently by the angry Furies, is tortured by intensely passionate and anguished longing to have sexual intercourse with her father. Her Nurse who, like Shakespeare's, loves and helps her mistress to achieve her heart's desire, arranges for Myrrha to enter her father's bedroom and consummate her desire. These incestuous acts lead to tragic catastrophe. The pregnant Myrrha, burdened with overwhelming guilt and grief, begs to be metamorphosed into a tree. As a tree, she gives birth to a son, Adonis, who figures in Ovid's tale that follows – which Shakespeare adapts in his narrative poem *Venus and Adonis*. Myrrha's tale functions as a spectral trace or unconscious memory in Shakespeare's play, bringing with it a shift in focus to Juliet's desires, underscoring her passionate love for Romeo and moving relationship with her Nurse. Shakespeare's alteration of Juliet's age from sixteen in *Romeus and Juliet* to almost fourteen makes his Juliet much more of a "daughter" figure than a grown woman, but one who boldly speaks her own desire, like Myrrha.

The character of Shakespeare's Nurse much more closely resembles the Nurse in Ovid's tale than Brooke's poem. Ovid's Nurse reaches out to the desperate Myrrha, reminding her that she had nurtured her as a baby, "shewing her her emptie dugges and naked head all gray, / Besought her for the paynes shee tooke with her both night and day / In rocking and in feeding her" and offering to help with "charms and chanted herbs" (*Metamorphoses* X, 440–4, 50).[31] Ovid's Nurse devises a way for Myrrha to be able to sneak into her father's room to have sexual relations without him knowing her identity; she acts as a go-between, bringing her charge to the bed of her father. Clearly, Ovid's Nurse intervenes only out of pure love and devotion for her mistress; she has no ulterior motive. On the other hand, Brooke's

Nurse is a bit more mercenary: Juliet has to offer her a bribe to get her to help in her plan to meet Romeus. Shakespeare continues the use of the Nurse as a device to unite Juliet with Romeo in his play, but his characterization of her far exceeds that of Brooke's poem. I contend that Shakespeare infuses his Nurse with the spirit of Ovid's, which is particularly evident in her anecdotes about her days nursing her own child and Juliet, referring to her "dug[s]" (*Romeo and Juliet* I, iii, 29), and in her genuine love and well-intentioned (even if often misguided) care for Juliet that is evident in their scenes together, such as Act two, scene four and Act three, scenes two and five. Like Ovid's Nurse, Shakespeare's needs no bribe from Juliet to offer help (although she does get paid, after refusing, by Romeo), but rather is eager to play Juliet's "drudge," to "toil in . . . [her] delight" (II, v, 74). The intensity of that relationship and the character of Juliet herself hearken back to Ovid's tale of Myrrha. This tale, intertwined with Pyramus and Thisbe, provides uncanny, spectral perspectives on Ovidian lovesickness and death, themes that undergird this play.

Ovid uncannily returns as the figure of lovesickness – and theatricality – in *As You Like It*, which was most likely written in 1599, the year in which Q2 of *Romeo and Juliet* was printed. In this comedy, Ovid's specter appears through the character of Rosalind, especially as Ganymede, and in the citings of Marlowe-as-Ovidian poet and the historical Ovid himself. Touchstone evokes Marlowe's death and his play, *The Jew of Malta*, by referencing "a great reckoning in a little room" (III, iii, 14). As the Ovidian Ganymede, Rosalind echoes Ovid, in particular *Ars Amatoria* and *Remedia Amoris*, in her advice to the lovelorn Orlando. Momentarily embodying Marlowe-as-Ovid, Phebe, in response to her instantaneous lovesickness for Ganymede, conjures Marlowe's memory by evoking his "Passionate Shepherd to His Love" and *Hero and Leander*: "Dead shepherd, now I find thy saw of might, / 'Who ever lov'd, that lov'd not at first sight?'" (*Hero and Leander*, 176). And, of course, Silvius pines for lovesickness over Phebe, who has fallen for Rosalind-as-Ganymede, making *As You Like It* a comedic romp of Ovidian lovesickness, without the supernatural metamorphoses of *Midsummer*.

Moreover, like *Midsummer*, Shakespeare links Ovidian melancholy with theatricality. The melancholy Jacques's famous "All the world's a stage, / And all the men and women merely players" speech (*As You Like It* II, vii, 139–66) punctuates the play's investment in Ovidian metamorphic illusion and melancholy. Conversely, Rosalind exudes the positive creative energy of theatricality in her Ovidian role-playing, metadramatically commenting on the combination of metamorphic illusion and comic lovesickness of Shakespeare's play.

Invoking Ovid's ghost, Touchstone characterizes him as the figure attacked by moralists who, as noted above, appropriated Ovid in their antitheatrical discourses. Comparing himself to Ovid in exile, Touchstone tells Audrey that he is "here with thee and they goats, as the most capricious poet, honest Ovid, was among the Goths" (III, iii, 6–8). As James has noted, the Goths in Touchstone's reference suggest moralists like Stephen Gosson and the bishops who banned and burned an edition of John Davies's satires bound with Marlowe's translation of *All Ouid's Elegies* in 1599.[32] Marlowe and Ovid, fused into one spectral figure, thus represented the dangers and pleasures of poetry and theatre. Shakespeare, in this play about lovesickness and role-playing, champions that theatrical metamorphic illusion through ghostly apparitions of Marlowe's Ovid, whose memory was bound up with lovesickness and theatricality, from his translation *All Ouid's Elegies* to his tour-de-force of Ovidian lovesickness, *Dido, Queen of Carthage*, among his other plays.[33] For Shakespeare and others, such as Ben Jonson, spectral Ovids were distinctly Marlovian.

4. Ovidian Lovesickness and Antitheatricality in *Poetaster*

Reflecting back on the previous age of Ovid on the early modern English stage, Ben Jonson stages Ovid as a spectral character explicitly linked with Marlowe and Shakespeare in his satirical play, *Poetaster*. Jonson appropriates Shakespeare in a farewell scene between Ovid and Julia that resembles the one in *Romeo and Juliet*, as Jonathan Bate has also pointed out.[34] Jonson's play not only clearly identifies Shakespeare as one of the followers of Ovid, but also it singles out *Romeo and Juliet* as a play that explores lovesickness and the legacy of Marlowe's Ovid. In this comedy, written in response to the infamous War of the Theatres (or *Poetomachia*) in 1601, Jonson gently mocks playwrights John Marston and Thomas Dekker and implicitly censures Marlowe and Shakespeare as Ovidian playwrights by appropriating classical writers as characters and interpreting them for his own time. The play centers on a contest between ancient Roman poets Ovid and Virgil, with Horace (most likely representing Jonson himself) as moderator and Emperor Augustus as judge, but it includes many comic bits that align Ovid with lovesickness and theatricality, as opposed to the ridiculous antitheatrical sentiments expressed by comic characters.

Jonson's Ovid appears as a radical poet who pursues poetry against his father's wishes for him to study law and a melancholy lover who swoons over Augustus's married daughter Julia. Like Shakespeare in *As You Like It*, Ovid-as-character is a composite of the mythic Ovid via Marlowe. Reciting from a marginally altered version of Marlowe's translation of Ovid's *Amores*, elegy 1.15 (*Poetaster* I, i, 1–2),[35] Ovid invokes not only his own ghost but also Marlowe's, the quotation resurrecting them both and adding spectral layers to this play. And, of course, Marlowe's Ovid-as-character exudes the spirit of lovesickness, which by this time was fused with the image of "Ovid." Jonson sprinkles lines referring to love-melancholy in scenes with the Roman elegists Tibullus and Propertius, who align the Roman elegy with lovesickness, waxing melancholic on the "grief" and "wounds" of love (II, ii, 42–53). Comically referring to the masochistic threat of lovesickness, the shattering of the self, Tibullus warns his friend, "Publius, thou'lt lose thyself" (I, iii, 44). To counter its miseries, Ovid expresses the exhilaration of his lovesickness for Julia, by exclaiming, "my passion so transports me" (I, iii, 2). Later, Julia responds with "Methinks I love him, that he loves so truly" (II, ii, 57), a moment that satirizes the stance of Ovid and his fellow elegists.

Moreover, like Shakespeare, Jonson conflates Ovidian lovesickness with theatricality and antitheatricality in *Poetaster*, situating it within the discourses described above. Although Ovid denies that he has anything to do with playwriting or acting, declaring that "I am not known unto the open stage, nor do I traffic in their theatres" (I, ii, 60–1), the denial is futile. Through Marlowe, Ovid-as-character becomes synonymous with the playwright. His father associates poetry with playmaking, citing Ovid's lost play *Medea*. He complains that his son has frittered away his future as a lawyer to "become Ovid the playmaker" (I, ii, 7–8), expressing disgust at the thought of his son working as a "stager" (I, ii, 10–16). This scene then ridicules the positions of antitheatricalists who appropriated "Ovid": Luscus rails against the players as idle, ill-behaved rascals, mainly because they personate and mock those of his class on the stage (I, ii, 35–42); Tucca, a disbanded soldier, condemns the players as "rogues" that have become "licentious" in their mocking of soldiers on the stage. Of course, in this play, Jonson is ridiculing Luscus and Tucca both, along with other hypocritical moralists. In her note on these lines (II, i, 14–16), Margaret J. Kidnie explains that "the arguments presented in this scene in opposition to acting would have pointed resonance for an Elizabethan audience accustomed to the rhetoric of anti-theatrical polemics."[36] I would add that the audience would also have associated this rhetoric with "Ovid," whose spectrality Jonson is fully engaging in this play – both as satire and tribute. As a comedy staged at the close of the Ovid wave, *Poetaster* could be seen to mark the end of the Ovidian theatre in its banishment of Ovid.[37]

Similarly, Shakespeare stages a farewell to the Ovidian stage in *The Tempest*, while simultaneously reviving it.[38] Prospero relishes the power of Ovidian metamorphic illusion before rejecting it, and although he renounces his creative ability, he nevertheless reiterates its potency. Appropriating Golding's translation of Medea from *Metamorphoses* (VII, 265–777), Prospero conjures Ovid's specter in a metadramatic moment that foregrounds the dual-nature of theatricality (V, i, 33–57). When Prospero cites Medea's claim that she "call[s] up dead men from their graves" (*Metamorphoses* VII, 275), he confesses that he also has "waked" the dead in their graves "and let 'em forth" (*Tempest* V, i, 48–9), bringing to mind the spectral nature of theatre itself. As noted above, actors were thought to be ghost-like shadows or transient essences. Through this appropriation of Ovid's Medea, Shakespeare appears to comment on the previous age of Ovid on the English stage, luxuriating in metamorphic illusion while also cautioning against its potential risks. Prospero drowns his book – perhaps a physical copy of Golding's 1567 *Metamorphosis* – and thus his magic skills, purging the stage of theatrical power at the conclusion of a play that celebrated that power by resurrecting Ovid's ghost and reveling in the thrill of theatrical artifice.

5. Ovids Ghost

"Ovid" makes another uncanny return during the interregnum in *Ovids Ghost*, this time as a literal ghost who is forced into the closet, as it were. Appropriated to critique the Puritan values that banned the pursuit of sensual pleasures and the staging of plays, Ovid haunts the new era as a specter representing lovesickness and theatricality. In contrast to Jonson's character Ovid, however, here Ovid's Ghost functions more as a mouth-piece for the poet than a character, lecturing those who suffer from love-melancholy. The play revolves around themes related to meanings that Ovid had accumulated in his afterlife – the threat of male submission to lovesickness, corresponding misogyny, and antitheatricality – but during a period in which Puritan rule had outlawed the decadence that the icon came to represent, particularly the metamorphic power of love and theatrical illusion. The closet-drama revives the Roman poet through appropriations of *Ars Amatoria*, conjuring the Ovidian theatre – but with a difference. This Ovid is fully spectral, literally and figuratively, a shadow of the earlier Ovidian stage, now a phantom lurking behind closed doors.

Although Ovid frames this odd closet-drama, his Ghost does not appear until Act four, when he is needed to advise the lovelorn. The play opens with Venus, melancholy, complaining to Cupid about their lack of "victims" in the modern world. Cupid vows to spread lovesickness throughout the land, which then sets up for the character visits in Act two: a "Love-sick souldier," who is afraid that he will be mocked for falling in love; a Tradesman who is haunted by love; and a Courtier who complains to Ovid that he who toyed with lovesick girls has now fallen prey to lovesickness himself. Cupid's Cryer then enters in Act three to teach the lovesick men how to win their ladies, followed by examples of three Country Men, each in love with their own lasses, who follow Cupid's messenger.

Finally, Ovid's Ghost, with book in hand, appears to deliver lectures appropriated loosely from *Ars Amantis* (*De Arte Amandi* is printed on the title page) on how to find love and manage love affairs, and he makes a direct reference to the banned pastime of playgoing. In Lecture 1, "To those who are not yet, but would be in love," Ovid suggests going to plays, echoing the moralists' claims: "But the chiefe place the Poets say, / To find them's at the acting of a Play; / There honey pots enough yee may espie."[39] Ovid's Ghost adds, "And ever since the stage hath been a trap, in which all young Gallants catch their Ladies."[40]

Ovid's Ghost continues with a mix of misogyny, early modern rape culture, and the anxiety surrounding male submission. He draws from *Metamorphoses* in Lecture 2, "To those who begin to be in Love," for examples of passionate females (Mirra) and those who need to be deceived to be won (Europa and Io). These examples are intertwined with misogyny from Ovid's other poems, as in this counsel: look like a gentleman, for "[t]hey who on virgins would commit a rape, / Must favour more o'th'man, lesse of the Ape";[41] do not overdrink (or, if you do, pretend you're "lovesick"); and blazon your beloved.[42] The Ghost tells the lovers that women mean yes when they say no, for "[t]hey say they'r forc'd," but "yet such force is welcome to them still," as in the example of Helen of Troy and Paris. If the woman will not yield, Ovid advises, take her by force, for "love [is] a warefare."[43] Ovid adds that in the current day, a man must seduce a woman with money, not poetry, for the latter no longer works as it did in the past,[44] and that to maintain an affair, the man should let the woman win sometimes, to use as leverage later on, and praise his lover profusely.[45]

Finally, in Lecture 3, "To those more deeply engaged," Ovid's Ghost indirectly attacks Puritan morality, flouting marital indiscretions and infidelities. In this final lecture, Ovid's Ghost provides additional guidance on affair maintenance, with hints on managing jealousy, deceiving and cheating on your lover, and avoiding cuckoldry. Compliment your lover, the Ghost suggests, even if the compliments are lies, "mitigate[ing] the faults which you espie."[46] Once Ovid's Ghost concludes the lectures, he returns to the afterlife: "Thus having done that for which I come," he exclaims, "I'll visit once againe Elysium."[47] The Epilogue then punctuates the lectures by underscoring Ovid's poetry as instructional reading: "Thy lines let lovers read, / They will conduct 'em to their Ladies bed."[48] Fittingly, this little play is published with a poem entitled "The Wife-Hater," which follows it in this volume.

It is difficult to discern how much, if any, of Ovid's ironic tone is attempted in this play or how much of the poet's misogynistic advice is taken at face value. Ironic or not, the play clearly attempts to resurrect an Ovid who is closeted as a poet, not a "stager," carrying a book as prop and spouting out appropriated maxims from his poems. This move, perhaps, is a surface attempt to remake "Ovid" of the previous century as a poet, not a playmaker, thereby reducing the Roman poet to a misogynistic wit doling out advice on finding, keeping, and ending affairs. Nevertheless, the play does so in dramatic form, closeted or not. Therefore, despite this token gesture to disassociate Ovid from Marlowe and remove Ovid from the taint of theatre, the play brings back the poet's Ghost to challenge Puritan values of that era and to champion the theatrical Ovid from the past. As an icon of lovesickness, "Ovid" is inseparable from Marlowe and the illusions of the playhouse.

Ovids Ghost may have been an attempt to disengage Ovid from the taint of theatricality, to make the poet acceptable in an age that was hostile to the power of theatricality, while simultaneously questioning the antitheatrical assumptions of that age. Nevertheless, the uncanny return of Ovid's Ghost when the stage was condemned dramatized the inextricable link between Ovid, lovesickness, and the theatrical experience – from the actor's personation to the audience's vulnerability to metamorphic illusion. Spectral Ovids on the early modern English stage served as a reminder that players and playgoers, like the lovelorn characters onstage, were ever susceptible to Cupid's arrows.

Notes

1. Many thanks to Daniel G. Lauby, Miriam Jacobson, Sujata Iyengar, and Christy Desmet (in loving memory) for their feedback on earlier drafts of this chapter.
2. This play is also referred to as *Cupid's Grand Polititian* (1657). The only extant copy of it is housed in the Folger Shakespeare Library. On its date, authorship, cataloguing, and early brief commentary on, see McInnis, "*Cupid's Grand Polititian*." As McInnis notes, there have not been any previous contemporary critical analyses of this play published.
3. Calbi, *Spectral Shakespeares*, pp. 2–4.
4. Derrida, *Specters of Marx*, pp. 10, 22, 40; Calbi, *Spectral Shakespeares*, pp. 1–2.
5. Derrida's emphasis, *Specters of Marx*, p. 11.
6. Calbi, *Spectral Shakespeares*, p. 19.
7. Golding, "Epistle," pp. 7, 288–9. See also Starks-Estes, *Violence, Trauma, and* Virtus, p. 5.
8. Meres, *Palladis Tamia*, p. 282.
9. See Starks-Estes, "*Julius Caesar*, Ovidian Transformation," and Starks, "Ovidian Appropriations, Metamorphic Illusion."
10. Starks-Estes, "*Julius Caesar*, Ovidian Transformation," pp. 104–6, and Starks, "Ovidian Appropriations, Metamorphic Illusion."
11. Gainsford, *The Rich Cabinet*, sig. Q4r.
12. Nashe, "Pierce Penilesse," I, 212.
13. Roach, *The Player's Passion*, p. 42; Roach cites Heywood, *An Apology for Actors*, E4.
14. Roach, *The Player's Passion*, p. 42.
15. Ibid. p. 28. See also Starks-Estes, "*Julius Caesar*, Ovidian Transformation," pp. 118–19.
16. I discuss Ovid's Proteus in relation to theatricality and Marlowe's *The Jew of Malta* in "Ovid's Proteus."
17. Burton, *The Anatomy of Melancholy*, I.2, p. 257.
18. See Starks-Estes, "*Julius Caesar*, Ovidian Transformation," pp. 120–1.
19. See Dawson, *Lovesickness and Gender*, p. 5.
20. Dawson, *Lovesickness and Gender*, pp. 20–2.
21. Gosson, *The Schoole of Abuse*.
22. Prynne, *Histrio-mastix*, sig. 5X4r. See also Starks-Estes, "*Julius Caesar*, Ovidian Transformation," pp. 104–6.
23. I deal with this topic and *A Midsummer Night's Dream* in "Ovidian Appropriations, Metamorphic Illusion."
24. See Lehmann, *Shakespeare's Romeo and Juliet*, pp. 3–58.
25. All citations of Shakespeare's plays are to Shakespeare, *Shakespeare*.
26. All citations of Christopher Marlowe's *Hero and Leander* are to Marlowe, *Hero and Leander*.

27. James, "The Ovidian Girlhood," p. 111.
28. Ibid. p. 119.
29. Ibid. p. 120.
30. James points out that Juliet in Q2 resembles other Ovid's girls: Medea, Scylla, Byblis, Iphis – as well as Myrrha, but she does not discuss Myrrha at length. See James, "The Ovidian Girlhood," p. 112.
31. All citations of Golding's translation of Ovid's *Metamorphoses* are to Ovid, *Ovid's Metamorphoses*.
32. See James, "The Ovidian Girlhood," p. 120.
33. On lovesickness and adaptation in Marlowe's *Dido, Queen of Carthage*, see Daniel G. Lauby's chapter in this volume, "Queer Fidelity: Marlowe's Ovid and the Staging of Desire in *Dido, Queen of Carthage*."
34. Bate, *Shakespeare and Ovid*, p. 167.
35. All references to Ben Jonson's *Poetaster, or, The Arraignment*, are to Jonson, *Poetaster*, pp. 1–101.
36. Kidnie, *Ben Jonson*, p. 430.
37. See Jacobson, *Barbarous Antiquity*, pp. 42, 49.
38. I discuss this point more fully in "Ovidian Appropriations, Metamorphic Illusion."
39. Fuscus, *Ovids ghost*, p. 10.
40. Ibid. p. 11.
41. Ibid. p. 19.
42. Ibid. pp. 20–1.
43. Ibid. p. 24.
44. Ibid. p. 26.
45. Ibid. p. 27.
46. Ibid. p. 35.
47. Ibid. p. 35.
48. Ibid. p. 38.

Bibliography

Bate, Jonathan, *Shakespeare and Ovid* (Oxford: Clarendon Press, 1993).
Burton, Robert, *The Anatomy of Melancholy*, Holbrook Jackson (ed.) (New York: New York Review of Books, 2001).
Calbi, Maurizio, *Spectral Shakespeares: Media Adaptations in the Twenty-First Century* (New York: Palgrave Macmillan, 2013).
Dawson, Lesel, *Lovesickness and Gender in Early Modern English Literature* (Oxford and New York: Oxford University Press, 2008).
Derrida, Jacques, *Specters of Marx: The State of the Debt, the Work of Mourning, and the New International*, Peggy Kamuf (trans.) (New York and London: Routledge, 1994).
Fuscus, Edvardus, *Ovids ghost, or, Venus overthrown by the Nasonian polititian: with a remedy for love-sick gallants, in a poem: on the dispraise*

of all sorts of wives: severall other occasionall verses and characters (London: Printed for the author, 1657). Folger Shakespeare Library, F2566.5.

Gainsford, Thomas (trans.), *The Rich Cabinet*, Giovanni Della Casa (author) (London: Printed by Iohn Beale for Roger Iackson and are to be sold at his shop neere Fleete Conduit, 1616).

Golding, Arthur, "Epistle," in John Frederick Nims (ed.), *Ovid's Metamorphoses: The Arthur Golding Translation of 1567* (Philadelphia: Paul Dry Books, 2000).

Gosson, Stephen, *The Schoole of Abuse* (Printed at London: for Thomas Woodcocke, 1579), sigs. CIr–C2r.

Heywood, Thomas, *An Apology for Actors* (New York and London: Garland, 1973).

Jacobson, Miriam, *Barbarous Antiquity: Reorienting the Past in the Poetry of Early Modern England* (Philadelphia: University of Pennsylvania Press, 2014).

James, Heather, "The Ovidian Girlhood of Shakespeare's Boy Actors: Q2 Juliet," *Shakespeare Survey* 69, 2016, pp. 106–22.

Jonson, Ben, *Poetaster, or, The Arraignment*, in Margaret Jane Kidnie (ed.), *Ben Jonson, The Devil is an Ass and Other Plays*, Oxford World's Classics (Oxford: Oxford University Press, 2000), pp. 1–101.

Kidnie, Margaret J. (ed.), *Ben Jonson, The Devil is an Ass and Other Plays*, Oxford World's Classics (Oxford: Oxford University Press, 2000).

McInnis, David, "*Cupid's Grand Polititian* (1657)," *Early Theatre* 16.2, 2013, pp. 157–64.

Marlowe, Christopher, *Hero and Leander*, in Roma Gill (ed.), *The Complete Works of Christopher Marlowe*, vol. 1 (Oxford: Clarendon Press, 1987).

Meres, Francis, *Palladis Tamia, Wits Treasury* (At London: Printed by P. Short, for Cuthbert Burbie, and are to be solde at his shop at the Royall Exchange, 1598).

Nashe, Thomas, "Pierce Penilesse; His Supplication to the Devil," in R. B. McKerrow (ed.), *Works of Thomas Nashe* (Sidgwick & Jackson, [1592] 1910).

Ovid, *Ovid's Metamorphoses: The Arthur Golding Translation of 1567*, John Frederick Nims (ed.) (Philadelphia: Paul Dry Books, 2000).

Prynne, William, *Histrio-mastix* (London: Printed by Edward Allde, Augustine Mathewes, Thomas Cotes and William Iones for Michael Sparke, and are to be sold at the Blue Bible, in Greene Arbour, in little Old Bayly, 1633).

Roach, Joseph R., *The Player's Passion: Studies in the Science of Acting* (Ann Arbor: University of Michigan Press, 2008).

Shakespeare, William, *Shakespeare: Complete Works*, Revised edn, The Arden Shakespeare (London and New York: Bloomsbury, 2014).

Starks, Lisa S., "Ovidian Appropriations, Metamorphic Illusion, and Theatrical Practice on the Shakespearean Stage," in Christy Desmet, Sujata

Iyengar, and Miriam Jacobson (eds), *The Routledge Handbook of Shakespeare and Global Appropriation* (New York and London: Routledge, forthcoming).

Starks, Lisa S., "Ovid's Proteus and the Figure of the Male Jew in Marlowe's *The Jew of Malta*," in John Garrison and Goran Stanivukovic (eds), *Ovid and Masculinity in English Renaissance Literature* (forthcoming).

Starks-Estes, Lisa S., "*Julius Caesar*, Ovidian Transformation and the Martyred Body on the Early Modern Stage," in Andrew James Hartley (ed.), *Julius Caesar: A Critical Reader*, Arden Early Modern Drama Guides (London: Bloomsbury, 2016).

Starks-Estes, Lisa S., *Violence, Trauma, and* Virtus *in Shakespeare's Roman Poems and Plays: Transforming Ovid* (Basingstoke: Palgrave Macmillan, 2014).

Medea's Afterlife: Encountering Ovid in *The Tempest*

John S. Garrison

Prospero promises to tell "the story of my life" towards the end of Shakespeare's *The Tempest*, yet one of his most revealing speeches does not seem to be about his life at all (V, i, 308).[1] Instead, he draws his language from Ovid and claims as his own the experiences of Medea as described by the ancient author. In the final act of Shakespeare's play, Prospero inventories his feats – many of which, including the ability to restore the dead to life, we have not seen on stage (V, i, 42–60). The speech derives from the sorceress Medea's incantation in Book 7 of Ovid's *Metamorphoses*, and Shakespeare scarcely alters the language from Arthur Golding's early modern translation of Ovid's poem into English. The appropriation of Ovid intriguingly transports the language not only across time but also across genders and narratives.[2] Curiously, though, Shakespeare and Prospero simultaneously invoke Ovid and his Medea at the same time that they elide them by claiming these ancient figures' words as their own. They thereby engage in a form of appropriation where the "element itself is neither living nor dead, present nor absent: it spectralizes"; that is, *The Tempest* offers an intriguing case study for Jacques Derrida's notion of "hauntology."[3] Derrida in fact uses the ghost of Hamlet's father as one of his case studies for the operations of this concept, and Maurizio Calbi has argued that hauntology has even further purchase on the work of Shakespeare.[4] The spectralization of older elements in Prospero's speech bolsters his power and instantiates how "appropriation is intrinsic to building a self."[5] The story of Prospero's life – both within the play and in subsequent film adaptations of it – attains dimension when we trace its debt to the phantom presence of Ovid.[6]

1. The Presence of Absence

In Ovid's poem, Medea's speech occurs during a scene where she revivifies her lover Jason's father. Golding's version of the speech reads:

> Ye Ayres and windes: ye Elves of Hilles, of Brookes, of Woods alone,
> Of standing Lakes, and of the Night approche ye everychone.
> Through helpe of whom (the crooked bankes much wondring at
>   the thing)
> I have compelled streames to run cleane backward to their spring.
> By charmes I make the calme Seas rough, and make the rough Seas
>   plaine,
> And cover all the Skie with Cloudes and chase them thence againe.
> By charmes I raise and lay the windes, and burst the Vipers jaw.
> And from the bowels of the Earth both stones and trees doe draw.
> Whole woods and Forestes I remove: I make the Mountaines shake,
> And even the Earth it selfe to grone and fearfully to quake.
> I call up dead men from their graves: and thee lightsome Moone
> I darken oft, though beaten brasse abate thy perill soone.
> Our Sorcerie dimmes the Morning faire, and darkes the Sun at Noone.
>   (VII, 188–200)[7]

Although Shakespeare's version of this speech sounds very much the same, there are some noteworthy alterations. The playwright condenses the meter that he inherits from Ovid and Golding, rendering the language more contemporary as he aligns it with the poetics of his day. He also removes the reference to raising stones from the ground, perhaps because it has no plausible corollary in the play. However, he does not remove the claim to resurrecting the dead. In some instances, the playwright's rewording causes Prospero's magic to appear more aggressive than Medea's. While Prospero has "'twixt the green sea and azured vault / set roaring war," Medea tells us that she can "make the calme Seas rough, and make the rough Seas plaine" (V, i, 43–4). Prospero has "call'd forth the mutinous winds" (V, i, 42). Medea might "cover all the Skie with Cloudes," but she also will "chase them thence againe"; she will "raise *and* lay the windes" (my emphasis). Medea uses her power to maintain balance, it would seem, rather than to enforce her will on others. Her claim to raising the dead follows these lines almost immediately, suggesting that these resurrections are meant to balance some other force in the world. Such a reading finds support in her choice to return to a balanced pair of the sun and moon at the end of the speech.

Given the context of Medea's claim about raising the dead (both that the act appears alongside depictions of quelling the weather and that the act is an expression of love for Jason), I believe that it goes too far to suggest, as one scholar does, that Prospero "recoils from the thought of what he has done, recalling such resurrections with the same horror as did Medea."[8] Prospero's speech mixes assertions about things he has and has not done, while Medea's speech strikes me as one tinged with themes of reconciliation rather than horror. I favor an interpretation such as Katherine Heavey's, which sees Prospero as "doubly Medea-like, echoing her words and, through his cruelty to Ariel, inadvertently revealing his similarity to the Medea-like Sycorax."[9] In Gordon Braden's words, the magician's speech functions as "a boast and threat."[10] He deploys older words in the service of power. In doing so, he elides the more temperate elements of Medea's character and magic.

Although it appropriates the words of Medea, Prospero's speech could be construed to track to at least some of what the audience has viewed or heard described on stage. Perhaps he has "bedimmed / The noontide sun" in the sense the he initiated the storm that brought the sailors to the island. Moreover, the assertion could meta-theatrically refer to Shakespeare's convincing audience members that they witness nighttime during an afternoon at the theatre (V, i, 41–2). It is the speech's final claim, however, that is the most striking and might give us the most pause: "graves at my command / Have waked their sleepers, oped, and let 'em forth / By my so potent art" (V, i, 48–50). It is the only claim that cannot be located easily in the narrative. On the one hand, we might interpret Prospero's allusion to resurrection as meta-theatrical: he ends the highly orchestrated events on the island by gathering characters who have assumed that each other has drowned. On the other hand, his speech invites the specters of two figures – Ovid and his character Medea – onto the Renaissance stage.[11]

While the audience never witnesses Prospero bringing a dead character to life, the play itself does seem to brim with phantom figures that instantiate a Derridean "logic of the ghost" that "points towards a thinking of the event that exceeds a binary or dialectical logic."[12] It is not simply that Prospero conjures the ghost of Medea in his speech. Instead, he engages with a chain of narrative resurrections. He resuscitates the ancient figure and claims her powers of revivification by ventriloquizing her voice from a scene where she herself restores to life the dying Aeson. The very act of subsuming the story of her life into the story of Prospero's renders visible a chain of absent women haunting the play. Melissa E. Sanchez has identified several figures who accompany Miranda as "ghostly surrogates"; she notes that the play names Sycorax, Claribel, and Dido, and I would add the unnamed Medea to Sanchez' list of *The Tempest*'s spectral female figures.[13]

Perhaps Medea haunted Shakespeare's literary memory, as she seems to haunt other figures and relationships in this work. In *The Merchant of Venice*, Ovid's sorceress is connected closely to Portia. Bassanio describes how his future wife's hair hangs "on her temples like a golden fleece, / Which makes her seat of Belmont Colchis' strand, / And many Jasons come in quest of her" (I, i, 170–2). Portia represents both the fleece and Medea, for her bodily appearance positions her as simultaneously the material treasure and the desired lover. The powers of revivification appear in the play as Portia saves Antonio from a death sentence and symbolically resurrects Shylock when he is forcedly reborn a Christian. Success in their voyage to Belmont engenders a transformation among the men, tying them, too, back to an ancient narrative. Gratiano proclaims, "We are the Jasons; we have won the fleece," once the marriages to Portia and Nerissa are secured (III, iii, 240). The presence of multiple Jasons in *The Merchant of Venice* underscores that the story from Ovid is multivalent for Shakespeare. What remains absent, of course, is any sense of what will happen to the marriages after the events of the play. The ambiguous placement of the marriages in the middle of the play complicates our expectations of whether we are supposed to interpret the ending of the play as effective ordering and whether we are supposed to identify this as a tragedy or a comedy. Yet Portia's triumphs in the closing scenes of *The Merchant of Venice* might be interpreted as an alternate ending for the tale of Jason and Medea, one in which the sorceress might be capable of retaining her husband and a degree of control over their relationship.

The ghost of Medea looms over another relationship in the play. Jessica likens her night-time elopement with Lorenzo to "such a night / Medea gather'd the enchanted herbs / That did renew old Aeson" (V, i, 13–15). The comparison is not necessarily positive, as the conversation also invokes the figures of Cressida, Dido, and Thisbe (V, i, 6–12). Thus, on some level, the comparison to Medea falls in line with the others to suggest that Lorenzo eventually will leave her, despite sacrifices she might make for him. At the same time, the reference to the resurrection of Aeson suggests Jessica's own rebirth (as a wife and as a Christian), in turn inviting us to consider Medea as a figure who signifies second chances. If Medea can revive old Aeson and grant him a second chance at life, perhaps the union of Jessica and Lorenzo might endure longer and more peacefully than that of Medea and Jason.[14] While Jessica's description of the doomed couples seems to threaten failure for her and Lorenzo, it also nods to the way that adaptations, because they are wholly aware of their predecessor texts, can deliver new narratives and new outcomes.

Certainly, Jason uses Medea in the same way that Bassanio uses Portia in order to obtain wealth. However, whereas Medea is abandoned by her husband for another beloved, Portia sees this threat and obviates it when she asks her husband's beloved Antonio to serve as "surety" for their marriage (V, i, 254). Medea will eventually murder her husband's new bride. Portia, on the other hand, enrolls into her marriage the rival for her husband's affections. Salerio, early on in the play, suggests that Antonio's sadness directly relates to sea voyages, choosing a term that relates closely to the story of Medea and Jason. He suggests, "Your mind is tossing on the ocean, / There where your argosies with portly sail" (I, i, 8–9). The term "argosies" refers to Antonio's investment in ships and ties closely to the name of Jason's ship, the Argo. The term appears three more times in the play, each time referring to Antonio's ships. The final use is by Portia, who informs him that

> Antonio, you are welcome;
> And I have better news in store for you
> Than you expect: unseal this letter soon;
> There you shall find three of your argosies
> Are richly come to harbor suddenly:
> You shall not know by what strange accident
> I chanced on this letter. (V, i, 272–8)

With the addition of the curious information at the end here, we learn that Portia has access to texts with occluded origins. Through her access to information and to texts, she has now laid claim to knowledge of Antonio's fortunes. By welcoming him to her and her husband's home, she demonstrates the power to extend hospitality. This represents a striking divergence from Medea's fate as she will end up a stranger in a foreign land through her marriage to Jason. It would seem that Portia, as a new Medea, directs her own fate by rewriting unwanted elements of her classical predecessor's life story.

Whereas the sailors in *The Merchant of Venice* find their Medea in Portia and Lorenzo finds his in Jessica, *The Tempest*'s sailors and lovers encounter the phantom Medea in Prospero's power and in his words. Might we say, then, that this later play without many women is a play about missing women? Miranda does not remember her mother, though she does recall a group of women who attended to her. Sycorax died before Prospero arrived. The possibility that Ariel might be female – adduced when he takes the form of a harpy and when Prospero refers to him as "my chick" – is foreclosed (V, i, 320). Ovid's Medea is an unnamed voice at the climax of the play. She is subsumed into Prospero's speech, just as Ovid's own play entitled *Medea* (his only known work of drama) has been lost to us.

One of the most intriguing of Prospero's additions to Medea's speech is his mention of the "printless foot" that marks the presence of the helper entities addressed in the speech (V, i, 36). While this might seem to allude to the invisible movements of spirits such as Ariel, the phrase also recalls the poetic footsteps of Shakespeare's Ovid. Consider Sir Philip Sidney's concern that "others' feet still seemed but strangers in my way" when his poetic speaker attempts to woo his beloved.[15] Barbara A. Mowat's description of Prospero's sorcery aptly describes his use of source texts: "a serious master of spirits and a stage-or-romance wizard who also reminds us . . . of a Renaissance magus and a Jacobean street magician."[16] The notion of Prospero as a stage or street performer recently found expression in a production of the play directed by the Las Vegas magician Teller (of the performing duo Penn and Teller) that features a number of old-school tricks. I think that the sleight of hand to which Mowat alludes helps us to imagine the speech as a feat of *sprezzatura*. Here, Prospero draws upon his learned study to produce this short speech, re-articulating words written by an earlier writer, as one might do in courtly performance. Jonathan Baldo notes that Prospero is in the business of flaunting his memory, evinced when the character informs Miranda of her history, reminds Ariel of his torment by Sycorax, and recalls the past betrayals by the visitors to the island. We could easily add the speech appropriated from Ovid's Medea to Baldo's list, especially given how it places into "the assumption of the superiority of European memory," which Baldo traces within the play.[17] In light of Sarah Beckwith's claim that "Prospero's project of restitution . . . is utterly tied up with the question of recall and memory," the hauntological operations of the play become clearer as the ghosts (of figures and of texts) are conjured as forces of wanted or unwanted forms of remembrance.[18]

Imagining the speech as *sprezzatura*, a seemingly spontaneous courtly performance of a memorized text, helps us understand why

Stephen Orgel interprets the adopted words from Medea to signal that Prospero's "most potent art" is "revealed as translation and interpretation" as the ancient sorceress first becomes incorporated into the figure of Sycorax and is then shown to be an aspect of Prospero himself.[19] This magician's performance is not just translation, though. More specifically, it is an instance of *translatio et studii imperii* because his very command of a classical voice links to his power. Indeed, Orgel suggests that "the absent, the unspoken" constitutes "the most powerful and problematic presence in *The Tempest*."[20] Reinforcing Orgel's interpretation, James Kearney suggests that the "Absent Present" at the heart of the play is Prospero's book, rather than his wife or other female figures.[21] As we will see, these two readings – that the predominant absence is the book itself and that it is the female figure – ultimately conflate.

In their speeches, both Prospero and Medea admit that their capabilities rely upon the aid of other entities. Both Medea and Prospero nod to help from "elves," and *The Tempest* describes Ariel and his "meaner ministers" performing supernatural feats during the play. It seems that Prospero's way is to put everyone to work. This is hardly the utopia envisioned by Gonzalo, when the aging courtier is asked how he'd envision the perfect island society. He depicts a community with "use of service, none" and "no occupation; all men idle, all" (II, ii, 151–5). In Prospero's utopia, everyone is working – that is, everyone but him and Miranda. And these workers in the play have connections to tropes of resurrection. The ways in which Prospero displays mastery over the island – the labors of everyone on it, and even the words of others that enable such control – instantiate Derrida's claim that Shakespeare understood the "phantomilization of property centuries ago and said it better than anyone."[22] Shakespeare and Prospero perform ownership over the words and characters of previous authors by way of scant citation. Because they do not overtly name their sources, they implicitly assert that authority to call the power of past figures is their own.

2. Textual Transfers of Power

Whereas the stories in the *Metamorphoses* often share the theme of change, the tale of Medea specifically depicts how enabling another's transformation might also make possible a transfer of power. That is, Medea's transmittal of her capabilities to Jason and to Jason's father lays the conceptual architecture for how her powers might be transferred to later literary figures. As we trace the transmission of Medea's power from Ovid's text to Prospero's speech, we see an instance of Derrida's notion that "appropriation, in general, we would say, is *in the condition of the other* and of the *dead* other."[23] By way of textual transfer, Prospero takes on the conditions of Medea's life in ways similar to how characters in the *Metamorphoses* do. In Ovid's narrative, the sorceress mixes herbs together to help Jason achieve his aims in her homeland. The subsequent power he receives is framed not only as a direct acquisition of Medea's own power but also as an instance of learning: "*creditus acceptit cantatas protinus herbas / edidicitque usum laetusque in tecta recessit*" ["she believed; and straight he received the magic herbs and learned their use, then withdrew full of joy"] (VII, 98–9).[24] In fact, Jason's learned embodiment of Medea's magic enables him to cast a spell very similar to one that Prospero will cast. The ancient hero is able to cause others to fall asleep when:

> *Hunc postquam sparsit Lethaei gramine suci*
> *Verbaque ter dixit placidos facientia somnos,*
> *Quaemare turbatum, quae concita flumina sistunt,*
> *somnus in ignotos oculos sibi venit, et auro*
> *heros Aesonius potitur spolioque.*
> [After Jason had sprinkled upon him the Lethaean juice of a certain herb and thrice had recited the words that bring peaceful slumber, which stay the swollen sea and swift-flowing rivers, then sleep came to those eyes which had never known sleep before, and the heroic son of Aeson gained the golden fleece.] (VII, 152–6)

The scene presages the moment from *The Tempest* when Miranda drifts to sleep at her father's command. We also see here Jason able to control the elements, just as Prospero does when he conjures the storm. It is only sixty lines after the resurrection that Medea will begin the speech that Prospero ventriloquizes, a speech which articulates her claims to command rivers and seas. Here the *Metamorphoses* models how Medea's power might be co-opted by men, where Jason obtains them through herbs and Prospero does so through knowledge of ancient texts. However, both men seem to forget the debt they owe to women, as Jason will eventually abandon Medea (who in turn will poison his new bride) and Prospero's lack of citation may have him making claims to power he does not possess. Forgetting absent women has consequences.

The *Metamorphoses* makes quite clear that Medea's power, by nature, can be transferred to other individuals. The means by which she revivifies Jason's father Aeson involves a ritual that transmits her life essence to the older man. Ovid describes the scene this way:

> *stricto Medea recludit*
> *ense senis iugulum veteremque exire cruorem*
> *passa replete sucis*
> [Medea unsheathed her knife and cut the old man's throat; then, letting the old blood all run out, she filled his veins with her brew.]
> (VII, 285–7)

Scrutiny of the Latin here underscores the theme of power transfer. It is not simply that Medea uses her potion to enact magic. Instead, she imbues Aeson's body with her magic. What the Loeb editors translate as "brew" in the quoted passage, Golding translates as "boyled juice." According to the *Oxford Latin Dictionary*, the Latin "*sucis*" can mean not only "a medicine or healing lotion" or "a magic drug" derived from a plant but also the "vitality" of human beings. Like many scholars, Agnès Lafont notes that Ovid's "mythology is not only a source material for the Elizabethan arts, but a creative process in itself."[25] The ways in which Medea's magic emboldens Jason and Aeson to perform remarkable feats present an apt blueprint for *translatio studii et imperii*, where Shakespeare and Prospero draw vital energies from ancient texts to breathe life into their language.

As noted above, for Prospero and for Medea, feats described in their speeches owe to the assistance of others. For Prospero, of course, the actual text of the speech owes to the help of other entities and of previous writers. Yet appropriation, as Christy Desmet reminds us, "signifies, at least historically, both theft and donation, giving and taking."[26] Writing in the humanist tradition, early modern writers so often seek to revivify dead voices within their own. In doing so, they keep ancient voices alive in the shared consciousness of public readers and audiences.

3. Cinematic Reception

The spectral presence of Medea in *The Tempest* finds intriguing expression in Julie Taymor's decision to re-imagine Prospero as a female "Prospera" in the director's recent film version titled *The Tempest*. The ease with which the character becomes female can be attributed in part to Helen Mirren's strong embodiment of the role.

However, we can also take it as a sign of how palpably Ovid hovers beneath Shakespeare's story. Interestingly, Taymor describes her decision to cast a female actor in the principal role as motivated by her own realization that Prospero's speech was drawn from one by the Ovidian Medea.[27] So inspired, Taymor makes several decisions regarding her film. For example, Prospera is expelled from Milan not only because of her brother's zeal for power but also because of rumors he spreads about her having killed her husband. To drive home the linkages between Prospero/a's sorcery and witchcraft, Taymor interpolates into the script the line "knowing that others of my sex have burned for far less."

The intertwined operations of translation and transformation characterize the adaptation of Ovid across Shakespeare's and Taymor's enterprises. Medea's life story becomes Prospero's life story in Shakespeare's play just as Ovid's words become Shakespeare's words. Prospero transforms into Prospera in Taymor's film, at once returning the character to its arguably original gender just as the text is adopted for a new medium. Lisa S. Starks-Estes puts nicely the ways in which Renaissance writers seized upon Ovid, "this method of one tale morphing into the next . . . is based on the poetics of transformation they saw in Ovid's *Metamorphoses*."[28] This claim can be extended to Taymor's use of Shakespeare and Ovid as twin source texts. As the contemporary of Shakespeare, Frances Meres, famously says of him: "the sweet witty soul of *Ovid* lives in mellifluous & honey-tongued *Shakespeare*."[29] The playwright absorbs and voices Ovid, just as Prospero does Medea.

Let us imagine for a moment that the speech by Prospero expresses a fragment memorized from his own commonplace book. Such a hypothesis invites us to interpret these words to instantiate how Shakespeare's use of the *Metamorphoses* involves – as Starks-Estes puts aptly – "piecing together a bricolage of myths, grafting features of tales onto others."[30] Taken within Starks-Estes' framework, Shakespeare and Prospero do not simply retell a story from Ovid. Instead, they actively blend and reconfigure the ancient poet's fictional elements in order to nurture hybrid forms that foster their own self-fashioning. When we acknowledge his roles as a reader and as a writer, we can see Prospero practicing what Orgel has recently characterized as "humanistic, secular magic."[31] The sorcerer's speech then feels like the familiar act of commonplacing, as it functions as a list of accomplishments to which a natural philosopher might aspire.[32] When we imagine Prospero's use of Medea's speech as related to commonplacing, we can see how his acts of adaptation link surprisingly to those of twenty-first-century adapters of Shakespeare. Maurizio Calbi has characterized the recent mode of adaptation as "essentially an ensemble of fragments."[33] We could claim that Prospero (and by extension Shakespeare) is already doing what contemporary filmmakers are beginning to do today.

If Prospero plans to drown a book in which he has jotted down fragments from other writers, then his promise that "I'll drown my book" constitutes a farewell not just to magic but to elements of his memory (V, i, 66). Because memory relies upon, as Derrida remarks, "the condition of finitude," Prospero needs this act of closure in order to effectively place his sorcerous ways in the past.[34] To drown the book is to forget things he knows or has learned, including perhaps the stories of Ovid that he had confused as his own.

Peter Greenaway's film adaptation of *The Tempest* offers a messy – and attractive – adaptation of this play where we cannot disaggregate readings and voices. Writing in the journal *Shakespeare*, Christy Desmet and Sujata Iyengar have recently challenged scholars to embrace the difficulties of sorting through issues of adaptation and appropriation of the playwright's work not by "abandoning theoretical analysis altogether" but rather by "exploring the oscillation between these concepts as attitudes toward artistic production, consumption, and social regulation."[35] Such an approach urges literary scholars to eschew fidelity and attribution as critical markers of the value of an adaptation. Even in their absence from the stage, the book or books that Prospero promises to drown offer a constant reminder of the Derridean, textual phantoms that power the narrative of the play and, in turn, inspire later versions of *The Tempest*. Greenaway's *Prospero's Books* intriguingly points to an interpretation where the unseen books might be selections from Ovid's *Metamorphoses*. John Gielgud plays Prospero and voices the lines of all of the other characters, dramatizing the polyvocality in Shakespeare's play where Prospero's words are permutations of Medea's words. *Prospero's Books* is divided into chapters, each one named for one of the magical books possessed by the island's magician. It is not a stretch of the imagination to posit that these titles could point to Ovid's works as they include the terms "mythologies," "Orpheus," "minotaur," and "love." In the film, Prospero both reads these books and actively writes in them. In this way, Greenaway's film conflates interpretations of the magic books as source texts from classical antiquity and commonplace journals composed in the Renaissance present.

At times, those of us tracing Ovid's influence on Shakespeare (or any other later writer) may find ourselves suffering from what Derrida characterizes as "archive fever":

> It is to burn with a passion. It is never to rest, interminably, from searching for the archive right where it slips away. It is to run after the archive. . . . It is to have a compulsive, repetitive, and nostalgic desire for the archive, an irrepressible desire to return to the origin, a homesickness, a nostalgia for the return to the most archaic place of absolute commencement.[36]

I suggest that Prospero's appropriation of Medea's speech in *The Tempest* reminds us of just how prosperous this burning affliction can be. While we should resist the desire to identify and circumscribe a definitive archive for any given text or author, we should embrace the ways in which the study of adaptation and appropriation demands that we render visible the very instability of archives and the texts that draw upon them. Taymor and Greenaway emphasize that Prospero's voice inevitably constitutes multiple voices and that the figure of Medea in the text, like that of Prospero's book(s), might best serve us if it remains evocatively un-locatable. It is their absence – and their relationship to each other – that urges further study.

Notes

1. All quotations from Shakespeare draw from *The Norton Shakespeare*.
2. I choose the term "appropriation" here because Shakespeare does not so much adapt the story of Medea as much as he treats it as a useful fragment for his character to draw upon. I find useful the distinction that Julie Sanders draws between adaptation and appropriation: while both have an origin text, the latter involves a "journey away from the informing source into a wholly new cultural product and domain." Such a distinction certainly holds true, as Shakespeare's use of Medea's speech moves it from poetry to prose and to a notably dissimilar story. Sanders, *Adaptation and Appropriation*, p. 26.
3. Derrida, *Specters of Marx*, p. 63.
4. See Calbi, *Spectral Shakespeares*, pp. 1–2, for an early application of Derrida's notion to Shakespeare's work.
5. Desmet and Iyengar, "Adaptation, Appropriation, or What You Will," p. 5.

6. The following discussion draws from and builds upon my study *Shakespeare and the Afterlife*, where I discuss Medea and Ovid as resurrected figures in *The Tempest*. See Garrison, *Shakespeare and the Afterlife*, pp. 103–13.
7. All references to Golding's translation draw from the Perseus Digital Library (Ovid, *Ovid*).
8. Benson, "The Resurrection of the Dead," p. 16.
9. Heavey, *The Early Modern Medea*, p. 141.
10. Braden, "Ovid's Witchcraft," p. 126.
11. Because Prospero will renounce his powers shortly after this speech, Sean Benson suggests that "having resurrected the dead, Prospero had apparently unleashed a kind of nightmarish world." However, such a claim extends beyond what the evidence supports, and I believe an Ovidian reading of the play generates a more nuanced explanation. Such a claim is even more startling when we note that Shakespeare's audience may have believed resurrection was possible, but really only for Christ and for humans at the Second coming. Benson, *Shakespearean Resurrection*, p. 182.
12. Derrida, *Specters of Marx*, p. 78.
13. Sanchez, "Seduction and Service in *The Tempest*," p. 52.
14. For a discussion of how Portia's character parallels Medea and even echoes some of her lines for Ovid, see Zuckert, "The New Medea."
15. Sidney, "sonnet 1," p. 1084.
16. Mowat, "Prospero's Book," p. 29.
17. Baldo, "Exporting Oblivion in *The Tempest*," p. 114.
18. Beckwith, *Shakespeare and the Grammar of Forgiveness*, p. 160.
19. Orgel, "Prospero's Wife," p. 11.
20. Ibid. p. 1.
21. Kearney, "The Book and the Fetish," p. 463.
22. Derrida, *Specters of Marx*, p. 51.
23. Ibid. p. 134.
24. All references to Ovid's Latin draw from the Loeb edition (Ovid, *Metamorphoses*). Shakespeare draws upon both Golding's English version (Ovid, *Ovid. Metamorphoses*) and Ovid's Latin. For a discussion of prior scholarly work on this, see Braden, "Ovid's Witchcraft," p. 128.
25. Lafont, "Interacting with Eros," p. 1.
26. Desmet, "Recognizing Shakespeare, Rethinking Fidelity," p. 42.
27. Available at <http://www.cbr.com/the-tempest-julie-taymor-gathers-a-perfect-storm/> (last accessed 12 December 2016).
28. Starks-Estes, *Violence, Trauma, and* Virtus, p. 10.
29. Meres, *Palladis Tamia* (1598), qtd in Macdonald, *Bedford Companion*, p. 32.
30. Starks-Estes, *Violence, Trauma, and* Virtus, p. 10.

31. Orgel, "Secret Arts and Public Spectacles," p. 83.
32. For an interesting discussion of how the "bookish" humanist practice of commonplacing gave way to writing practices central to the rise of "modern" science in the seventeenth century, see Blair, "Humanist Methods."
33. Calbi, *Spectral Shakespeares*, p. 81.
34. Derrida, *Specters of Marx*, p. 18.
35. Desmet and Iyengar, "Adaptation, Appropriation, or What You Will," p. 8.
36. Derrida, *Archive Fever: A Freudian Impression*, p. 91.

Bibliography

Baldo, Jonathan, "Exporting Oblivion in *The Tempest*," *Modern Language Quarterly* 56.2, June 1995, pp. 111–44.

Beckwith, Sarah, *Shakespeare and the Grammar of Forgiveness* (Ithaca: Cornell University Press, 2011).

Benson, Sean, "The Resurrection of the Dead in *The Winter's Tale* and *The Tempest*," *Renascence* 61.1, Fall 2008, pp. 3–24.

Benson, Sean, *Shakespearean Resurrection: The Art of Almost Raising the Dead* (Pittsburgh: Duquesne University Press, 2009).

Blair, Ann, "Humanist Methods in Natural Philosophy: The Commonplace Book," *Journal of the History of Ideas* 53, 1992, pp. 541–51.

Braden, Gordon, "Ovid's Witchcraft," in William Brockliss, Pramit Chaudhuri, Ayelet Haimson Lushkov, and Katherine Wasdin (eds), *Reception and the Classics: An Interdisciplinary Approach to the Classical Tradition* (Cambridge and New York: Cambridge University Press, 2012), pp. 124–33.

Calbi, Maurizio, *Spectral Shakespeares: Media Adaptations in the Twenty-First Century* (New York: Palgrave Macmillan, 2013).

Derrida, Jacques, *Archive Fever: A Freudian Impression*, Eric Prenowitz (trans.) (Chicago and London: University of Chicago Press, 1995).

Derrida, Jacques, *Specters of Marx: The State of the Debt, the Work of Mourning, and the New International*, Peggy Kamuf (trans.) (New York and London: Routledge, 1994).

Desmet, Christy, "Recognizing Shakespeare, Rethinking Fidelity: A Rhetoric and Ethics of Appropriation," in Alexa Huang and Elizabeth Rivlin (eds), *Shakespeare and the Ethics of Appropriation* (New York: Palgrave Macmillan, 2014), pp. 41–57.

Desmet, Christy and Sujata Iyengar, "Adaptation, Appropriation, or What You Will," *Shakespeare* 11.1, 2015, pp. 1–9.

Garrison, John S., *Shakespeare and the Afterlife* (Oxford: Oxford University Press, 2019).

Heavey, Katherine, *The Early Modern Medea: Medea in English Literature, 1558–1688* (New York and Basingstoke: Palgrave Macmillan, 2015).

Kearney, James, "The Book and the Fetish: The Materiality of Prospero's Text," *Journal of Medieval and Early Modern Studies* 32.3, Fall 2002, pp. 433–68.

Lafont, Agnès, "Interacting with Eros: Ovid and Shakespeare," in Agnès Lafont (ed.), *Shakespeare's Erotic Mythology and Ovidian Renaissance Culture* (Farnham and Burlington: Ashgate, 2013), pp. 1–16.

Macdonald, Russ (ed.), *The Bedford Companion to Shakespeare: An Introduction with Documents* (New York: Bedford/St. Martin's, 2001).

Mowat, Barbara A., "Prospero's Book," *Shakespeare Quarterly* 52.1, 2001, pp. 1–33.

Orgel, Stephen, "Prospero's Wife," *Representations* 8, Autumn 1984, pp. 1–13.

Orgel, Stephen, "Secret Arts and Public Spectacles: The Parameters of Elizabethan Magic," *Shakespeare Quarterly* 68.1, 2017, pp. 80–91.

Ovid, *Metamorphoses: Books 1–8*, 3rd edn, Frank Justus Miller (trans.), revised by G. P. Goold (Cambridge, MA and London: Harvard University Press, 1977).

Ovid, *Ovid. Metamorphoses*, Arthur Golding (trans.) (London: W. Seres, 1567), Perseus Digital Library, Gregory R. Crane (ed.) (Tufts University), <http://www.perseus.tufts.edu/hopper/> (last accessed 10 December 2016).

Oxford Latin Dictionary, P. G. W. Glare (ed.) (Oxford: Oxford University Press, 1982).

Prospero's Books, film, directed by Peter Greenaway. Santa Monica: Miramax Films, 1991.

Rosenberg, Adam, "*The Tempest*: Julie Taymor Gathers a Perfect Storm," CBR.com, 4 October 2010, <http://www.cbr.com/the-tempest-julie-taymor-gathers-a-perfect-storm/> (last accessed 12 December 2016).

Sanchez, Melissa E., "Seduction and Service in *The Tempest*," *Studies in Philology* 105, 2008, pp. 50–82.

Sanders, Julie, *Adaptation and Appropriation* (London and New York: Routledge, 2006).

Shakespeare, William, *The Norton Shakespeare, Based on the Oxford Edition*, 2nd edn, Stephen Greenblatt, Walter Cohen, Jean E. Howard, and Katharine Eisaman Maus (eds) (New York: W. W. Norton, 2008).

Sidney, Philip, "sonnet 1," in Stephen Greenblatt, Katharine Eisaman Maus, George Logan, and Barbara K. Lewalski (eds), *The Norton Anthology of English Literature, Volume B: The Sixteenth Century and the Early Seventeenth Century*, 9th edn (New York and London: W. W. Norton, 2012).

Starks-Estes, Lisa S., *Violence, Trauma, and* Virtus *in Shakespeare's Roman Poems and Plays: Transforming Ovid* (Basingstoke: Palgrave Macmillan, 2014).

The Tempest, film, directed by Julie Taymor. Burbank: Walt Disney Studios Motion Pictures, 2010.

Zuckert, Michael, "The New Medea: On Portia's Comic Triumph in *The Merchant of Venice*," in Joseph Alulis and Dennis Bathory (eds), *Shakespeare's Political Pageant: Essays in Literature and Politics* (New York: Rowman and Littlefield, 1996), pp. 3–36.

Chapter 7

Remnants of Virgil, Ovid, and Paul in *Titus Andronicus*

Catherine Winiarski

Many recent surveyors of adaptation studies have wondered how we might imagine infidelity to the persistent "fidelity paradigm," which imposes ideological categories like "faithful" and "unfaithful," and "original" and "derivative," on the texts it examines. Christy Desmet, for example, has proposed a model of dialogic appropriation, and Douglas Lanier a model of Deleuzian rhizomatics, to complicate our current conceptions of adaptation.[1] Linda Hutcheon has offered an especially viable alternative to fidelity theory in a theory of "cultural selection:" "[l]ike evolutionary natural selection, cultural selection is a way to account for the adaptive organization, in this case, of narratives. Like living beings, stories that adapt better than others (through mutation) to an environment survive."[2] In place of "original" and "derivative" texts, Hutcheon and her co-author Gary R. Bortolotti propose "ancestor" and "descendent" texts; they go on to conceive narratives as "replicators" that seek to adapt to various cultural environments through concrete "vehicles."[3] Thus, all (manifest) versions of a (latent) narrative can be understood as vehicles of adaptation, the "source" text as much as the "derivative" one. What Hutcheon and Bortolotti do not address directly, in their exploration of "a homology between biological and cultural adaptation," is cultural competition among narratives.[4]

Shakespeare's *Titus Andronicus* demonstrates an intertwining of biological and cultural adaptation, including competition among narratives, in its treatment of the survivor, or remnant, in three distinct dimensions: first, in the play's thematics of survival and remains; second, in the relations among its fragmentary allusions to Virgil's *Aeneid* and Ovid's *Metamorphoses*; and third, in its Renaissance project of adapting ancient Roman culture to a new time and place. As the survivors of a devastating war – a biological, political, and cultural catastrophe – both the Roman and Gothic characters of *Titus Andronicus* work to adapt to circumstances of decimation and then to renew hostile competition in adaptive ways. The text also employs tropes of fragmentation and remaindering within its many allusions to Virgil and Ovid.[5] As readers of the play like Jonathan Bate, Cora Fox, and Lisa S. Starks-Estes have explained, its characters employ strategies from Virgil's and Ovid's narratives to express the abjection of mourning and sorrow, the trauma of violence, and the manic enthusiasm of vengeance.[6] These characters also understand their status as survivors – and enter into renewed competition with their rivals – through the cracked lenses of these two ancestor narratives. In one more dimension of adaptation, within Renaissance culture, the play experiments with adapting the remnants of pagan, Roman culture to a Protestant Christian environment rooted in the texts of St. Paul.

Titus Andronicus shows its Roman and Gothic war survivors divided by their concepts of the remnant, which they adapt from competing Virgilian and Ovidian ancestor texts. The Romans experience their history, especially their descent from Trojan origins, as a subtraction or decimation. They seem trapped in the abjection of the Fall of Troy, of Book 2 of the *Aeneid*, with the Goths as a new set of scheming Greeks inflicting undeserved ruin on an innocent, unsuspecting people. In this conception of human history, death continuously extends its empire, decimating the living in a long execution line of time.[7] The remainder left in the present, while well-adapted and resistant to the pain of traumatic loss, is ultimately non-regenerative. Stoicism – and perhaps even a perverse death wish – seems to be the only response available to *Titus*'s Romans. The Goths, on the other hand, introduce an actively adaptive, transformative, and regenerative kind of remnant, by way of Ovid. Strategic allusions to episodes in Ovid's *Metamorphoses* oppose the cultural and political power of Greece to Scythia, Thrace, Troy, and finally Rome. In this way, Shakespeare evokes Ovid's logic of metamorphosis, which evinces a reversal, in the fullness of time, of the political and moral dynamic between Greece and its "barbaric" opponents, through the survival and vindication of a remnant of Greece's defeated enemy. This metamorphic logic opens up the potential of retributive violence, especially female violence, against the Romans' stoic male victimhood. If the Virgilian remnant continuously erodes, in stoic suffering without redemption, the Ovidian remnant transforms and strikes back against its oppressor. The Ovidian narrative eventually converts the Virgilian Titus to its strategy. Its success, however, has an ironic limit: it succeeds against its competitors only at the expense of its own survival.

The remnant understood as a non-regenerative decimation is evident in Titus's addresses to the Roman people in Act one, where Titus adapts Virgil to evoke a tragic loss which is nonetheless felt as petty compared with Rome's heroic past. Mourning his lost sons, Titus expresses the fragmentation of his Trojan legacy: "Romans, of five-and-twenty valiant sons, / Half of the number that King Priam had, / Behold the poor remains alive and dead" (I, i, 79–81).[8] While the number of Titus's offspring may still strike readers as mythically abundant, Titus sees his reproductive output – and the potential for military service that comes with the production of sons – as reaching only half that of the legendary Trojan king. He feels his appearance on the historical scene to be determinately late, with decadence and decay built necessarily into the passage of time. We witness a double decimation here, both by degeneration inherent in the passage of time and by Rome's relentless pursuit of empire. Only a "poor remains" is left, "poor" in the sense that it is drained of the implied wealth of the whole but also "poor" because it can evoke the pity of the Roman people, who are its appointed spectators. The quantification of the classical tradition here – its rendering into fractions – suggests its conception as a formal sum of divisible, equivalent, abstract parts that constitute a value through their sheer quantity; the content of that legacy seems subordinate to its form.

In Titus's conception of the dynamic between life and death, death, made concrete in the monument of the Andronici, continually decimates the living, making endless claims that are never repaid. Titus laments death's unbalanced and excessive claim on his family in this apostrophe and rhetorical question addressed to the monument itself:

> O sacred receptacle of my joys,
> Sweet cell of virtue and nobility,
> How many sons of mine hast thou in store,
> That thou wilt never render to me more! (I, i, 92–5)

The personified tomb hoards Titus's reproductive wealth and its attendant happiness. Virtue and nobility, the expected return for the warrior's sacrifice and his father's, are here objectified as a valuable substance, like honey, stored up in the tomb's "cells" and inaccessible to the father. In his exclamation, Titus calls attention to the an-economic nature of his relationship with the tomb: it makes an absolute and never-ending claim, never "rendering" back the sons it claims from the father. Roman fatherhood appears here as a permanent state of mourning mixed with, arguably, a kind of necrophilia. Titus offers this consolation to his dead sons: "In peace and honour rest you here, my sons, / Rome's readiest champions, repose you here in rest, / Secure from worldly chances and mishaps!" (I, i, 150–2). The chiastic repetition and reversal of "rest you here, my sons" in the next line, "champions, repose you here in rest," encloses the sons in a verbal tomb of ritualized sameness.

Shakespeare adapts the world and worldview of Virgil's *Aeneid*, Book 2, a tragic origin point for the Roman Empire, in order to conjure Rome's fatalistic, late-imperial period in *Titus Andronicus*. Titus's identification with Priam, in particular, evokes this worldview. Here, Virgil gives a vision of decimation: Priam's immense reproductive wealth is destroyed, as his sons are killed before his eyes. Panthus's lament describes a Troy that is extinct in the present and has entered the past tense: "Troyans we were; and Troye was sometime, / And of great fame the Teucrian glory erst: / Fierce Jove to Greece hath now transposed all."[9] Here, it is the cruel and capricious will of the gods that makes an absolute claim on Trojan life and empire, conceived as movable property that can be "transposed" to the Greeks in the logic of *translatio imperii*. Although this is not where Book 2 ultimately ends, Virgil certainly gives a powerful vision of non-regenerative destruction here. Seen from this perspective, Titus's Pyrrhic victories seem no less devastating than the fall of Troy itself. Late-imperial Rome has returned to its origins in the destruction of Troy.

Titus adapts the oppositional logic of the *Aeneid*, Book 2, in which civilized and innocent Trojans are attacked by "scheming" and even barbaric Greeks, to his conflict with the Goths, seeing himself and the Romans as representatives of civilization locked in an eternal conflict with barbarism, in this instance, the "barbarous Goths" (I, i, 28). In her plea for her son's life, Tamora undertakes a radical critique of this opposition between civilization and barbarism and proposes an extension and universalization of Roman values.[10] The scene of supplication between Titus and Tamora, Roman conqueror and Gothic captive, presents a tableau of the interlocking oppositions of civilized/barbarian, free/bonded, and male/female. Against these radicalized oppositions, Tamora asserts parental love as a universal value and even seeks to universalize the traditional Roman value of piety, embodied by *Pius Aeneas*, founder of Rome, and sustained in the present by "Pius" Andronicus:

> And if thy sons were ever dear to thee,
> O, think my son to be as dear to me . . .
> O, if to fight for king and commonweal
> Were piety in thine, it is in these. (I, i, 107–15)

Pietas, or piety – defined as duty to family, country, and the gods – is consistently asserted as a ground of Roman identity in the play. Tamora also invokes quantities and equations in her counterargument against the excessive claim of Titus: "Sufficeth not that we are brought to Rome / To beautify thy triumphs, and return / Captive to thee and to thy Roman yoke" (I, i, 109–11). In this assertion of sufficiency – the sufficiency of Gothic captivity to demonstrate Roman triumph publicly and spectacularly – Tamora proposes to "call it even" between Romans and Goths. Titus insists upon "one more." When Titus refuses Tamora's call for mercy and seizes her eldest son for sacrifice, she, rising from her kneeling position, declares a reversal in the terms of the opposition between pious Roman and cruel barbarian: "O cruel, irreligious piety!" (I, i, 130). If piety means to offer or to take just enough to achieve reciprocity or justice, cruelty means to take an excess. The "civilized" Roman virtue of piety – and the "barbarian" vice of cruelty – can be understood in the quantifiable, economic terms of sufficiency and excess.

The Goths, as much as Titus, understand themselves as the remnants left over after the decimation of war, but they only initially adapt Virgilian concepts of tragic decimation to their situation. Demetrius at first echoes Titus's death wish, exalting the peace and security of death in comparison to the suffering that accompanies life: "Alarbus goes to rest and we survive / To tremble under Titus' threat'ning look" (I, i, 133–4). Survival for enslaved captives means something quite distinct from survival for victorious Roman warriors, however. The surviving captive persists in a state of "trembling," which expresses the anxiety of the bonded state, in which the violence of previous war and capture is held in reserve and indiscriminately unleashed within an ostensibly civilized and peaceful legal order. Attacks in war give way to "threats" in slavery, and the exaction of excess penalty from Alarbus. As survivors, the Goths see their national identity as Goths to have been shattered and now placed in the past tense, as expressed in Demetrius's parenthesis: "The selfsame gods . . . May favour Tamora, the Queen of Goths / (When Goths were Goths, and Tamora was queen)" (I, i, 136–40). This certainly echoes the abjection expressed by Panthus in the *Aeneid*, Book 2, but that abjection is soon transformed to active vengeance, by way of Ovidian allusions.

Chiron uses the language of fragmentation to respond to Titus's condemnation of their brother, by way of an Ovidian reference to "barbarous Scythia" and the multiplication of its legacy in the present day of imperial Rome:

> Chiron: Was never Scythia half so barbarous.
> Demetrius: Oppose not Scythia to ambitious Rome. (I, i, 131–2)

Here, Chiron confronts the Romans' assumed representation of civilization against the "barbarous Goths," in Marcus's phrase (I, i, 28). Effecting an ironic reversal of the usual referents of "barbarous" and "civilized," Chiron asserts that Rome has exceeded even the notoriously barbarous Scythians in barbarism. Demetrius asserts that Rome has become singular in its "ambition," transgressing all bounds of comparison and opposition. Entering into a kind of second-order exceptionality, Rome has become the exception to the exception. Scythia, a model of barbarism that used to stand alone, in independent wholeness, is now reduced to a fragment: not even "half" of Rome's whole. A crucial point of reference for the "barbarous Scythian" is Ovid's tale of the primeval meeting between the Athenian Triptolemus and Scythian Lyncus, who tries to kill his guest in order to steal and take credit for the technology of agriculture:

> The savage king had spite and, to th'intent that of so rare
> And gracious gifts himself might seem first founder for to be,
> He entertained him in his house and, when asleep was he,
> He came upon him with a sword. But as he would have killed him,
> Dame Ceres turned him to a lynx . . . (V, 806–10).[11]

This attempted murder and theft represents a failure of hospitality and gratitude on the part of the barbarian, whose ethical failure is registered in his metamorphosis to an animal. Beyond the intent to shed innocent human blood, "barbarity" in this episode can be seen in the violation of hospitality, in the spite directed at the gods' chosen ones (the "civilized" Athenians), in the refusal to enter into a social contract, and in the taking of excess. An ethical line is drawn more clearly by Ovid here than in later episodes of the *Metamorphoses*. An opposition between civilization and barbarism seems firmly established. In this allusion, Shakespeare's play casts Rome back to a primeval confrontation between civilization and barbarism, between Athens and Scythia. In Book 15 of the *Metamorphoses*, Ovid offers an ironic celebration of the Roman Empire as the culmination and end of aeons of progressive metamorphosis, suggesting in fact that Rome will undergo the same transformations as every other empire before it. Shakespeare unleashes Ovidian metamorphosis in the setting of the late Roman Empire, recasting the Romans as the new barbarians. Titus is accused of barbarism – the taking of excess and failure to form a just social contract with the other – in his demand for Alarbus's death.

This logic of reversal between civilization and barbarism, enacted through the transformation of remnants, is evident in Shakespeare's references to Ovid's Hecuba in Act one and Ovid's Philomela in later acts. An accidental cultural alliance emerges between Titus, who casts himself in the role of Priam, and his defeated Gothic enemy, Tamora, who is identified with Hecuba by her son Demetrius. In their competition for possession of the Trojan legacy and for survival and power in the late Roman Empire, the two fall unexpectedly into the roles of husband and wife, king and queen of Rome's tragic ancestral city. However, the Goths' Hecuba belongs to Ovid, not to Virgil. While Virgil's Hecuba merely counsels Priam in stoicism, in the futility of an old man's arming himself against the Greeks' attack, Ovid's Hecuba is a survivor or remnant of the destruction of Troy who becomes her children's avenger.[12] As a reaction to Alarbus's slaughter and the Goths' further subjection and decimation by the Romans thereby, Demetrius alludes to Ovid's account of Hecuba's revenge upon the treacherous Polymestor in Book 13 of the *Metamorphoses*:

> Then, madam, stand resolved, but hope withal
> The selfsame gods that armed the Queen of Troy
> With opportunity of sharp revenge
> Upon the Thracian tyrant in his tent
> May favour Tamora, the Queen of Goths (I, i, 135–9)

Unlike Titus, who expresses loss as a fragmentation of the Trojan legacy, Demetrius conjures a vision of the complete restoration of that legacy, in the service of revenge. The "selfsame gods" that aided Hecuba in her revenge may be able to restore the Goths to their selfsame identity. Hecuba in Ovid does not appear as the "poor remains" of the Trojan War; she is transformed by grief for her children into a powerful revenger. In Ovid's telling of this episode from the aftermath of the Trojan War, Thracian Polymestor ("the Thracian tyrant") violates a contract of adoption and protection he made with Priam by slaughtering Priam's son Polydorus and stealing the treasure Priam sent with Polydorus. Hecuba's vicious act of vengeance against Polymestor (tearing out his eyes) is punished with her metamorphosis to a dog; however, her howls of sorrow touch all (Trojans, Greeks, and the gods) with sympathy:

> Long mindful of her former ills, she sadly for the same
> Went howling in the fields of Thrace. Her fortune moved not
> Her Trojans only but the Greeks, her foes, to ruth. Her lot
> Did move even all the gods to ruth, and so effectually
> That Hecub to deserve such end even Juno did deny. (XIII, 684–8)

In comparison to the metamorphosis of Lyncus, the ethical significance of Hecuba's metamorphosis is notably ambiguous. Though condemned for her vicious wrath, she is also universally pitied, defying the political boundaries between Trojan and Greek. If Ovid had cast the Trojans as the "barbarians" in the conflict between Greece and Troy because of Paris' lustful stealing of Helen and his violation of hospitality, Hecuba is made the moral exception; her maternal despair and subsequent revenge are seen as justified and her metamorphic punishment excessive. The ethical line between civilization and barbarism is not as clear in this episode. In Demetrius's allusion to this episode from Ovid, he reframes Titus's purported act of sacrifice as a violated contract, like that between Priam and Polymestor. Tamora's revenge may cost her her humanity, but her cause may achieve universally recognized justice. The ambiguity of the Thracian, as geographically and politically intermediate between Greece and Troy, is projected onto Titus and Rome.

Demetrius's allusion to Hecuba in Thrace also evokes her confrontation with the ghost of Achilles in the *Metamorphoses*. Achilles, like Titus, demands an additional sacrifice after war hostilities have concluded, the sacrifice of Hecuba's daughter Polyxena over his grave:

> Achilles with a threatning look did like resemblance make
> As when at Agamemnon he his wrongful sword did shake
> And said, "Unmindful part ye hence of me, O Greeks? And must
> My merits thankless thus with me be buried in the dust?
> Nay, do not so! But to th'intent my death due honour have,
> Let Polyxene in sacrifice be slain upon my grave . . . (XIII, 530–5)

Demetrius's reference to Titus's "threat'ning look" appears to be a direct quotation of this moment from Golding's translation of Ovid, cementing an association between Achilles and Titus (I, i, 134). The story suggests that Achilles's ghost violates a civilized principle of proportionality in war by demanding yet more sacrifice on the already defeated Trojan side. It seems appropriate that Achilles's singular and excessive wrath would continue to demand "one more" victim, even after his death. Titus risks the same kind of excess in his demand for "one more" victim in the person of Tamora's son.

Ovid's tale of Procne and Philomela in the *Metamorphoses*, to which Shakespeare alludes in Act two and after, problematizes and transforms the opposition between civilization and barbarism even more than the tale of Hecuba. Here, Ovid presents another "Thracian tyrant," intermediate between civilized Athenian and barbaric Scythian, this time attacking his sister-in-law, the daughter of the Athenian king Pandion. In kidnapping his wife's sister, raping her, and then imprisoning her, all under the pretense of transporting her for a visit to Thrace, Tereus is guilty of excessive and violent desire, as well as the violation of hospitality, like Lyncus and Paris. Procne, like Hecuba, is an empowered female revenger, attacking male tyranny.[13] Unlike Hecuba, Procne disavows maternal bonds for sisterly ones, striking at Tereus's tyranny by attacking his heir and her own son. What makes this story distinctive is the metamorphosis of all three characters at the conclusion, Thracian and Athenian alike. The birds into which the characters are transformed represent the remnants of the Thracian kingdom now bereft of its sovereign line. The moral condemnation of Tereus seems clear, but the transformation of Procne and Philomela, justified in their sense of injury but perhaps unhinged in their pursuit of revenge, reflects the same moral ambiguity that Ovid created in Hecuba's case. Shakespeare takes from Ovid the idea that internecine conflict between civilization and barbarism ultimately turns both sides barbaric. The consumption of both Romans and Goths in their revenge plots in *Titus Andronicus* reflects this Ovidian idea.

Tamora's Ovidian transformations are especially complex and ambiguous, constructing her as a righteous avenging mother, a cruel barbarian, and eventually, in a literal metamorphosis, a bird and a beast. Combining the figures of Hecuba and Tereus, she authorizes and urges on the lust of her sons (aligned with Tereus), complicating it with a maternal desire for revenge (aligned with Hecuba); rape becomes a tool of her revenge. The role of Hecuba the avenging mother hardens into a personification of Revenge itself; here, Tamora's metamorphoses take her into the conventions of medieval allegory and revenge tragedy. From the personification of the abstract, she finally materializes as the literal flesh of Ovid's metamorphoses. Lucius pronounces exposure of her corpse to be the best punishment for her bestial behavior: "But throw her forth to beasts and birds of prey; / Her life was beastly and devoid of pity" (V, iii, 197–8). As food for "beasts" and "birds," Tamora is naturalistically and literally transformed to Hecuba's dog and Tereus's bird. Crucially, the role of Ovidian female revenger, which Tamora takes up, is contagious to the Romans: Titus imitates Tamora in the taking up of Procne's role and even in his declaration of revenge.[14] Tamora declares, "Ne'er let my heart know merry cheer indeed / Till all the Andronici be made away" (II, iii, 188–9). We hear an uncanny echo of this declaration when Titus finally abandons abject sorrow and embraces a course of revenge: "I shall never come to bliss / Till all these mischiefs be returned again / Even in their throats that hath committed them" (III, i, 271–3). Each conditions his or her own happiness on the fulfillment of revenge, conceived as a whole, as "all," in contrast with the fragmented state in which they find themselves as victims. Titus's declaration may represent the triumph of Ovid's vindictive and regenerative remnant over Virgil's stoic and non-regenerative remnant.

I would like to suggest another context for *Titus Andronicus* which, I would argue, presents a third type of remnant and continues the metamorphosis of Roman and barbarian through the decline of the Roman Empire and the rise of its successor. Shakespeare's play, with its late-Roman setting and Ovidian universe of references, obscures the Christian context put forth by the prose history, "The Tragical History of Titus Andronicus," which is regarded by some critics as a source for the play. The prose history asserts its time period as that of the Roman Empire's greatest extent, under the Christian emperor Theodosius, in the late fourth century CE. The assumption is that the Roman Empire had been fully Christianized by this time; its invaders, the Goths, are "a barbarous people, strangers to Christianity."[15] The category of "barbarian," normally opposed to "Greek" or "Roman" in those contexts, is here opposed to "Christian." This controversial source suggests that there may be a hidden Christian context, in some way indicative of Shakespeare's Protestant Christian England, lodged within the play. Perhaps this "cloaking" of the Christian narrative is a strategy of adaptation and survival for it, especially in an environment of religious censorship and persecution like the Protestant Reformation in England. It enables the play to explore, indirectly, the violent foundations of the Christian community of the present.

I would argue that Shakespeare's Ovid mediates between Virgil and Paul, opening up the potential for the social transformations that Paul calls for, that is, the formation of a new social body, the "body of Christ," out of remnants of civilized and barbarian communities. However, the Ovidian characters in *Titus* are violently purged, to enable the formation of a Pauline Christian community.

The epistles of St. Paul conceive of the transformation of Greek and Roman ethnic and legal categories, including opposed categories of civilization and barbarism so essential to Virgil and Ovid, in the articulation of a new Christian community and identity. Paul's transformative claim famously appears in the epistle to the Galatians: "There is neither Iewe nor Grecian: there is neither bonde nor free: there is neither male nor female: for ye are all one in Christ Iesus" (Gal. 3: 28).[16] Paul uses the term "barbarian" in the epistle to the Romans to limn a fourth distinction in his thought: "I am detter bothe to the Grecians, and to the Barbarians, bothe to the wisemen & unto the unwise" (Rom. 1: 14). As we have seen, Ovid assumes these oppositions between barbarian and civilized, defining them in relation to social contract and reciprocity. In an ironic proclamation at the end of the *Metamorphoses*, Ovid imagines the "Roman" and the "civilized" eventually overwhelming and cancelling out all particular barbarian identities. Shakespeare stages Paul's particular conception of these opposed identities vividly in Act one of *Titus Andronicus*: in the scene of supplication between Titus and Tamora, we see an opposition between barbarian and civilized, bond and free, female and male. This is a subtle, structural allusion to Paul, but legible nonetheless. Shakespeare's play ultimately performs a transformation of these categories by way of Paul's distinct kind of remaindering.

Paul performs a kind of metamorphosis upon the identities and oppositions of the Roman Empire, reflected in Ovid, producing a new kind of remnant. Giorgio Agamben's reading of the epistle to the Romans asserts that the Pauline Christian is not a universal subject but a "remnant" of Paul's re-divisions of the divisions of Hebrew and Roman law. Agamben contends that in his treatment of the law, Paul respects the root of the Greek term for law, *nomos*, which is *nemo* ("to divide"). Thus, the function of the law is to establish divisions. Agamben notes that the opposition Jew/Greek (*Ioudaios/ Hellen*) – elsewhere written in the epistles as Jew/Gentile (*Ioudaios/ ethne*) – is the "fundamental partition" of Jewish law.[17] The opposition bond/free (*doulos/eleutheros*) marks the fundamental division of Roman law, the other juridical discourse Paul was working within in his effort to conceptualize a new Christian identity and community.

Agamben argues that Paul in fact performs "a separation to the second power, a separation which, in its very separateness, divides and traverses the divisions of the Pharisaic laws."[18] Paul imposes a second division on the divisions of Jewish law: that of flesh/spirit (*sarx/ pneuma*). Thus, the category of Jew is divided into Jews of the flesh ("the outward Jews") and Jews of the spirit ("the inward Jews"). The category of non-Jew is divided according to the same opposition of flesh and spirit. These re-divisions bear out Paul's pronouncement that "all they are not Israel, which are of Israel" (Rom. 9: 6). These re-divisions of Pauline messianism produce a remnant that prevents the sum of Jews and non-Jews from constituting "all." According to Paul, this remnant fulfills Isaiah's prophesy about the fate of Israel, which Paul quotes in Romans: "Thogh the nomber of the children of Israel were as the sand of the sea, *yet* shal *but* a remnant be saved" (Rom. 9: 27).

The conclusion of *Titus Andronicus* witnesses the formation of a Pauline community of Romans and Goths based on the violent production of remnants which are then merged into a new body politic. The members of each community who are committed to revenge grounded in Ovidian narratives and in their ethnic identities as Romans or Goths – Titus, Saturninus, Tamora, Chiron, Demetrius, and even Lavinia, tragically – are consumed in their revenge plots and ultimately cut out of the body politic. The remaining Andronici and the Gothic army they lead are integrated through the workings of grief and pity. In a fascinating move, the narrative at first threatens to return to the *Aeneid*, Book 2, when Marcus calls on Lucius to narrate the events that have transpired just as Aeneas did when he told "[t]he story of that baleful burning night / When subtle Greeks surprised King Priam's Troy" (V, iii, 82–3). However, Lucius refuses to perpetuate this narrative (maladapted to these new circumstances?) and describes a different interaction between Goths and Romans, between invading barbarians and invaded civilization, from that of Virgil's text. He describes his banishment from Rome and plight as a survivor (like Aeneas) but then his appeal to and acceptance by Rome's enemies, the Goths (unlike Aeneas):

> The gates shut on me, and turned weeping out,
> To beg relief among Rome's enemies,
> Who drowned their enmity in my true tears,
> And oped their arms to embrace me as a friend. (V, iii, 104–7)

This scene of supplication repeats and reverses the scene of supplication in Act one. The body politic seems to experience an opening and liquefaction here that integrates the "poor remainder of the Andronici" as the head of a new body politic and the leaderless community of compassionate and "just" Goths as its in-grafted members (V, iii, 130). Two remnants merge into a new body politic that expresses the dream of the Pauline community – and its cost. This is perhaps the play's pro-spective (and critical) vision of a "Holy Roman Empire."

Shakespeare's stake in the logic of the remnant can perhaps be best understood in the context of the Protestant Reformation, the cultural environment to which Virgilian and Ovidian narratives arguably attempt to adapt in *Titus*, as part of a Renaissance project of cultural integration between past and present, pagan and Christian. Protestant writers and leaders posed the same challenge to the Catholic Church that Paul had posed to Israel. They re-instantiated Paul's division or cut within the Christian community, producing a remainder or remnant; they divided Christians of the spirit (Protestants) from Christians of the flesh (law-bound Catholics, who attempted to determine righteousness themselves, according to outward practice alone). John Calvin, for example, looks at Paul's pronouncement that "not all those of Israel are Israel" and draws an analogy with present circumstances: "just as in present day the Papists would fain under this pretext [claiming the name of the Church for themselves] substitute themselves in place of God."[19] In other words, "not all those of the Church are the Church." It is God's "secret election" that divides the saved from the damned, forming a "righteous remnant" that perhaps remains an invisible community. The conclusion of *Titus Andronicus* settles remnants of the Roman and Gothic nations into an incorporate Pauline community. Shakespeare adapts Ovidian narratives to break down the binary opposition of Roman and Goth, civilized and barbarian; the Pauline narrative of the play completes that breakdown but also produces violent social excisions that mark the transition from late imperial to early Christian Rome. What are excised from the Pauline community are the remnants of Ovid: figures of metamorphic passion and revenge.

Notes

1. I am indebted to Lisa Starks, editor of this collection, for helpful references to the most current theories of adaptation, insightful feedback on this chapter, and patience with my revision process. See Desmet, "Recognizing Shakespeare," and Lanier, "Shakespearean Rhizomatics."

2. Hutcheon, *A Theory of Adaptation*, p. 167.
3. Hutcheon and Bortolotti, "On the Origin," p. 447.
4. Ibid. p. 444. On the subject of narrative competition, Heather James perceives Virgil and Ovid as competing versions of the classical tradition, as tradition and counter-tradition, in terms of their contrasting genres, ideological perspectives on empire, and treatment of gender. See James, *Shakespeare's Troy*.
5. Many readers of the play have commented on its "mutilations" of texts from Virgil and Ovid. See especially James, *Shakespeare's Troy*, and St. Hilaire, "Allusion and Sacrifice," pp. 311–31.
6. Jonathan Bate has argued that Shakespeare was most interested in Ovid's depiction of human beings transported by extreme emotion, which represents moments of internal and psychological metamorphosis, according to the metaphorical readings of Ovid in the Renaissance. See Bate, *Shakespeare and Ovid*, p. 28. In *Ovid and the Politics of Emotion in Elizabethan England*, Cora Fox examines how Shakespeare employs Ovid to analyze the connections between internal, often hidden, emotion and external action, revenge most crucially. Lisa S. Starks-Estes provides a comprehensive study of Ovidian intertexts in Shakespeare through the lenses of ancient, early modern, and modern trauma theory. In particular, she argues how Shakespeare employs Ovidian allusions to attempt to represent the unrepresentable impacts of traumatic violence and even to depict the fundamental fragmentation of the self, as analyzed by Lacan. See Starks-Estes, *Violence, Trauma, and Virtus*. I am also concerned with fragmentation in Shakespeare's adaptation of Ovid, in the social and cultural senses of the remnant.
7. Eric L. De Barros calls attention to Shakespeare's use of Ovid as a counterpoint to the "death-obsessed literalism within the Roman literary tradition." See De Barros, "'My fleece of woolly.'"
8. All references to *Titus Andronicus* are to Shakespeare, *Titus Andronicus*.
9. Howard, *Poetical Works of Henry Howard*, p. 156. All references to the *Aeneid* in English are to this 1557 translation. The passage in the original Latin: "*fuimus Troes, fuit Ilium et ingens / Gloria Teucrorum; ferus omnia Iuppiter Argos / transtulit*" (Virgil, *Aeneid*, II, 325–7).
10. Both Nicholas Moschovakis and Danielle A. St. Hilaire have noted the Virgilian precedent for Lucius and Titus's demand for Alarbus's sacrifice. According to their readings, Lucius's call for a victim to appease the shades of his brothers may refer to Aeneas's sacrifice of Italian captives over Pallas's grave in Book 11, treated briefly and unceremoniously by Virgil. It may also refer to Aeneas's more dramatic claim to sacrifice Turnus to the shade of Pallas, at the very conclusion of the epic. See St. Hilaire, "Allusion and Sacrifice," and Moschovakis, "'Irreligious Piety,'" pp. 460–86.
11. All references to Ovid in English translation are to Ovid, *Ovid's Metamorphoses*.

12. Fox reflects on how Hecuba's extreme grief is transformed to revenge in Ovid and how that grief is politicized: political agency (in revenge) seemingly arises from "a feminized position of impotence" (Fox, *Ovid and the Politics*, p. 109). I extend this argument by noting that Hecuba's grief and revenge actually overcome political differences between Trojan and Greek, in the shared experience of pity for her.

13. Jane Newman analyzes the dynamic between two classical traditions pertaining to the representation of rape. Livy's Lucretia story "blames the victim, allows her to internalize guilt, and defines her as an agent of political change solely in terms of a male's ability to avenge her." Ovid's Philomela represents "the countertradition of vengeful and violent women associated with Bacchic legend." See Newman, "'And Let Mild Women,'" p. 305. Fox analyzes the process by which the extreme emotional states of Ovid's characters (especially female) produce the individual agency of revenge. See Fox, *Ovid and the Politics*, Chapter 3. My focus is on how Ovidian emotion and revenge can transform identity, especially within the civilization/barbarism opposition of Roman political ideology.

14. Starks-Estes elaborates further on the multiple Ovidian transformations Tamora undergoes. She also argues that Titus "moves from a figure of Stoic Roman masculinity to one of feminine laments and brutal revenge." See Starks-Estes, *Violence, Trauma, and* Virtus, Chapter 2. Fox sees Titus as appropriating feminine Ovidian violence, which she sees as "rewritten finally as male" (Fox, *Ovid and the Politics*, p. 123). My intervention in critical discussion of Tamora and Titus's Ovidian roles and revenge plans is to examine the logic of the remnant at work.

15. "The Tragical History of Titus Andronicus," p. 196.

16. References to the Bible are to *The Geneva Bible*.

17. Agamben, *The Time that Remains*, p. 47.

18. Ibid. p. 46.

19. Calvin, *Institutes of the Christian Religion*, 3.215.

Bibliography

Agamben, Giorgio, *The Time that Remains: A Commentary on the Letter to the Romans*, Patricia Dailey (trans.) (Stanford: Stanford University Press, 2005).

Bate, Jonathan, *Shakespeare and Ovid* (Oxford: Oxford University Press, 1993).

Calvin, John, *Institutes of the Christian Religion*, Henry Beveridge (trans.) (Grand Rapids, MI: Eerdmans, 1997).

De Barros, Eric L., "'My fleece of woolly hair that now uncurls': Shakespeare's *Titus Andronicus*, 'Black' Hair, and the Revenge of Postcolonial Education," unpublished manuscript.

Desmet, Christy, "Recognizing Shakespeare, Rethinking Fidelity: A Rhetoric and Ethics of Appropriation," in Alexa Huang and Elizabeth Rivlin (eds), *Shakespeare and the Ethics of Appropriation* (New York: Palgrave Macmillan, 2014), pp. 41–57.

Fox, Cora, *Ovid and the Politics of Emotion in Elizabethan England* (New York: Palgrave Macmillan, 2009).

The Geneva Bible: A Facsimile of the 1560 Edition (Madison, Milwaukee, and London: University of Wisconsin Press, 1969).

Howard, Henry, *Poetical Works of Henry Howard, Earl of Surrey, Minor Contemporaneous Poets, and Thomas Sackville, Lord Buckhurst*, Robert Bell (ed.) (London: J. W. Parker and Son, [1557] 1854).

Hutcheon, Linda *A Theory of Adaptation* (New York: Routledge, 2006).

Hutcheon, Linda and Gary R. Bortolotti, "On the Origin of Adaptations: Rethinking Fidelity Discourse and 'Success'—Biologically," *New Literary History* 38.3, 2007, pp. 443–58.

James, Heather, *Shakespeare's Troy: Drama, Politics, and the Translation of Empire* (Cambridge: Cambridge University Press, 1997).

Lanier, Douglas, "Shakespearean Rhizomatics: Adaptation, Ethics, Value," in Alexa Huang and Elizabeth Rivlin (eds), *Shakespeare and the Ethics of Appropriation* (New York: Palgrave Macmillan, 2014), pp. 21–40.

Moschovakis, Nicholas, "'Irreligious Piety' and Christian History: Persecution as Pagan Anachronism in *Titus Andronicus*," *Shakespeare Quarterly* 53.4, 2002, pp. 460–86.

Newman, Jane, "'And Let Mild Women to Him Lose Their Mildness': Philomela, Female Violence, and Shakespeare's *The Rape of Lucrece*," *Shakespeare Quarterly* 45.3, 1994, pp. 304–26.

Ovid, *Ovid's Metamorphoses: Translated by Arthur Golding*, Madeleine Forey (ed.) (Baltimore: Johns Hopkins University Press, [1567] 2002).

Shakespeare, William, *Titus Andronicus*, Eugene M. Waith (ed.) (Oxford: Oxford University Press, 2008).

St. Hilaire, Danielle A., "Allusion and Sacrifice in *Titus Andronicus*," *SEL* 49.2, 2009, pp. 311–31.

Starks-Estes, Lisa S., *Violence, Trauma, and* Virtus *in Shakespeare's Roman Poems and Plays: Transforming Ovid* (Basingstoke: Palgrave Macmillan, 2014).

"The Tragical History of Titus Andronicus," in Eugene M. Waith (ed.) *Titus Andronicus* (Oxford: Oxford University Press, 2008), pp. 196–203.

Virgil, *Aeneid*, H. Rushton Fairclough (ed.) (Cambridge, MA: Harvard University Press, 1999).

Part III

Affect, Rhetoric, and Ovidian Appropriation

Power, Emotion, and Appropriation in Ovid's *Tristia* and Shakespeare's *Henry V*

Jennifer Feather

At its heart, the issue of adaptation or appropriation is an issue of textual relations and authority.[1] An appropriation, while necessarily not the original, must raise the presence of an original. Linda Hutcheon describes adaptation as "a derivation that is not derivative – a work that is second without being secondary."[2] In other words, the concept of "literary appropriation" posits a specific relationship between the author who adapts or alludes to a text and the text itself, raising the question of which party has authority. Of course, the idea of textual authorities suggests a slavish subservience to the original, but the Renaissance appropriation of Ovid posits a much different notion of authority. While Ovid enjoyed an important place in early modern education, part of what attracted many early modern authors to Ovid were those less respectable portions that persistently flout authority. To model oneself on Ovid would seem in some cases to be a rejection of authorities altogether.[3] In examining early modern appropriations of Ovid, then, I suggest we analyze Ovid's relationship to authority by interrogating his understanding of sovereign power and how this understanding appears in early modern texts.

To explore the traces of a broader form of textual borrowing, I analyze two texts not typically discussed together – Ovid's *Tristia* and Shakespeare's *Henry V*. *Henry V* is not the typical text for discussions of Ovid in Shakespeare's work, nor is the *Tristia* the typical Ovidian text to which critics turn. Many other texts are more directly allusive to Ovid, and the play's English rather than Roman, Greek, or Italian setting seems in some ways more divorced from the realities of Ovid's poetry than plays such as *Titus Andronicus* and *Midsummer Night's Dream*.[4] However, at a crucial moment in *Henry V*, Henry indirectly invokes the figure of Actaeon and thereby Ovid just as he is exercising his famously ambiguous form of authority. Many would argue that this allusion to the story of Actaeon is too faint an echo to be considered in discussions of appropriation and adaptation. Hutcheon argues that "allusions to and brief echoes of other works would not qualify as extended engagements," a critical element of her understanding of adaptation.[5] However, Ovid's *Tristia* explores the same questions of hegemonic power that Shakespeare's play does, and therefore these textual patterns may be attributed to Ovid. Both texts examine the role of affect in the operation of imperial power, or more precisely, in two contexts on the cusp between shifting forms of government. *Henry V* articulates the rise of national sentiment while dramatizing the history of dynastic monarchy. Ovid's *Tristia* analyzes the imperial power of Augustan Rome. Without much direct reference to Ovid, Shakespeare's vision of power in *Henry V* comes from his sustained engagement with versions of authority in Ovid. We might call these echoes as Douglas M. Lanier does, "unmarked adaptations"; or, following Christy Desmet, we might think of them as a form of recognition that involves a dialogic process.[6] As Elizabeth Rivlin and Alexa Huang elucidate, "ethics is an essential, often missed, term in discussions of Shakespeare and appropriation," and the ethical issues appropriation raises frequently have to do with authority.[7] Looking specifically at the relationship between these two texts, so deeply concerned with issues of political authority, one can see a relationship between the political and the emotional that otherwise remains obscured by a rhetoric of sovereign resolve. The ethical issues of appropriation, thus, offer special insight into the operation of political authority.

For some time, scholars have considered early modern writers' relationships to hegemonic political power. Not least, Stephen Greenblatt's hallmark analysis of containment and subversion has indelibly shaped generations of scholarship.[8] This chapter focuses particularly on Shakespeare's *Henry V* because of the especially thorny relationship to hegemonic power it presents. At the play's center is a particularly ambiguous sovereign who at turns seems the grave monarch and the playful tavern companion. Moreover, the play has been understood as a confirmation of the Tudor monarchy and a critique of hegemonic power.[9] Both the ambiguous figure at its center and the historical context of its performance have received considerable critical attention, but situating them in terms of Ovidian appropriation highlights the issue of authority in crucial ways.[10] Ovid's exile only reinforces his image as recalcitrant in the face of authority. However, his poetry of exile presents a complicated relationship to authority that defies the idea of an absolute sovereign entirely guided by reason. Ovid's depiction of the operation of emotion in the judgments of hegemonic power plays a crucial role in Shakespeare's understanding of political sovereignty in *Henry V*.

Conceptions of authority, both in intertextual and political relationships, frequently rely on an assertion of sovereign resolve that eschews emotional influence. The figure of the dispassionate ruler, steadfast in his judgments and guided by reason rather than emotion, circulates in the early modern period as an ideal of sovereign authority. In early modern political theory, this invulnerability to emotional appeal defends against tyranny. One version of this valorization of emotional fortitude figures the ruler as literally immovable: as Julius Caesar says of himself in Shakespeare's play, he alone "unassailable holds on his rank, / Unshaked of motion" (*Julius Caesar*, III, i, 70–1).[11] Shakespeare's enigmatic and ambiguous Henry V expresses the same sort of stalwart refusal to waver. The French Constable reports to the Dauphin that Henry is "terrible in constant resolution" (II, iv, 35). Moreover, both classical authors such as Aristotle and Cicero and their early modern counterparts extol temperance as a kingly virtue. However, this idealization of constancy does not abrogate the necessity for a monarch to be able to inspire emotions in others. Indeed, temperate self-control is in part a virtue precisely because it enables the monarch to detach himself enough to influence the emotions of others.

Henry would seem to be a model in this regard. From Henry IV's pleas to his son to present himself with more *gravitas* to Henry's own appeals to his troops at Agincourt, the *Henriad* can be understood as an extended meditation on the importance of emotional temperance on the one hand and of the elicitation of strong emotions from one's subjects and peers on the other.[12] This vision of sovereignty, however, suggests an authority that, while deeply concerned with the emotions of others, is aloof from them, not swayed by emotional appeal. Indeed, attempts to make sense of Henry's famously ambiguous character as he shifts from affable prince to resolute sovereign rely on the presumption that Henry is not so moved by emotional appeal as to influence his judgment. The fellow-feeling he shows toward his subjects in this reading is merely an emotional performance calculated to maintain his authority.

This assumption bears on the supposition that, as Claire McEachern puts it, "the exercise of state power stands in an unequivocally negative relation to human bonds."[13] Contrary to these assumptions, McEachern argues that the personification of state power operating in the figure of Henry serves in early modern political discourse to create "fellowship and hegemony . . . [as] complicit forms of social existence" rather than as mutually exclusive states.[14] Ovid's depiction of hegemonic power in the *Tristia* not only shares a sense of the complicity between fellowship and hegemony but actually relies on it for its argumentative force. The sovereign's democratic sympathy for his peers and subjects is crucial to Ovid's pleas for pity, and he envisions the authority to which he appeals not as aloof, not swayed by the emotions of others, but as an exercise of authority precisely through emotion. Ovid highlights the emotional nature of political relationships that would seem to be devoid of emotion.[15] Examining Ovid's depiction of sovereignty illuminates how what seems to be a performance of emotional transcendence, a triumph of steadfast reason over passion, involves an emotional state in itself.

The process of appropriation raises the same issues of authority and emotion. In the introduction to their edited collection, *Shakespeare and Appropriation*, Christy Desmet and Robert Sawyer remind us that "[d]iscussion of appropriation as an aesthetic phenomenon raises questions of individual agency and therefore demands a theory of textual relations."[16] To think about appropriation is instantly to situate the author in relationship to previous texts. Moreover, this set of relations has both political and personal implications. In discussing Paul Robeson's account of performing *Othello*, they remind us that the process of appropriation is "at once political and intensely emotional."[17] This chapter considers further the "at once" nature of the political and the intensely emotional in the process of appropriation and how this simultaneity shapes a particular understanding of political authority. To insist that these two states – the political and the intensely emotional – occur simultaneously in some, if not all, acts of appropriation is also to indicate that in other situations they are understood as distinct realms. Early modern ideals of sovereignty suggest that politics often is or should be devoid of emotion. Appropriation unsettles that divide. Similarly, the issue of appropriation troubles any easy understanding of individual agency by situating the author within a broader set of textual relations. Shakespeare takes up these concerns, where the political and emotional intersect around issues of agency, as he explores the nature of sovereignty in the character of Henry V.

If the processes of appropriation, adaptation, and allusion necessarily raise questions of authority and personal agency, this chapter looks to depictions of sovereign authority to understand the emotional nature of that process. Conversely, if political authority operates through emotion rather than by transcending it, this chapter analyzes faint echoes as a form of appropriation that can draw attention to a sustained engagement with earlier texts that might otherwise remain obscure. Henry V's allusion to the story of Actaeon at the moment when he accuses his peers of betraying him is such an echo. It points to issues of sovereign authority and the operation of emotion in a play that can be understood as a meditation on precisely those issues. In what follows, I trace Ovid's articulation of the political operation of emotion through the *Tristia* and show how Shakespeare uses a subtle allusion to draw his audience's attention to his sustained engagement with Ovid's conception of sovereign power.

Ovid's understanding of hegemonic power is nowhere more stark than in his poetry of exile, where his relationship to imperial power becomes vital to his pleas for redress. In the *Tristia*, Ovid overtly seeks amelioration of his exile and, as Matthew McGowan argues, simultaneously critically analyzes the operation of imperial power.[18] The redress he asks for is not only practical but emotional: he attempts to indict hegemonic power and reveal its contingency as much as he attempts to secure his return to Rome. In this exploration of how Caesar's power operates, Ovid understands mercy and punishment in terms of affective disposition and associates the cruelty of betrayal with the northern and eastern lands of his exile. Figuring merciless power in terms of the harsh geography of his exile, he understands the landscape of the Black Sea region as an extension of Caesar's imperial power.[19] In so doing, however, Caesar and those friends who have betrayed him become not simply devoid of feeling but possessed of an emotional disposition likened to the world of Tomis. Ovid finds himself literally swept up in this political and affective system, describing his own emotions in terms of the turmoil of the Pontus. This description portrays Roman political power as operating through emotion and therefore susceptible to the emotional states of others. Ovid overtly praises Augustus, who, following ideals of temperance set forth in Aristotle and Cicero, presents himself as a model of heroism and moral rectitude. However, Ovid interrogates this very ideal by presenting sovereign power not as aloof from emotion but as an affective relationship.[20]

In the *Tristia*, Ovid understands his fate as a direct result of Caesar's wrath (*ira*), and his appeals make his case largely in emotional terms. He prays to the gods that Caesar may feel what the gods already know – that his transgression was a mistake rather than a crime: "*quod vos scitis, poenae quoque sentiat auctor*" ["that what you know he too, author of my punishment, may feel"] (I, iii, 39). Using the verb "*sentiat*," Ovid understands the remedy not in terms of knowledge but in terms of feeling. The gods know, "*scitis*," but Caesar must feel, "*sentiat*." Caesar's feelings about the crime must be changed, and his understanding is figured in emotional terms. This way of perceiving Caesar's power, as exercised through an emotion, wrath, that must be mollified, runs throughout the poem. Ovid later hopes that his friend's prayers may be efficacious because his own "*quae pro me duros non tetigere deos*" ["did not affect the cruel gods"] (I, ix, 4). The key to the relief of his suffering is to change the emotional disposition of the powerful, especially Caesar. Ovid writes about this change in terms of emotional transformation. The cruel gods (*duros deos*) must be affected (*tetigere*), literally touched, as if to make an impression. Cruelty under these circumstances is figured as a particular affective disposition, a lack of feeling that refuses to be swayed by emotional appeal. Relief of suffering is achieved through an emotional entreaty that softens this lack of feeling, making an impression on the powerful. What changes is not what Caesar knows about the situation but what he feels. Thus, in Ovid's depiction, political power enacts an emotion, rage; and therefore, in addressing power, he addresses not the rational powers of judgment but the feelings of the ruler.

In contrast to Ovid's implicit contention that political power operates in and through emotion, emotional imperviousness is frequently understood in early modern texts as foundational to state power. The monarch should ideally be moved solely by reason and never by emotion. For example, Thomas Elyot commends continence "whiche kepeth the pleqasaunt appetite of man under yoke of reason" and explains the virtue of constancy saying that the

> man which in childehode is brought up in sondry vertues: if eyther by nature or els by custome, he be nat induced to be all way constant and stable, so that he meve nat for any affection, griefe or displeasure, all his vertues will shortly decay.[21]

Moreover, Shakespeare offers us a model of this form of kingship in the figure of *Julius Caesar*, when Cimber pleads for the return of his brother from exile. Like Augustus Caesar's continued anger against Ovid, Julius Caesar's refusal to grant Publius Cimber's return is a refusal to be moved. In the play, Caesar proclaims:

> I must prevent thee, Cimber.
> These couchings and these lowly courtesies
> Might fire the blood of ordinary men,
> And turn pre-ordinance and first decree

Into the lune of children. Be not fond,
To think that Caesar bears such rebel blood
That will be thaw'd from the true quality
With that which melteth fools; I mean, sweet words,
Low-crooked court'sies and base spaniel-fawning. (III, i, 36–44)

Caesar understands Cimber's pleas as attempts to "fire his blood" and turn that blood from the decree of banishment. He refuses this appeal, saying that his blood will not be "thaw'd from the true quality / With that which melteth fools." His blood is constant as if it were frozen solid, and this constancy maintains the blood in its "true quality." From Caesar's point of view, the exercise of power involves the imperviousness to emotional manipulation, "sweet words, / Low-crooked court'sies and base spaniel-fawning." These sorts of appeals are only efficacious, according to Caesar, in that they "melteth fools."

However, even as manuals like Elyot's and figures like Caesar praise a certain kind of imperviousness, they recognize in this model of state power, designed to control the affections and thereby prevent tyranny, the significant possibility of the abuse of power. Elyot, for instance, uses Caesar as an example of tyranny (Book II, Chapter V). Similarly, Mettelus's plea, a deliberate strategy to detain Caesar to make way for the conspirators' attack, provokes the very imperiousness that the conspirators claim necessitates Caesar's death. Indeed, in the context of a play that so thoroughly examines state power, this treatment of the appeal for the return of an exile exemplifies how the imperviousness to sympathy produces the very tyranny it aims to prevent. Caesar's claim in the play to be "constant as the Northern star" may indeed echo Ovid's own sardonic praise of Caesar in the last book of the *Metamorphoses*.[22] This disposition toward constancy is, thus, a central but contested feature of state power.

Ovid refuses the image of the dispassionate monarch that Elyot and his classical sources present as an ideal, persistently highlighting the emotional nature of Caesar's exercise of power even as he describes Caesar's terrible constancy. In the *Tristia*, Ovid uses the word *crudelem*, the Latin word most etymologically related to the English "cruel," only very rarely. Rather those words most often translated as "cruel" are in Ovid's Latin *saevus* (I, iv, 27), *durus* (I, v, 73), and *ferus* (II, i, 176), all words that he also uses to describe the area to which he has been exiled and its people. While death, warfare, and his enemies are *saevus* (IV, i, 78), so are the raging waters of the Pontus (I, x, 8) on which he is exiled and the winds of Boreas that blow across it (III, x, 51). Similarly, a treacherous friend is *"dure"*

or "cruel one" (I, xviii, 14); the gods who are not affected by his
prayers are "*duros*" (I, ix, 4); and the winter of his exile, where the
seas can be crossed by carriages, are "*durus*" – literally, like Caesar's blood, hardened to the point of freezing solid. The wild roar
of the sea is "*ferus*" (I, xi, 7), and the people around him are a cruel
race, "*fera gens*" (III, x, 5). However, a treacherous enemy, "*ferox*,"
also assails him, attacking the shadow of his former self with bitter
words (III, xi, 31). These terms move back and forth from describing "natural" phenomena – the rough seas of the Pontus, the bitter
cold of the north, and the wildness of its people – and the emotions
and dispositions of Ovid and especially of the powers with which he
pleads. Figuring emotional states as a dynamic landscape situates his
relationship to the powerful in terms of his physical circumstances.
Ovid's connection of both emotional states and the operation of
power to the ambient environment insistently figures the exercise of
authority as emotional.

At moments, the location of Ovid's exile figures forth the internal disposition of the exiled himself. For instance, in the epilogue to
the first book of the *Tristia*, Ovid exclaims, "*ipse ego nunc miror
tantis animique marisque / fluctibus ingenium non cecidisse meum*"
["I myself now marvel that amid such turmoil of my soul and of the
sea my powers did not fail"] (I, xi, 9–10). The turmoil ("*fluctibus*")
is both the uproar of the sea and of his soul, both of which are pos-
sessive. There is no syntactic distinction between the two, strength-
ening the connection between external surroundings and his internal
state. Ovid uses this deliberate sliding between external and internal,
between those forces that act upon a person and those which are
most personal to him, repeatedly to characterize how power functions in the poem. The powerful unsettling of the sea is the equally
alarming upheaval in his own soul, and his "powers" ("*ingenium*")
are barely able to withstand the assault, which is simultaneously a
contest between powerful forces beyond his control and the turbu-
lent emotions of his own being. Ovid's use of these metaphors blurs
the boundaries of an individual subject, even the emperor, figuring
the emotional world of both ruler and ruled as coterminous with a
broader landscape.

Caesar's constancy is similarly described in natural terms, mark-
ing it as an emotional state. While some form of "*durus*" is used to
describe the hardness of both the frozen waters of the Pontus and the
disposition of Caesar or other powerful figures, other examples of
this slippage between external forces and internal disposition abound.
One prominent example is the manifestation of Jove's power, the

lightning bolt. When describing how friends began to distance them-selves after his fall, Ovid writes, *"saeva neque admiror metuunt si fulmina, / quorum ignibus adflari proxima quaque solent"* ["I won-der not if they dread the fierce lightnings whose flames are wont to blast everything nearby"] (I, ix, 21–2). Though not directly referenc-ing Jove, in using lightning to describe the power that has descended on him, he is associating Caesar's wrath and power with the king of the gods, as he similarly compares Augustus and Jove in the *Meta-morphoses*.[23] This lightning, a manifestation of Caesar's power that implies his proximity to Jove, is *"saeva."* Elsewhere, Ovid explicitly connects Caesar's power to Jove's lightning bolt, writing *"me quo-que, quae sensi, fateor Iovis arma timere"* ["I too admit – for I have felt it – that I fear the weapon of Jupiter"] (I, i, 81). He describes the power of Jove's bolt using the word *"saevi,"* exclaiming *"vidi ego pampineis oneratam vitibus ulmum, / quae fuerat saevi fulmine tacta Jovis"* ["I have seen an elm laden with the tendrils of a vine even after it has been blasted by the thunderbolt of angry Jove"] (I, i, 81). While the description is clearly meant to refer to the power of the thunderbolt, *"saevi"* modifies not *"fulmine"* but *"Jovis."* Jove him-self is cruel or savage, not, as elsewhere, the bolt. Again, the adjec-tives Ovid uses to describe cruelty and power are as likely to describe the harshness of the natural environment as they are to describe indi-vidual dispositions.

The easy slippage between these two usages connects the opera-tion of power to individual dispositions through natural metaphors. A few lines after Ovid describes Jove's bolt, he writes of his own feel-ings, *"ac veluti ventis agitantibus aequora non est / aequalis rabies continuusque furor"* ["As in the winds that buffet the seas there is no steady, no constant madness"] (II, 149–50). The fury of his inner turmoil ebbs and flows like the winds that buffet the seas. The easy assignation of terms to both emotional experience and environmen-tal forces connects these figures in an emotional ecology, the ecol-ogy of cruelty and pity in which cruelty is a frozen solidity that is mollified by sympathy and pity. Thus, not only does Ovid couch his appeal in emotional terms, but he also embeds both himself and Cae-sar in the environment. He figures this environment not simply as emotionally charged but also as coterminous with the experience of sovereign and subject. This way of thinking about emotion situates both Ovid and Caesar in the same emotional medium through which power must be negotiated.

Shakespeare uses a subtle reference to Ovid to evoke this under-standing of sovereign power. At an iconic moment, Henry refers obliquely to the story of Actaeon, saying to the noblemen who have conspired against him,

> The mercy that was quick in us but late,
> By your own counsel is suppress'd and kill'd:
> You must not dare, for shame, to talk of mercy;
> For your own reasons turn into your bosoms,
> As dogs upon their masters, worrying you. (*Henry V*, II, ii, 76–80)

We are accustomed to reading this moment as yet another instance of the type of political theatre that Henry routinely creates. Having pardoned a man who rails against his person against the advice of these conspirators, Henry constructs a scenario where the conspirators are in part responsible for their own condemnation. However, Henry formulates their fate in terms that harken back to the story of Actaeon that Ovid uses repeatedly to analyze the whims of imperial power. This formulation is a curious one because Ovid himself uses it to explore the just operation of sovereign power and its abuses. In this context, Henry clearly means to insinuate that the fate of the conspirators is just, but for those familiar with Ovid's understanding of political power, the assignation of justice is anything but clear. This moment of appropriation transforms the nature of the scene and our understanding of the sovereign power exerted in it. Henry is not simply a master manipulator, exerting imperial power; but also he deploys a very Ovidian sense of the operation of emotion in the execution of justice.

In the *Tristia*, Ovid uses the story of Actaeon to assert a particular operation of sovereign power. As he does in describing Caesar's wrath, he depicts that power as operating through emotion rather than through reason. Ovid emphasizes Actaeon's blamelessness, calling him "*inscius*" ["unwitting"] (II, 105), and then remarks that "*scilicet in superis etiam fortuna luenda est, / nec veniam laeso numine casus habet*" ["Clearly, among the gods, even ill-fortune must be atoned for, nor is mischance an excuse when a deity is wronged"] (II, 107–8). Here he indicates that the exertion of state power is not limited by culpability. Indeed, sometimes that power, swayed by a slight to its majesty, must be exerted – Ovid uses the gerundive of obligation here signaling the sense of requirement – even if the transgression is "*fortuna*" ["mischance"] rather than deliberate crime. The raging goddess must be mollified, and the assault on her dignity demands a response that will ease her emotional state. In the *Tristia*, references to Actaeon's fate allow Ovid to invoke circumstances in which power, which might seem to be aloof, is exerted because of an emotional response to a mistake rather than a rational judgment against wrongdoing.

Henry's reference to dogs turning upon their masters recalls this story, but with a substantial difference: the conspirators are not "*inscius.*" They have knowingly betrayed Henry, so the image of dogs turning on their masters vividly describes their disloyalty. It also suggests the intimacy of the bond that they have transgressed in their treachery. Their reasons have turned against them, biting the hand that feeds them, so to speak, just as they have turned against Henry. In this context, Henry's treatment is justified by their disloyalty far more clearly than Diana's treatment of Actaeon justifies his fate. Shakespeare inserts an allusion that questions sovereign power and indicates its susceptibility to emotion, even as Henry uses it to justify that power. This reference makes it difficult to see this moment as merely affirming the King's power. Henry uses it to indicate the justice with which he punishes the conspirators, having just shown his sympathetic side to the man he released, but the allusion to Ovid undercuts the sympathetic relationships Henry creates. Echoing Ovid, thus, invites us to see not a just King operating totally based on reason, but rather one whose political decisions are deeply influenced by his emotions.

Ovid's telling of the Actaeon story in the *Metamorphoses*, like his use of it in the *Tristia*, highlights the emotional dimension of sovereign power. The transformation at the center of the story is the result of Diana's emotional state, her wrath when she discovers that Actaeon has seen her unclothed in her bath. Diana's rage causes a set of feelings: it causes Actaeon to feel the helplessness she feels at having been surprised by him. The entire story centers around an emotional exchange enabled by the bleeding of boundaries between human and animal. While Henry tries to hide his own feelings of betrayal behind his infamous emotional machinations, the reference to this story brings them to light.

The tale in the *Metamorphoses* ends with a debate over whether or not Actaeon's fate is just. The question is not so much whether Actaeon acted deliberately but whether, regardless of his intention, womanhood needs to be safeguarded. In Golding's translation of the *Metamorphoses*, Ovid ends the tale of Actaeon as follows:

Much muttring was upon this fact. Some thought there was extended
A great deale more extremitie than neded. Some commended
Dianas doing: saying that it was but worthely
For safegarde of hir womanhod. Eche partie did applie
Good reasons to defende their case. (III, 305–9)

Diana's actions are the subject of some debate, and each party to the debate is able to defend his or her case with "good reasons." However, Ovid's Latin is slightly more ambiguous. It reads: "*Rumor in ambiguo est; aliis violentior aequo / visa dea est, alli laudant dignamque severa / virginitate vocant: pars invenit utraque causas*" ["Common talk wavered this way and that: to some the goddess seemed more cruel than just; others called her act worthy of her austere virginity; both sides found good reasons for their judgment"] (III, 253–5). As noted, Miller translates "*violentior aequo*" as "more cruel than just," suggesting not just the extremity of the punishment but its cruelty. Moreover, whereas Golding translates "*causas*" as "good reasons," the word also has the sense of a motive or even a pretext. Also, the verb "*invenit*" ordinarily means something more like "to find out" or "to discover" rather than "to apply" as Golding translates. Overall, Golding leaves the impression of a reasoned debate, whereas Ovid implies something more like a heated discussion. Thus, Ovid presents Actaeon's fate as posing a thorny question in which all parties are emotionally invested. Judgment is, as we have seen elsewhere in the *Tristia*, less a calm application of reasoned argument than an exchange of emotions. Shakespeare, who was influenced by Golding's translation, nonetheless preserves the sense of an emotional exchange present in Ovid's original and in his overall formulation of sovereign power.

Inserting a reference to this tale, and no doubt to Ovid's multiple tellings of it, into Henry's speech changes our understanding of the dynamic of the encounter substantially. It brings into Henry's act of judgment against the conspirators the specter of sovereign power over-reaching at a moment when we are inclined to sympathize with Henry not as a terrifying ruler but as a vulnerable human being, and it also questions the categories and oppositions whereby we typically understand sovereign power. It sees that power, as Ovid does, not as working apart from emotion but through it. Prominent constructions of the ideal monarch in early modern England suggest a divide between operations of hegemonic power and emotion, but Ovid persistently questions this divide, not least in his use of the Actaeon story. Seeing the relationship to Ovid's construction of political sovereignty at this moment in the drama, Shakespeare provides a picture of Henry not as aloof from the emotions involved in the encounter but as engaged in negotiating a situation in which all parties are emotionally invested. The reference makes Henry's claim that "[t]ouching our person seek we no revenge, / But we our kingdom's safety must so tender, / Whose ruin you have sought" ring somewhat hollow (*Henry V*, II, ii, 170–2). The entire scene confounds the distinction he tries to draw here between rational judgment and emotional vengeance. He remarks in reflecting on the betrayal of one as close to him as Scrope that "'[t]is so strange / That though the truth of it stands off as gross / As black on white, my eye will scarcely see it," indicating that the reality of the situation defies reason and that his feeling of betrayal makes it hard for him to see Scrope's treachery clearly (II, ii, 99–101).

In identifying the emotional component of hegemonic power, Ovid attempts not to obscure how power functions through the manipulation of public sentiment but to show the susceptibility of that power to emotional influence. Similarly, if we recognize that Henry is not the master manipulator aloof from emotional appeal but a player in a larger emotional drama, then we can see how the operation of power Shakespeare examines in his play is not one where the monarch is untouched by the emotional circumstance in which he rules. Ovid develops such an understanding of power to provide the opportunity for redress of his exile, both in terms of literal relief but also in terms of readjusting the relative position between himself and Caesar. He implies that the rage of the powerful is indeed "more cruel than just" rather than a more rationally guided response to a crime. Applying this idea to Shakespeare's *Henry V*, one can see Henry's actions not simply as rational calculations but as the emotional responses they are. His authority is not unassailable but part of a larger system in which he convinces himself as well as others. The understanding of Henry runs throughout the rest of the play as much as in this episode, where his authority repeatedly functions through emotion and he is repeatedly influenced by emotion.

This understanding of authority can also inform our view of the process of appropriation. If Shakespeare understands authority in *Henry V* in ways similar to Ovid's understanding in the *Tristia*, he also enters into a specific kind of affective relationship with Ovid's texts. Ovid's work exerts a continued and sustained force on the playwright by giving him a model for the affective operation of power even as that power claims to be purely rational. Examining this relationship foregrounds the affective in the ethical quandaries of appropriation. It presents appropriation as insistently dialogic even when ideals of sovereignty might call for isolated authority. Analyzing the operation of political authority in this moment of recognition between texts highlights the role of emotion in the exercise of sovereignty. It reads the political in terms of the textual and politics in terms of transmission.

Notes

1. Since this chapter hopes to trouble the kinds of textual borrowings that count in these discussions, I will not go through an extended analysis of the differences here. For considerations of the possible uses of these terms and others, see Sanders, *Adaptation and Appropriation*, and Desmet and Iyengar, "Adaptation, Appropriation, or What You Will."
2. Hutcheon, *A Theory of Adaptation*, p. 9.
3. For a discussion of Ovid's anti-authoritarian appeal to Renaissance writers, see Starks-Estes, *Violence, Trauma, and Virtus*. Bate points out that Marlowe's *Amores* were banned in 1599, bringing the fate of Marlowe's sixteenth-century translation in line with Ovid's. Bate, *Shakespeare and the Renaissance Ovid*, p. 32. While some argue that the Bishops' Ban of 1599 was directed mostly at John Davies's *Epigrams* rather than Marlowe's *Elegies*, others note the particular imbrication of political authority and overt sexual content in the ban. See Clegg, *Press Censorship in England*, p. 199, and Boose, "The 1599 Bishops' Ban," respectively. In either case, appropriating Ovid was, at the very least, a delicate process, and many writers found his vexed relationship to authority appealing. See James, "Ovid in Renaissance English Literature," esp. pp. 425–32.
4. Bate comments on the deliberateness with which Golding "Englished" Ovid by bringing in a "robust vernacular vocabulary," bringing the *Metamorphoses* into a more English setting, but Shakespeare's plays do not always do the same. Bate, *Shakespeare and Ovid*, p. 29.
5. Hutcheon, *A Theory of Adaptation*, p. 9.
6. Lanier, "Afterword," p. 300.
7. Huang and Rivlin, "Introduction," p. 2.
8. Greenblatt, *Shakespearean Negotiations*.
9. Wells, "The Fortunes of Tillyard," pp. 391–403.
10. The definitive formulation of this critical ambivalence is Rabkin, "Rabbits, Ducks, and *Henry V*."
11. All citations of Shakespeare's plays are from Shakespeare, *The Norton Shakespeare*.
12. Dawes, "Emotional Education and Leadership," pp. 108–15.
13. McEachern, "*Henry V* and the Paradox," p. 47.
14. Ibid. p. 44.
15. Cora Fox posits that Ovid's works served as "emotional scripts" for early modern writers as they negotiated political relationships. Fox, *The Politics of Emotion*.
16. Desmet and Sawyer, *Shakespeare and Appropriation*.
17. Ibid. p. 18.
18. McGowan, *Ovid in Exile*.
19. Ovid was exiled to a Roman colony in Tomis in what is now Romania on the coast of the Black Sea. Ovid and early modern English writers typically refer to the Black Sea as the "Pontus" or "Euxine" sea.

20. Ovid's praise of Augustus is ambiguous, and some scholars take it at face value while others see it as a covert criticism of the regime. Feldherr, *Playing Gods*; Hinds, "Generalising About Ovid"; Millar, "Ovid and the Domus Augusta."
21. Elyot, *A Critical Edition of Sir Thomas Elyot's The Boke*, pp. 218, 224.
22. Shakespeare, *Julius Caesar*, III, i, 61; Ovid, *Metamorphoses*, XV, 848–9; for further discussion of Shakespeare's simile as an echo of Ovid, see Starks-Estes, *Violence, Trauma, and* Virtus, pp. 138–9.
23. Ovid, *Metamorphoses*, I, 201–5. For further analysis of the comparison see James, "Ovid and the Question of Politics."

Bibliography

Bate, Jonathan, *Shakespeare and Ovid* (New York: Oxford University Press, 1993).

Boose, Lynda, "The 1599 Bishops' Ban, Elizabethan Pornography, and the Sexualization of the Jacobean Stage," in Richard Burt and John Michael Archer (eds), *Enclosure Acts: Sexuality, Property, and Culture in Early Modern England* (Ithaca: Cornell University Press, 1994), pp. 185–202.

Clegg, Cyndia Susan, *Press Censorship in England in Jacobean England* (Cambridge: Cambridge University Press, 2001).

Dawes, Martin, "Emotional Education and Leadership in the Henriad," in R. S. White, Mark Houlahan, and Katrina O'Louglin (eds), *Shakespeare and Emotions: Inheritances, Enactments, Legacies* (New York: Palgrave Macmillan, 2015), pp. 108–15.

Desmet, Christy, "Recognizing Shakespeare, Rethinking Fidelity: A Rhetoric and Ethics of Appropriation," in Alexa Huang and Elizabeth Rivlin (eds), *Shakespeare and the Ethics of Appropriation* (New York: Palgrave Macmillan, 2014), pp. 41–57.

Desmet, Christy and Sujata Iyengar, "Adaptation, Appropriation, or What You Will," *Shakespeare* 11.1, 2015, pp. 1–10.

Desmet, Christy and Robert Sawyer (eds), *Shakespeare and Appropriation* (New York and London: Routledge, 1999).

Elyot, Thomas, *A Critical Edition of Sir Thomas Elyot's The Boke Named the Governour*, Donald Rude (ed.) (New York: Garland Publishing, 1992).

Feldherr, Andrew, *Playing Gods: Ovid's* Metamorphoses *and the Politics of Fiction* (Princeton: Princeton University Press, 2010).

Fox, Cora, *Ovid and the Politics of Emotion in Elizabethan England* (New York: Palgrave Macmillan, 2009).

Greenblatt, Stephen, *Shakespearean Negotiations: The Circulation of Social Energy in Renaissance England* (Los Angeles: University of California Press, 1988).

Hinds, Stephen, "Generalising about Ovid," *Ramus* 16.2, 1987, pp. 4–31.

Huang, Alexa and Elizabeth Rivlin, "Introduction: Shakespeare and the Ethics of Appropriation," in Alexa Huang and Elizabeth Rivlin (eds),

Shakespeare and the Ethics of Appropriation (New York: Palgrave Macmillan, 2014), pp. 1–20.

Hutcheon, Linda, *A Theory of Adaptation* (New York: Routledge, 2006).

James, Heather, "Ovid and the Question of Politics in Early Modern England," *ELH* Summer 2004, pp. 343–73.

James, Heather, "Ovid in Renaissance English Literature," in Peter E. Knox (ed.), *A Companion to Ovid* (Malden, MA: Blackwell, 2009), pp. 423–41.

Lanier, Douglas M., "Shakespeare / Not Shakespeare: Afterword," in Christy Desmet, Natalie Loper, and Jim Casey (eds), *Shakespeare / Not Shakespeare* (New York: Palgrave Macmillan, 2017), pp. 293–306.

McEachern, Claire, "*Henry V* and the Paradox of the Body Politic," *Shakespeare Quarterly* 45.1, 1994, pp. 35–47.

McGowan, Matthew, *Ovid in Exile: Power and Poetic Redress in the* Tristia *and* Epistulae ex Ponto (Boston: Brill, 2009).

Millar, Fergus, "Ovid and the Domus Augusta: Rome Seen from Tomoi," in Hannah M. Cotton and Guy M. Rogers (eds), *Rome, The Greek World, and the East: Volume 3: The Greek World, the Jews, and the East* (Chapel Hill, NC: University of North Carolina Press, 2002), pp. 321–49.

Ovid, *Metamorphoses: Books 1–8*, 3rd edn, Frank Justus Miller (trans.), revised by G. P. Goold (Cambridge, MA and London: Harvard University Press, 1977).

Ovid, *Ovid's Metamorphoses: The Arthur Golding Translation of 1567*, John Frederick Nims (ed.) (Philadelphia: Paul Dry Books, 2000).

Ovid, *Tristia. Ex Ponto*, 2nd edn, A. L. Wheeler (trans.), revised by G. P. Goold (Cambridge, MA: Harvard University Press, 1996 and London: William Heinemann, 1988).

Rabkin, Norman, "Rabbits, Ducks, and *Henry V*," *Shakespeare Quarterly* 28.3, 1977, pp. 279–96.

Sanders, Julie, *Adaptation and Appropriation* (London and New York: Routledge, 2006).

Shakespeare, William, *The Norton Shakespeare*, 3rd edn, Stephen Greenblatt, Walter Cohen, Suzanne Gossett, Jean E. Howard, Katharine Eisaman Maus, and Gordon McMullan (eds) (London: W. W. Norton, 2015).

Starks-Estes, Lisa S., *Violence, Trauma, and* Virtus *in Shakespeare's Roman Poems and Plays: Transforming Ovid* (Basingstoke: Palgrave Macmillan, 2014).

Wells, Robin Headlam, "The Fortunes of Tillyard: Twentieth-Century Critical Debate on Shakespeare's History Plays," *English Studies* 66.5, 1985, pp. 391–403.

Chapter 9

Appropriating Ovid's Tyrannical Raptures in *Macbeth*

John D. Staines

> Better be with the dead,
> Whom we, to gain our peace, have sent to peace,
> Than on the torture of the mind to lie
> In restless ecstasy. (*Macbeth*, III, ii, 19–22)[1]

Near the midpoint of his tragedy, Macbeth – soldier, thane, tyrant – describes living "in restless ecstasy," always stretched out upon the rack.[2] His equivocations about "peace" hide from his wife, and from himself, their unspeakable desires and crimes. Forced to speak nothing but such deformed and twisted words, his mind is seized by ecstatic visions of the traumas secreted in evasions and silences. Having killed untold numbers battling for his king, and now killed that king himself, Macbeth admits he is tormented so badly that rather than live in such fear, he would "let the frame of things disjoint" and destroy the order of all creation (III, ii, 16). Later, when he sees Banquo's blood but hears Fleance lives, "Then comes my fit again," he says, and is seized by the vision of a ghost taking his seat (III, iv, 20). Macduff flees to the peace of England; so in fury, Macbeth seizes his home, leaving the father haunted by his murdered wife and babes. Haunted by those ghosts and others, Lady Macbeth will kill herself. At the end of that sequence of violent, ecstatic seizures, Macbeth will realize the meaningless "sound and fury" of it all (V, v, 27), though even after achieving that insight, he will struggle against death's peaceful nothing until the final blow. In this play, history appears to be nothing more than the repetition of tyrannical violation, rapture, and transformation, a vision that can be found in Ovid, where the model applies not just to the succession of political authority but to the transformations and translations of culture across time.

If we follow Douglas Lanier's use of the decentered, asymmetrical rhizome to understand adaptation and appropriation, we can start to appreciate the creative multiplicity that Shakespeare found in Ovid, and that we can find in both, and discover models for reading them through their collisions, fragmentations, and re-formations.[3] A rhizome "is always in the middle, between things, interbeing," write Gilles Deleuze and Félix Guattari.[4] It records changing and becoming, but not being. Ovid and Shakespeare connect and branch out, grow together and apart, in a record of how one poet read, adapted, and appropriated his ancient predecessor, whom he only experienced through the mediating work of other poets, teachers, scholars, editors, and translators. Readers and critics of both poets continue to create additional connections, and to strengthen, weaken, or fracture existing ones, within this constantly evolving rhizome. Today's readers can only know an Ovid already translated and appropriated into Shakespeare's poetry, and from there into thousands of other texts.

This model is less a slow-growing tuber than a system sustained by conflict: "The rhizome operates by variation, expansion, conquest, capture, offshoots."[5] The violence implicated in the rhizome points to the traumas that fragment the past and to the seizures of material pulled out from the ruins. Translated and transformed, these appropriations are rearranged in new assemblages, to borrow another concept from Deleuze and Guattari.[6] Ovid's episodic narratives, which invite readers to break him into pieces for reuse, are assemblages of fragments drawn from the cultures that had come into contact, often violently, as Greece and Rome expanded, conquered, captured, and sent out offshoots, and were each in turn captured, conquered, exiled, transformed. Stories and characters from those cultures connect at seemingly arbitrary moments, woven together by Ovid's imagination, which generates meaning not just by telling separable narratives but by arranging and fixing them into place within larger poems where readers can make connections as they follow the linear narrative – Daphne to Philomela to Medea – or as they read and re-read stories retrospectively and at will, jumping in and around the text as their interests dictate. Following themes or characters, they can form links among the different poems that carry Ovid's name – the Philomela of *Metamorphoses* to the Lucretia of *Fasti*, the powerful Medea of *Metamorphoses* to the suffering lover of *Heroides* – and from there to a boundless range of texts across time.

At the end of a ruinous century, Jacques Derrida was drawn to Hamlet's assertion that "[t]he time is out of joint" (I, v, 188), that time, history, culture, seem not where, not when, they should be.[7]

Shakespeare, who learned not only Latin but the art of character from translating Ovid's voices,[8] has his melancholy prince imagine a shattered world haunted by ghosts of lost times, places, and texts, like his father's spirit arisen from a Senecan revenge tragedy. Macbeth, who wants to "let the frame of things disjoint," is slow to realize that the "terrible dreams" that haunt him are signs his world is already out of joint (III, ii, 18). That disjointed world is made of fragments and ghosts. These fragments seem destined for continual appropriation and reappropriation, always able, and always needed, as Derrida observes, to say something new, yet uncannily familiar, "the Thing that . . . *engineers* [s'ingénie] a habitation without proper inhabiting, call it a *haunting*, of both memory and translation."[9] Each of the texts we recognize as Ovidian is haunted by a different ghost of Ovid, conjured up to answer distinctive needs: the Ovid of Rome, or Pontus; the *Ovide moralisé*; the Elizabethan schoolroom Ovid; Golding's Ovid, or Shakespeare's, or Freud's. Today we might encounter a mythological sourcebook, an embodiment of the classical canon, or a rebel giving voice to women's complaints against patriarchy. Each cultural moment gives rise to its own Ovid, or Ovids, and judges by different standards the fidelity of those creations to the original, who is not fixed in time but always becoming another, evolving according to the interests, methods, and media of the moment. John Frederick Nims describes Arthur Golding's 1567 translation as "metamorphosing Ovid" so that "the sophisticated Roman" now inhabits the body of "a ruddy country gentleman."[10] Although today that lively vernacular Ovid might seem more faithful to a Tudor market town than Augustan Rome, that creative fusion served the needs of its time, opening new connections between the ancient and modern and shaping the emerging voice of English poetry. Such a "performative interpretation," as Derrida puts it in his account of *hauntology*, is "the interpretation that transforms the very thing it interprets."[11] In conceiving of the translation and transmission of premodern texts as encounters with specters, I want to suggest that the uncanny experiences traced in contemporary media by Maurizio Calbi in *Spectral Shakespeares* are not new phenomena but intensifications of the hauntings that arise from the earliest of texts and the earliest of myths. Ovid models such hauntings when he narrates the translation of human minds into alien bodies, and he produces sublime emotions from the struggle to animate new tongues. Ghosts trapped in bodies out of joint, they transform the forms into which they are translated. That creative violence has led me in this chapter to prefer the term "appropriation" to "adaptation": to appropriate is to seize and make one's own, a violent act that transforms both subject and object while never fully achieving the appropriator's original goal of possessing the other, whose identity can never be perfectly known. The most powerful of such ghosts, ones capable of enacting performative interpretations of history, arise from great trauma: the sack of Troy, or Rome; the collapse or foundation of empires, religions, ideologies; the seizure, enslavement, murder, and rape of individuals and nations.

Ovid's *raptus*, where a character is carried away, violated, and raped, can serve as a figure for appropriation, where one poet's text or tongue is seized, reassembled, and translated into something new. Shakespeare's rapture of Ovid creates a new text in a new medium, metamorphic epic translated to the stage, which, as Leonard Barkan suggests, may be one reason Shakespeare returns obsessively to Philomela's story, where competing mimetic media – poetry, rhetoric, weaving, dramatic action – take up the challenge of voicing trauma.[12] *Macbeth* may not seem the most Ovidian of plays, but that is a function of how, by this stage in his career, Shakespeare has fully appropriated Ovid, who haunts his poetry even as the direct references become less obvious.[13] Jonathan Bate calls these "moments of recognition" as opposed to allusions.[14] In *Macbeth*, though, I see not just moments where audience members might recognize a surprising source but a play shaped by the appropriation of Ovid's poetic method itself. Shakespeare recognizes how Ovid uses *raptus* to explore the dangerous pleasures of sublime words. As Lynn Enterline observes, "In an Ovidian universe, subjects may be just as 'carried away' by words (the original sense of *raptus*) as by implacable lovers."[15] While some critics reject the founding of a male poetics on *raptus* and sexual violence, Enterline values how Ovid's unsettling effects often come from his "transgendered *prosopopoeiae*," his ability to speak not only in the male voice but in the female; in "Ovidian ventriloquism," the tongue of the male poet speaks in other mouths, allowing ironic counterpoints to arise and undermine the fantasies of tyrannical masculinity.[16]

Words, which might come from another tongue, or from within one's own mind, share with desire the terrifying power to carry the mind and body to extremes of feeling. Desire for the Greeks and Romans is "both the most private and voluntary and the most alien and invasive of emotions," Melissa E. Sanchez writes, "both choice and compulsion," a tyranny that comes from within and without, potentially destructive in its mix of pleasure and pain.[17] When Macbeth is seized in rapture by witches voicing his desires, he experiences an Ovidian metamorphosis. Moreover, in Ovid, the paradoxes of desire produce boundary-defying ironies where sublime terror can be followed by comic absurdity or can simultaneously provoke both fear and laughter. Ovid's appropriations from myth and literature mix piety with irreverence, and Shakespeare embraces what Heather James calls his "interrogative, even transgressive imitations."[18] This Ovidian attitude shows when a drunken porter responds to the ominous knocking at the castle gate by telling knock-knock jokes about equivocation. Then, when Lennox evokes the sublime terror conjured by the murder of the Lord's anointed – "Lamentings heard i'th'air; strange screams of death, / And prophesying, with accents terrible" (II, iii, 56–7) – Macbeth responds with deadpan litotes, "'Twas a rough night" (61). That wry joke is soon followed by shouts of "horror, horror, horror!" (64).

Ovid's first exploration of the raptures of desire and poetry begins as a mock-heroic parody of Homeric warriors challenging one another to a battle for glory, but the farce quickly turns to violence and rape. After a boastful Apollo ridicules the boy Amor (Cupid), Venus's son promises he will show which of them is greater: "*quantoque animalia cedunt / cuncta deo, tanto minor est tua gloria nostra*" (I, 464–5).[19] Golding translates, "And looke how far that under God eche beast is put by kinde, / So much thy glorie lesse than ours in shooting shalt thou finde" (561–2), his interpolation, "by kinde," evoking a natural order of gods over beasts. Amor's violence, however, shows that this order is fragile since even the divine mind is subject to the tyranny of desire. Losing control over his passions and will, the male god is compelled to force his will upon a nymph who has been hit by an opposing arrow compelling her to resist. Every living creature or *animalia* is defined by its *anima*, its breath, life-force, and living soul, which the god seizes when taking the body in *raptus*, though his ultimate goal is to control the other's *animus* or mind.[20] This sequence of wounding and pursuit, wounding and flight, corresponds to the ruptures and proliferations of identity and meaning – territorialization, deterritorialization, reterritorialization – that are essential characteristics of the rhizome.[21] Force and resistance are thus essential parts of the process. Although, as Enterline shows, Daphne initiates her ironic transformation by praying that her divine father take away her ravishing beauty (*forma*), which results instead in a complete change of shape (*forma*), her transformation changes neither her *animus* nor Apollo's.[22] Even in her wooden form, Daphne's mind and body continue to flee, her unending resistance captured in Golding's unsettling couplet, "And in his armes embracing fast hir boughes and braunches lythe, / He proferde kisses to the tree, the tree did from him writhe" (681–2).

The graceful movements of the laurel, so "lithe," are revealed in the rhyme to be, horrifically, the soul and body that "writhe" as her mind rejects the rapist's touch.

Finally, Apollo offers to turn Daphne into the eternal symbol of Roman triumph, another ironic transformation given Amor's victory over them both. She seems to respond: "*factis modo laurea ramis / adnuit utque caput visa est agitasse cacumen*" (566–7). The ambiguous wording makes it difficult to translate the lines, which may signify consent or just show the movement of some branches: the laurel nodded, or approved, "*adnuit*," with her new-made branches, so that her head seemed, "*visa est*," to have stirred, or nodded, "*agitasse*," her top. What is Daphne's *animus* intending to communicate, if anything? Does her *anima* move the laurel's high branches, or does the breeze? Has Apollo's "*Paean*" (566) won her mind despite Amor's shot, or is he just translating random movements into words of consent? And in any case, does a nod signify agreement, or submission? Golding erases some but not all of the ambiguity: "The Lawrell to his just request did seeme to condescende, / By bowing of hir newe made boughs and tender braunches downe, / And wagging of hir seemely toppe, as if it were hir crowne" (698–700). In the original, Ovid's narrator does not come forward to declare that Apollo gives a "just request," leaving readers to assess the god's interpretation of the wordless swaying branches. Today's critics are split: Heather James, for instance, emphasizes the ambiguity, while Thomas M. Greene supports Apollo.[23] Each competing translation and interpretation of what is seen in those swaying branches posits a different Ovid and a different sense of the Ovidian, identifying him and his poetics either with the *animus* of a male god interpreting as he wishes, or with the *animus* of a female trapped into a silent, doubtful consent.

Tereus begins like Apollo, a powerful male seized by desire. As Philomela's beauty ravishes him, Ovid compares him to dry leaves bursting into flame: "*quam si quis canis ignem supponat aristis / aut frondem positasque cremet faenilibus herbas*" (VI, 456–7). Passion drives him to plot rape but also makes him eloquent: "*facundum faciebat amor*" (469). By showing how the king's eloquence manipulates others into serving the lusts he hides behind fine words, Ovid points to the political significance of these crimes. Tereus is a tyrant, while Philomela's soaring to the sublime heights of eloquence links her tragic resistance to republican heroism. Golding's translation emphasizes this theme, employing "tyrant" and related words more often than their equivalents appear in the Latin, as when he translates Philomela's opening accusation, "*o diris barbare factis / o cruedelis*"

(533–4), as "O cankerd Carle, O fell / And cruell Tyrant" (676–7). Golding then makes "cruel tyrant" Tereus's epithet.

Once Tereus gets Philomela alone in his house in the woods, Ovid's narrator says he *"fassusque nefas"* (524), literally "confessed the unspeakable crime," a sort of euphemism for the obscenity of rape that Golding renders, "bewraide / His wicked lust" (666–7). Immediately after the act, though, Philomela announces she will undo that equivocation: *"ipsa pudore / proiecto tua facta loquar"* (544–5). Golding makes the connection explicit by using the same verb for both *fassus* and *loquar*: "Yea I my selfe rejecting shame thy doings will bewray" (694). Given the unspeakable nature of the "doings" he bewrayed to her, Tereus might have expected the young virgin never to bewray them "in open face of all the world" (696), as Golding writes in a line not found in the Latin. As Lisa S. Starks-Estes shows, in Ovid's trope of *fassusque nefas*, a voice struggles to express the unspeakable. In putting that experience into words, Ovid has the victim re-inflict the traumatic wound upon herself, and his readers, while also, paradoxically, repairing some of the violations against her own integrity and against the larger community both inside and outside the poem.[24] Promising to speak in full the taboo, polluting words behind the word *nefas*, Philomela claims the power to destroy male authority with her eloquence, predicting she will "make the stones to understand" (698), *"conscia saxa movebo"* (547), using a rhetorical term (*movere*) for drawing an audience to a position by moving the passions.[25]

To prevent this orator of the unspeakable from filling city and countryside with her grief and indignation, Tereus commits the act of a savage tyrant (*"feri . . . tyranni,"* 549) moved by anger (*"ira,"* 549) and fear (*"metus,"* 550): "The cruell tyrant being chaaft and also put in feare" (700). By using his epithet "cruel tyrant" for *"feri . . . tyranni,"* which in Ovid points to the savagery of the Thracian barbarian, Golding puts attention squarely on the political nature of this crime. Through rape and incest, Tereus has seized, violated, and thrown Philomela's body and social identity into disorder – *"omnia turbasti"* (537), she says, "Behold thou hast confounded all" (682) – but when he realizes that her mind and voice remain free to speak the unspeakable, anger and fear drive him to seize her tongue in a brutally literal sense. Her fragmented body is transformed into a symbol for silenced eloquence:

> The stumpe whereon it hung
> Did patter still. The tip fell downe and quivering on the ground
> As though that it had murmured it made a certaine sound.

> And as an Adders tayle cut off doth skip a while: even so
> The tip of Philomelaas tongue did wriggle to and fro,
> And nearer to hir mistresseward in dying still did go. (710–15)

Ovid's nightmare imagery and onomatopoeic verbs – "*radix micat ultima linguae, / . . . tremens inmurmurat atrae / . . . / palpitat et moriens dominae vestigia quaerit*" (557–60) – inhabit the sounds and images of the vernacular translation, even if, to modern ears, Golding verges on comic bad taste. That image of the murmuring, palpitating tongue, throbbing like a mangled snake's tail, seeking out the footsteps of the woman who once ruled it, is at once grotesque and sublime. Her eloquent tongue seized, Philomela loses not just her voice but her autonomy, a dominance Tereus reaffirms by returning to rape her again and again (561–2).

Ironically, Macbeth is at his freest and most autonomous when serving his king at war. The first we hear of "brave Macbeth" is the Sergeant's gleeful report of a self-sufficient, hyper-masculine killer who, "with his brandish'd steel," all alone through a mass of bodies "carv'd out his passage" (I, ii, 16–19). A terrifying figure of phallic penetration and destruction, Macbeth "unseam'd [the rebel Macdonwald] from the nave to th' chops / And fix'd his head upon our battlements" (22–3). That Macbeth never appears on stage. Although he says he will "dare do all that may become a man" (I, vii, 46), repeatedly the words of the witches and his wife, and Banquo's wordless ghost, and other words and signs, seize control of him, his rapt tongue suggesting that his masculine self-control and authority have been rendered impotent.[26]

Macbeth is silenced by the witches after he speaks just two lines. His first is a paradox, a figure that expresses the extra-rational knowledge associated with the sublime: "So foul and fair a day I have not seen" (I, iii, 38).[27] His second commands the witches to prove they have voices and reveal their identities, knowledge that might dispel the fears they provoke: "Speak, if you can: what are you?" (47). When they speak, they give voice to desires that, till then, have remained hidden in Macbeth's mind, apparently voiced aloud to no one but his wife. Hearing the witches ventriloquize his secret words, he is stunned into silence. Banquo, who never loses control of his tongue, tells them, "My noble partner / You greet with present grace, and great prediction / Of noble having and of royal hope, / That he seems rapt withal" (54–7), attributing Macbeth's rapture to "the great prediction" and "royal hope." Two lines earlier, though, he perceived a different emotion: "why do you start, and seem to fear /

Things that do sound so fair?" (51–2). Sublime rapture seizes Macbeth's body, tongue, soul, and face with fear, or maybe hope. At this point, the audience does not get to hear the secrets of Macbeth's mind and must judge by the player's performance. He gets his tongue back and commands the witches answer his questions: "Speak, I charge you" (78). They vanish at once, as if to show him his impotence.

When the power of the witches' words appears to be confirmed by the news of his new title, Macbeth is again struck silent. Banquo once more is the one who notices: "Look how our partner's rapt" (142). This time, Macbeth's soliloquy takes the audience into his rapt mind to hear the secrets of an *animus* gripped by

> horrible imaginings:
> My thought, whose murther yet is but fantastical,
> Shakes so my single state of man that function
> Is smother'd in surmise, and nothing is
> But what is not. (138–42)

The rapture of his "single state of man," his identity or *animus*, comes both externally from the witches' voices and internally from his own fantasies, where thinking and doing become confounded. As David L. Sedley has shown, the early modern sublime arises out of and together with the irresistible skepticism of modernity.[28] The feeling of the sublime arises during moments of uncertainty that press against the limits of human knowledge. In Shakespeare, as in Ovid, we see those moments occurring when a body and mind are seized and fragmented, leading to the failure of rational knowledge and communication. Macbeth cannot speak, move, or think, all mental "function . . . smother'd in surmise," his *anima* choking under the weight of his imagination. The line between reality and fantasy disappears, "nothing is but what is not."

Macbeth's letter to his wife reassembles the events the audience has just witnessed, reframing his rapturous discovery that the witches "have more in them than mortal knowledge" (I, v, 3). The witches, he declares, know beyond what a mortal body should know, "mortal" being of course an equivocation. That teasing knowledge ravishes Macbeth so that, he writes, he "burnt in desire to question them further" (4), recalling Apollo, pricked by Amor's arrow, and Tereus, set on fire and ravished by desire. Tyranny begins with the loss of the self to desires that can never be sated. Macbeth's letter, though, omits mentioning that he was rapt by their first words to him and for a time rendered speechless, a moment of impotence that paradoxically begins his transformation into a tyrant. He does accurately record that when he questioned them, "they made themselves air, into which they vanish'd," but then writes that he was left "rapt in the wonder of it" (4–6). The pronoun "it" ambiguously could refer to either the mystery of their vanishing or the knowledge they have spoken. Sedley shows that in Renaissance poetics, "Knowledge inspires wonder," *admiratio*, which is distinguished from the feelings inspired when reason fails to reveal truth, the awe and fear that were coming to be known as *sublime*.[29] Macbeth's letter transforms the shock and fear that Banquo, the witches, and the audience saw into the wonder of knowledge, misrepresenting his uncertain mind, which does not find the knowledge he's gained to be a wondrous revelation as much as an amazing, confusing terror. His letter then continues to equivocate, neglecting to mention that after the royal messengers greeted him with the news the king had translated him into Thane of Cawdor, he was rapt again. That is a significant omission since this fit was triggered by the (apparent) proof of the witches' prophetic powers.

The audience hears Lady Macbeth's voice ventriloquize this letter of rapture and metamorphosis, and speaking those words prompts her to reinforce the prophecy. "[Thou] shalt be / What thou art promis'd," she insists before immediately voicing her fear that he does not possess the cruelty of a tyrant: "Yet do I fear thy nature, / It is too full o' th' milk of human kindness / To catch the nearest way" (I, v, 15–18). Milk, which bonds mother and child, represents the feelings of kindness and kinship that suppress the desire to "catch," seize, kill, rape. The things we choose to share, both the food and the words we put into other bodies, form and sustain ties of kinship. The choice of whether or not to eat a given thing as food, or whether or not to share a meal with a person, inevitably ruptures some bonds even as it forges others.[30] Against nourishing milk, Lady Macbeth will use poisonous rhetoric, beckoning to her husband, "That I may pour my spirits in thine ear, / And chastise with the valor of my tongue" (26–7). Like Tereus, she abuses eloquence.

Although Medea's rituals in *Metamorphoses* might be one source for the witchcraft Lady Macbeth performs to exorcise maternal love, Ovid's account of the murder of her children is not. *Metamorphoses* devotes just two dry lines to the crime, its only reference to her even being a mother, a repudiation of the way most writers shape the plot of her life so that it climaxes in lurid child-murder (VII, 396–7). Since Ovid treats the entire story of her abandonment by Jason as only worth mentioning so that he can move on to more exciting events in her life, his more pointed models for killing maternal kindness are Procne and Philomela. After asking, "*Quid faciat . . . ?*" (VI, 572),

Philomela appropriates the loom to speak for her missing tongue. Golding connects this moment to Tereus's original *fassusque nefas* by rendering the phrase "*indicium sceleris*" (578) as "bewraide / The wicked deede of Tereus" (737–8). This shocking message from her dead sister silences Procne. Just as Philomela's dying tongue searched for its mistress ("*quaerit*," 560), Procne's seeks in vain for words capable of expressing her outrage: "*verbaque quaerenti satis indignantia linguae / defuerunt*" (584–5). Upon seeing Itys, vengeful Procne is struck by the image of the father in her son and looks at him with pitiless eyes ("*oculisque . . . inmitibus*," 621). Once he embraces and kisses her, though, she hesitates. Golding elaborates on the pathos: "The mothers heart of hirs was then constreyned to relent, / Asswaged wholy was the rage to which she erst was bent, / And from hir eyes against hir will the teares enforced went" (794–6). Her piteous maternal heart battles her will until she looks at her sister, "*rapta . . . lingua*," whose tongue had been ravished from her, and is unmothered: "*quam vocat hic matrem, cur non vocat illa sororem?*" (632, 633). Golding's imitation of Ovid's tightly parallel line, "as well why calles not she / Me sister, as this boy doth call me mother?" (800–1), doesn't quite capture the metamorphosis from mother to sister. In ending her question with the word, "*sororem*," Procne transforms herself: where her husband's crimes had once confounded her kinship bond with Philomela, she now rejects the name and identity her son has given her and becomes all sister. When the terrified boy throws his arms around her and calls out her old name – "*mater! mater!*" – she kills him without even changing the look on her face (640–2). Procne and Philomela then confirm their sisterhood in a frenzy of dismemberment. Fittingly, in a foreshadowing of the poet Orpheus's fate in Book 11, Procne has rescued her sister from captivity under the cover of the rites of Bacchus, stealing her away disguised as one of the celebrants (587–600).

Lacking her own sisterhood – the Scottish noblewomen are notably isolated, the rites of the Weïrd Sisters offering the play's only glimpse into female friendship – Lady Macbeth instead prays to the spirits to unmother her:

> unsex me here,
> And fill me from the crown to the toe topful
> Of direst cruelty! Make thick my blood,
> Stop up th' access and passage to remorse,
> . . . .
> Come to my woman's breasts,
> And take my milk for gall, you murth'ring ministers. . . .

Her prayer, a perversion of Daphne's, locates the sources of pity in her humours and sex organs, but whatever the effect of those words upon her body and mind, they do not translate all the mother from her. Lady Macbeth will be the one to hesitate when the sleeping Duncan looks like her father, and remorse for murder will murder her sleep, make her see bloodstains on her hands, and drive her to madness and suicide. Her words to her husband, though, spur on a more complete metamorphosis. Macbeth, after hesitation, will remove all "the milk of human kindness" from his temperament and seize what is promised, and more, not recognizing until too late that he is the one who has been seized.

In Macbeth's final moment of hesitation, his imagination puts together an assemblage of fragmented memories of Ovid's ravishers:

> Now o'er the one half world
> Nature seems dead, and wicked dreams abuse
> The curtain'd sleep; witchcraft celebrates
> Pale Hecat's off'rings; and wither'd Murther,
> Alarum'd by his sentinel, the wolf,
> Whose howl's his watch, thus with his stealthy pace,
> With Tarquin's ravishing strides, towards his design
> Moves like a ghost. (II, i, 49–56)

In this walking nightmare, Macbeth imagines witches offering sacrifices to Hecate, whose name calls to mind her most celebrated devotee, Medea, and the bloody rites she performs in *Metamorphoses*. Macbeth then imagines himself as the personification of Murther, alarmed by the howl of a wolf, stepping with the stealth of Tarquin.

"Tarquin's ravishing strides" evoke not just a rapist but a tyrant who cannot resist using his power to fulfill his desires. Critics often identify Seneca as the source for the paradoxical conception of tyranny as a desire for total mastery that becomes a loss of control to mad *furor*.[31] However, Shakespeare also finds the idea in Ovid, who describes Tarquin possessed by the *furor* of desire: "The royal youth caught furious fire" ["*furiales ... ignes / concipit*"], "and seized by blind love, he raved" ["*et caeco raptus amore furit*"] (*Fasti* II, 761–2).[32] Indeed, the "fatal vision" of the dagger (II, i, 36) that leads Macbeth on and spurs him to draw his own steel is another ghostly fragment of Tarquin's tyrannical masculinity:

> It was night, and there was not a light in the whole house. He rose, and drew his sword from his gilded scabbard and came into your chamber,

virtuous wife. And as he pressed down upon the bed, "My sword, Lucretia, is with me," the son of the king said. "I am a Tarquin who speaks." (792–6)

Tarquin's drawn sword, a symbol of the masculine force the Roman state harnesses and directs outward for defense and conquest, leads his invasion of the domestic space of this embodiment of Roman female virtue ("*nupta pudica*," 794). His threat, "*ferrum, Lucretia, mecum est*" (795), suggests a parallel to Macbeth's "brandish'd steel," which once carved up Duncan's enemies but now comes to rape him. Ovid's description of Tarquin drawing the sword hints at the violent sexual perversity of tyranny: he frees the sword ("*liberat ensem*," 793) to force a woman's will, and he frees it from a gilded scabbard ("*aurata vagina*," 793) that first suggests luxurious, even decadent wealth but ultimately signifies the rape he intends. The word for scabbard, *vagina*, had been used euphemistically since at least the time Plautus made an obscene joke about soldiers putting their swords into a woman's scabbard.[33] Ovid uses the phrase "*vagina liberat ensem*" one other time: when Tereus draws his sword to cut out Philomela's tongue (*Metamorphoses* VI, 551).

Tarquin's threats give rise to the next symbol from Macbeth's soliloquy as Ovid compares him to a wolf pouncing on a trembling lamb. Since Ovid uses the same simile to describe Philomela's shock immediately after Tereus rapes her but before her mind settles enough to challenge him (*Metamorphoses* VI, 528–9), the three tyrants and victims come together at this point. Tarquin, Tereus, and Macbeth are all tyrannical wolves preying on the defenseless, which in Shakespeare's Christian culture also connects their victims to the iconography of the innocent sacrificial lamb. Lucretia becomes that lamb when confronted with the power of a male body, backed by a warrior's steel phallus and the patriarchal authority contained in the royal family's name:

> She said nothing. She had neither voice nor power to speak, nor any thought in her whole heart. But she trembled, just as when at times a little lamb, caught after having strayed from the fold, lies still under the predatory wolf. (*Fasti* II, 797–800)

Her voice and words were part of what first impelled Tarquin to seize her ("*verba placent et vox*," 765), so it is fitting that he begins the *raptus* by seizing her tongue. She can think but not speak a series of questions whose answers increase her terror: "*Quid faciat? pug-net?* . . . / *clamet?* . . . / *effugiat?* . . ." (801–3). The *nefas* itself is an obscene lacuna in the story, filled with the narrator's address to Tarquin, lines that might have given Macbeth pause: "Why do you rejoice, victor? This victory will destroy you. / Alas, how one night will cost you your kingdom!" (811–12). The next day, Lucretia will not be able to speak the words that name Tarquin's crime – "'Must I speak [*eloquar*],' she said. 'Must I speak, unhappy me, my shame myself?'" (825–6) – so she will take up the symbol of masculine force and sheathe the steel into the scabbard of her breast, acting out the unspeakable, just as Philomela found another medium to express the words stolen from her.

Macbeth's description of the sublime terror or "present horror" (II, i, 59) he feels as he, ravished, approaches the royal body he will seize, translates Ovid's similes to emphasize how tyranny results from a man's loss of self-control. Ovid's similes make simple, if moving, analogies between the rapists and wolves, but Shakespeare transforms the beast into Murther's howling sentinel to represent Macbeth's fear, which, the allusions to Tarquin and especially Tereus remind us, is the passion that combines with furious desire to compel tyrants to act. This appropriation of Ovid's rapists, moreover, transforms Duncan into a silent sacrificial lamb and a raped woman, confounding (as elsewhere in the play) the simplistic gender binaries that many characters unwisely long for.[34] Beginning with "wither'd Murther," Shakespeare builds up that sequence of phrases, metaphors, and allusions to end (like a Latinate periodic sentence) with the verb and a final simile: "Moves like a ghost." Haunted by a host of Ovid's ghosts – Tarquin, Lucretia, Medea, Philomela, Tereus – Macbeth fears enacting the words he has sworn, words pulled from his imagination by witches, by his wife, by his own desires, and by the ghosts of history. As the ghost of a dead monarchy whose tyrannical act ensured that he would neither become king nor "get kings" (I, iii, 67), Tarquin continues to haunt Macbeth. He soon imitates Lucretia's acting out of Tarquin's *nefas* by sheathing his steel into the guards' bodies, but his dramatic performance of revenge does not unite the witnesses cathartically but divides them by drawing attention to his failures to represent his emotions convincingly. A more complete rhizomatic sketch of all these appropriations would be further complicated by Shakespeare's adaptation of his own *Rape of Lucrece*, whose voluble heroine is less like Lucretia, the silenced lamb who cannot speak, than Philomela, the orator of *nefas* who, after recovering from what Golding wonderfully calls her "mazed-nesse" (VI, 674), turns her eloquence against the tyrant. Being amaz'd, a word often used for sublime rapture, ironically is one of the jumble of emotions that Macbeth cites to explain why he killed and silenced Duncan's guards, a speech that is a notable rhetorical failure (II, iii, 108).

Although rape is never named as one of Macbeth's crimes, the climax of his tyranny comes when his agents stealthily invade a home to ravish a mother, "*nupta pudica*," and her children, who are all ideologically the king's children. Terrified, Lady Macduff asks, "Whither should I fly?" (IV, ii, 73), echoing Lucretia, Philomela, and so many victims of *raptus*. The last we see her, she is fleeing men with daggers covered in her son's blood, symbols of tyrannical masculine force. Her offstage fate is unspeakable. Lady Macbeth, who knows "[h]ow tender 'tis to love the babe that milks me" but claims the ability to "[h]ave pluck'd my nipple from his boneless gums, / And dash'd the brains out" (I, vii, 55–8), has given her unsexed spirit to her husband. Without pity, he has become Procne taking revenge on her son for her sister's rapt tongue, but without a cause beyond his loss of control to ambition and pride – and, like Tereus, to anger and fear. In turn, Macbeth's tyranny transforms Macduff into a fury of vengeance. He names himself "[s]inful Macduff, / . . . naught that I am" (IV, iii, 224–5), feeling himself transformed into both a wicked man and a nothing, an equivocal prophecy "of no woman born" (V, viii, 31). Unless he kills Macbeth, he believes, "My wife and children's ghosts will haunt me still" (V, vii, 16). He will fight no one else, leaving his blade virginal, sheathed "with an unbattered edge" (V, vii, 19), unless he gets to sheathe it into Macbeth.

Macduff does finally bring out the tyrant's head so all may see that "the time is free" (V, ix, 21), but has Macduff really freed time and gained our peace? The play's ending promises a return to the order upset by the tyrant, yet the play begins with a parallel scene of Macbeth beheading a usurper. This Ovidian universe consists of the endless appropriation of power and texts, and the endless return of ghosts and tyrants, murders and rapes, uncanny but always imperfect in their representations of what came before, their bodies and minds out of joint. The tragedy's sublime terror is not purged in catharsis. Rather, the violence done to secure our peace brings the "restless ecstasy" of endless cycles of metempsychosis that parody Pythagoras's lecture at the end of *Metamorphoses*. Such traumatic seizures, violations, and appropriations haunt time and continue to leave their marks upon ravished bodies and minds.

Notes

1. Quotations follow Shakespeare, *The Riverside Shakespeare*.
2. Calbi, *Spectral Shakespeares*, analyzes how Klaus Knoesel's 2001 adaptation *Rave Macbeth* translates this pleasurable terror into the drug ecstasy (pp. 115–35), a translation that marks the difference between a culture shaped by a war over religion, where the technologies used by the state to monitor the mind loomed large, to one shaped by consumer capitalism, where the technologies used to produce psychological pleasure and pain, and to define the boundaries between the healthy and the ill, and the real and the delusional, are inescapable.
3. Lanier, "Shakespearean Rhizomatics" and "Afterword," pp. 293–306. My discussion of appropriation draws on Sanders, *Adaptation and Appropriation*; Huang and Rivlin, "Introduction," pp. 1–20; Desmet, "Recognizing Shakespeare," pp. 41–57; Desmet and Iyengar, "Adaptation, Appropriation," pp. 10–19; Desmet et al., "Introduction," pp. 1–22.
4. Deleuze and Guattari, *A Thousand Plateaus*, p. 25.
5. Ibid. p. 21.
6. Cf. Drew Daniel's exploration of the Renaissance culture of melancholy in Daniel, *The Melancholy Assemblage*.
7. Derrida, *Specters of Marx*, pp. 19–30.
8. Enterline, *Shakespeare's Schoolroom*.
9. Derrida, *Specters of Marx*, p. 20.
10. Nims, "Introduction," p. xxxi.
11. Derrida, *Specters of Marx*, p. 63.
12. Barkan, *The Gods Made Flesh*, pp. 243–51. On Ovid, mythical appropriations, and artistic creation, see Sanders, *Adaptation and Appropriation*, pp. 80–104.
13. Burrow, *Shakespeare and Classical*, pp. 92–132.
14. Bate, *Shakespeare and Ovid*, p. 200.
15. Enterline, *The Rhetoric*, p. 78.
16. Ibid. p. 88; on Ovidian ventriloquism, see pp. 1–38 and *passim*. Leo Curran initiated the current critical debate by demonstrating Ovid's focus on the terror of the victims of *raptus*. Curran, "Rape and Rape Victims," pp. 213–41.
17. Sanchez, *Erotic Subjects*, "Introduction," para. 3.
18. James, *Shakespeare's Troy*, p. 63.
19. For *Metamorphoses*, I cite the Loeb Classical Library (Ovid, *Metamorphoses*) and Golding's translation (Ovid, *Ovid's Metamorphoses*). I have consulted the Perseus Digital Library, available at <http://data.perseus.org/texts/urn:cts:latinLit:phi0959.phi006> (last accessed 4 November 2018).
20. Enterline, *The Rhetoric*, pp. 49–67.

21. Deleuze and Guattari, *A Thousand Plateaus*, pp. 9–12.
22. Enterline, *The Rhetoric*, pp. 63, 67–83.
23. James, *Shakespeare's Troy*, pp. 45–6; Greene, *The Light in Troy*, p. 129.
24. Starks-Estes, *Violence, Trauma, and* Virtus. On *nefas*, see Enterline, *The Rhetoric*, pp. 3–4.
25. Shugar, *Sacred Rhetoric*, p. 211.
26. See Janet Adelman on *Macbeth*, male anxiety about maternal power, and the fantasy, or nightmare, that men can excise the female from their bodies, minds, and social bonds. Adelman, *Suffocating Mothers*, pp. 130–46; and Starks-Estes, *Violence, Trauma, and* Virtus, on transformations of masculine *virtus* in Ovid and Shakespeare's Roman plays.
27. Useful recent studies on the sublime include Shaw, *The Sublime*, and Doran, *The Theory of the Sublime*.
28. Sedley, *Sublimity and Skepticism*, pp. 1–17.
29. Ibid. p. 11.
30. Using Derrida's late work on sovereignty, Calbi, *Spectral Shakespeares* (pp. 21–38), explores "incorporation and its uncanny effects" (p. 22) in recent postmodern adaptations of *Macbeth*, noting that they introduce it at particularly self-referential moments, just as (I suggest) Ovid connects food, tongues, love, power, and art.
31. Braden, *Renaissance Tragedy*, and Bushnell, *Tragedies of Tyrants*. On *Macbeth* and debates over the royal succession and resistance to tyrants, see Norbrook, "*Macbeth* and the Politics," pp. 78–116; Hadfield, *Shakespeare and Renaissance Politics*, pp. 78–86.
32. For *Fasti*, I follow the Loeb Classical Library Online Edition. I produced this translation while consulting Frazer's and the Perseus Project, available at <http://data.perseus.org/texts/urn:cts:latinLit:phi0959. phi007> (last accessed 4 November 2018).
33. Plautus, *Pseudolus* IV, vii, 79–80.
34. Adelman, *Suffocating Mothers*, p. 133.

Bibliography

Adelman, Janet, *Suffocating Mothers: Fantasies of Maternal Origin in Shakespeare's Plays, "Hamlet" to "The Tempest"* (New York and London: Routledge, 1992).

Barkan, Leonard, *The Gods Made Flesh: Metamorphosis and the Pursuit of Paganism* (New Haven: Yale University Press, 1986).

Bate, Jonathan, *Shakespeare and Ovid* (Oxford: Clarendon Press, 1993).

Braden, Gordon, *Renaissance Tragedy and the Senecan Tradition: Anger's Privilege* (New Haven: Yale University Press, 1985).

Burrow, Colin, *Shakespeare and Classical Antiquity* (Oxford: Oxford University Press, 2013).

Bushnell, Rebecca W., *Tragedies of Tyrants: Political Thought and Theater in the English Renaissance* (Ithaca and London: Cornell University Press, 1990).

Calbi, Maurizio, *Spectral Shakespeares: Media Adaptations in the Twenty-First Century* (New York: Palgrave Macmillan, 2013).

Curran, Leo, "Rape and Rape Victims in the *Metamorphoses*," *Arethusa* 2, 1978, pp. 213–41.

Daniel, Drew, *The Melancholy Assemblage: Affect and Epistemology in the English Renaissance* (New York: Fordham University Press, 2013).

Deleuze, Gilles and Félix Guattari, *A Thousand Plateaus: Capitalism and Schizophrenia*, Brian Massumi (trans.) (Minneapolis and London: University of Minnesota Press, 1987).

Derrida, Jacques, *Specters of Marx: The State of the Debt, the Work of Mourning, and the New International*, Peggy Kamuf (trans.) (New York and London: Routledge Classics, 2006).

Desmet, Christy, "Recognizing Shakespeare, Rethinking Fidelity: A Rhetoric and Ethics of Appropriation," in Alexa Huang and Elizabeth Rivlin (eds), *Shakespeare and the Ethics of Appropriation* (New York: Palgrave Macmillan, 2014), pp. 41–57.

Desmet, Christy and Sujata Iyengar, "Adaptation, Appropriation, or What You Will," *Shakespeare* 11.1, 2015, pp. 10–19.

Desmet, Christy, Natalie Loper, and Jim Casey, "Introduction," in Christy Desmet, Natalie Loper, and Jim Casey (eds), *Shakespeare / Not Shakespeare* (New York: Palgrave Macmillan, 2017), pp. 1–22.

Desmet, Christy, Natalie Loper, and Jim Casey (eds), *Shakespeare / Not Shakespeare* (New York: Palgrave Macmillan, 2017).

Doran, Robert, *The Theory of the Sublime from Longinus to Kant* (Cambridge: Cambridge University Press, 2015).

Enterline, Lynn, *The Rhetoric of the Body from Ovid to Shakespeare* (Cambridge: Cambridge University Press, 2000).

Enterline, Lynn, *Shakespeare's Schoolroom: Rhetoric, Discipline, Emotion* (Philadelphia: University of Pennsylvania Press, 2012).

Greene, Thomas M., *The Light in Troy: Imitation and Discovery in Renaissance Poetry* (New Haven and London: Yale University Press, 1982).

Hadfield, Andrew, *Shakespeare and Renaissance Politics* (London: Methuen Drama, 2004).

Huang, Alexa and Elizabeth Rivlin, "Introduction: Shakespeare and the Ethics of Appropriation," in Alexa Huang and Elizabeth Rivlin (eds), *Shakespeare and the Ethics of Appropriation* (New York: Palgrave Macmillan, 2014), pp. 1–20.

Huang, Alexa and Elizabeth Rivlin (eds), *Shakespeare and the Ethics of Appropriation* (New York: Palgrave Macmillan, 2014).

James, Heather, *Shakespeare's Troy: Drama, Politics, and the Translation of Empire* (Cambridge: Cambridge University Press, 1997).

Lanier, Douglas M., "Shakespeare / Not Shakespeare: Afterword," in Christy Desmet, Natalie Loper, and Jim Casey (eds), *Shakespeare / Not Shakespeare* (New York: Palgrave Macmillan, 2017), pp. 293–306.

Lanier, Douglas, "Shakespearean Rhizomatics: Adaptation, Ethics, Value," in Alexa Huang and Elizabeth Rivlin (eds), *Shakespeare and the Ethics of Appropriation* (New York: Palgrave Macmillan, 2014), pp. 21–40.

Nims, John Frederick, "Introduction," in John Frederick Nims (ed.), *Ovid's Metamorphoses: The Arthur Golding Translation of 1567* (Philadelphia: Paul Dry, 2000), pp. xiii–xxxv.

Norbrook, David, "*Macbeth* and the Politics of Historiography," in Kevin Sharpe and Steven N. Zwicker (eds), *Politics of Discourse: The Literature and History of Seventeenth-Century England* (Berkeley: University of California Press, 1987), pp. 78–116.

Ovid, *Fasti*, James G. Frazer (ed. and trans.) and G. P. Goold (ed.), Loeb Classical Library Online Edition (Cambridge, MA: Harvard University Press, 1931), DOI: 10.4159/DLCL.ovid-fasti.1931.

Ovid, *Metamorphoses*, 3rd revised edn, Frank Justus Miller (ed. and trans.) and G.P. Goold (ed.), Loeb Classical Library (Cambridge, MA: Harvard University Press, 1977).

Ovid, *Ovid's Metamorphoses: The Arthur Golding Translation of 1567*, John Frederick Nims (ed.) (Philadelphia: Paul Dry Books, 2000).

Plautus, *Pseudolus*, F. Leo (ed.), Perseus Digital Library, <http://data.perseus.org/texts/urn:cts:latinLit:phi0119.phi016>.

Sanchez, Melissa E., *Erotic Subjects: The Sexuality of Politics in Early Modern English Literature*, Kindle edn (Oxford: Oxford University Press, 2011).

Sanders, Julie, *Adaptation and Appropriation*, 2nd edn (London and New York: Routledge, 2016).

Sedley, David L., *Sublimity and Skepticism in Montaigne and Milton* (Ann Arbor: University of Michigan Press, 2005).

Shakespeare, William, *The Riverside Shakespeare*, 2nd edn, G. Blakemore Evans et al. (eds) (Boston: Houghton Mifflin, 1997).

Shaw, Phillip, *The Sublime*, 2nd edn (London and New York: Routledge, 2017).

Shugar, Debora Kuller, *Sacred Rhetoric: The Christian Grand Style in the English Renaissance* (Princeton: Princeton University Press, 1988).

Starks-Estes, Lisa S., *Violence, Trauma, and Virtus in Shakespeare's Roman Poems and Plays: Transforming Ovid* (Basingstoke: Palgrave Macmillan, 2014).

Chapter 10

Ovid and the Styles of Adaptation in *The Two Gentlemen of Verona*

Goran Stanivukovic

The Two Gentlemen of Verona, written sometime between 1590 and 1591, marks the beginning of Shakespeare's long-lasting appropriations of Ovid.[1] Ovid's influence on Shakespeare ranges from direct references and specific citations to motivation and style. The imprint of Ovid's works in Shakespeare's writing is deep; it is one of the most varied and authentic of Shakespeare's engagement with a classic. This chapter explores stylistic correspondences between *The Two Gentlemen of Verona* and the *Heroides*. Specifically, it explores Shakespeare's appropriation of the Heroidean verse-epistle in the creation of lovers' emotional interiority. The Heroidean verse-epistle gave Shakespeare a new voice, and it added stylistic vivacity and affective immediacy to the lover as a speaking subject. The affinities between the emotional and stylistic exuberance of Ovid's amatory works and the ornamental richness of Shakespeare's Ovidian poetry suggest that Shakespeare turned to Ovid because he read him a great deal and because, being "the sexiest poet from antiquity,"[2] Ovid resonated with the linguistic freedom with which Shakespeare freed love poetry from inherited convention.

The process of transformation of Ovid's verse into Shakespeare's dramatic poetry is a testimony to a complex and often complicated relationship between adaptation, appropriation, and imitation. Intertwined, these processes are both philological and cultural. Both theory and practice of imitation showed "a bewildering variety of positions."[3] Two of the positions that Shakespeare seems to have engaged particularly in the 1590s, and that made him consistent with the theory of imitation of the period, concern "a method for enriching one's writing with stylistic gems" and another that "provides the competitive stimulus necessary for achievement."[4]

Thomas M. Greene has suggested that "Renaissance imitation at its richest became a technique for creating etiological constructs of unblocking . . . the blockages in transmission"[5] of one text into another. Shakespeare's relationship with Ovid in the early years of the playwright's entry into the London theatre scene illustrates how this unblocking works. In those early years, Shakespeare experimented not only with the transformation of stories and plots but also with an appropriation of styles and rhetoric.

Recent theory of adaptation has highlighted the ethical aspect of Shakespeare's method of transformation that responds to a "diversified" application and use of Shakespeare in "a multitude of agendas" and that, therefore, emphasizes the ethics of, and in, adaptation.[6] As a process of creative and critical assimilation of Ovid, transformation was also part of the complex process of what Liz Oakley-Brown has called "the cultural politics of translation"[7] of Ovid into a generically diverse body of early modern English literature. Adaptation that focuses on "often unspoken ethical tenets that inform our understanding of the process of adaptation"[8] approaches the subject of transmission from outside the text, from our "increasingly globalized"[9] culture, thus engaging with the Shakespearean text externally while also profiting from the rich and textured layers of the ethics of those texts themselves. Such adaptation is a larger and both culturally and textually motivated process that concerns both the larger ethical ramification of the text as well as how the adaptation benefits from the formal, linguistic, and thematic properties of Shakespeare's works.

But the kind of adaptation that I explore in this chapter turns the critical method back on the text itself. I uncover how philological, linguistic, and rhetorical features of the originating text, Ovid's, gave rise to a new style of amorous writing in drama in a new, Shakespeare's, text. In this new formalist approach to both the idea and practice of transformation, it is Shakespeare's own affinity with the kind of writing he encountered in Ovid that acts as "a transformational force"[10] in turning, and appropriating, a classical model into new forms of dramatic representation. As a poet who "does not abandon love"[11] in any of his works, even when he changes poetic forms, Ovid was an obvious choice for Shakespeare, who was ambitiously engaged in developing his own poetic discourse of love within a culture of literary appropriation.

The Two Gentlemen of Verona came out of the medieval tradition of romance, Petrarchism, and Neoplatonic love philosophy. When Shakespeare grafted the Ovidian style and the verse-epistle onto these influences, he balanced emphasis on the love plot and narrative with a new linguistic medium through which love and desire were experienced. H. Moore has argued that the rhetorical and thematic richness of the Ovidian narrative means that Elizabethan fiction is "saturated" with copious *exempla* from the *Heroides*[12] because the status of *Heroides* "validates . . . female experience in love."[13] Yet the Heroidean love-epistle also transmitted to Shakespeare's early romantic comedy stylistic and verbal techniques of expression that fictionalized men employed to speak their passion, articulate their desire, and reveal their fragile, wounded, but fearless selves as romantic lovers, no longer as heroes of the Ovidian love world. The "epistolary eloquence"[14] from the *Heroides* thus became a stylistic universe[15] through which the intensity of men's amorous emotions was released in soliloquies.

The verse-epistle shapes "a principle of pairing"[16] of friends and of lovers – upon which this comedy is based. Letters are also crucial to the structure and plot of this play and as props; and to "the tearing of letters." Alan Stewart contests they represent a way by which Shakespeare revises his source, Jorge de Montemayor's "hugely popular"[17] 1559 *Diana*, a work of romance fiction that abounds in letters. Shakespeare turns elements of the story from this fiction into the plot and story of his drama. But he replaces the prose letters that circulate in the Spanish pretext with the verse-epistle form in Ovid, and thus appropriates the epistolary form more suitable to verse drama and, more importantly, to a drama in which letters are the medium through which passions and interiority are revealed to the audience, just as they were to Ovid's classical and neoclassical readers. Letters, however, are more than material objects exchanged between characters. They are textual places through which love is performed rhetorically as a feature of Ovidian aesthetics that gives this play its distinctiveness. It was the *Heroides*, more than a prose romance, that became a major resource presenting love in *The Two Gentlemen of Verona*.

The Two Gentlemen of Verona has been described as a "failure"[18] and has been one that "bears upon it . . . obvious marks of immaturity,"[19] but Shakespeare's handling of the Ovidian verse-epistle demonstrates that, for Shakespeare, "'Ovid' meant for [Renaissance readers] . . . a greater variety to it than modern critics can easily keep in their heads when they generalize about the 'Ovidian.'"[20] By appropriating the Heroidean style of writing about love as an interior monologue, Shakespeare makes the lover the agent of his own longing and grief, not the passive victim of love's unpredictable course.

Ovid's influence on *The Two Gentlemen of Verona* can be illustrated by different kinds of evidence. They include the two earliest occurrences of the word "metamorphosed" in the Shakespearean canon (I, i, 66 and II, i, 28); a direct reference to Phaëton (III, i, 153–6), alluding to the tragedy ensuing from the unbridled ambition of youth; an invocation of Orpheus (III, ii, 77), though for the purpose of drawing attention to the broken strings of his lute, which Jonathan Bate links with Shakespeare's fascination "by the extremes of harmony and violence in the Orpheus story,"[21] which is particularly important in this play; and Julia's allusion to Proteus's name, by way of a reference to the story of Ariadne and Theseus, suggesting unjustness and untrustworthiness (IV, iv, 164–5). The Ovidian world of this play centers on masculine desire, friendship, love, and self-mastery; "the most 'Ovidian' element," however, is "the attempted rape" of Silvia.[22] This theme connects the play to the *Metamorphoses* and *Ars amatoria*. But Shakespeare's appropriation of the Ovidian style shows that Ovid was not only a resource but that it added a flair of modernity in the stylizing of passions because Ovid himself sounded "modern."[23] Shakespeare's way of appropriating Ovid through style in *The Two Gentlemen of Verona* shows that philological transformation is not a kind of adaptation in which Ovid is used to fit, or be accommodated to, an already formed dramatic genre. Rather, Shakespeare appropriates Ovid's style to free his love idiom from inherited clichés and formulas.

To the extent to which themes like love, friendship, and desire inform Shakespeare's imagination and the world of *The Two Gentlement of Verona*, we can assume Philip Hardie's claim that "[i]n Ovid's erotic world desire never exists apart from texts"[24] is tempered by its reliance on Ovidian effect to represent men's interior world. The male and female figures in Ovid's poetry are driven by violent desires that tear them apart. As such, these figures could hardly have been models for the friends in Shakespeare's early comedy. Ovid himself voices skepticism at the notion of friendship that is idealized to the extent that it contrasts the naturalism and extremes of desire and sex when, in the third elegy in *Ex ponto*, he says "[t]hat once revered name of friendship is exposed for sale, awaiting gain like a courtesan."[25] Ovid's ironic voice does not escape us. When about thirty years after *The Two Gentlemen of Verona* was written a contemporary hand, identified in the Folger Shakespeare Library record as belonging to one Paul Gosnold, copied in a commonplace book under the entry "*De amicitia*" the same line from *Ex ponto*, "*Illud amicitiae quanda venerabila nomen Prostat, / et in quastu pro meretrice ist est*" (20^r),[26] we are not only reminded that humanists raised questions about the idealized nature of friendship, but also that Ovid provided an unlikely source for thinking about friendship.

That Ovid has less to say about friendship than love and desire, and that Shakespeare builds the conflict between friendship and desire in key episodes at the heart of which is the Ovidian verse-epistle that exposes the emotional life of a man, tells us that Shakespeare's preoccupation is, at best, with exploring the tension between the discourse of affective friendship and the Ovidianism of hetero-erotic love. This strand of Ovidianism, which gives men romantic agency, is important because it provides a counterpoint to a more prevailing argument among scholars that Ovidian myths were predominantly appropriated for new discourses of what Sarah Carter has called "sexual deviance"[27] and the discourses of non-procreative sexualities.

The *Metamorphoses* and *Tristia* were two Ovidian texts extensively read as part of the classical education in the grammar school curriculum in sixteenth-century England.[28] Evidence garnered in commonplace books compiled by the early readers of Ovid shows that *Ex Ponto* often appeared on the reading lists in that curriculum. These three texts were also included in the teaching at most levels of classroom instruction in the elite schools like Eton, Westminster, and Ruthin (North Wales).[29] Grammar school education was a male-only undertaking, and *Ex ponto* resonated with educated male youth attentive to both the learning and social experience lived during their grammar school days, of "Ovidian banter" being absorbed in the discourse of affectionate friendship.[30] Our knowledge of this experience of reading Ovid in school extends our awareness as modern readers of the role Ovid's works played in the imitation of the love narratives and fictions, and in social interaction between men.

In the first Ovidian epistle in the play, Julia reads a letter by "Love-wounded Proteus," a love letter "[t]hat, some whirlwind bear / Unto a ragged, fearful, hanging rock / And throw it thence into the raging sea" (I, ii, 121–3). This Shakespearean verse-letter appropriates the Heroidean verse-epistle 18 and Leander as its subject. "[T]he raging sea" (123) echoes "the surging Seas" (G6^r) and the "raging waters" (J6^v), which form the liquid element that frames the narrative of Leander's effort to love Hero, as the sea is rendered in the most important early English translation of the *Heroides* by George Turberville (1570?). The rough sea not only represents the raging love within the swimming Leander, or within Proteus's fluid subjectivity as both a friend and lover, but also captures the crisis and ecstasy of love in a play in which the expression of love is freed from the ornamental clichés and blazons of Petrarchan love poetics and the Neoplatonic aetiology of love that dominate love poetry of the 1590s. Lines such as, "I throw thy name [Julia] against the bruising stones / Trampling contemptuously on thy disdain" (112–13), could be read as the Ovidian reaction to the formulaic rhetorical performances of the pining lover in the Petrarchan love sonnet of the 1590s. But the "force of forward streames," which "drench . . . top and tasle" (G6ʳ) of the swimming lover in the *Heroides*, is not unlike the force of "some whirlwind" that "bear[s]' / Unto a ragged, fearful, hanging rock" (I, ii, 121–2), which throws Proteus's name around, as this Ovidian lover pushes on towards amorous satisfaction. This Ovidian image is based on movement; it rests on the idea of directing the lover towards the desired love object; it also plunges the subject, "[p]oor forlorn Proteus," "passionate Proteus" (125), or Leander, in the sea current that flows between and keeps the lovers apart.

The Ovidian poetry in this passage shows that the issue of adaptation becomes perhaps more evident if we compare modern with early modern rendering of the same passage. The 1570s adaptation of the Heroidean epistle evokes a story of separated lovers and youthful longing. A modern English translator has rendered the same passage by emphasizing the physical effort exerted by the lover in overcoming the obstacle placed between him and the beloved:

> Thrice have I laid down my garments upon the dry sand; thrice, naked, have I tried to enter on the heavy way—the swollen billows opposed the old attempts of youth, and as I swam, my head was covered by the fronting surge. (XVIII, 25)[31]

Is Shakespeare in dialogue with Turberville? Would he have been familiar with Turberville when he was pupil in the Stratford grammar school (if he indeed attended it), or at any point later, but close in time to his writing of *The Two Gentlemen of Verona*? At this point, Shakespeare's appropriation of Ovid does not carry "strong overtones of agency," a characteristic of adaptation that Alexa Huang and Elizabeth Rivlin argue connect the "appropriated" and the "appropriator" in a "political, cultural, and . . . ethical advocacy."[32] The degree of appropriation here is philological, as it is style and affect that Shakespeare transposes. Although there is no direct evidence that Shakespeare knew Turberville's text, it is unlikely that Shakespeare could have avoided knowing about it.

Ovid was crucial not only to Shakespeare's imitation of his stories, but his works were also deeply embedded in the creation of new forms and styles in all genres of literary and artistic expression just at the time when Shakespeare's own poetic imagination was shaped by Ovid.[33] The *Heroides* was one of the most popular texts in grammar school teaching of imitation and the classics.[34] The Ovidian letter from the *Heroides*, as Victoria Rimell suggests, is "a loaded act."[35] This letter captures emotion at its most intense. When love moves the feeling subject, that subject undergoes interior transformation.[36] The billowing waves, "the troubled sea . . . boiling with horse-voiced waters," and the arduous swim ahead of Leander are the natural correlative to the interior torment experienced by the separation. Attempts at swimming across the Hellespont, the undressing on the shore, and the naked swim against "the fronting surge" that threatens to drown the self as it pushes forward towards the beloved, liberate the self in love. They also have a titillating appeal, drawing the reader's and the spectator's gaze to Leander's naked body standing on the shore, about to plunge into the rough sea. It is in Ovid that Shakespeare finds a model for such scenes of amorous intensity, in which style becomes an index of interiority.

Shakespeare's affinity for adapting voice and reworking style in his poetry of love and desire that draws on Ovid is especially pronounced in his recasting of the voice of a male lover who nervously and frustratingly yearns for the beloved who is "so near yet so far."[37] When Ovid's style enables masculinity, a gap that divides the lovers is also the space in which masculinity is tested. In moments like that, appropriation raises questions about the moral basis of masculine agency. In the *Heroides*, Philip Hardie reminds us that "Leander tries to face-out the hyper-masculine wind-god Boreas."[38] But Shakespeare removes such obstacles (unless the Duke of Milan, the voice of normative order, counts as one) and replaces the young lover's confrontation with hyper-masculinity through a socially equal opponent: a rival friend. As the passages quoted from the *Heroides*, Epistle 18, show, Ovid's signature style is not only irony, but also the rhetoric of emotional quandary. This rhetoric stylizes the kind of "Ovidian emotion"[39] that lies at the heart of the adaptation of love's discourse in *The Two Gentlemen of Verona*. The Ovidian language of emotions brims with images, metaphors, and adjectives signifying emotional disturbance, since, as Valentine says, "in revenge of my contempt of love / Love hath chased sleep from my enthralled eyes, / And made them watchers of mine own heart's sorrow" (II, iv, 128–30). The pessimism of these lines shows the close association between Ovidian and Shakespearean rhetorical styles of writing about love where ful-fillment and happiness often tend to be overshadowed by anguish and hopelessness. In Valentine's speech, adjectives like "contemning," "imperious," "penitential," and "heart-sore" resonate with pessi-mism; and references to contempt, tears, sorrow, and sleeplessness ("Love hath chased sleep from my enthralled eyes") evoke dissolu-tion of a loving subject, showing how Shakespeare creatively inter-prets Ovid in his appropriation.[40]

This emotional depth, revealed from within this Ovidian speech, balances off the "noticeably regular and relatively simple" blank verse[41] for which Shakespeare's model lies elsewhere, in Christopher Marlowe. Turberville's translation of the *Heroides* 18 illustrates one of the thorny issues of adaptation: what is the degree of fidelity that exists between an imitated text and its adaptation? One way of understanding fidelity in adaptation is to think of it as "an ideal of exact duplication";[42] another is to consider it as loyalty to the other – that is, as not replicating the original but emulating its key elements in an adaptation. In his adaptation of Ovid, Turberville renders the story of Ovid's original:

> Thrise laide I downe my robes
>   to safe and sandie shore:
> And naked thrise assayed to swimme,
>   as oft I had before:
> But swelling waters made
>   me of my purpose saile,
> And by the force of forward streames
>   did drench me top and taisle.[43]

Turberville is more interested in getting the gist of the narrative than in appropriating the style and mood of the original. In contrast, Shakespeare invests his creative energy in channeling Ovid's height-ened style into emotion. Shakespeare's method of adaptation is thus more comprehensive in that it shows that adaptation is an "evolving category," moving from narrative to style and emotion.[44] In a play containing more verse than prose, the Ovidian style produces a new aesthetics of love. Proteus is "astounded"[45] by the "braggardism" (II, iv, 162) of Valentine's verses. But the stylistic affinity with the Ovidian intertext in Valentine's verses helps the exchange of emo-tion between friends and between male and female lovers in men's soliloquies. Shakespeare turns the ethics and agency of the Ovidian original into a new subject creation in this comedy.

What is new in *The Two Gentlemen of Verona* has neither impressed nor baffled critics. Jonathan Bate's point, that "[w]e cannot exactly praise Shakespeare for the originality of his invention in this play,"[46] illuminates Shakespeare as an imitator who does not stray too far away from his narrative source. The focus of Bate's judgment is the plot and story of an old lost play of Felismena and Felix. When read against Turberville's translation, Valentine's speech shows how Shakespeare reshaped and enriched the Ovidian original so that it fits the purpose that the soliloquy is given on the stage of a public theatre, as "the art of a character's self-examination at moments of emotional crisis."[47] Although the *Heroides* was "written from the point of view of women in mythology who are deserted by their lovers,"[48] Shakespeare turned this practice around and made his fictional men speak such intimate expositions.

In a play that is largely homosocial because of the friendship theme while containing the most brutal scenes of rape in all of Shakespeare's drama, Shakespeare appropriates Ovid's verse-epistles so that the emotional weight they carry compromises the romantic lover. Namely, by shifting the focus in his narrative on men writing verse-epistles as monologues of the self in love, Shakespeare not only reacts against grammar school teaching of the *Heroides*, but also shows that his play is more authentic than critics have been willing to give it credit. The material letter, imagined as a prop, complements the stylistic effect of the Ovidian verse-epistle. Julia rips up the letter she reads and imagines its pieces tossed in the sea just as the love theme in the play is tossed between a series of opposites, or "issues and tensions," which Tony Tanner identifies as "commitment and disloyalty, pursuit and rejection, love and betrayal, constancy and change."[49] The text showing the torn-up letter that Proteus has written to Julia closes, rather than confirms, the gap between distant lovers.

Around the same time when Shakespeare appropriated Ovid, debates about the goal of imitation dominated rhetorical historiography. Helen Moore has demonstrated in detail how Erasmus's comprehensive manuals of letter writing, *De conscribendis epistolis* (1522), and Angel Day's treatise on letter writing, *The English Secretorie* (1586), enabled examples of letters embedded in Elizabethan prose fiction, where they served as spaces through which male and female characters open themselves up to the scrutiny of the lover from whom they are separated. Such letters are carriers of secret desires and private thoughts, but also of the Ovidian styles of writing about love. Although one could argue that the same manuals of epistolary composition lie behind the form and rhetoric of the verse-epistles in Shakespeare's comedy, contemporaneous views of Ovid provide some evidence of what drew early modern writers to appropriate Ovid in their love writing.

In 1589, a year or two years before the *The Two Gentlemen of Verona* was written, George Puttenham's influential theory of poetry, *The Art of English Poesy*, contributed to the cultural debate about the fashion for Ovidian appropriations. Puttenham addressed the "reprehenders" among the poets of his time, who, like some of their medieval predecessors, "esteemed nothing that savoreth not of theology" and "care[d] for nothing but matters of policy and discourses of estate."[50] He urged such unpolished poets to abandon religious and political themes and devote their efforts to "the trifling poems" of love and passion written by Homer, Ovid, Virgil, and Catullus. "These poets were," Puttenham continues, "not of any gravity and seriousness, and many of them full of impudicity and ribaldry, as are not these of ours, nor for any good in the world should have been."[51] Puttenham's version of humanism is reflected in the space he devotes to commenting on humorous and erotic poetry.

There were other relevant views. Written probably in 1599, William Scott's *The Model of Poesy* is a lively discussion of the nature of poetry that complements Sir Philip Sidney's poetical treatise. It also provides direct evidence of the period's use of Ovid as a model for new writing. Scott addresses Ovid's impact on his contemporaries by pointing out that despite the thematic and therefore also expressive crudities of Ovid's poetry, Ovid proves to be an irresistible influence on those writers willing to show that "neither doth anything sound well that is not graced with some of Ovid's gross fables of their esteemed gods . . . so unreverend are Ovid's fictions of their divinities; and we thoroughly imitate them."[52] Scott acknowledges that the appropriation of irreverent and gross – massive, luxuriant (with a hint of deviance), and excessive – tales of gods' desires and bodies from Ovid's writing challenges and calls into question the imitations of Christian religious iconography in poetry.

Yet the divine inspiration that moves Shakespeare to craft new poetry of love in what is probably his earliest play is not the Christian God but Orpheus, Ovid's god of somber love music, as presented in *Ars amatoria* (III, 590). In response to Duke's comment that "much is the force of heaven-bred poesy" (III, ii, 71), Proteus replies that "Orpheus' lute was strung with poets' sinews / Whose golden touch could soften steel and stones, / Make tigers tame, and huge leviathans / Forsake unsounded deeps to dance on sands" (III, ii, 77–80).

The phrase "unsounded deep" contains traces of the Ovidian style, evident in the pairing of nouns with adjectives, like "troubled sea," "raging deep," or "fronting surge," which the reader can find in the *Heroides* (XVIII, 25). Scott would have been familiar with the trend of turning to Ovid, not the reformed Church of England, for stylistic models and emotional, especially amorous, fulfilment. He suggests, in this long passage in which he credits new imitations of Ovid as a refreshing move in writing poetry in his age, that Ovid's works became the target of criticism launched by theologians. However, Arthur Golding, the most influential translator of Ovid in the sixteenth century, was a devout Calvinist who defended Ovid in the dedicatory epistle to Robert, Earl of Leicester, a piece of text which precedes the 1567 edition of his translation of the *Metamorphoses*.[53] This criticism did not slow down the tempo of Ovidian appropriation in late Elizabethan England. Thus, Georgia Brown has argued, that "[t]he reinterpretation of Ovid [was] the catalyst for cultural change in the 1590s," and she documented that Ovid played a major role in redefining "late Elizabethan literary practice."[54]

At the heart of this poetic redefinition undertaken in the spirit of the humanist thinking about learned interiority, Shakespeare's *The Two Gentlemen of Verona* can be regarded a comedic masterpiece in the growing repertoire of the new comedy written and staged in the early 1590s. Although critics still tend to treat *The Two Gentlemen of Verona* as if it were an unsatisfying play, the play's distinctive Ovidian flavor connects it with some of the most authentic and striking aesthetic re-envisaging of Ovid in the 1590s. It is evident, for instance, that Shakespeare was attracted to the boldness of Leander as an unstoppable lover when he invokes him by the name, this time in relation to Valentine, as "bold Leander" embarking on the "adventure" (III, i, 120) of climbing "a ladder quaintly made of cords" (117) to Silvia's bedroom. As Roger Warren suggests, these lines are most likely a "conflation" of two passages from *Ars Amatoria*.[55] This conflation, however, anticipates a more extensive appropriation of the Ovidian poetic form that follows, the letter-form modelled on the *Heroides*.

The Duke of Milan finds Valentine's letter written to Silvia inside Valentine's cloak, which the lover left next to the rope ladder that he used to climb into Silvia's room. Shakespeare uses the letter to segue into a soliloquy, treating Valentine's interiority as a lover's public display of amorous emotions. In this instance, Ovid provides Shakespeare with both the form and content that fill this letter. The lover's thoughts are presented as a form of wished-for enslavement:

My thoughts do harbour with my Silvia nightly,
And slaves they are to me, that send them flying.
O, could their master come and go as lightly,
Himself would lodge where, senseless, they are lying. (III, i, 140–3)

Valentine's unmistakably Ovidian epistle shows the influence of Ovid's gross and "unreverend" fable, to echo Scott; it illustrates how such Ovidian style is both about "choice-making implicit in a writer's language" as well as "his showmanship in language."[56] In both Valentine's letter and in Leander's Ovidian Epistle 18, senses and thoughts are the text's subject. The letter provides Valentine with space and isolation to speak his amorous anguish in a way that Shakespeare will continue to develop in his later drama, as he makes his soliloquies more nuanced, stylistically more complicated, and ethically more complex. Ovid's epistle spoken by a romantic lover, gushing out language while speaking about the longing for Hero, provides a stylistic model for Shakespeare to imagine a similar lover, Valentine, enwrapped in thoughts about his missing beloved, Silvia. Valentine composes a speech arising from his "pure bosom" (III, i, 144) out of which this Elizabethan lover "heralds" (III, i, 144) his thoughts of love, as his classical model does, too.

Shakespeare's creative revival of Ovid's style shows that appropriation is as much essential to the formation of the amorous self and the notion of romantic love as it is central to the adaptation of themes and engagement with politics, including gendered politics, and the discourse of history. Appropriation, Christy Desmet and Sujata Iyengar have argued, has been "intrinsic to building a self" and proven to be "political in import."[57] Shakespeare's aesthetic appropriation of Ovid shows both how the persona of the male lover is created in dramatic poetry and how the politics of friendship defines social and romantic relationships in the play. The Ovidian verse-epistle shows how Ovid was appropriated as a linguistic and especially stylistic model for representing the lover's inner turmoil caused by separation. Critics who have written about the use of rhetoric in Elizabethan writing have typically, and rightly, focused on assessing the role numerous manuals played in shaping individual composition. Yet in a culture that looked back at classics as models for composition, classical literary writers, not just theoreticians, were equally important sources of linguistic and stylistic rules and formulas that were both appropriated and reacted against.

In her brief but influential critical summary of style, rhetoric, and decorum that characterize Shakespeare's writing in the first half of the 1590s, Lynne Magnusson has asked the question that offers itself to any critic engaging with Shakespeare's earliest plays, plays whose fate in their own time was sometimes diametrically opposed to the neglect they have often suffered in modern criticism. Magnusson asks, "What, above all, set the youthful Shakespeare in the 1590s on a course that would make him the most widely admired both of canonical and of popular authors in English was his astonishing aptitude with language."[58] Magnusson proceeds to explain this effect of Shakespeare's writing: "What especially fostered his talents for verbal risk-taking and display and created an audience that took pleasure in performative language was a renewed emphasis in sixteenth-century education on rhetoric."[59] Magnusson is one of the critics who have documented the scope of the rich indebtedness of Shakespearean eloquence rhetorical theory and practice, and classroom education, especially showing how effects of classical rhetoric emerged.[60] The Shakespeare of *The Two Gentlemen of Verona* is deeply indebted to Ovid as a stylistic and a linguistic model. Ovid aids Shakespeare in shaping the kind of language that brings moving intensity and emotional naturalness, allowing male romantic heroes to speak in ways that such heroes had not fully spoken to their contemporary audiences before.

Because criticism has been invested in demonstrating how Shakespeare reconfigures Ovid's ideology of love and sexuality, and less on exploring how Shakespeare appropriated Ovid's style and strategies of amorous persuasion, the Ovidian influence on the comedic style of the 1590s has only recently become the subject of sustained and exciting new critical evaluation.[61] "The youthful Shakespeare in the 1590s," from Magnusson's account,[62] owes as much to the style of Ovid as a model for linguistic composition as he does to the love stories and myths that Shakespeare imitated from the beginning to the end of his career. Shakespeare's engagement with Ovidian style and language was as extensive as it was in his encounter with other classical authors used as models for *imitatio*, such as Cicero, Virgil, Quintilian, or Horace, as Lynn Enterline has demonstrated recently. Although Enterline does not take up *The Two Gentlemen of Verona* as a play related to the classroom practice of Ovidian imitations, her methodological question concerning how "grammar school training influence . . . counted as genteel masculinity," that in turn affected "experiences of sexuality and desire,"[63] encourages us to think of Shakespeare's Ovidian appropriations of the style of men's emotional turmoil as an expression of romantic masculinity with which the Shakespearean comedy of the 1590s became preoccupied.

The Ovidian soliloquy, telling about love's pain as spoken in situations describing men's separation from women, shows the romanticized masculinization of the Ovidian eloquence of lament in the verse-epistle turned into the subject of comedy. And verse-epistle is already a form of rhetorical performance. This performance of style – a male lover masculinizes the rhetoric of a female verse-epistle – is gendered in the *Heroides*, where Ovid gives as much space to male as to female voices. The passions of classical characters foster in Shakespeare's drama new styles of writing about such emotions. The analysis of the Ovidian style of the verse-epistle, which gives men's subjectivity a new emotional voice, illustrates on a limited set of examples the extent to which the study of letters as aesthetic, poetic, and literary facts only extends what scholars of the material letter have recently flagged as a methodological problem. When James Daybell and Andrew Gordon write that "[t]he study of early modern letters finds itself poised at a crossroads,"[64] they consider the material letter, not verse-epistle or such poetic letters turned into dramatic poetry framed as letters. But they encourage scholars to consider letter writing as a rhetorical performance, and from a different perspective, where the styles of fictional epistles played a key role in making *The Two Gentlemen of Verona* a deeply Ovidian play.

Notes

1. I have adopted the date proposed by the editors of the Oxford *Complete Works* of Shakespeare, 2nd edn (Shakespeare, *The Complete Works*). This date is also confirmed by Roger Warren, the editor of the single edition of the Oxford Shakespeare, from which I quote Shakespeare's text throughout this chapter (Shakespeare, *The Two Gentlemen of Verona*).
2. Burrow, *Shakespeare and Classical Antiquity*, p. 92.
3. Pigman, "Versions of Imitation," p. 2.
4. Ibid. p. 2.
5. Greene, *The Light in Troy*, p. 19.
6. Huang and Rivlin, *Shakespeare and the Ethics*, p. 2.
7. Oakley-Brown, *Ovid and the Cultural*, p. 4.
8. Ibid. p. 3.
9. Ibid. p. 2.
10. Ibid. p. 3.
11. Armstrong, *Ovid and His Love Poetry*, p. 140.
12. Moore, "Elizabethan Fiction," p. 42.
13. Ibid. p. 43.
14. Ibid. p. 43.

15. I have adapted Thomas M. Greene's phrase "semiotic universe" to describe a process of transmission of the language matrix from a source to its recipient, in his study of imitation in the Renaissance. Greene, *The Light in Troy*, p. 21.
16. Bate, *Shakespeare and Ovid*, p. 33.
17. Stewart, *Shakespeare's Letters*, p. 61.
18. Wells, "The Failure of *The Two Gentlemen*," p. 49.
19. Chambers, *The Two Gentlemen of Verona*, p. 49.
20. Braden, "Translating the Rest of Ovid," p. 46.
21. Bate, *Shakespeare and Ovid*, p. 110.
22. Carroll, "'And above you 'gainst,'" p. 57.
23. Burrow, *Shakespeare and Classical*, p. 95.
24. Hardie, *Ovid's Poetics*, p. 50.
25. The original in a modern edition of Ovid reads as follows: "*[I]llud amicitae quondam venerabile nomen / prostat et in quaestu pro meretrice sedet.*" Quoted from *Ex ponto*, II, iii, 19–20 in Ovid, *Tristia*.
26. See translation in note 25.
27. Carter, *Ovidian Myth and Sexual Deviance*, p. 4.
28. Bolgar, "Classical Reading," p. 21, elaborates on this point.
29. Bolgar, "Classical Reading," pp. 20–1; Bolgar, *The Classical Heritage*, pp. 185–9; and Martindale and Martindale, *Shakespeare and the Uses*, pp. 45–90, provide evidence of the role the *Metamorphoses* and *Tristia* in grammar school education.
30. Brown, *Friendship and Its Discourses*, p. 71.
31. The Latin original reads as follows: "*Septima nox agitur, spatium mihi longius anno, sollicitum raucis ut mare fervet aquis. / his egosi vidi mulcentem pectora somnum / noctibus, insani sit mora longa freti! / rupe sedens aliqua specto tua litora tristis / et, quo non possum corpose, mente feror. / lumina quin etiam summa vigilantia turre / aut vide taut acies nostra videre putat. / ter mihi deposita est in sicca vestis harena; / ter grave temptavi carpere nudus iter—/ obstitit inceptis tumidum iuvenalibus aequor, / mersit ed advesis ora natantis aquis*" (25–36). Ovid, *Heroides*, p. 246.
32. Huang and Rivlin, *Shakespeare and the Ethics*, p. 2.
33. See Keith and Rupp, *Metamorphosis: The Changing Face*, and Lafont, *Shakespeare's Erotic Mythology*.
34. Bate, *Soul of the Age*, p. 117.
35. Rimell, *Ovid's Lovers*, p. 125.
36. Fox, *Ovid and the Politics*, and Starks-Estes, *Violence, Trauma, and Virtus*.
37. Hardie, *Ovid's Poetics*, p. 142.
38. Ibid. p. 142.
39. Fox, *Ovid and the Politics*, p. 59.
40. I borrow Desmet and Iyengar's point about appropriation being both "interpretative and creative"; see Desmet and Iyengar, "Adaptation, Appropriation," p. 11.

41. McDonald, *Shakespeare and the Arts*, p. 94.
42. Lanier, "Afterword," p. 296.
43. Turberville, *The heroycall epistles*, sigs. G5v–G6r.
44. Kidnie, *Shakespeare and the Problem*, p. 5.
45. Charney, *Shakespeare's Style*, p. 29.
46. Bate, *The Genius of Shakespeare*, p. 134.
47. Bate, *Soul of the Age*, p. 117.
48. Ibid. p. 117.
49. Tanner, *Prefaces to Shakespeare*, p. 60.
50. Puttenham, *The Art of English Poesy*, p. 199.
51. Ibid. p. 199.
52. Scott, *The Model of Poesy*, p. 42.
53. Ovid, *Ovid's Metamorphoses*, pp. 5–22.
54. Brown, *Redefining Elizabethan Literature*, p. 36.
55. Shakespeare, *The Two Gentlemen of Verona*, p. 128, note to lines 119–20.
56. Magnusson, "Style, Rhetoric and Decorum," p. 17.
57. Desmet and Iyengar, "Adaptation, Appropriation," p. 14.
58. Magnusson, "Style, Rhetoric and Decorum," p. 17.
59. Ibid. p.17.
60. Magnusson, "Mixed Messages," pp. 132–55.
61. See Weaver, *Untutored Lines*; Burrow, *Shakespeare and Classical*, pp. 92–132; Wiseman, *Writing Metamorphosis*; and Enterline, "Elizabethan Minor Epic," pp. 253–89.
62. Magnusson, "Style, Rhetoric and Decorum," p. 17.
63. Enterline, *Shakespeare's Schoolroom*, p. 22.
64. Daybell and Gordon, "Introduction," p. 19.

Bibliography

Armstrong, Rebecca, *Ovid and His Love Poetry* (London: Duckworth, 2005).
Bate, Jonathan, *The Genius of Shakespeare* (London: Picador, 1997).
Bate, Jonathan, *Shakespeare and Ovid* (Oxford: Oxford University Press, 1994).
Bate, Jonathan, *Soul of the Age: The Life, Mind and World of William Shakespeare* (London: Penguin Books, 2008).
Bolgar, R. R., *The Classical Heritage and Its Beneficiaries* (Cambridge: Cambridge University Press, 1977).
Bolgar, R. R., "Classical Reading in Renaissance Schools," *Durham Research Review* 6, 1955, pp. 18–24.
Braden, Gordon, "Translating the Rest of Ovid: The Exile Poems," in K. Newman and J. Tylus (eds), *Early Modern Cultures of Translation* (Philadelphia: University of Pennsylvania Press, 2016).

Brown, Cedric C., *Friendship and Its Discourses in the Seventeenth Century* (Oxford: Oxford University Press, 2016).

Brown, Georgia, *Redefining Elizabethan Literature* (Cambridge: Cambridge University Press, 2004).

Burrow, Colin, *Shakespeare and Classical Antiquity* (Oxford: Oxford University Press, 2013).

Carroll, William C., "'And above you 'gainst the nature of love': Ovid, Rape, and *The Two Gentlemen of Verona*," in A. B. Taylor (ed.), *Shakespeare's Ovid: "The Metamorphoses" in the Plays and Poems* (Cambridge: Cambridge University Press, 2000), pp. 49–65.

Carter, Sarah, *Ovidian Myth and Sexual Deviance in Early Modern English Literature* (New York: Palgrave Macmillan, 2011).

Chambers, E. K., *The Two Gentlemen of Verona*, in *Shakespeare: A Survey* (London: Sidgwick and Jackson, [1925] 1963), pp. 49–57.

Charney, Maurice, *Shakespeare's Style* (Madison and Teaneck, NJ: Fairleigh Dickinson University Press, 2014).

Daybell, James, and Andrew Gordon, "Introduction: The Early Modern Letter Opener," in James Daybell and Andrew Gordon (eds), *Cultures of Correspondence in Early Modern Britain* (Philadelphia: University of Pennsylvania Press, 2016), pp. 1–26.

Desmet, Christy and Sujata Iyengar, "Adaptation, Appropriation, or What You Will," *Shakespeare* 11.1, 2015, pp. 10–19.

Enterline, Lynn, "Elizabethan Minor Epic," in Patrick Cheney and Philip Hardie (eds), *The Oxford History of Classical Reception in English Literature: Vol. 2: 1558–1660* (Oxford: Oxford University Press, 2015), pp. 253–89.

Enterline, Lynn, *Shakespeare's Schoolroom: Rhetoric, Discipline, Emotion* (Philadelphia: University of Pennsylvania Press, 2012).

Fox, Cora, *Ovid and the Politics of Emotion in Elizabethan England* (New York: Palgrave Macmillan, 2009).

Gosnold, Paul, "De amicitia," ms. V.a.478 (The Folger Shakespeare Library, 1625).

Greene, Thomas M., *The Light in Troy: Imitation and Discovery in Renaissance Poetry* (New Haven and London: Yale University Press, 1982).

Hardie, Philip, *Ovid's Poetics of Illusion* (Cambridge: Cambridge University Press, 2002).

Huang, Alexa and Elizabeth Rivlin (eds), *Shakespeare and the Ethics of Appropriation* (New York: Palgrave Macmillan, 2014).

Keith, Alison and Stephen Rupp (eds), *Metamorphosis: The Changing Face of Ovid in Medieval and Early Modern Europe* (Toronto: Centre for Reformation and Renaissance Studies, 2007).

Kidnie, Margaret Jane, *Shakespeare and the Problem of Adaptation* (London and New York: Routledge, 2009).

Lafont, Agnès (ed.), *Shakespeare's Erotic Mythology and Ovidian Renaissance Culture* (Farnham and Burlington: Ashgate, 2013).

Lanier, Douglas M., "Shakespeare / Not Shakespeare: Afterword," in Christy Desmet, Natalie Loper, and Jim Casey (eds), *Shakespeare / Not Shakespeare* (New York: Palgrave Macmillan, 2017), pp. 293–306.

McDonald, Russ, *Shakespeare and the Arts of Language* (Oxford: Oxford University Press, 2001).

Magnusson, Lynne, "Mixed Messages and Cicero Effect in the Herrick Family Letters of the Sixteenth Century," in James Daybell and Andrew Gordon (eds), *Cultures of Correspondence in Early Modern Britain* (Philadelphia: University of Pennsylvania Press, 2016), pp. 132–55.

Magnusson, Lynne, "Style, Rhetoric and Decorum," in Silvia Adamson, Lynette Hunter, Lynne Magnusson, Ann Thompson, and Katie Wales (eds), *Reading Shakespeare's Dramatic Language: A Guide* (London: Thomson Learning, 2007), pp. 17–30.

Martindale, Charles and Michelle Martindale, *Shakespeare and the Uses of Antiquity: An Introductory Essay* (London and New York: Routledge, 1990).

Moore, H., "Elizabethan Fiction and Ovid's *Heroides*," *Translation and Literature* 9, 2000, pp. 40–54.

Oakley-Brown, Liz, *Ovid and the Cultural Politics of Translation in Early Modern England* (Farnham and Burlington: Ashgate, 2006).

Ovid, *Heroides. Amores*, 2nd edn, Grant Showerman (trans.), revised by G. P. Goold (Cambridge, MA: Harvard University Press and London: William Heinemann, 1986).

Ovid, *Ovid's Metamorphoses: Translated by Arthur Golding*, Madeleine Forey (ed.) (Baltimore: Johns Hopkins University Press, 2001).

Ovid, *Tristia. Ex Ponto*, 2nd edn, A. L. Wheeler (trans.), revised by G. P. Goold (Cambridge, MA: Harvard University Press, 1996 and London: William Heinemann, 1988).

Pigman III, G. W., "Versions of Imitation in the Renaissance," *Renaissance Quarterly* 33.1, 1980, pp. 1–32.

Puttenham, George, *The Art of English Poesy*, F. Whigham and W. A. Rebhorn (eds) (Ithaca and London: Cornell University Press, [1589] 2007).

Rimell, Victoria, *Ovid's Lovers: Desire, Difference, and the Poetic Imagination* (Cambridge: Cambridge University Press, 2006).

Scott, William, *The Model of Poesy*, Gavin Alexander (ed.) (Oxford: Oxford University Press, [1599?] 2013).

Shakespeare, William, *The Complete Works*, 2nd edn, J. Jowett, W. Montgomery, G. Taylor, and S. Wells (eds) (Oxford: Oxford University Press, 2005).

Shakespeare, William, *The Two Gentlemen of Verona*, R. Warren (ed.) (Oxford: Oxford University Press, 2008).

Starks-Estes, Lisa S., *Violence, Trauma, and* Virtus *in Shakespeare's Roman Poems and Plays: Transforming Ovid* (Basingstoke: Palgrave Macmillan, 2014).

Stewart, Alan, *Shakespeare's Letters* (Oxford: Oxford University Press, 2008).

Tanner, Tony, *Prefaces to Shakespeare* (Cambridge, MA and London: The Belknap Press of Harvard University Press, 2010).

Turberville, George, *The heroycall epistles of the learned poet Publius Ouidius Naso, in English verse* (London: Henrie Denham, 1570?), STC 18942.

Weaver, William P., *Untutored Lines: The Making of the Epyllion* (Edinburgh: Edinburgh University Press, 2012).

Wells, Stanley, "The Failure of *The Two Gentlemen of Verona*," in Stanley Wells, *Shakespeare on Page & Stage: Selected Essays* (Oxford: Oxford University Press, 2016), pp. 49–57.

Wiseman, Susan, *Writing Metamorphosis in the English Renaissance, 1550–1700* (Cambridge: Cambridge University Press, 2014).

Part IV

Ovid Remixed: Transmedial, Rhizomatic, and Hyperreal Adaptations

"Truly, and very notably discharg'd": The Metamorphosis of Pyramus and Thisbe and the Place of Appropriation on the Early Modern Stage

Louise Geddes

Literary studies has traditionally constructed appropriation as a derivative act that emerges as a parasitic offshoot to the source text, creating a space between an author's own appropriative practices and contemporary reimaginings.[1] Recent work on transformative Shakespeares, however, articulates new ways to think about the larger networked relationships that span centuries of intellectual and creative "use." As Douglas M. Lanier notes in his essay, "Post-Textual Shakespeare," twentieth-century popular culture is "marked by repeated efforts to loosen the ties between Shakespeare and the words he wrote in an effort to recover Shakespeare's cultural authority for a wider popular appropriation," expanding the meaning of a source text far beyond narrative or linguistic structures.[2] As Lanier makes clear, the site of adaptation is no longer to be found in the language alone, but instead, through a looser identification of author or text – one that also encompasses a "transmedial set of objects" that converge to constitute a given work.[3] The contemporary recognition of a fragmented source ties modern Shakespeare appropriations to a larger practice of textual deconstruction and circulation that was common on the early modern stage and is evidenced in Shakespeare's use of Ovid in *A Midsummer Night's Dream*.

To recognize a nebulous and ever-shifting notion of source as the uncertain ground upon which later artists build work is to destabilize the understanding of appropriation as a strictly linear series of reworkings and reject approaches that privilege fidelity. Instead, as Margaret Jane Kidnie rightfully notes, the process is the dominant feature of the appropriative act, which allows the "cultural, geo-graphical, or ideological differences between work and adaptation" to be mapped onto a network of diverse texts into complex relation-ships with one another.[4] Such approaches recognize appropriation as "a study of reception" and positions appropriators as both consum-ers and producers simultaneously.[5] Appropriation, then, constructs a "dialogic transaction" between the metacritical practices of the early modern stage and Ovid's own use of his source material, suggest-ing a wider network of use than source study generally allows for.[6] Shakespeare's use of Pyramus and Thisbe is a pivotal transmedial remix of Ovid that embodies the core appropriative theory of the transformative text as unfinished artifact brought to fruition by the contemporary artist. Moreover, as Shakespeare's overwriting of Ovid takes hold, it alters the generic identity of Pyramus and Thisbe and offers instruction on how to treat remixed material.

As Lanier argues, rhizomatic theories of appropriation welcome erratic and shifting points of contact that arise as an appropriative culture evolves around a given text, suggesting that "the Shakespeare rhizome is never a stable object but an aggregated field in a per-petual state of becoming."[7] The rhizomatic approach is part of a broader appropriative theory that "thinks less about relationships between discrete objects than of networks of relationships consti-tuted by agents, both human and non-human."[8] The rhizome rejects the linearity that characterizes studies of Shakespeare's sources, as it rejects any understanding of appropriation as derivative, and asks critics to rethink Shakespeare's relationship to Ovid. Jonathan Bate's seminal critical study, for example, refers to *A Midsummer Night's Dream* as a "displaced dramatization,"[9] characterizing the work as a well-constructed "*imitatio*"[10] rather than recognizing a rich network of work that encapsulates Shakespeare's own remediating practice, which would displace the notion of a core canonical text and instead imagine a de-territorialized text that allows practitioners the liberty of tapping into the "spirit"[11] of Shakespeare or Ovid, through a com-plex, and often abstract network of associations.

Bate's assumption of a linear progression of influence that sees Shakespeare as demonstrating a cool-eyed appraisal of "his great original, as a good imitator should," is echoed in a critical meth-odology that is resistant to ceding part of Shakespeare's greatness to his collaborators.[12] A. B. Taylor affirms Shakespeare's genius by suggesting that the use is "complex, drawing on a varying array of eclectic, copious secondary sources, 'englysshe,' and with deep, reso-nant mythic undertones."[13] Questions of the collaborative nature of theatre production aside,[14] such reading is predicated on a notion of textual purity and isolates Shakespeare from his own network of transformative and transforming works. What this chapter intends to show is early modern period's own participation in a culture of remixing material and, in particular, how an affirmation of "fannish" enthusiasm at the heart of the remediated Pyramus and Thisbe is a justification for transformative appropriation that reflects "the processes, products, and politics of signification"[15] that concerned Ovid. Ovid himself shaped his erotic texts as an "ongoing process of interaction" with Roman culture, offering text as a bricolage of subversive explorations of mythology.[16] Moreover, as Lowell Edmund notes, Ovid used humor to draw attention to his own remixes of Roman sources through playfully erroneous citation, to suggest the subjectivity inherent in Rome's construction of its own identity.[17] As such, the early modern remixes of Pyramus and Thisbe assert a fidelity to the spirit of Ovid, while satirizing those who invest too deeply in textual authority.

When appropriated by Shakespeare, Pyramus and Thisbe's critique of the creative impulse fruitfully unsettles the determinacy of the playwright's vision, bringing Shakespeare's commentary of authorial identity in line with contemporary discourses such as performance studies, remix theory, and fan studies, all of which share a common investment in more participatory iterations of a given work. Performance theory's insistence on a clear distinction between "work" and "event"[18] "asserts a richly materialized semiosis, one that enforces an intellectual, sensory, affective encounter with an estranged worldliness, representation balanced within the process of its presenting."[19] Likewise, remixing, which is the reconfiguration of one or more extant works, blended to suit the technological platforms available, is a popular and legally contentious practice among digital practitioners, born out of a fan-like appreciation of a given text. Remixing, envisioned as a practice of "reconceptualizing found footage,"[20] is production-as-consumption that celebrates appropriation through its primary focus on the skills of the remixer or DJ. It is dependent on the new technology at hand, whether it be beatbox, turntable, digital music, or video software. Remixing centers itself around an irreverent yet appreciative claim on its source text. Although it recognizes the remixer's own skill, remixing emerges from a place of fan-like enjoyment of the transformative text. Both performances and remixes enforce an unabashed desire to remodel the original text into a visible demonstration of transformation and, in Pyramus and Thisbe's example, repeatedly subjects the Ovidian text to the material conditions of its reproduction. Moreover, remixing heavily incorporates the visual arts; Pyramus and Thisbe, with its emphasis on tableaux, the thrill of seeing a lion, and the intoxicating presence of blood, could easily mirror the "digital utterance expressed across the verbal, the aural, and the visual"[21] that characterizes remix praxis.

Furthermore, to privilege fan practice as an essential part of Pyramus and Thisbe's remix is to undermine the assumption of a strictly derivative relationship between the multiple texts at play in this history and emphasize affective enthusiasm of the everyday cultural consumer. Pyramus and Thisbe succeeds as the case study for a more visible process of appropriation because *A Midsummer Night's Dream* authorizes fans to engage with the work on their own terms, consistent with twenty-first-century theories of participatory culture. Fan cultures demonstrate near boundless enthusiasm for their subjects, and one of the most common by-products of this devotion is derivative art – tributes, or explorations, in art, literature, and video. Fans remix, recreate, and retell variations of their chosen text, celebrating their identity as fans as well as the processes of recycling that allow the canon of what constitutes the text continuously to expand. Moreover, there is a subversive element to fan practices, as they challenge the traditional model of consumption that relegates the appropriator to a subservient and passive position in regards to the "original" text. It rejects the notion of the limits placed on the source object, instead recognizing an ongoing transformation that is dependent on the energies of the consumer and the technology available to manifest new iterations. Participatory culture ideally provides "opportunities to create and share culture"[22] with an aspiration of building stronger networks between art and its communities. Shakespeare's remix, which focuses on a parody of staging techniques and blends the well-worn tragedy with a satire on medieval guild plays, is well-positioned to exemplify the value of fan-oriented remixes as a model of appropriative critical study, particularly when applied to the transition between print and performance. The metacritical identity in which Shakespeare divests Ovid's lovers sets in motion a new network of appropriation that empowers the framework of amateur performance by drawing attention to the process as a product of affective pleasure. Pyramus and Thisbe quite literally becomes Grossman's "affective billboard"[23] for its combination of literary pleasure, commercial aspirations, and the unadulterated enthusiasm of the artisans, who blend their beloved text with all the affordances of their medium. As such, Pyramus and Thisbe transitions from work to event, activated and reactivated by further remixing the text with new performative forms and technologies.

By the late sixteenth century, as Lisa S. Starks-Estes notes, "reading Ovid was intrinsic to Renaissance theories of learning and translation," and this practice was manifest in a dual pedagogical emphasis on allegorical and historical reading.[24] Pyramus and Thisbe's relative ubiquity in the medieval and early modern classroom[25] facilitated a regular output of appropriative iterations, many of which were infused with the medieval emphasis on a didactic principle that recognized intemperance as the source of the tragedy, overlooking the Ovidian playfulness that identifies tragedy as a generative source in itself. As Liz Oakley-Brown notes, "the type of hermeneutic that Ovid's narrative invites is one placed within the context of translation and transformation";[26] and during the late sixteenth century, Ovid was both translated and transformed. Pyramus and Thisbe emerged randomly in literary ephemera – in miscellanies, frontispieces of books, and broadsides, all of which contributed to the text's reputation as a juvenile, and largely unremarkable, tragedy. The rise of the "new Ovidianism"[27] that peaked during the 1590s manifested itself in new transformative works that drew from Ovid's own enthusiasm for remixing his sources and found inspiration in *The Metamorphoses'* free-wheeling structure and tonal instability. This new approach to translating Ovid was characterized by the work of Arthur Golding, who "remained faithful to the spirit of Ovid's original – its energy and vitality – while adapting it to his own culture and landscape."[28]

Shakespeare visited Pyramus and Thisbe twice around 1595, once as a recontextualized adaptation that absorbed medieval visual reworkings of Ovid, and then as a remix that more carefully explores the principles of transmedial appropriation.[29] Although, as Starks explores within this volume, Shakespeare's use of Ovid is a rhizomatic structure that incorporates Arthur Brooke's 1562 *Romeus and Juliet*, his final images in *Romeo and Juliet* directly intersect with Pyramus and Thisbe, drawing on the more static representations of Thisbe in the image of Juliet lamenting her forbidden lover's suicide. Although Shakespeare alters the theatrical device to keep his lovers from convening (as *A Midsummer Night's Dream* makes evident, the lion is simply too absurd to stage with any efficacy), his text, like medieval appropriations of Ovid, essentially relies on tableaux, offering a more formal adaptation that is consistent with the structured fight scenes and set-pieces that characterize the play. *Romeo and Juliet's* remediation onstage suggests a moralistic homage to an Ovid that has been filtered through Chaucer, Gower, and Golding.

The lovers' lamentations and suicides are a stilted, passive recontextualization of Ovid, but the new medium of theatre invited a more rambunctious form of play. In *A Midsummer Night's Dream*, Shakespeare remixes Pyramus and Thisbe more aggressively, examining the media at his disposal in *Romeo and Juliet*, to play with theatrical conventions and engender collaboration by carving out a space for the clowns to play. Pyramus and Thisbe is used to consider the stage as medium, and to rethink the relationship between the performer and their text. Through Pyramus and Thisbe, Shakespeare critiques, celebrates, and, ultimately, manages the populism of the actors in his company by curtailing the actor's improvisational impulse, striking a delicate balance between amateur enthusiasm and clear-eyed professionalism that will in turn be exploited by later artists, who will use Ovid's own metacritical awareness as tacit authorization to privilege remediated use over textual fidelity.

The failure of the would-be Proteus is crucial to the success of Pyramus and Thisbe, resulting in a focus on the visibility of the appropriative process, rather than the end product. Thomas P. Harrison suggests that "the Pyramus play becomes comic only through the actors, never the plot,"[30] but Shakespeare goes further and uses Pyramus and Thisbe to celebrate fan enthusiasm and affirm the value of affective investment in art. In the play-within-a-play, Shakespeare remixed the popular Ovidian tragic archetype with the form of satire evident in the medieval guild tradition from which the artisans drew; indeed, the failed artistry of Bottom and company recalls the inept workmen of the York Play of the Crucifixion, or as Clifford Davidson notes, those in the Coventry cycle.[31] The remix is given new life by a conscious juxtaposition of the older technologies of stagecraft, evidenced in the concern with the casement window; with the more modern theatrical spectacle represented by the fairies and lovers in the Athenian wood; and with the transformation that overcomes Bottom. By making the artisans blissfully unaware of their archaic stage practices, Shakespeare sets them up to fail, only to redeem them through another theatrical device – the audience within an audience, which simultaneously encourages our laughter and our sympathy.

Moreover, the artisans' unbridled enthusiasm for the art form in which they are aspiring to participate redeems their failure and transforms the tragedy into a comedy of overblown ambition and a celebration of fan passion. Bottom's enjoyment of literature in general is repeatedly illustrated in his wholesale commitment to his artistry, and his deference to Peter Quince's ability to realize his dreams in ballad form. Nick Bottom is his own affective billboard. His enthusiasm is infectious, and it reinvigorates the terrible performance of Pyramus and Thisbe, promising entertainment for anyone willing to meet the work halfway. Following Theseus's admonition, that terrible actors are "no worse, if imagination amend them" (V, i, 212),[32] Hyppolita allows herself to invest in the performance and is rewarded accordingly. Arguably, even the derisive commentary that the Athenians offer the mechanicals constitutes a form of participation and ensures that the watching audience in the playhouse commits to understanding and enjoying their failure. Shakespeare remediates Pyramus and Thisbe by the presence of the double audience and furthermore infers that there is a hubristic quality to a structurally faithful adaptation, parodying the mimetic approach in a play that otherwise joyfully embraces the protean nature of the artist.

Framed by the theatrical metamorphoses of *A Midsummer Night's Dream*, Shakespeare's appropriation of Pyramus and Thisbe renders Ovid clearly recognizable and affiliates it with the juvenilia that Quince presumably remembered from the schoolroom. And yet, the playful remix of the tragedy for comedic purposes remains recognizably Ovidian, particularly when situated as part of the larger transformative erotics of *A Midsummer Night's Dream*. However, Pyramus and Thisbe's well-crafted and compact dramaturgy appealed as an event in itself and, in the early seventeenth century, it was annexed from the play as a whole, with the attribution shifting away from Ovid and towards Shakespeare. The continuation of the text as tragedy was largely consistent with its presence in print; the ongoing life of the text as a comedy occurred in the theatre where it could transform every point of contact with new artists and new stage practices. In print, Pyramus and Thisbe was relegated to a kind of flyover status in texts such as Francis Davidson's 1611 *A Poetical Rapsodie*, William Lisle's 1631 *The Faire Ethiopian*, Dunstan Gale's forgettable 1616 tragedy, and a wealth of smaller references in anonymous pamphlets such as *Pyramus and Thisbe: Love's Masterpiece*. In 1624, however, a private performance of an unnamed text for the Bishop of Lincoln resulted in the host being fined for producing the entertainment on a Sunday, and "the court also decreed that a principal player of the unnamed play be put in the stocks, wearing an ass's head with a bundle of hay at his feet."[33] While these small citations are not conclusive or even strong evidence that the text was in greater circulation as a comedy, if one considers the network of iterations that communicated the text to Andreas Gryphius, through Daniel Schwenter and the English

Comedians, James Shirley's *Masque of Beauty*, and anonymous drolls, such as *The Merry Conceited Humours of Bottom the Weaver*, it is not unreasonable to assume that the remix of Pyramus and Thisbe was in wide enough circulation to be a recognizable trope.

The evidence from such texts as the anonymous 1646–7 droll, entitled *The Merry Conceited Humours of Bottom the Weaver*, suggests that Pyramus and Thisbe retained theatrical life during the interregnum, and circled back to the spirit of Ovid, if not directly to the text itself. *Bottom the Weaver* employs Titania and Oberon's quarrel as a plot device that only exists to serve the main drama of the play's rehearsal. The droll begins with the mechanicals meeting to practice their plays and, from that point, follows Shakespeare's outline of the artisan scenes with a large degree of dramaturgical fidelity. Oberon arrives with his servant spirit, Pugg, plotting revenge on Titania's refusal to acquiesce to his claim on her page. In spite of Pugg's decision to adorn Bottom with an ass's head, he and Oberon generally demonstrate a more reduced agency, watching Titania and Bottom play out their comic scenes, as a chorus might, with little or no interference. The dislocation of context that occurs with the excision of Pyramus and Thisbe invokes the allegorical potentiality that Ovid's poem inspires when it rejects background detail in order to affirm the significance of metamorphosis.

In *Bottom the Weaver*, an emphasis remains on Bottom as a player, and the redaction of the play results in a streamlined slapstick comedy that gives free rein to the playful theatrics of Shakespeare's mechanicals licensing further appropriation through an emphasis on the transformative experience of performance. It is, however, the emphatically theatric, and not the poetical languages that Pugg retains, that allows us to more vividly regard the slapstick humor induced by the sight of Bottom clad in the ass's head. The text retains Shakespeare's comic speeches, for example keeping Puck's description of how the fearful mechanicals flee bottom and "madly sweep the sky" (II, iii, 23). Pugg's image describes the men scattering, and in a speech that could well operate as a stage direction, capturing the cacophony of sound and activity that accompanies their frenzied exit. Pugg's narration identifies the droll as drawing from a more physical comic tradition, characterized by his common English vernacular, celebrating the performance as the highlight of the text.

Bottom the Weaver's self-identification as "humour" also inserts it quite distinctly into a Restoration critical vernacular that emphasizes its ordinariness by using the everyday prose of Shakespeare's artisans to foreground character by limiting the appropriation to a textual renovation that is more generally linked to adaptive work. Moreover, the assertion of the droll as a lower-class entertainment, and the reduction of Bottom to no more than a product of his humors, looks back to Shakespeare's own complex relationship with the rustic clown and the excision of the subtle nods to Ovid that exist in the larger taxonomy of *A Midsummer Night's Dream*. Isolated, Shakespeare's remix of Pyramus and Thisbe transforms not only the genre, but also the attribution of authorship, by placing the blame for the adaptation squarely on the shoulders of the over-reaching artist, even as this figure, when performed well, becomes the locus of a successful comic performance.

On the continent, a parallel process was unfolding, appropriating the remixed and satiric Pyramus and Thisbe for popular entertainment. Andreas Gryphius's *Absurda Comica Oder Peter Squentz*, written in either 1648 or 1649 and later published in 1658, dislocates the performance of Pyramus and Thisbe from the larger framework of *A Midsummer Night's Dream*, ostensibly presenting a tragedy from the "pretty book, *Memoriumphsis*" written by "the ancient holy churchman Ovid" (I, 53–4).[34] This passing reference to Ovid, along with a brief synopsis of the tragedy, not only points to Shakespeare's own literary obscurity at the time but also directs the audience to seek out comedy through Squentz's ridiculous mischaracterization of Ovid. Gryphius uses the structure of Shakespeare's playlet as a means of foregrounding extra-textuality, without acknowledging the restrictions that the remainder of *A Midsummer Night's Dream* places on its clown.[35] In doing so, this new appropriation elides the larger classical allusions and metamorphic themes of *A Midsummer Night's Dream* in favor of a more overt satire on pretentious artists and the culture to which they aspire to belong. The value of Bottom (or in Gryphius's usage, Peter Squentz) shifts from object of satire to satirist, and his limitation is his inability to master the medium through which the lamentable tragedy is performed, bringing into sharp focus the nature of the genre he attempts. As a result of this shift, Ovid's tragic lovers are now defined by the paucity of their verse, and the text makes a mockery of the poet who harbors visions of artistic greatness.

Rather than representing a shift away from Ovid, the *Absurda Comica* makes visible the stages of recalibration that occur as a text mutates across time and space. Gryphius is thought to have inherited Shakespeare's text secondhand, adapting a version that a scholar named Daniel Schwenter pirated from the English Comedians as they toured Shakespeare's text through Europe.[36] Scant information survives on strolling players, but what we do know is that itinerant companies both in the Provinces of England and on the Continent were equipped to offer a variety of entertainments. An application to perform in the city of Dansk in 1622 described the Comedians' program as offering "not only beautiful religious but secular comedies and tragedies, during all of which beautiful and pleasant music will be performed just as during said comedies and tragedies excellently beautiful ballets, disguisings and English dancing will be seen."[37] Their emphasis on "clowning, dancing, tumbling, music, pantomime, roaring and shouting"[38] was an energetic attempt to elide the demands of linguistic similitude as a performance moved from one culture to another. This transnational piracy is appropriation at its most basic, transforming the text to meet the very specific cultural and material needs of the artists who use it, with little regard for textual fidelity.

The text Gryphius received was only minimally adapted from the Shakespearean work. Gryphius then changed his names to localize the text to its German setting – Bottom becomes Pickelherring; Peter Quince becomes Peter Squentz; and they perform not in Athens, but in the town of Rumpelskirchen – and his plot more or less follows the same trajectory as that of *A Midsummer Night's Dream*'s fifth act. The artisans form a company, assign roles, and ineptly perform the tragedy of Pyramus and Thisbe for a derisive court. As the title suggests, the playwright's role is expanded, and Gryphius makes the performative elements a more apparent source of comedy. In the *Absurda Comica*, Peter Squentz assumes the role of the over-ambitious buffoon that Shakespeare ascribed to Nick Bottom, and Squentz's scenes with the nobility are expanded to allow him more interaction with the upper classes as well as an extensive prologue and epilogue. By doing so, Gryphius's diverges from Shakespeare's containment of the over-zealous performer in order to present an overreaching scribe who fails because of his insistence on fidelity to his vision of his text. Gryphius's Pyramus and Thisbe enacts the appropriative desires that drive Bottom, Peter Quince, and Peter Squentz and reinforces Shakespeare's use-based iteration of Pyramus and Thisbe, which allows ongoing opportunities to respond to new cultural stimuli and poorly executed amateur enthusiasm.

In Germany, Pyramus and Thisbe became necessarily more physical: one staging of the play recounts the lioness giving birth on Thisbe's mantle, a spectacle that was presented using a jug of blood and a litter of real kittens who ambled around the stage.[39] Johannes

Von Rist's account of a performance he witnessed in Germany in the early seventeenth century describes the production's dependence on slapstick. He describes how

> the King and all the gentlemen and ladies laughed themselves almost to death to see Pickelherring with his round red beard, and prettily dressed in women's clothing, strolling up and down. He walked mincingly and talked in a tiny voice, as though he were a ten-year old girl.[40]

Ironically, by transferring the story into German and annexing Pyramus and Thisbe from the script of *A Midsummer Night's Dream*, the text centralizes and celebrates the appropriative practice that desecrates the value of the so-called original. Gryphius recalibrates the extant material that he has available by conflating Ovid's cultural capital with Shakespeare's narrative and creating an entirely new text that parodies conservative approaches to Ovidian use.

The delightful failure of Squentz's Pyramus and Thisbe lies at the feet of the over-officious author, whose continuous interruptions sabotage his text by insisting on his right to dominate the interpretive space. Even as his insistence on fidelity destroys his tragedy, Squentz continues to fight the collaborative processes of theatre and make an ass of himself. Squentz's overly intellectual analysis of his text as it happens prevents any sustainable theatrical disbelief and prohibits any empathetic association with Pyramus. In parodying the playwright's role (particularly while producing a tragedy concurrently), Gryphius insists on the incompatibility of the authorial presence with successful appropriation. Squentz's grim determination that "nothing will go wrong by a single inch" (III, 101) is not an affirmation of his faith in the theatrical spectacle, but a failed attempt at imposing textual regulation on a text as it is subjected to remediation. Squentz's dogged adherence to doing "right by what's there in the book" (III, 136–7) misses the ephemerality and subjectivity that defines both performance and successful appropriation, and his threat "from the truth I will not flinch" (III, 100) ignores the *communitas* of the theatre he attempts to produce. Moreover, Gryphius's appropriation of Shakespeare builds its own network by parodying older, outmoded forms of German drama in his comedy;[41] but, unlike Shakespeare, in the *Absurda Comica*, the playwright is the culprit as much as it is the cure.

The final appropriation that this chapter will discuss uses Shakespeare's satire derisively, and in doing so, inadvertently affirms Squentz's overwrought investment in his holy churchman. James

Shirley's 1646 masque, *The Triumph of Beauty*, appropriates Shakespeare's framework of incompetent working-class artisans for his anti-masque. Shirley's indirect use of Shakespeare illustrates the extent to which the Shakespearean remix of Pyramus and Thisbe had taken hold in the early modern imagination. As eighteenth-century musical parodies of the text illustrate, Pyramus and Thisbe evolved from medieval tragedies to become representative of a particular type of self-parody, staging the appropriative processes and making visible the network of confluences that generate new Ovids and new Shakespeares. Shirley's interpretation, however, stands as a rebuttal to Gryphius's use, illustrating the way in which Shakespeare's iteration of Pyramus and Thisbe sets in motion an ongoing debate about the definitions of "good" art, which Pyramus and Thisbe, by its emerging reputation as enjoyably "bad" art, cannot escape.

Shirley's masque opens with an abridged rewrite of the mechanicals scene from *A Midsummer Night's Dream*. A group of rural shepherds, identifiable by their appropriately rustic names – Hobbinol, Crab, Toadstool – are led by Bottle through a forest at the base of Mount Ida, in search of the Trojan prince, Paris, whom they intend to entertain out of his melancholy. Like Peter Quince's men, the shepherds decide to present an unambiguously tragic Ovidian tale and turn their attentions to Jason's journey to acquire the golden fleece. From here, Shirley turns the genres within Shakespeare's playlet inside out and uses the rustics' foolishness to validate Paris's subsequent melodrama when the goddesses descend upon him in his dream. The performers, not fully comprehending their rightful place in Paris's melancholy in this world, decide to jolly the prince out of his mood by ineptly performing their play. Bottle assures Crab that "if he do not laugh at every man of us, I'll lose my part of the next posset."[42] Although Shirley inverts the structure, the effect is the same: consumed by their desire to perform superlative classical tragedy, the clowns entirely misread their audience; and the humor stems from their failure, not their artistry. Ironically, their parody of Jason's tragedy becomes an anti-masque in itself as the actors torment Paris with their "unseasonable mirth"[43] until Mercury descends and engineers Paris's escape through enforced sleep. Shirley's text denies the compromise between audience and performer that allows collaborative imagination to elevate mediocre drama, instead allocating full responsibility for the success or failure of the piece onto the artist's ability to shape an elegant text, which Shirley demonstrates in Paris's dream in which three goddesses – Pallas Athena, Venus, and Juno – visit him and demand that he choose the fairest among them. Shirley himself appropriates the role of Peter Quince, rebuking Shakespeare's gentle scorn and restoring the poet to the primary creator of a text. A clear debate about art begins to emerge when Shirley presents his masque: bad art can and must, he suggests, be rescued by the presence of the controlling author. The shift from Pyramus and Thisbe to the golden fleece narrative is consistent with Shirley's loftier ambitions. Pyramus and Thisbe, to Shirley's mind, clearly belongs to drolls and lower-class entertainment, while Jason's story is more fitting for a masque of gods and princes.

Bottle attempts to entertain Paris with a verse that is appropriately poor, proudly reciting, in true Quincian style, lines such as "her breast is as soft as any down / Beneath which lies her maiden down";[44] but, in spite of Bottle's gleeful self-awareness of the paucity of his verse, Paris is not entertained. The shepherds threaten to amuse Paris with indiscriminate abandon, promising what the audience recognizes as the anti-masque "with fear and wit, or without fear and wit."[45] The masque itself is a solemn affair, and Bottle's attempt at comedy fails because Shirley intends to make the point that truly refined theatre transcends weak parody. Shirley does not allow the characters to perform their actual burlesque, only their antic dance whose "strange rudeness"[46] falls short of the dream that follows. Shirley then disempowers the artisans by denying them the low comedy that might have justified their buffoonery. And yet, the masque's claim on the imagination is not entirely divorced from the less courtly reiterations of Pyramus and Thisbe – any form of theatre must enthrall its audience. Shirley's masque goes on to represent Paris's dream, in which he is offered imaginative gifts from the goddesses Pallas Athena, Juno, and Venus, once more evoking the process of artistic creation as one that is interactive and participatory. By demanding that Paris choose the art form that best pleases him, Shirley enacts Shakespeare's own processes of audience engagement and illustrates the aesthetic rewards available to those who embrace acts of co-creation.

The subsequent history of Pyramus and Thisbe illustrates the endurance of Shakespeare's metacritical appropriation, and subsequent rise of Shakespeare veneration has not only generically converted Pyramus and Thisbe to a comedy but has also made the text synonymous with the interrogation of artistic processes. The comic masques of Lampe, and Leveridge, in the mid-eighteenth century, used Pyramus and Thisbe to Italian operatic styles, just as the short stories by Henry James and Louisa May Alcott in the late nineteenth century abstracted the idea of Pyramus and Thisbe to consider the imaginative potentialities of the American realist novel. In the twentieth century, the playlet's popularity in sketch comedy during the rise of television in the 1950s and 1960s set forth an aesthetic debate about popular culture's relationship to the theatre as it newly displaced the theatre as a mass media.[47] All of these appropriations draw, directly or indirectly, from Shakespeare's reworking and emphasize a self-awareness that derives pleasure from the vast network of associations that recognize Shakespeare as a source of authority, ironically enough, through Shakespeare's own language. That is to say, appropriators who have adopted Shakespeare's Pyramus and Thisbe as a text in its own right deconstruct the very authority that Shakespeare is presumed to stand for, not unlike the use that Shakespeare made of his Ovid.

Moreover, this practice parallel's Shakespeare's own attempt to reclaim Ovid's irreverence and slyly leads us back to Ovid's intertextuality. Ovid's own self-aware practice of appropriation is one that is predicated on the pleasure of getting it wrong and exposing perceived textual authority as fiction. As John F. Miller suggests, Ovid's own colored, or flawed, rememberings of literary allusions is often a "playfully extravagant"[48] reference that draws attention to prior literary traditions and representations of history, appealing to the contemporary reader by invoking the performative nature of the tales being told. Shakespeare's remix of Pyramus and Thisbe attunes the reader willing to return to Ovid to the subtleties of language that construct Ovid's lauded irony and pave the way for an excess that is unabashedly sentimentalized in the medieval tradition. In the Pyramus and Thisbe episode in *The Metamorphoses*, Louis A. Perraud notes, "the basic incongruity created by the use of apostrophe"[49] in the speeches of the two lovers consistently resists clear and direct address to one another, keeping the lovers apart.

Thus, the history of Pyramus and Thisbe returns us, unexpectedly, to the self-reflexivity and playful critique of contemporary writing that is the hallmark of Ovid's own writing. What Pyramus and Thisbe's strange history reveals is the deep and complicated network that accrues around an appropriated text. The authority for self-critique with which Shakespeare imbued his appropriation reinforces the idea that the remixed text owes as great a debt to the remixer as it does the source text itself. Instead of a linear process, whose valuation comes from a misguided notion of fidelity, more is yielded when we consider the text as an object to be used, and which, through appropriation, becomes a gateway for contemporary critical analysis.

Notes

1. See Sanders, *Adaptation and Appropriation*, and Marsden, *The Appropriation of Shakespeare*.
2. Lanier, "Post-Textual Shakespeare," p. 148.
3. Lanier, "Afterword," p. 295.
4. Kidnie, *Shakespeare and the Problem of Adaptation*, p. 43.
5. Desmet, "Recognizing Shakespeare," p. 43.
6. Ibid. p. 43.
7. Lanier, "Shakespearean Rhizomatics," p. 30.
8. Desmet and Iyengar, "Adaptation, Appropriation, or What You Will," p. 15.
9. Bate, *Shakespeare and Ovid*, p. 131.
10. Ibid. p. 132.
11. Lanier, "Afterword," p. 299.
12. Bate, *Shakespeare and Ovid*, p. 39.
13. Taylor, *Shakespeare's Ovid*, p. 5.
14. See Worthen, *Shakespeare and the Authority*.
15. Oakley-Brown, *Ovid and the Cultural Politics*, p. 8.
16. Lafont, *Shakespeare's Erotic Mythology*, p. 6.
17. Edmunds, *Intertextuality and the Reading*, p. 136.
18. See Lehmann, *Postdramatic Theatre*.
19. Worthen, *Shakespeare Performance Studies*, p. 50.
20. Kuhn, "The Rhetoric of Remix," 1.1.
21. Ibid. 1.5.
22. Jenkins et al., *Participatory Culture in a Networked Era*, p. 181.
23. Grossberg, "Is there a Fan in the House?," p. 58.
24. Starks-Estes, *Violence, Trauma, and* Virtus, p. 4.
25. Glendinning, "Pyramus and Thisbe in the Medieval," p. 54.
26. Oakley-Brown, *Ovid and the Cultural Politics*, p. 11.
27. Starks-Estes, *Violence, Trauma, and* Virtus, p. 8.
28. Ibid. p. 8.
29. Amy Reiss and George Walton Williams note that this is not the only time Shakespeare parodies his own work. See Reiss and Williams, "Tragical Mirth," pp. 214–18.
30. Harrison, "*Romeo and Juliet, A Midsummer Night's Dream*," p. 210.
31. See Davidson, "'What hempen home-spuns have we,'" pp. 87–99.
32. All references to *A Midsummer Night's Dream* are to Shakespeare, *The Complete Works*.
33. Williams, *Our Moonlight Revels*, p. 36.
34. Brennecke, *Shakespeare in Germany*, p. 74.
35. See Geddes, "Playing No Part But Pyramus," pp. 70–85.
36. See Brennecke, *Shakespeare in Germany*, pp. 54–6.
37. Brandt and Hogendoorn, *German and Dutch Theatre*, p. 71.
38. Brennecke, *Shakespeare in Germany*, p. 5.

39. Brennecke suggests that in spite of the text's marginalization of the character, the lion became one of the more popular characters of Pyramus and Thisbe on the German stage. See Brennecke, *Shakespeare in Germany*, p. 66.
40. Qtd in ibid. p. 64.
41. Atkin, "The Comedies of Andreas Gryphius," p. 120.
42. Shirley, "The Triumph of Beauty," p. 322.
43. Ibid. p. 326.
44. Ibid. p. 327.
45. Ibid. p. 328.
46. Ibid. p. 328.
47. See Geddes, *Appropriating Shakespeare*.
48. Miller, "Ovidian Allusion and the Vocabulary," p. 156.
49. Perraud, "Amatores Exclusi," p. 138.

Bibliography

Atkin, Judith P., "The Comedies of Andreas Gryphius and the Two Types of European Comedy," *The Germanic Review* 63, 1998, pp. 114–20.

Bate, Jonathan, *Shakespeare and Ovid* (Oxford: Oxford University Press, 1993).

Brandt, George W. and Wiebe Hogendoorn, *German and Dutch Theatre, 1600–1848* (Cambridge: Cambridge University Press, 1993).

Brennecke, Ernest, *Shakespeare in Germany, 1590–1700* (Chicago: Chicago University Press, 1964).

Davidson, Clifford, "'What hempen home-spuns have we swagg'ring here?' Amateur Actors in *A Midsummer Night's Dream* and the Coventry Civic Plays and Pageants," *Shakespeare Studies* 19, 1987, pp. 87–99.

Desmet, Christy, "Recognizing Shakespeare, Rethinking Fidelity: A Rhetoric and Ethics of Appropriation," in Alexa Huang and Elizabeth Rivlin (eds), *Shakespeare and the Ethics of Appropriation* (New York: Palgrave Macmillan, 2014), pp. 41–57.

Desmet, Christy and Sujata Iyengar, "Adaptation, Appropriation, or What You Will," *Shakespeare* 11.1, 2015, pp. 10–19.

Edmunds, Lowell, *Intertextuality and the Reading of Roman Poetry* (Baltimore: Johns Hopkins University Press, 2000).

Geddes, Louise, *Appropriating Shakespeare: A Cultural History of Pyramus and Thisbe* (Teaneck, NJ: Fairleigh Dickinson University Press, 2017).

Geddes, Louise, "Playing No Part but Pyramus: Restructuring the Clown in *A Midsummer Night's Dream*," *Medieval and Renaissance Drama in England* 28, 2015, pp. 70–85.

Glendinning, Robert, "Pyramus and Thisbe in the Medieval Classroom," *Speculum: A Journal of Medieval Studies* 61.1, 1986, pp. 51–78.

Grossberg, Lawrence, "Is there a Fan in the House?: The Affective Sensibility of Fandom," in Lisa A. Lewis (ed.), *The Adoring Audience: Fan Culture and Popular Media* (London: Routledge, 1992), pp. 50–65.

Harrison, Thomas P., "*Romeo and Juliet, A Midsummer Night's Dream*: Companion Plays," *Texas Studies in Language and Literature* 13, 1971, pp. 209–13.

Jenkins, Henry, Mizuko Ito, and danah boyd, *Participatory Culture in a Networked Era: A Conversation on Youth, Learning, Commerce, and Politics* (New York: Polity Press, 2015).

Kidnie, Margaret Jane, *Shakespeare and the Problem of Adaptation* (London and New York: Routledge, 2009).

Kuhn, Virginia, "The Rhetoric of Remix," *Transformative Works and Cultures* 9, 2012, doi: 10.3983/twc: 2012.0358.

Lafont, Agnès (ed.), *Shakespeare's Erotic Mythology and Ovidian Renaissance Culture* (Farnham and Burlington: Ashgate, 2013).

Lanier, Douglas M., "Post-Textual Shakespeare," *Shakespeare Survey* 64, 2011, pp. 145–62.

Lanier, Douglas M., "Shakespeare / Not Shakespeare: Afterword," in Christy Desmet, Natalie Loper, and Jim Casey (eds), *Shakespeare / Not Shakespeare* (New York: Palgrave Macmillan, 2017), pp. 293–306.

Lanier, Douglas, "Shakespearean Rhizomatics: Adaptation, Ethics, Value," in Alexa Huang and Elizabeth Rivlin (eds), *Shakespeare and the Ethics of Appropriation* (New York: Palgrave Macmillan, 2014), pp. 21–40.

Lehmann, Hans Theis, *Postdramatic Theatre*, Karen Jürs-Munby (trans.) (London: Routledge, 2006).

Marsden, Jean, *The Appropriation of Shakespeare: Post-Renaissance Reconstructions of the Works and the Myth* (London: St. Martin's Press, 1992).

Miller, John F., "Ovidian Allusion and the Vocabulary of Memory," *Materiali e Discussioni per l'Analisi Dei Testi Classici* 30, 1993, pp. 153–64.

Oakley-Brown, Liz, *Ovid and the Cultural Politics of Translation in Early Modern England* (Farnham and Burlington: Ashgate, 2006).

Perraud, Louis A., "Amatores Exclusi: Apostrophe and Separation in the Pyramus and Thisbe Episode," *The Classical Journal* 79.2, 1983, pp. 135–9.

Reiss, Amy, and George Walton Williams, "Tragical Mirth: From Romeo to Dream," *Shakespeare Quarterly* 43.2, 1992, pp. 214–18.

Sanders, Julie, *Adaptation and Appropriation*, 2nd edn (London and New York: Routledge, 2016).

Shakespeare, William, *The Complete Works*, 2nd edn, Stanley Wells and Gary Taylor (eds) (Oxford: Clarendon Press, 2005).

Shirley, James, "The Triumph of Beauty," in William Gifford and Alexander Dyce (eds), *The Dramatic Works and Poems of James Shirley*, vol. 1 (London: Murray, [1646] 1883).

Starks-Estes, Lisa S., *Violence, Trauma, and* Virtus *in Shakespeare's Roman Poems and Plays: Transforming Ovid* (Basingstoke: Palgrave Macmillan, 2014).

Taylor, A. B., *Shakespeare's Ovid: The Metamorphoses in the Plays and Poems* (Cambridge: Cambridge University Press, 2006).

Williams, Gary Jay, *Our Moonlight Revels: A Midsummer Night's Dream in the Theatre* (Iowa City: University of Iowa Press, 1997).

Worthen, W. B., *Shakespeare and the Authority of Performance* (Cambridge: Cambridge University Press, 1997).

Worthen, W. B., *Shakespeare Performance Studies* (Cambridge: Cambridge University Press, 2014).

Chapter 12

The Golden Age Rescored?: Ovid's *Metamorphoses* and Thomas Heywood's *The Ages*

Liz Oakley-Brown

1. Heywood and Adaptation Before-the-Letter

As I was writing this chapter on Ovid's *Metamorphoses* and Thomas Heywood's *The Ages* (1611–1635)[1] – the prolific premodern author's quintet of plays generally based on William Caxton's *Recuyell of the Historyes of Troye* (*c.*1474)[2] – the British Broadcasting Company (BBC) began screening an eight-week television series *Troy: The Fall of a City* (2018) as part of its leading channel's Saturday evening schedule.[3] Though separated by nearly five centuries of historical and cultural differences, these versions of Troy's siege, a narrative thoroughly inscribed in Western sensibility, had four key similarities. Firstly, *The Ages* and *Troy: The Fall of a City* are episodic. In this structural respect, there is precedent in Caxton's translation of Raoul Lefèvre's French romance,[4] the first book printed in England that entered the vernacular via a collection of stories (as its title makes plain). Secondly, the seventeenth- and the twenty-first-century Trojan transpositions dramatize the classical narrative for popular consumption on London's Red Bull Theatre's stage[5] and Britain's public service broadcaster respectively. Thirdly, while canonical Greek and Roman poets nest the archetypal conflict within their larger works (for example, Homer's *Iliad* and *Odyssey*, Virgil's *Aeneid* and Ovid's *Heroides* and the *Metamorphoses*, Caxton's *Troye*), *The Ages* and *Troy: The Fall of a City* are wholly concerned with the location's demise.[6] Finally, and with this current volume's focus in mind perhaps most importantly, Heywood's five plays and the television series correspond in their adaptive strategies.

Adaptation studies' refutation of originality and fidelity in favor of "process, ideology and methodology" has enjoyed considerable traction in Anglo-American contexts since the late twentieth century.[7] It seems significant, then, that the opening credits for *Troy: The Fall of a City* inform its audience that the series has been "Created and Written by David Farr" and subsequently "Inspired by Homer and the Greek myths." The BBC's decision to situate the British author and sometime director of the Royal Shakespeare Company above his motivating material emphasizes the contemporary writer's worth for the BBC while retaining the Greek poet's cultural capital in politically savvy ways.[8] By using a term that suggests an organic rather than parasitic relationship between Farr and Homer,[9] *Troy: The Fall of a City's* use of the verb "to inspire" ("to breathe or blow upon or into")[10] rather than "to adapt" ("to make . . . suitable or fit for a purpose")[11] avoids falling into the problematic hierarchical binary opposition of "original" and "copy." As we shall see, the television series' call to "inspiration" as a description for textual production shares some common ground with premodern England's mode of rendering classical literature into the vernacular. Produced in a period yet to settle on the dualistic concepts of original/copy, Heywood's *The Ages* are adaptations before-the-letter.

The individual title pages of the printed editions of the five plays comprising *The Ages* place emphasis on the staging of classical set pieces as much as a linear narrative:

THE GOLDEN AGE OR The lives of *Jupiter and Saturne*, with the deifying of the Heathen Gods.

THE SILVER AGE, *INCLUDING* the love of *Jupiter* to *Alcmena*: The birth of *Hercules*. AND The Rape of PROSERPINE. *CONCLUDING*, with the Arraignement of the Moone.

THE BRAZEN AGE *The first Act containing*, The death of the *Centaure Nessus*, THE SECOND, The Tragedy of *Meleager*: THE THIRD The Tragedy of *Jason* and *Medea*. THE FOURTH *VULCANS NET*. THE FIFTH. The Labours and death of *HERCULES*:

THE IRON AGE: Contayning the Rape of *Hellen*: The siege of *Troy*: The Combate betwixt *Hector* and *Ajax*: *Hector* and *Troilus* Slayn by Achilles: *Achilles* slaine by *Paris*: *Ajax* and *Ulisses* contend for the Armour of *Achilles*: the Death of *Ajax*, &c.

THE Second Part of the Iron Age Which contayneth the death of *Penthesilea, Paris, Priam*, and *Hecuba*: The burning of *Troy*; the deaths of *Agamemnon, Menelaus, Clitemnestra, Hellena, Orestes, Egistus, Pillades*, King *Diomed, Pyrrhus, Cethus, Synon, Thersites*, &c.

In concert, these thirty-five episodes help illustrate Mark Bayer's point that *The Ages* "draw on classical epic to trace Roman mythical history from the birth of Jupiter to the fall of Troy."[12] The title pages overtly offer a structured narrative, and the central play, *The Brazen Age*, even divides its five classical highlights over that play's five acts. However, it is worth noting that in their effort to spotlight microcosmic aspects of Troy's violent end, Parts One and Two of *The Iron Age* cannot sustain the forgoing methods of categorization: the ampersands delineate excess. This tension between semiotic order and chaos is at the heart of Heywood's *Ages*, and it is telling that no Greek or Latin sources appear on the title page, just the printed line "Written by Thomas Heywood." On the one hand, Heywood is acutely aware of the politics of authorship and ownership. In *The Golden Ages'* preface "To the Reader" he complains about "[t]his Play comming accidently to the Presse" and how he was "loath (finding it mine owne) to see it thrust naked into the world, to abide the fury of all weathers, without either Title for acknowledgement, or the formality of an Epistle for ornament" (3). Heywood makes a related grievance about the piratical publication of classical material that originally appeared in his prose tract *An Apology for Poetry* (1609). At the start of *The Brazen Age*, he tells the Reader that

> a Pedant about this Towne . . . turn'd *Pedagogue*, & once insinuating with me, borrowed fromme certaine Translations of *Ouid*, as his three books *De Arte Amandi*, & two *De Remedio Amoris*, which since, his most brazen face hath most impudently challenged as his own . . . But courteous Reader, I can onely excuse him in this, that this is the *Brazen Age*. (167–8)[13]

On the other hand, Heywood integrates such a range of materials into his own works that it is difficult to tell where Heywood's own writing begins and ends.[14]

Premodern pedagogical works such as Roger Ascham's *The scholemaster* (1570) show how the mid-sixteenth century tried to differentiate between translation and imitation. In a section called "The Ready Way to the Latin tong," Ascham's scheme proposes that "There be six wayes appointed by the best learned men, for the learning of tonges, and encreace of eloquence, as 1. Translatiolinguarum. 2. Paraphrasis. 3. Metaphrasis. 4. Epitome. 5. Imitatio. 6. Declamatio."[15] However, as scholars and theoreticians have comprehensively discussed, the boundaries between these rhetorical devices were – and remain – hard to maintain. Massimiliano Morini, for instance, concludes:

> sixteenth-century translation was still in a phase of instability: with original writing, imitation, paraphrase and exegesis, it still made pairs which could be seen as conflicting as well as harmonic; and the borders between different literary discourses had not clearly been defined. The seventeenth century, with its insistence on "imitation" rather than translation as the only way to reproduce the rhetorical qualities of a text, would mark a new phase of development . . . [16]

Located in the interstices between Morini's distinctive phases of sixteenth-century translation and seventeenth-century imitation, Heywood's *Ages* betray an uneasy textual practice that defies contemporaneous definition. Richard Rowland's discussion of Heywood and "Stages of Translation in Early Modern England" works out from mid-seventeenth-century Royalist translation practices before reviewing the topic from the early decades of the sixteenth century.[17] The discovery of the incomplete manuscript of an English version of the *Captivi* of Plautus's at New College helped Rowland to closely consider its relationship to Heywood's 1624 comedy *The Captives* and his "approach to commercial theatre."[18] Through a comparison of the Plautine fragments and Heywood's play, Rowland comments that Heywood's "acts of translation were by no means free of error, and some of his anachronistic interpolations were less happy than others."[19] After M. L. Stapleton, Rowland sums up Heywood's processes of translation as "a 'rough wooing' of the Roman originals."[20]

In a series of plays so markedly concerned with dissolution, Heywood makes striking use of Greek and Roman material as embellishments rather than scaffolding. As Stapleton puts it, "*The Ages* plays epitomize the fascination with classical culture, history, and mythology that one finds in the rest of his dramatic work, studded as it is with Latin tags and allusions to Greek and Roman literature."[21] The *OED* suggests that the earliest use of the word "adaptation" in English is around the turn of the sixteenth century:[22] a period coterminous with *The Ages*. What might now be termed Heywood's adaptation of Ovid's *Metamorphoses* thus takes place at a time when the model itself was just coming into view.

Alongside these "Latin tags" and "allusions to Greek and Roman literature," Homer functions as a kind of synecdoche for Heywood's indiscriminate use of classical material. In the first three plays, Heywood uses the Greek poet as "a chorus figure"[23] to guide his audience through *The Ages*' numerous classical vignettes which take the form of dialogues, songs, dumbshows and spectacle. As with the BBC's twenty-first-century television audience, Homer has "cultural capital"[24] for seventeenth-century London theatregoers, and Heywood appropriates the Greek poet for his own dramaturgical purposes. Charlotte Coffin reminds us that *The Ages*

> are contemporary with the later installments of George Chapman's translation of the *Iliad*: the first twelve books printed by Humphrey Lownes for Samuel Macham in 1608–9, and the complete edition of *The Iliads Homer Prince of Poets*, printed by Richard Field for Nathaniell Butter in 1611.[25]

In this context, it is not altogether surprising that *The Golden Age*, *The Silver Age*, and *The Bronze Age* situate Homer quite literally on The Red Bull's stage to steer the audience through the dramatic action.[26] The entire *Ages* cycle begins thus:

> Actus I. Scaena I
> *Enter old Homer*
> The Gods of Greece, whose deities I rais'd
> Out of the earth, gaue them diuinity,
> The attributes of Sacrifice and Prayer
> Have giuen old *Homer* leaue to view the world
> And make his owne presentment. I am he
> That by my pen gaue heauen to *Jupiter*,
> Made *Neptunes* Trident calme, the curled waves,
> Gaue *Aeolus* Lordship ore the warring winds;
> Created blacke hair'd *Pluto* King of Ghosts,
> And regent ore the Kingdomes fixt below.
> By me *Mars* warres, and fluent *Mercury*
> Speakes from my tongue. I place'd diuine *Apollo*
> Within the Sunnes bright Chariot. I made *Venus*
> Goddesse of Loue, and to her winged sonne
> Gaue severall arrows, tipt with Gold and lead.
> What hath *Homer* not done, to make his name
> Liue to eternity? (5)

The opening lines of *The Golden Age* make much of Homer's descriptive abilities, arguably the epitome of the period's Plutarchian endeavors to make "poetry a speaking picture."[27] Coffin is right to argue that

> [t]he repetition of the first personal pronoun and the series of verbs emphasizing creation and control underline Homer's agency – the verbs also play on etymology, recalling that the poet is a "maker." Because Homer is here acting as a Prologue, he initiates the transfer of authority from poetry to theatre and may speak both for the poet and the playwright.[28]

In the midst of this Homeric remediation from epic verse to popular theatre, there may not quite be the profound elision between Homer and Heywood that Coffin detects.[29] Though indebted to Coffin's highly insightful observations about Homer's significance for Heywood's plays and her article's overarching argument that the "*Ages* can be approached as a dramatic response to Chapman's *Iliad*,"[30] I contend that the five plays comprising *The Ages* provide a tacit response to the poet's opening question: "What hath Homer not done, to make his name / Live to eternity?" In what follows, I suggest that Heywood's mythopoetic quintet of plays take up and develop the classical material that the Greek poet vividly bequeathed first to Rome and then to England. As *The Ages* progress, Heywood's "chorus figure" fades from view and ultimately gives London its own brand of classical narrative, which is notably Heywoodian: a dramaturgical *translatio imperii* achieved by techniques that chime with (rather than cite) Ovid's *Metamorphoses*.

To paraphrase Christy Desmet, Natalie Loper, and Jim Casey, *The Ages* rely on the dynamic between classical/not classical – Ovid/not Ovid – to bring the text into being.[31] Or rather, becoming. Since 2010, adaption studies' extant disruption of the binary relationship between original and copy has been substantially augmented by Douglas Lanier's use of Gilles Deleuze and Félix Guattari's (DG's) concept of the rhizome for his thinking about Shakespeare. In "Shakespearean Rhizomatics: Adaptation, Ethics, Value," for instance, Lanier considers how "[a]t the heart of DG's philosophy is an emphasis in differential 'becoming' rather than Platonic 'being.'"[32] By comparison with arborescent structures, DG's rhizome has no linear or teleological rationale: it is an "ever-expanding, ever-changing aggregate"[33]comprised of "lines of flight" and regions of amplification called "plateaus." In some respects, Elizabethan and Stuart England is a kind of Ovidian plateau, a "space where particular meanings or energies temporarily intensify and 'territorialize.'"[34] Heywood's *The Ages* might thus be called another "self-vibrating region of [Ovidian] intensities."[35]

2. Heywood's *Metamorphoses*

Though scholars have made short references to his "dramatizations of tales from the *Metamorphoses* [that] were being performed at the popular playhouse the Red Bull,"[36] Heywood avoids the explicit mention of Ovid's poem in *The Ages* plays and throughout his works in general. His first extant publication turns to Ovid's *Heroides* and transposes the Fifth Letter from Oenone to Paris into an English *epyllion*. It is frustrating that Heywood's *Oenone and Paris* (1594) is missing its title page, though the brief dedication "To the Curteous Readers" is intact. Neil Rhodes observes that "it was in the context of print publication that theorizing about the nature of translation tended to take place."[37] Heywood was not adverse to these kinds of explanations. Heywood's 1608 translation of Sallust's *The Conspiracy of Catiline and The War of Jugurtha* via a French intermediary (Louis Meigret Lyonnais's mid-sixteenth-century rendition) includes a twenty-page "Preface, dedicated to the Courteous Reader, upon the occasion of the frequent Translations of these latter times" (np). There is no such discussion of the verse as a translation or an imitation in his prefatory address accompanying *Oenone and Paris*. Instead, Heywood tells his audience, "Heare you haue the first fruits of my indeavours, and the Maiden head of my Pen" (A2r). Heywood also invokes the story of Oenone and Paris in Canto 10 of his *Troia Britannica or Great Britaines Troy* (1609), an annotated narrative *Poem Deuided into XVII. seuerall Cantons, intermixed with many pleasant Poeticall Tales. Concluding with an Vniuersall Chronicle from the Creation, untill these present Times.*

Notably, a short scene in the first part of *The Iron Age* (1632) dramatizes the emotionally charged meeting between Paris and his first wife (271–3). Richard Tarrant explains how Ovid

> often recasts his writing by incorporating it into a subsequent work. Recycling of this kind is not the result of flagging inspiration: part of its attraction surely lay in giving existing material a new meaning by placing it in a new context.[38]

As this brief case study of Oenone and Paris demonstrates, Heywood's reworking of his own material is Ovidian. And that Heywood is an Ovidian in very general terms is very clear to see. In his well-known treatise *The Apology for Actors* (1612), for instance, Heywood draws explicit attention to his knowledge of Ovid's Latin *Amores, Remedia Amores Ars Amatoria, Tristia,* and *Ex Ponto.*[39] Similarly, Heywood's *Gynaikeion: or, Nine bookes of various history. Concerninge women inscribed by ye names of ye nine Muses* (1624), produces a redaction of Ovid's epic poem called "An Abstract of all the Fables in the fifteene bookes of Ouids Metamorphosis, as they follow in the Poem."[40] By comparison, *The Ages* remain curiously – perhaps even stubbornly – silent about their explicit Ovidian debt, in Latin or the vernacular.

Ovid's *Metamorphoses* makes stage appearances in Shakespeare's *Titus Andronicus* (1594) and *Cymbeline* (1611). Act four, scene one of the Elizabethan play opens with Lavinia "running after" Young Lucius who is carrying a copy of the Ovidian poem which allows her to communicate Demetrius and Chiron's violent assault. While the classical text takes a more static role in *Cymbeline*, its significance as Innogen's bedtime reading looms large.[41] Closer to *The Ages* themselves, a character in *Fortune by Land and Sea* (*c*.1607–9), a play co-written by Thomas Heywood (with William Rowley) and also likely to have been performed at The Red Bull Theatre, makes a passing reference to "*Ouids* Metamorphosis" in terms of transformations of the self.[42] Even though Felix Emmanuel Schelling stated in 1908 that Heywood "sat" with a "copy of the *Metamorphoses* on his left hand and translated it into five plays, omitting little and extenuating nothing," *The Ages* make no obvious non-verbal or verbal reference to the Ovidian text.[43] It is highly likely, of course, that Heywood used a Latin or English copy of the poem as he worked on his plays. At the time of the first three plays' publication, the only available vernacular translation was Arthur Golding's mid-Tudor moralization *The. xv. bookes of P. Ouidius Naso, entytuled Metamorphosis, translated oute of Latin into English meeter*. Originally published in 1567, Golding's Ovid was republished in 1603 and 1612. By the time of the *Iron Age* plays' publications, John Brinsley's *Ouids Metamorphosis translated grammatically, and also according to the propriety of our English tongue, so farre as grammar and the verse will well beare. Written chiefly for the good of schooles* (1618) and George Sandys's *Ovid's Metamorphosis Englished* (1626) were available. However, in spite of Schelling's confident assertion, it is difficult to call *The Ages* a translation in the fulsome way that he describes. What Schelling needed was a vocabulary to help describe Heywood's complex navigation of classical material. And in any case, critics have largely overlooked the fact that *The Ages'* fundamental engagement with the *Metamorphoses* is related to structure rather than the mythic content itself.

Most evidently, the individual titles of the plays map onto Ovid's description of the four ages from Book 1 of the *Metamorphoses*:

> Golden was that first age, which, with no one to compel, without a law, of its own will, kept faith and did the right. There was no fear of punishment, no threatening words were to be read on brazen tablets . . . men knew no shores except their own . . . After Saturn had been banished to the dark land of death, and the world was under the sway of Jove, the silver race came in . . . Jove now shortened the bounds of the old-time spring, and through winter, summer, variable autumn, and brief spring completed the year in four seasons . . . In that age men first sought the shelter of houses . . . Next after this and third came the brazen race, of sterner disposition and ready to fly to arms savage, but not yet impious. The age of hard iron came last. Straightway all evil burst forth into this age of baser vein. (I, 90–129)[44]

Historiography forms a generic seam in Heywood's large corpus of work, and this brand of Ovidian teleology allows Heywood to exploit and explore that interest. *The Ages* thus join his chronicle play *Edward IV* (1599), the aforementioned *Troia Britannica or Great Britaines Troy*, and his translation of Sallust, which opens with a discussion of classical authors such as Livy who

> wrote worthily of Military and civill government, with the Office of an Historiographer. His histories intreat almost of al Nations which were of any reputation in his time, or somwhat before, (viz) from the CXXIIII. *Olimpiad*: that is, from the worlds Creation 3680. to the year three thousand seauen hundred, sixtie six, . . . And as he was an excellent Historiographer, so was hee a verie good Phylosopher:)[45]

Viewed through this historiographical lens, *The Ages'* alignment with the *Metamorphoses'* linear trajectory, its Augustinian delineation of the world out of chaos through to the foundation of Rome, and Caesar's apotheosis is clear to see. Furthermore, Heywood's titular emphasis on *The Silver Age*'s "Arraignment of the Moon," an episode from *Metamorphoses* Book 5 (V, 565–72) that recounts the division of the seasons following Proserpine's travels between earth and the underworld, underscores Heywood's extant interests in teleology and temporality. By comparison, the *Metamorphoses'* keen awareness of corporeal transformation and its overarching compulsion to speak of "bodies changed into new forms" (I, 1) remains firmly embedded within the plays. Beyond the finality of death's transformative effects, the title pages efface mutability.

Accordingly, it is no coincidence that Robert G. Martin comments that *The Brazen Age* – the series' central play – "has most frequent recourse to Ovid."[46] With theatrical brilliance, I.1 dramatizes *Metamorphoses* Book 9's contest between Achelous and Hercules over Deianira (IX, 1–97). The stage directions announce "Enter at one doore the river [god?] Achelous, his weapons borne in by Water-Nymphes. At the other Hercules" (173). The river-god draws attention to his preternatural prowess thus:

> When we assume the name of Demi-god
> Not *Proteus* can trans-shape himselfe like vs,
> For we command our figure when we please.
> Sometimes we like a serpent run along
> Our meadowy bankes: and sometimes like a Bull
> Graze on these strands we water with water with our streames.
> We can translate our fury to a fire,
> And when we swell, in our fierce torrents swallow
> The Champian plaines, and flow above the hils,
> Drowne all the continents by which we run . . . (174–5)

Punctuated by a propensity to "trans-shape" with ease and to weaponize his emotions, he "can translate . . . fury to a fire," Achelous's dexterous speech delineates his transformative power in content and form. As the battle progresses, and by way of some canny staging involving offstage costume changes and pyrotechnics, the river-god takes his promised "shape of a Dragon" (s.d.175), a Bull (s.d.176), and even fire (s.d.175). The fight concludes as Hercules "tugs with the Bull, and pluckes off one of his horns. Enter from the same place Achelous with his forhead all bloudy" (s.d.176). In a clear disavowel of "Magicke, or inchanting spell" that "Have no power over virtue and true fortitude" (s.d.176), Hercules' opponent concedes.

The subsequent scene juxtaposes a rather more tender example of transformation. In its portrayal of Venus and Adonis, the myth from *Metamorphoses* Book 10 (X, 725–39) made famous by Shakespeare's 1593 publication, Act two of this pivotal play dramatizes the youth's shift from animate subject to inanimate object following his fatal wounding by the boar. Venus exits with these words:

> Earth shall thy trunke deuoure
> But thy liues blood I'le turne into a flower,
> And every Month in sollemne rights deplore,
> This beauteous Greeke slaine by *Dianaes* Boare. (194)

Retaining Ovid's sense of the goddess's repeated memorialization, here monthly rather than annually, the narrative also recalls and arguably challenges Homer's opening statement in *The Golden Age* that he "made *Venus* / Goddesse of Loue." Heywood's episode hints at the Latin poet's propensity for metamorphic range combined with a complex loop of self-reflexive creativity.

"When Heywood wrote the *Ages*," Joseph Quincy Adams explains, "he was an actor and full sharer in the Queen's Company, and was employed as its chief playwright."[47] Given this immersion in offstage and onstage dramaturgy, Ovidian notions of transformation might have appealed to Heywood's own creative scope. As Jean E. Howard's discussion of the writer as a "dramatist of London and playwright of the passions" observes, Heywood was "Fully attuned to the theatrical world of which he was part" and "was a notable dramatic innovator, turning received genres to new purposes and inventing new theatrical devices to heighten the emotional impact of his dramas."[48] Specifically, his *Apology for Actors* delineates how "plays *do things* to spectators"[49] and, as Tanya Pollard states, the ways in which "dissimulation [is] at the core of theatrical performance."[50] While the *Metamorphoses*' teleology is aligned with Heywood's historiographical pursuits, the poem's shape-shifting outlook simultaneously engages with tropes of theatrical transformation. In so doing, however, Heywood fashions a seventeenth-century Ovid which, for all of its dynamic enterprise and showy theatricality, hits a downward cadence at odds with the Roman poet's apotheotic objective. Ellen R. Belton's perceptive appraisal of "The Unity of Thomas Heywood's *Ages*" concludes:

> Essential to an understanding of Heywood's conception of the ages is an awareness of the fact that the pristine happiness conventionally associated with the golden age cannot be located anywhere in the cycle. At the end of *The Golden Age* Jupiter suggests that the really good times are still to come, yet in *The Silver Age* the newly raised deities are already experiencing frustration and conflict, and men are beginning to defy their laws and fight against their own limitations. By the time we reach *The Brazen Age* we find Homer yearning for a more fortunate and virtuous past, while in *The Iron Age* the previous ages seem to have been forgotten. Heywood's characters are always either working towards a future-good or drifting away from a good that is past. Prisoners of time, they are always in motion, and the *"golden rest"* retrospectively associated with the first of the ages (*Brazen*, Induction, p. 171).[51]

If Ben Jonson conceived of *The Golden Age Restor'd. In a Maske at Court* (1616) and depicted the English poets Chaucer, Gower, Lydgate and Spenser exclaiming that "strife," "hate," "feare," and "paine . . . all cease,"[52] this piece is Heywood's golden age rescored: an altogether less positive outlook for the public theatre's broader ideological domain. While responding to the period's enthusiasm for Ovid's etiological epic, *The Ages'* cumulative reticence to name the *Metamorphoses* might suggest the Latin poem's articulation of relentless mobility is far too unsettling for Stuart selfhoods. Indeed, Heywood's own dedicatory signature to Thomas Mannering accompanying *The Second Part of the Iron Age* – "ever remaining, Yours, not to be chang'd" (354) – accentuates deep-rooted personal and cultural disquiet for mutable masculinities and "bodies changed into new forms."

3. Conclusion: Transformation and Adaptation

I began this chapter by thinking about Heywood's *Ages* plays from a twenty-first-century perspective, an approach which draws attention to some synchronicities between premodernity's and postmodernity's storytelling techniques. In many ways, Heywood's refusal to work within the available paradigms of "translation" and "imitation" anticipate "adaptation," a textual practice that, as Julie Sanders explains, is

> inevitably involved in the performance of textual echo and allusion, but this does not usually equate to the fragmentary bricolage of quotation more commonly associated with postmodern intertextuality. In French, bricolage is the term for "do-it-yourself" (DIY), which helps to explain its application in a literary context to those texts that assemble a range of quotations, allusions and citations from an often diverse range of existent works of art. A parallel form in fine art is the creation of collage by assembling found items to create a new aesthetic object, or in contemporary music the creative act of "sampling."[53]

Sanders' reference to adaptation as "echo," "allusion," "collage," and "sampling" are terms which could easily be applied to Heywood's Ovid. Likewise, and as we saw at the outset of my discussion, Lanier's use of DG's rhizome as a means of delineating a creative process exempt from notions of origins, sources, and copies helps to realize obscured Ovidian plateaus. Yet Heywood's novel compression of the *Metamorphoses* – the re-siting of Troy's ruin within Ovid's own temporal scheme – clearly underplays the Latin poet's unremitting examination of translation and transformation itself. From our contemporary vantage point that sets out to examine *Ovid and Adaptation in Early English Theatre*, *The Ages* work hard to replace Ovidian concepts of becoming for ontological security more commonly thought of as being.

Notes

1. The plays' periods of production are contested. In 1919, Joseph Quincy Adams stated that "the Ages in the form we now have them were certainly the product of Heywood in 1610–12." Adams, "Shakespeare, Heywood, and the Classics," p. 336. I am using the dates recorded on the published editions. All quotations are from Heywood, *The Dramatic Works of Thomas Heywood* and given in the text.
2. Martin, "Notes on Thomas Heywood's Ages," p. 23.
3. Synopsis of the 2018 BBC series available at <https://www.bbc.co.uk/programmes/b09szdtr/episodes/guide> (last accessed 10 August 2018).
4. Caxton, *Here begynneth the volume.*
5. See further Griffith, *A Jacobean Company and its Playhouse*, pp. 17–18, 224.
6. John. S. P. Tatlock makes the point that Caxton and John Lydgate's *Troy Book* (*c*.1420) "gave the whole story of Troy in order, while Homer, Virgil and Ovid gave only parts." Tatlock, "The Siege of Troy in Elizabethan Literature," p. 681, n. 10.
7. See the discussion of the term "adaptation" in Sanders, "What is Adaptation?," pp. 21–34, esp. p. 24.
8. I am indebted to Douglas Lanier's use of Pierre Bourdieu's notion of "cultural capital." Lanier, "Recent Shakespeare Adaptation," p. 104.
9. It is significant to note that the BBC series did not avoid public criticism. For a summary of and response to the discussion that unfolded on social media, see Ling, "No, the BBC is not 'blackwashing' *Troy: Fall of a City*," available at <https://www.radiotimes.com/news/tv/2018-08-10/troy-fall-of-a-city-blackwashing-casting-black-actors-greek-myth/> (last accessed 10 August 2018).
10. 1.a. *OED Online*. Oxford University Press, <http://www.oed.com.ezproxy.lancs.ac.uk/view/Entry/96990?redirectedFrom=inspire#eid> (last accessed 18 December 2018).
11. 1.a. *OED Online*. Oxford University Press, <http://www.oed.com.ezproxy.lancs.ac.uk/view/Entry/2110?rskey=BrvzMa&result=2&isAdvanced=false#eid> (last accessed 18 December 2018).
12. Bayer, "Heywood's Epic Theatre," p. 372.

13. See further Stapleton, "Introduction," pp. 3–4.
14. Stapleton notes that "Heywood was not above plagiarism himself" but then considers the term's anachronism. Stapleton, "Introduction," p. 20, n. 32.
15. Ascham, *The scholemaster or plaine and perfite way*, p. 33.
16. Morini, *Tudor Translation in Theory*, p. 24.
17. Rowland, "Introduction," pp. 157–72.
18. Ibid. p. 166.
19. Ibid. p. 171.
20. Ibid. p. 172.
21. Stapleton, "Introduction," pp. 1–2.
22. "adaptation, n. . . . 1. 1597 tr. R. Bacon *Mirror Alchimy* 16 As all things haue proceeded from one, by the meditation of one, so all things haue sprung from this one thing by adaptation. . . . 2. 1610 J. Healey tr. St. Augustine *Citie of God* xviii. lii. 743. They made a very ingenious adaptation of the one to the other." *OED Online*. Oxford University Press, <http://www.oed.com.ezproxy.lancs.ac.uk/view/Entry/2115?redi rectedFrom=adaptation#eid> (last accessed 1 June 2018).
23. Coffin, "Heywood's *Ages* and Chapman's Homer," p. 71. For a further discussion of the relationship between Homer and *The Ages,* see Kenward, "Sights to Make an Alexander," pp. 89–97.
24. Coffin, "Heywood's *Ages* and Chapman's Homer," p. 75.
25. Ibid. pp. 55–6.
26. Ibid. p. 74.
27. As recorded by Plutarch in *De gloria Atheniensium* [*On the Glory of Athens*], 3.347a, the phrase "Poema pictura loquens, pictura poema silens [poetry is a speaking picture, painting silent poetry]" is credited to Simonides of Keos.
28. Coffin, "Heywood's *Ages* and Chapman's Homer," p. 72.
29. Coffin acknowledges that Homer's texts are only a part of Heywood's cycle of plays.
30. Coffin, "Heywood's *Ages* and Chapman's Homer," p. 56.
31. I am referring to Desmet et al., *Shakespeare / Not Shakespeare*.
32. Lanier, "Shakespearean Rhizomatics," p. 27. See also Lanier, "Afterword," pp. 293–303.
33. Lanier, "Shakespearean Rhizomatics," p. 29.
34. Ibid. p. 29.
35. Ibid. p. 29.
36. Burrow, "Re-Embodying Ovid," pp. 309–10.
37. Rhodes, "Introduction," p. 48.
38. Tarrant, "Ovid and Ancient Literary History," p. 28.
39. This summary is based on Tanya Pollard's identification of Heywood's Latin quotations. See Pollard, "An Apology for Actors," pp. 213–54.
40. Heywood, *Gynaikeion*, pp. 48–56.
41. *Titus Andronicus* stage direction (s.d.) 41; *Cymbeline* II, ii, 1–47. All references to Shakespeare's plays are from Greenblatt et al., *The Norton Shakespeare*.

42. Heywood and Rowley, *Fortune by Land or Sea*, p. 14.
43. Schelling, *Elizabethan Drama*, p. 34. Cited in Martin, "Notes on Thomas Heywood's Ages," p. 23.
44. All references to Ovid's poem are from Ovid, *Ovid*.
45. Thomas Heywood, *The two most worthy and notable histories*, 4r. The Preface is a translation of Jean Bodin's *Methodus ad facilem historiarum cognitionem*. Kathman, "Heywood, Thomas," para. 16.
46. Martin, "Notes on Thomas Heywood's Ages," p. 23.
47. Adams, "Shakespeare, Heywood, and the Classics," p. 337.
48. Howard, "Thomas Heywood: Dramatist," pp. 120–1.
49. Ibid. p. 123.
50. Pollard, "Introduction," p. xiv.
51. Belton, "'A Plaine and Direct Course,'" p. 181.
52. Jonson, *The Golden Age Restor'd*, p. 1013.
53. Sanders, *Adaptation and Appropriation*, pp. 5–6.

Bibliography

Adams, Joseph Quincy, "Shakespeare, Heywood, and the Classics," *Modern Language Notes* 34.6, 1919, pp. 336–9.

Ascham, Roger, *The scholemaster or plaine and perfite way of teachyng children, to understand, write, and speake, the Latin tong* (London: Printed by Iohn Daye, 1570).

Bayer, Mark, "Heywood's Epic Theatre," *Comparative Drama* 48.4, 2014, pp. 371–91.

Belton, Ellen R., "'A Plaine and Direct Course': The Unity of Thomas Heywood's Ages," *Philological Quarterly* 56.2, 1977, pp. 169–82.

Burrow, Colin, "Re-Embodying Ovid: Renaissance Afterlives," in Philip Hardie (ed.), *The Cambridge Guide to Ovid* (Cambridge: Cambridge University Press, 2002), pp. 301–19.

Caxton, William, *Here begynneth the volume intituled and named the recuyell of the historyes of Troye, composed and drawen out of dyuerce bookes of latyn in to frensshe by the ryght venerable persone and worshipfull man.* (Bruges or Ghent, 1573)

Coffin, Charlotte, "Heywood's Ages and Chapman's Homer: Nothing in Common?," *Classical Receptions Journal* 9.1, 2017, pp. 55–78.

Desmet, Christy, Natalie Loper, and Jim Casey (eds), *Shakespeare / Not Shakespeare* (New York: Palgrave Macmillan, 2017).

Greenblatt, Stephen, Walter Cohen, Jean E. Howard, and Katharine Eisaman Maus (eds), *The Norton Shakespeare*, 2nd edn (New York: W. W. Norton, 2008).

Griffith, Eva, *A Jacobean Company and its Playhouse* (Cambridge: Cambridge University Press, 2013).

Heywood, Thomas, *The Dramatic Works of Thomas Heywood Volume III* (London: John Pearson, 1874).

Heywood, Thomas, *Gynaikeion: or, Nine bookes of various history. Concerninge women inscribed by ye names of ye nine Muses* (London: Printed by Adam Islip, 1624).

Heywood, Thomas, *The two most worthy and notable histories which remaine unmained to posterity (viz:) the conspiracie of Cateline, undertaken against the government of the Senate of Rome, and the warre which Jugurth for many yeares maintained against the same state. Both written by C.C. Salustius* (London: 1609).

Heywood, Thomas and William Rowley, *Fortune by Land or Sea* (London: John Sweeting and Robert Pollard, 1655).

Howard, Jean E., "Thomas Heywood: Dramatist of London and Playwright of the Passions," in Ton Hoenselaars (ed.), *The Cambridge Companion to Shakespeare and Contemporary Dramatists* (Cambridge: Cambridge University Press, 2012), pp. 120–33.

Jonson, Ben, "*The Golden Age Restor'd. In a Maske at Court,*" in *The workes of Benjamin Jonson* (London: William Stansby 1616), pp. 1010–15.

Kathman, David, "Heywood, Thomas, (c. 1573–1641), playwright and poet" *Oxford Dictionary of National Biography*, <http://www.oxforddnb.com.ezproxy.lancs.ac.uk/view/10.1093/ref:odnb/9780198614128.001.0001/odnb-9780198614128-e-13190> (last accessed 1 June 2017).

Kenward, Claire, "Sights to Make an Alexander," *Classical Receptions Journal* 9.1, 2017, pp. 79–102.

Lanier, Douglas, "Recent Shakespeare Adaptation and the Mutations of Cultural Capital," *Shakespeare Studies* 38, 2010, pp. 104–13.

Lanier, Douglas M., "Shakespeare / Not Shakespeare: Afterword," in Christy Desmet, Natalie Loper, and Jim Casey (eds), *Shakespeare / Not Shakespeare* (New York: Palgrave Macmillan, 2017), pp. 293–306.

Lanier, Douglas, "Shakespearean Rhizomatics: Adaptation, Ethics, Value," in Alexa Huang and Elizabeth Rivlin (eds), *Shakespeare and the Ethics of Appropriation* (New York: Palgrave Macmillan, 2014), pp. 21–40.

Ling, Thomas, "No, the BBC is not 'blackwashing' Troy: Fall of a City," *Radio Times Online*, <https://www.radiotimes.com/news/tv/2018-08-10/troy-fall-of-a-city-blackwashing-casting-black-actors-greek-myth/> (last accessed 10 August 2018).

Martin, Robert G., "Notes on Thomas Heywood's Ages," *Modern Language Notes* 33.1, 1918, pp. 23–9.

Morini, Massimiliano, *Tudor Translation in Theory and Practice* (Aldershot: Ashgate, 2006).

Ovid, *Ovid: The Metamorphoses, Volumes 1 and 2*, Frank Justus Miller (trans.) (Cambridge, MA: Harvard University Press, 1916).

Pollard, Tanya, "An Apology for Actors (1612): Thomas Heywood," in Tanya Pollard (ed.), *Shakespeare's Theatre: A Sourcebook* (Malden, MA: Blackwell, 2002), pp. 213–54.

Pollard, Tanya, "Introduction," in Tanya Pollard (ed.), *Shakespeare's Theatre: A Sourcebook* (Malden, MA: Blackwell, 2002), pp. x–xxv.

Rhodes, Neil, "Introduction," in Neil Rhodes, Gordon Kendal, and Louise Wilson (eds), *English Renaissance Translation Theory* (London: The Modern Humanities Research Association, 2013), pp. 1–70.

Rowland, Richard, "Introduction: Stage of Translation in Early Modern England," in Richard Rowland, *Thomas Heywood's Theatre, 1599–1639* (Farnham: Ashgate, 2010), pp. 157–72.

Sanders, Julie, *Adaptation and Appropriation*, 2nd edn (London and New York: Routledge, 2016).

Sanders, Julie, "What is Adaptation?," in Julie Sanders, *Adaptation and Appropriation*, 2nd edn (London and New York: Routledge, 2016), pp. 21–34.

Schelling, Felix Emmanuel, *Elizabethan Drama, 1558–1642* I (Boston: Houghton Mifflin, 1908).

Stapleton, M. L., "Introduction," in M. L. Stapleton (ed.), *Thomas Heywood's the Art of Love: The First Complete English Translation of Ovid's "Ars Amatoria"* (Ann Arbor: University of Michigan Press, 2000), pp. 1–29.

Tarrant, Richard, "Ovid and Ancient Literary History," in Philip Hardie (ed.), *The Cambridge Companion to Ovid* (Cambridge: Cambridge University Press, 2002), pp. 13–33.

Tatlock, John S. P., "The Siege of Troy in Elizabethan Literature, Especially Shakespeare and Heywood," *Publications of the Modern Language Association of America* 30.4, 1915, pp. 673–770.

Troy: Fall of a City, film, directed by Owen Harris and Mark Brozel. UK: BBC One, 2018, <https://www.bbc.co.uk/programmes/b09szdtr/episodes/guide> (last accessed 10 August 2018).

Chapter 13

"Materia conveniente modis": Early Modern Dramatic Adaptations of Ovid

Ed Gieskes

Colin Burrow's recent book *Shakespeare and Classical Antiquity* describes Shakespeare as a "practical humanist" who looked to the Latin tradition as a resource for his own work. This characterization is just as apt for writers like Christopher Marlowe and Ben Jonson, who found materials and models for their own work in the literature of classical antiquity.[1] Following this insight, this chapter investigates Ovid's place and use in stage representation. Ovid is, as many scholars have shown, a central figure for early modern writing of all sorts, including drama.

The words from the first poem of the *Amores* that I quote above describe a compositional disposition that guides Marlowe, Jonson, and Shakespeare in their uses of Ovid. *Materia* here refers to the content of the poem Ovid desires to write, *materia* that he hopes will come together (*conveniente*) with his *modis* or the measures of his verse. The *conveniente* Ovid speaks of here is, if not identical, similar in kind to what later writers do with Ovidian style and subject matter when producing their own *libelli* (to use Ovid's word). Ovid's *materia* was clearly suited to the stage, even though none of his plays survives to be translated or adapted. Stories out of the *Metamorphoses* appear on stage throughout the early modern period, and this chapter argues that the Ovidian *materia* lies as much in technique or structure as it does in the translation of poems or in retellings of stories out of the *Metamorphoses*. I will be discussing both aspects of the Ovidian *materia* of Shakespeare, Jonson, and Marlowe. They move between adaptation and appropriation as they translate classical work, model their new productions on those works, and deploy the representational resources of the varied traditions that they draw on and work within. Linda Hutcheon describes the process of adaptation as a process of translation and distillation that functions as a "recoding of a communication act into a new set of conventions."[2] Early modern playwrights are engaged in precisely this process when drawing on Ovid's *materia*.

1.

Ovid's place in the early modern English cultural imagination has long been the topic of scholarly attention. This fact attests as much to Ovid's hold on, say, Shakespeare's imagination as it does to Shakespeare's hold on ours. At the same time, pervasive critical commonplaces about how Ovid works in and for early modern culture can distort some of the particularities of cultural capital represented by the Ovidian corpus and the idea of Ovid himself. Similarly, critical attention to Shakespeare's explicit debts to Ovid tend to obscure other, less immediate (and less "Shakespearean") kinds of borrowings or uses of Ovidian precedents. This chapter begins with a discussion of Jonson's deployment of multiple versions of Ovid – as text, as character – in order to call attention to some of these complexities before turning directly to Shakespeare. Jonson's explicit and implicit references to *Amores* 1.15 point to the kind of less explicit uses of Ovidian poetics that I will be interested in in Shakespeare. Jonson enacts a layered series of appropriations in *Poetaster*, appropriations that operate as direct adaptation in the form of translation and in more mediated forms, including using an Ovid-character who speaks Marlowe's translation of Ovid's poem. In both of these modes of appropriation Jonson draws on the content and the cultural capital of the Ovidian "original."[3]

Jonson's play was performed for the first time in 1601, two years after Marlowe's translations of Ovid's *Amores* were banned and burned, and was likely composed closer to the date of the Bishop's Ban.[4] Jonson invokes a poem that quite literally was burnt on a kind of funeral pyre and secures the life of that poem (and the poet) in the face of quite literal forces of detraction, if not envy. Jonson's play preserves both Marlowe's translation of Ovid's poem and, at the level of the play's structure, reproduces the poem in a dramatic form. Nevertheless, the precise significance of this choice on Jonson's part in 1600–1 has been relatively unconsidered in criticism. The Cambridge Jonson's text of *Poetaster* subsumes the citation of this poem to the play's "anti-censorship theme."⁵ This point seems both true and insufficient. Tom Cain's Revels edition⁶ spends a bit more time on Jonson's use of Marlowe's Ovid, but he too focuses more on the exile of the poet at the close of the play than the effects of citing Marlowe's translation to open the play.

In her 1994 essay on the Bishops' Ban, Lynda Boose argues that the ban did not target "satire" per se, but a "newly sexualized, salacious tone with which many of them had been experimenting."⁷ This is the tone that Jonson purges at the end of the play. Jonson does not hesitate to purge (censor?) what he deems bad work, and the purge is quite specific about what has to go. Ovid's exile is more complicated, and that Jonson uses lines from the exilic poetry throughout *Poetaster* suggests that the poems are Ovid's (like Marlowe's) better part, which goes on to "aspire" in Jonson's revision of Marlowe's translation. Reviving (and modifying) Marlowe's text at this moment intervenes in the Poet's War and takes on its specific meaning in the context of both the Bishops' Ban and the Poet's War.⁸ Marlowe – just as much as Ovid – is not a target for the kind of criticism that Dekker and Marston receive in the play. Moreover, if Jonson were to dismiss 1590s Ovidian poetics by exiling Ovid, there are other poems that might be more effective than one about Envy. Instead, Jonson cites a poem about the problem the play grapples with, uses it to structure his play, and shows that he expects poetry – and Marlowe's words – to live.

2.

ergo etiam cum me supremus adederit ignis,
vivam, parsque mei multa superstes erit. (Ovid, *Amores* I, xv)

Then, when this body falls in funeral fire,
My name shall live, and my better part aspire. (Jonson, *Poetaster*)

Then though death rakes my bones in funeral fire,
I'll live, and as he pulls me down mount higher. (Marlowe, "*Ad invidos, quod fama sit poetarum perennis*" *All Ovids Elegies*)⁹

These lines from the end of the final poem of the first book of Ovid's *Amores* introduce *Poetaster*. All three versions point to the poet's triumph over death and envy. Jonson's version of Marlowe's translation emphasizes the endurance of the poet's name and the aspirations of his "better part" (Ovid's "*mei multa pars*"), while Marlowe's asserts that the poet will live, not just his name. In the play, they follow an induction in which Envy appears as a kind of interloping prologue. Envy's hope is

> [t]o blast your pleasures and destroy your sports
> With wrestings, comments, applications,
> Spy-like suggestions, privy whisperings,
> And thousand such promoting sleights as these.[10]

Envy's agents attempt to use "spy-like suggestions" and "privy whisperings" to condemn Horace as a traitor and lead Augustus to the "feast of sense" whose outcome is Ovid's banishment. In the Induction, Envy itself is suppressed by the play's Roman setting, which, according to Envy, cannot be forced to represent "the present state."[11] This is a peculiar (and incorrect) claim, as the play demonstrates by using Marlowe's translations of Ovid's poetry, which place its poetics firmly in the present state.[12] Envy's followers populate the play, driving much of the action, and the punishment of envious poets is the climactic scene. Envy's hopes are dashed at the end of the play when the brief successes of *delators* like Lupus meet defeat in Augustus's court, and Virgil reads from the *Aeneid* while seated on Augustus's throne. Ovid's poem to the envious is thus an appropriate place for the play proper to begin, and that Jonson uses a slightly altered version of Marlowe's translation offers a productive entry to the play.

Jonson aligns the Ovid of his play with Christopher Marlowe, a poet and playwright whose work Jonson treats much more appreciatively than that of Dekker and Marston, his main objects of criticism in the play.[13] Jonathan Bate argues that the Ovid in *Poetaster* is "initially recognizable as a poet like Marlowe" but that "there is a strong case for reading the character of Ovid as Jonson's composite representation of Marlowe and Shakespeare."[14] This identification, however tempting, is far from straightforward because of the specificity of the identification with Marlowe and a particular kind of erotic verse and because the character Ovid, despite being exiled, is not subjected to the purge at the close of the play. Bate's argument that Jonson's Ovid is a composite thus elides some of the particularities of Ovid's characterization by subsuming them into a picture of Shakespeare.[15] Marlowe's presence and influence is at the same time a sign of Ovid's, a poet to whose work the Horatian Jonson must also respond. Ovid's better part appears in Jonson's deployment of the structure of *Amores* 1.15 as a sort of framework for *Poetaster*. The play as whole is a response to Livor: the Prologue makes this clear as Livor sinks beneath the stage. Moreover, the sequence of events offers a kind of mirror of the poem and that suggests that Ovid's work is serving both the play's content and its form.

Poetaster opens with Ovid, Faustus-like, in his study, having settled his studies and made a decision to pursue a career in poetry.[16] This profession might be less dangerous in absolute terms than Faustus's turn to magic, but *Poetaster* presents poetry as dangerous in its own way. Over the course of the play, Ovid comes to represent one perhaps, though not certainly, less than ideal model of authorship, and ends up being exiled for participating in a masque that Augustus takes as blasphemous.[17] Ovid writes the last words of *Amores* 1.15 (in Jonson's revision of Marlowe's translation) in the opening scene and then revisits the whole of the text as a preparative to correcting the "hasty errors of our morning Muse" (I, i, 42).[18] The first scenes stage a confrontation between Ovid and his father about the value of poetry as an occupation – drawn, as much else in the play, from Ovid's work – with Ovid unsurprisingly preferring poetry to the law. His statement at I, ii, 235ff. on the lamentable place of poetry points to the way that poetry was once valued, but is now scorned, for

> [t]he time was once when wit drowned wealth: but now
> Your only barbarism is t' have wit and want.
> No matter now in virtue who excels,
> He that hath coin hath all perfection else. (I, ii, 254–7)[19]

His position here is not far from that of Jonson, who himself privileged his poetic talent over his relative poverty, and demonstrates that while Ovid may be a problematic figure, he does not merit only attack. The remainder of the first act associates Ovid with Gallus, Tibullus, and Propertius and sets up a poetic grouping united by their focus on love in their elegies.[20] Gallus and Tibullus appear in Jonson's version of *Amores* 1.15:

> Till Cupid's fires be out, and his bow broken,
> Thy verses (neat Tibullus) shall be spoken.
> Our Gallus shall be known from east to west:
> So shall Lycoris, whom he now loves best.
> The suffering ploughshare or the flint may wear,
> But heavenly poesy no death can fear. (I, i, 69–74)

The elegiac poets need not fear death because their works are "heavenly poesy," not the product of the "adulterate brains" and "jaded wits / That run a broken pace for common hire" (I, ii, 240, 242–3), as Ovid puts it. Gallus and Tibullus spend more time on stage in the play than Propertius, who has two brief speeches in II, ii and then is reported to have retired to Cynthia's tomb in IV, iii. The play thus echoes, if it doesn't duplicate, the poets' presence in *Amores* 1.15.

Ovid begins the poem by defending his time spent writing. Marlowe's version reads,

> Envy, why carp'st thou my time is spent so ill,
> And terms't my works fruits of an idle quill?
> Or that unlike the line from whence I sprung,
> War's dusty honours are refused, being young? (1–4)[21]

Defending his refusal to study the law, Ovid asserts that unlike a lawyer's, his "scope" is "eternal fame" (in both Marlowe's translation and Jonson's revision), and that the "mortal" scope of the law is thus not for him (ll, 5–8). The poem then catalogues poets from Homer to Ovid's contemporaries Virgil, Tibullus, and Gallus, whose verse "shall ne'er decay" (l, 32). The lines that close the poem and open Jonson's play include Ovid among those who are both safe from envy and immortal in fame after death.[22] While the play cannot be said to mirror the precise sequence of the poem, there are striking resemblances between the two works' trajectories and, more importantly, their arguments.[23]

Rather than offering a tightly structured narrative, Jonson's play proceeds by accreting episodes that illustrate the faults of Jonson's London and outline a poetics. Characters, to quote Augustus's lines from the final act, appear to "envy and detract," embodying ideas from *Amores* 1.15. Act five concludes with a trial scene where the envy-driven poetasters are judged, purged of their bad habits, and finally punished with a kind of educational program of reading the "best" authors. The trial articulates the difference between good and bad poetry and places good poetry out of the reach of Envy who, in Jonson's version of *Amores* 1.15, "twitts't" Ovid about wasting his time. Ovid's work is not mentioned specifically in Jonson's stage trial, but the play's return to the castigation of Envy brings it back to the Induction, and the trial at least implicitly endorses Ovid's position on envy. Augustus's final lines make this endorsement explicit:

> But let not your high thoughts descend so low
> As these despised objects. Let them fall
> With their flat, grovelling souls: be you yourselves.
> And as with our best favours you stand crowned,

So let your mutual loves be still renowned.
Envy will dwell where there is want of merit,
Though the deserving man should crack his spirit. (V, iii, 605–11)

The poetasters will fall, like the ashes of the funeral fire in *Amores* 1.15, while the true poets remain and will "be still renowned." Their better parts, in other words, go on to aspire further. In Jonson's play, Ovid figures as both a character and as a kind of narrative framework, and the "better parts" of both Ovid and Marlowe become a set of characters and a kind of poetic disposition. Shakespeare, to whom I turn now, is as deeply influenced by Ovidian poetics as Marlowe and Jonson, so my interest in what follows will be on how Shakespeare translates techniques of Ovidian narrative into his plays. In addition to adapting the content of Ovidian narratives, he is appropriating a characteristically Ovidian way of telling stories.

3.

Mota loco cur sim tantique per aequoris undas
advehar Ortygiam, veniet narratibus hora
tempestiva meis, cum tu curaque levata
et vultus melioris eris.[24]
[The right time will come for my narrating why I should have moved from my place and have been carried through the waves of such great seas to Ortygia when you will be relieved of care and are of a milder countenance.] (V, 498–501)

In Book 5 of the *Metamorphoses*, Ovid coins the word "*narratus*" as part of Arethusa's explanation to Ceres of how she knows of Proserpina's fate in the Underworld. The "right time" for this story comes about seventy lines later, once Ceres has recovered her daughter and she has a "milder" face.[25] Arethusa's deferral here produces Ceres' desire to hear the story, a desire that takes precedence over any other responsibilities she might have towards restoring the natural world disturbed by her grief over and quest to find the lost Proserpina. It mirrors and enacts a similar gesture made by the Muses in the frame narrative, when they disingenuously suggest that Minerva may be too busy to hear their song, saying "*sed forsitan otia non sint, / nec nostris praebere vacet tibi cantibus aures*" ["But perhaps there is not leisure, nor time to offer our songs to your ears"] (V, 333–4).[26] The Muses' suggestion encourages Minerva, if it doesn't actually coerce her, to invite a full (and word for word) recounting of Calliope's song. There is no actual deferral of the tale, only this effort aimed at eliciting the audience's desire for a song she might not otherwise wish or need to hear.[27] The layering of tale-within-and-around-tale in the Orpheus materials in Books 10 and 11 is the most extended version of this double emphasis on tale-telling in the poem, but the whole of the *Metamorphoses* works in the same way. Shakespeare picks up and, appropriately, transforms the self-consciousness of Ovid's narrative about narrating and narrators in his plays and poems as much as he does the content of the many stories. To use the language of adaptation theory, this double move transcodes/remediates the content of the poems as much as their technique.[28] It is both an act of adaptation and one of appropriation that might best be described in the literal meaning of translate: to carry over from one literary place to another. As Julie Sanders notes, the lines between adaptation studies and translation studies are of necessity blurry, and Shakespeare's practice blurs those lines as well.[29]

Arethusa's report of her sighting of Proserpina in the Underworld as "*regina*" and "*inferni pollens matrona tyranni*" (V, 507, 508) and her subsequent explanation of how she came to see Proserpina clearly articulate this narrative strategy. Her report itself appears in a tale being told to Minerva about the Muses' song-contest with the Pierides and is thus wrapped in several layers of narrative. After a paraphrase of the Pierides' entry in the *certamen*, the Muses introduce their own contribution:

> "*Hactenus ad citharam vocalia moverat ora:*
> *poscimur Aonides. Sed forsitan otia non sint,*
> *nec nostris praebere vacet tibi cantibus aures.*"
> "*Ne dubita, vestrumque mihi refer ordine carmen*"
> *Pallas ait nemorisque levi consedit in umbra.*
> ["Thus far her singing mouth moved to her lyre. We, the Muses, are
> called for. But, perhaps, there is neither leisure nor time for us to offer
> songs to your ears." "Doubt not, and bring your song in order to me,"
> said Pallas and sat in the pleasing shade of the grove.] (V, 332–6)

Golding translates this passage thus:

> This was the summe of all the tale which she with rolling tung
> And yelling throteboll to hir harpe before us rudely sung.
> Our turne is also come to speake, but that perchaunce your grace
> To give the hearing to our song hath now no time nor space.
> Yes yes (quoth Pallas) tell on forth in order all your tale:
> And downe she sate among the trees which gave a pleasant swale.[30]

Minerva, responding to the Muses' feigned worry that she is too busy to listen, tells them to sing the song "*ordine*," in order or exactly as it was told, unlike the song of the Pierides. Calliope's narrative begins with a disingenuous introduction, suggesting that Minerva might not have time to listen, which prefigures the deferral of Arethusa's tale to a "*tempestiva hora*," when Ceres might have both time and leisure to listen. In other words, not only does Ceres need to have a milder countenance, but she must also have leisure to listen, a leisure she lacks given the exigencies of her search for her daughter.[31]

In Calliope's song, Arethusa first delivers vital information about Proserpina's whereabouts, information that she gains during her journey from her native place to Ortygia; as a result of this information, Ceres recovers her daughter, and only then does Arethusa relate her own story. Arethusa appears without much introduction (save a reference to the location), surprising the reader/hearer and begging the question of where she came from. That question is suspended by Ovid and by Arethusa herself in her own story until a more opportune time. Within the narrative, Arethusa appears to calculate the relative importance of the stories she can tell here, deciding (probably correctly) that Ceres will be more immediately interested in the news of her daughter's location than the tale of how she came to acquire this knowledge. Once Ceres has recovered her daughter, Arethusa's opportunity to talk arrives. Calliope says:

> *Exigit alma Ceres, nata secura recepta,*
> *quae tibi causa fugae, cur sis, Arethusa, sacer fons.*
> *Conticuere undae: quarum dea sustulit alto*
> *fonte caput viridesque manu siccata capillos*
> *fluminis Elei veteres narravit amores.*
> [Fruitful Ceres, free from care, having recovered her daughter,
> demanded "What is your cause of flight, Arethusa, why are you a
> sacred spring?" The waters fell silent: from the deep spring the goddess
> lifted her head and drying her green hair with her hand, she narrated
> the ancient loves of the Elian river.] (V, 572–6)

Ceres demands (*exigit*) that Arethusa tell her tale, a story only marginally related to the overall plot of Calliope's song, demonstrating the success of her tactic from 200 or so lines earlier. Ceres' desire to hear the story delays Ceres' delivery of seeds to Triptolemus and the restoration of the land's fertility, both important actions needed to restore the disruptions caused by her search for Proserpina.[32] Ovid does not represent narrative economy, dramatic concision, or rapid pacing as being particularly valuable. Instead, nuanced fitting of story to hearer and occasion outweighs the value of forward movement. Ovid depicts a series of efforts at careful calibration of story to occasion and the needs or desires of the audience to those of the teller, calibrations that both narrate and imitate narration in ways that later readers of Ovid likewise imitate.

4.

"A sad tale's the best for winter."[33]

As critics have long noted, Shakespeare adapts Ovid directly in the statue scene – drawing on the Pygmalion story – but he is at the same time appropriating Ovidian methods. The play's attention to tale-telling in the final scene is strikingly Ovidian in the way that it layers a series of competing narratives best suited for particular times. The story of Perdita's return, how she was carried *"per aequoris undas"* back to her parents, is staged for the audience but withheld, if only temporarily, from Hermione and Leontes. Leontes, in the final lines of the play, turns to Paulina and asks her to

> [l]ead us from hence, where we may leisurely
> Each one demand and answer to his part
> Performed in this wide gap of time since first
> We were dissevered. (V, iii, 153–6)

The stories, of which there are several, are to be told at a time when there is leisure – the *otium*, perhaps, that Minerva has when listening to the nested narratives of Calliope in *Metamorphoses* V. It is not coincidental that these are tales of a daughter lost and found.

Stories told offstage – in the form of reports of those stories – are a recurring feature of the play, and many of those stories are of moments a theatre audience both could and would want to see.[34] Here, rather than being deferred, the narrative is related at a remove, as happens often in Ovid.[35] To take one example from the end of the play, in V, ii, Autolycus asks to hear a story:

> Autolycus: Beseech you, sir, were you at this relation?
> First Gentleman: I was by at the opening of the fardel, heard the old
> shepherd deliver the manner how he found it: whereupon, after a little

amazedness, we were all commanded out of the chamber; only this, methought I heard the shepherd say he found the child.
Autolycus: I would most gladly know the issue of it.
First Gentleman: I make a broken delivery of the business; but the changes I perceived in the king and Camillo were very notes of admiration. (V, ii, 1–11)

R. Rawdon Wilson points out that using "fardel," a bundle, a collection of things, a burden (sometimes of troubles, as in *Hamlet*), to refer to the story indicates a high level of self-consciousness that underscores the assembled nature of the story.[36] The First Gentleman's "broken delivery" is then supplemented by two other gentlemen's additions, both of whom call attention to the inadequacy of their delivery of the tale. The Second Gentleman exclaims that "the king's daughter is found: such a deal of wonder is broken out within this hour, that ballad-makers cannot be able to express it" (V, ii, 23–5) and goes on to say that "[t]his news, which is called true, is so like an old tale that the verity of it is in strong suspicion" (V, ii, 27–9).[37] The tale is delivered in fragments, and the whole of the reunion scene is recounted secondhand, heightening both the on- and offstage audiences' interest in and desire for the full tale. When the Second Gentleman confesses to not witnessing the meeting of the two kings, the Third tells him that he has "lost a sight that was to be seen, cannot be spoken of" before going on to try to speak of it. Throughout this scene, the Gentlemen describe events at a remove and remark on the power of the sights that they describe, sights that the audience never sees. At the end of this part of the scene, the Third Gentleman offers a closing appreciation of the events he has been describing. He recalls one of "prettiest touches," how during the "relation" of Hermione's death, Perdita weeps, and even the most "marble there changed colour" at her sorrow. His words prefigure the Ovidian transformation to come in the play's final scene. Act five, scene two, then, prepares the audience for the statue scene by whetting its appetite for seeing reconciliation scenes with these reports – framed as inadequate – and by hinting at the color change of the marble allegedly sculpted by Julio Romano.

Responding to Polixenes' wish to hear about what exactly happened to Hermione, Paulina remarks that, were this story to be told (like, say, the stories told in the preceding scene), they'd be "hooted at, like an old tale" (V, iii, 116–17). After Hermione steps down from the plinth and is embraced by Leontes, Paulina tells Hermione that her lost daughter has been found, and Hermione asks Perdita:

Where hast thou been preserved? where lived? how found
Thy father's court? for thou shalt hear that I,
Knowing by Paulina that the oracle
Gave hope thou wast in being, have preserved
Myself to see the issue. (V, iii, 124–8)

In a moment laden with Ovidian resonances, Paulina intervenes before Perdita can offer any answers to her long-missing mother's questions. "There's time enough for that" (V, iii, 129), she says, deferring Perdita's tale (which, of course, the audience already knows) until a better time – which does not come within the confines of the play. Here is a narrative deferred beyond the boundaries of its own narrating. More interesting than the unvoiced dramatic reason for the deferral is the suggestion that to begin Perdita's tale would be to invite interruption by "like relation" (V, iii, 131). To begin the story at this time would preclude its telling, because an unspecified "they" would insert their own similar stories.[38] Paulina's concern about "like relation" is borne out by the confusion of stories throughout the play – most immediately in the preceding scene – and leaves the tales to be told and retold in private and thus in the imagination and memory of the audience. Stories told, untold, or presented (or not) on stage, all combine to offer a picture of events, a picture that is not ever fully narrated, or even narratable.

5.

Jonson and Shakespeare, to use Hutcheon's vocabulary invoked at the beginning of this chapter, recode the Ovidian material they are responding to into dramatic forms in a species of adaptation that is complicated by particular engagements in the cultural field at the moment of composition/production. Their acts of translation, like Marlowe's, remediate classical poetry into contemporary forms. The question of what kind of cultural capital is being deployed – what this appropriation means – when Jonson uses Marlowe's Ovid in *Poetaster* can only be answered by a detailed awareness of the state of the literary field around 1600. In a similar way, Shakespeare's never-absolute move away from direct use of Ovidian stories towards using Ovidian strategies is to do with shifts in the literary field relating, perhaps, to changes in dramatic genres and in the shape of the subfield of narrative poetry. This chapter would take up those questions in more detail were there more time for narrating.

Notes

1. "Practical humanist" is a good description of a substantial number of early modern English writers.
2. Hutcheon, "From Page to Stage to Screen," pp. 40–1.
3. Both Sanders's *Adaptation and Appropriation* and Allen's *Intertextuality* call attention to the way that adaptation necessarily calls originality into question, and Jonson's practice makes this clear.
4. The works on the list were meant never to be printed again, but survive regardless.
5. Jonson, *Poetaster*, in Jackson (ed.), p. 32.
6. Jonson, *Poetaster*, in Cain (ed.), pp. 19–23.
7. Boose, "The 1599 Bishops' Ban," p. 187.
8. See Gieskes, *Representing* for an extended discussion of the Poet's War as a position-taking in the literary field.
9. I cite the *Amores* from the Oxford Classical Texts edition (Ovid, *Amores*), *Poetaster* from Tom Cain's Revels edition (Jonson, *Poetaster*, in Cain (ed.)), and Marlowe's translation from the Penguin edition of the poems and translations (Marlowe, *Complete Poems*).
10. Jonson, *Poetaster*, in Cain (ed.), Induction (Ind.) 23–6.
11. Ibid. Ind. 34. Envy may be vanquished by the setting, but the envious require a bit more effort to dismiss.
12. References specific to London make this link clear. See also Sinfield, "*Poetaster*," for a discussion of this connection and the play's engagement in the politics of poetry in Jonson's London.
13. See Shapiro, *Rival*. For more specific discussions of Jonson's relationship to Ovid's work, see Carr, "Jonson and the Classics"; Dane, "The Ovids of Ben Jonson"; and Mulvihill, "Jonson's *Poetaster* and the Ovidian Debate."
14. Bate, *Shakespeare and Ovid*, p. 170.
15. The composite becomes more about Shakespeare than either Marlowe or Ovid. That *Poetaster* invites such identifications is true, but the play is far from a simple allegory.
16. This opening resembles the first scene of Marlowe's *Faustus*. That the first words are based on Marlowe's translation of *Amores* 1.15 only reinforces the Marlovian *mise en scène*.
17. This trajectory resembles Faustus's fall; and though Tomis might not be Hell, Ovid's laments from exile treat it as nearly as bad.
18. Shapiro, among others, notes the strangeness of Jonson's including the whole poem in the play, particularly in the first scene. *Poetaster* ends with a reading from Virgil, but the whole play builds towards that ending. That this scene is one of revision points to the kind of relationship Jonson has to Marlowe and to Ovid.
19. These lines are a pastiche of sentiments from Horace's satires and Ovid's *Amores* 3.8 and the *Fasti* that indexes some of the ways that

the character Ovid in the play differs from the historical poet: Jonson's character is a synthetic figure representing contemporary poetry.

20. Cain notes that this grouping echoes that of Quintilian in *Institutio Oratoria* 10.1.93 as well as Ovid's systematizing of their work in his *Ars Amatoria*. Jonson, *Poetaster*, in Cain (ed.), p. 87.

21. I cite from the Penguin edition of Marlowe's poetry (Marlowe, *Complete Poems*). Jonson's version of these lines differs slightly – he changes a few words and reorders them – and the bulk of his translation is very close to Marlowe's. I use Jonson's version when discussing the play. Tom Cain's note to the full version recited in 1.1 argues that Marlowe's version was quite well known by the time Jonson wrote the play and that it makes sense to think that Jonson wanted his audience to recognize it as Marlowe's and not as plagiarism. And, as he notes, Dekker did not "accuse him of this theft" in *Satiromastix*. See Jonson, *Poetaster*, in Cain (ed.), p. 80.

22. That Marlowe is also among the dead is part of the point.

23. The play owes an important debt to Latin verse satire – directly as with the Horace episode and indirectly in the way that the play accretes incident more than it develops a plot – that complements the way it works with Ovid.

24. I am citing William S. Anderson's edition of *Metamorphoses*: Ovid, *Ovid's Metamorphoses*.

25. Most translators do not use "narrating" or "narrative" for the participle *narratus* here, preferring various circumlocutions that use "story" or "telling" or other cognates for the word. Golding's translation does not: he translates "*narratibus*" as "to tell."

26. In the introductory material, the Muses use cantus (a song) to describe their story, not *narratus* or some other word for story.

27. Barchiesi, "Narrative Technique" provides an excellent and succinct discussion of this issue. He discusses the Arethusa episode as well, and his work has influenced mine.

28. While much of adaptation studies understandably focuses on contents, I am interested more in Shakespeare's use of the techniques of Ovid's narrative poetry in the medium of drama.

29. See Sanders, *Adaptation and Appropriation*, pp. 9–10.

30. Golding's "rudely sung" and "yelling throteboll" seems unjustified by Ovid's Latin, expressing perhaps an assumption of the Muses' idea that this contest is unworthy of them. Golding, *The. xv. Booke of P. Ouidius Naso*.

31. Paulina's desire that Hermione delay the telling of the whole tale for a later (never seen) moment seems to me a related strategy, of which more below.

32. Barchiesi argues that the tale is relevant because it has a "threefold bearing on the threefold narrative frame: (i) it introduces a story which commands attention because of its parallelism with the Prosperpina

story, (ii) a story which is of interest to the nymphs and also (iii) a story which is of interest to Pallas" (Barchiesi, "Narrative Technique," p. 191). None of these reasons relates to narrative economy, but instead speaks to a desire to appeal to the multiple audiences for the story. If the Muses deserve their victory, it is less due to the excellence of their story as story than to its careful calibration to its audience, a calibration that the Pierides fail to make which results in their transformation into magpies.

33. Shakespeare, *The Winter's Tale*.
34. Could in the sense that these scenes would be easily stageable (unlike, say, the bear-eating Antigonus earlier in the play) and would in the sense that such affecting scenes have considerable emotional power.
35. See Wilson, "Narrative Reflexivity in Shakespeare," for a discussion of the reflexivity of this scene in the context of a more general consideration of narrative in the plays.
36. Wilson, "Narrative Reflexivity in Shakespeare," p. 782.
37. That Autolycus the ballad-monger is part of the onstage audience adds another layer of self-awareness about narrative to the scene.
38. This seems unlikely, given the story that Perdita has to tell, but it speaks to the ways that stories proliferate and interrupt each other in this play and in Ovid's poem.

Bibliography

Allen, Graham, *Intertextuality* (New York: Routledge, 2000).
Barchiesi, Alessandro, "Narrative Technique and Narratology in the *Metamorphoses*," in Philip Hardie (ed.), *The Cambridge Companion to Ovid* (Cambridge: Cambridge University Press, 2002), pp. 180–99.
Bate, Jonathan, *Shakespeare and Ovid* (Oxford: Oxford University Press, 1993).
Boose, Lynda, "The 1599 Bishops' Ban, Elizabethan Pornography, and the Sexualization of the Jacobean Stage," in Richard Burt and John Michael Archer (eds), *Enclosure Acts: Sexuality, Property, and Culture in Early Modern England* (Ithaca: Cornell University Press, 1994), pp. 185–200.
Burrow, Colin, *Shakespeare and Classical Antiquity* (Oxford: Oxford University Press, 2013).
Carr, Joan, "Jonson and the Classics: The Ovid-plot in *Poetaster*," *English Literary Renaissance* 8.3, 1978, pp. 296–311.
Dane, Joseph A., "The Ovids of Ben Jonson in *Poetaster* and *Epicoene*," *Comparative Drama* 13.3, 1979, pp. 222–34.
Gieskes, Edward, *Representing the Professions: Administration, Law, and Theatre* (Newark, DE: University of Delaware Press, 2006).
Golding, Arthur, *The. xv. Booke of P. Ouidius Naso, entytuled Metamorphosis*, Early English Books Online (London, 1567).

Hutcheon, Linda, "From Page to Stage to Screen: The Age of Adaptation," in Michael Goldberg (ed.), *The University Professor Lecture Series* (Toronto: University of Toronto Press, 2003).

Jonson, Ben, *Poetaster*, in Gabriele Bernhard Jackson (ed.), *The Cambridge Edition of the Works of Ben Jonson*, vol. 2 (Cambridge: Cambridge University Press, 2012).

Jonson, Ben, *Poetaster*, Tom Cain (ed.) (Manchester: Manchester University Press, 1995).

Marlowe, Christopher, *Complete Poems*, Stephen Orgel (ed.) (New York: Penguin, 1971).

Mulvihill, James D., "Jonson's *Poetaster* and the Ovidian Debate," *Studies in English Literature* 22, 1982, pp. 239–55.

Ovidi, *Amores, Medicamina Faciei Femineae, Ars Amatoria, Remedia Amoris*, E. J. Kenney (ed.) (Oxford: Oxford University Press, 1995).

Ovid, *Metamorphoses*, Arthur Golding (trans.) (London: W. Seres, 1567).

Ovid, *Ovid's Metamorphoses Books 1–5*, William S. Anderson (ed.) (Norman: University of Oklahoma Press, 1997).

Sanders, Julie, *Adaptation and Appropriation*, 2nd edn (London and New York: Routledge, 2016).

Shakespeare, William, *The Winter's Tale*, John Pitcher (ed.) (London: Arden Shakespeare, 2010).

Shapiro, James, *Rival Playwrights: Marlowe, Jonson, Shakespeare* (New York: Columbia University Press, 1991).

Sinfield, Alan, "*Poetaster*, the Author, and the Perils of Cultural Production," in Lena Cowen Orlin (ed.), *Material London, ca. 1600* (Philadelphia: University of Pennsylvania Press, 2000).

Wilson, R. Rawdon, "Narrative Reflexivity in Shakespeare," *Poetics Today* 10.4, 1989, pp. 771–91.

Chapter 14

Worse than Philomel, Worse than Actaeon: Hyperreal Ovid in Shakespeare's *Titus Andronicus*

Jim Casey

Within the past five or six years, some exceptional work has been done to expand our understanding of Shakespeare and adaptation, especially in the areas of intermediality, global Shakespeares, and theories of Shakespearean adaptation.[1] In this chapter, I want to invert the normal trajectory of exploration, which generally begins with Shakespeare and moves outward, and instead consider Shakespeare's own inspiration for *Titus Andronicus*. I will engage with powerful new theories of Shakespearean adaptation, normally used to discuss how recent works have adapted the plays of Shakespeare, in order to discover how the playwright himself reshaped his source material from Ovid's *Metamorphoses*. These various concepts and approaches to adaptation will inform specific moments from both *Titus Andronicus* and the *Metamorphoses* – especially regarding the performance of "unspeakable," "obscene," and "irreligious" acts – and consider the very act of adaptation itself.

In his *Metamorphoses*, Ovid recounts the story of young Actaeon accidentally seeing the "chaste Diana, huntress queen" bathing naked in her sacred grove.[2] Embarrassed and enraged, the goddess transforms the youth into a stag who is chased by his own dogs, "Till the whole pack, united, sank their teeth / Into his flesh"; with "fierce savagery," the hunting dogs, "tearing deep / Their master's flesh," literally rip Actaeon to pieces until his "countless wounds / Had drained away his lifeblood."[3] Later in the collection of tales, Ovid describes how the wicked Tereus drags the innocent Philomela – the sister of his wife – up to a remote cabin "[a]nd ravished her, a virgin, all alone"; after violating her, "he seized / Her tongue with tongs and, with his brutal sword, / Cut it away."[4] These two Ovidian myths provide a

set of powerful frames for Shakespeare's *Titus Andronicus*, both nar-
ratively and thematically, and each is specifically alluded to by the
characters. When Tamora is discovered in the woods with Aaron by
Lavinia and Bassianus, for instance, the empress retorts,

> Had I the power that some say Dian had,
> Thy temples should be planted presently
> With horns, as was Actaeon's, and the hounds
> Should drive upon thy new-transformèd limbs,
> Unmannerly intruder as thou art! (II, iii, 61–5)[5]

And later, when Lavinia is found by her uncle, Marcus immediately
suspects that "some Tereus hath deflowered" his niece (II, iv, 26). He
painfully observes that because Philomela only lost her tongue, the
mythical girl was still able to tell her story through sewing, "But, lovely
niece, that mean is cut from thee. / A craftier Tereus, cousin, hast thou
met, / And he hath cut those pretty fingers off / That could have better
sewed than Philomel" (II, iv, 40–3). Finally, when Titus initiates his
revenge against Chiron and Demetrius for the attack on his daughter, he tells the rapists, "Worse than Philomel you used my daughter, /
And worse than Progne I will be revenged" (V, ii, 193–4). In these
lines, Titus vows to outdo the vengeance of Philomel and her sister
against Tereus; he lives up to that promise by feeding Tamora both her
children (instead of just one) and then murdering her. This excessive
one-upmanship is mirrored by Shakespeare himself in his practice of
adapting the Actaeon and Philomela stories from the *Metamorphoses*
in such a way as to out-Ovid Ovid in violence and horror.

Before examining Shakespeare's alteration of these tales from the
Metamorphoses, however, I would first like to reflect on the way
early modern readers and audiences would have perceived Shakespeare's appropriation of Ovid's classical text. Jonathan Bate argues
that "[f]or the Renaissance, reading meant reading with a consciousness of the classics."[6] One important difference between reading
with present day practices and reading with a classical consciousness
is the reader's own awareness of the *hypotext* (the earlier text) being
referenced through the *hypertext* (the subsequent text).[7] Unlike most
postmodern allusive reading, which often relies on parody and pastiche, early modern reading revolves around the more conspicuous
utilization of imitation and allusion. The distinction here emphasizes
the opposition between the Renaissance's overt referencing of the
hypotext and today's more common dependence on humorous allusion (parody) or invisible allusion (pastiche). Fredric Jameson defines
pastiche as the "neutral practice" of stylistic mimicry "without the

satirical impulse, without laughter, without that still latent feeling that there exists something normal compared to which what is being imitated is rather comic. Pastiche is blank parody, parody that has lost its sense of humor."[8] More specifically, Jameson claims that in pastiche the particulars of the original referents have been lost, so that history and nostalgia are experienced "*metonymically*," without direct quotation or allusion.[9]

In contrast, early modern classical allusion depends on direct reference and acknowledgement for its experience of history and nostalgia – almost as a kind of anti-pastiche. According to Bate, imitations such as Shakespeare's treatment of the *Metamorphoses* in *Titus Andronicus* would have been essential to the reading and playgoing experience. He maintains that "the imitation is an allusion and is supposed to be recognized as such," meaning that "the source text is *brought into play* (from Latin *al-ludo*, to play with); its presence does significant aesthetic work of a sort which cannot be performed by a submerged source."[10] Bate stresses this anti-pastiche-like quality of Shakespeare's source-use in terms of aesthetic response, but I would add that the classical *hypotext* is brought into play in both senses of the word: its introduction creates both a playfulness in the *hypertext* and a tension between that text and the earlier *hypotext*, which is played out and then reeled back in throughout the reading experience.

Such textual allusions and quotations appear to be intentional and thematic in Shakespeare, but they are not simple citations or mere recitations of Ovidian *hypotext*. They are themselves complicated interpretive readings and interventions that sometimes rearrange and refigure the original, as when Marcus inverts the appearance of the nightingale in connection to Lavinia's means of expression:

> O, that delightful engine of her thoughts,
> That blabbed them with such pleasing eloquence,
> Is torn from forth that pretty hollow cage
> Where, like a sweet melodious bird, it sung
> Sweet varied notes, enchanting every ear. (III, ii, 82–6)

William W. Weber suggests that "[t]his simile immediately recalls the eventual fate of Philomela, being metamorphosed into a nightingale, but conflates this ending with the prehistory of the analogue. Lavinia has always been a Philomela in one way or another."[11] Yet even this seemingly straightforward allusion highlights the challenges of appropriately interpreting early modern references to classical myth and literature. For while it is true that Roman authors generally portray Philomela as the sister who transforms into a nightingale (unlike the Greek poets and playwrights, who usually depict Philomela as the swallow and Procne as the nightingale), Ovid himself does not specify which sister is metamorphosed into which bird. Instead, he groups them together as two Athenian women who seem to "float on wings! One daughter seeks the woods, / One rises to the roof; and even now / The marks of murder show upon a breast / And feathers carry still the stamp of blood"[12] ["*corpora Cecropidum pennis pendere putares: / pendebant pennis. quarum petit altera silvas, / altera tecta subit, neque adhuc de pectore caedis / excessere notae, signataque sanguine pluma est*" (VI, 667–70)]. Thus, despite Weber's claims to the contrary, Lavinia may not have always been a Philomela, because Philomela herself has not always been a nightingale.[13]

Nonetheless, Weber's main point is valid. The allusion – and the meta-allusive experience of Lavinia embodying Philomela to the audience – depends not on a perfect quotation and recollection of Ovid's original text, but instead on the idea of Philomela's violation in the *Metamorphoses*. As Weber asserts, Lavinia "need not quote a specific line of Latin, nor pick out the precise aspects of the story that apply to her; it is enough to bring the story to her audience's mind in an intentional, comparative way, for them to get the picture."[14] Texts experienced in this manner layer transparently over one another until the lines and boundaries of each one blur together in an intertwined matrix of reference and association. Playgoers familiar with Ovid need not see Chiron and Demetrius cruelly carve out the "delightful engine of [Lavinia's] thoughts" on stage because they will recall Philomela's tongue being cut out by Tereus in Ovid's tale. Moreover, the multidirectional nature of this allusive lattice means that some audience members will not only visualize Philomela's tongue as it "lay on the dark soil muttering / And wriggling, as the tail cut off a snake / Wriggles"[15] when they see Lavinia reenter with "her hands cut off and her tongue cut out, and ravished" (II, iv, 1 SD), but they will also imagine the "two branches" of Lavinia's arms "lopped and hewed" from her body (II, iv, 17–18) the next time they encounter Philomela's story in the *Metamorphoses*.

Linda Hutcheon refers to this feature of adaptations to eternally overwrite but never quite erase their affiliated intertexts as "palimpsestuous," a term she borrows from Scottish poet and scholar Michael Alexander.[16] For Hutcheon, conceptualizing the *hypertext* adaptation as connected but not inferior to the related *hypotext* allows readers to dismantle the creative hierarchy that normally privileges the "original" over the adaptation:

> seen through the perspective of its *process of reception*, adaptation is a form of intertextuality: we experience adaptations (*as adaptations*) as palimpsests through our memories of other works that resonate through

reception with variation. . . . Therefore, an adaptation is a derivation that is not derivative—a work that is second without being secondary. It is its own palimpsestic thing.[17]

Such a theory of adaptation also accommodates the way most people first encounter texts and their adaptations, that is, anachronistically. As Hutcheon observes, "we may actually read or see the so-called original *after* we have experienced the adaptation, thereby challenging the authority of any notion of priority. Multiple versions exist laterally, not vertically."[18] This is especially true of modern day encounters with Shakespeare. Very few people ever come upon culturally popular plays such as *Romeo and Juliet* or *Hamlet* (which themselves are adaptations) or even their more famous lines – such as "O Romeo, Romeo, / wherefore art thou Romeo?" (*Rom.* II, i, 74–5), or "To be, or not to be; that is the question" (*Ham.* III, i, 58) – without first encountering them elsewhere. Even with a relatively obscure play such as *Titus Andronicus*, there is a good chance that audience members will see the play only after first hearing the punk band *Titus Andronicus*, seeing one of the musicals *Titus Andronicus: The Musical!* or *Tragedy! A Musical Comedy*, hearing about Steve Bannon's strange obsession with the play (and his failed screenplay for a science fiction adaptation),[19] or, as is most likely, watching Julie Taymor's 1999 film *Titus*, starring Anthony Hopkins and Jessica Lange.

Of course, the same was true of early modern readers/audiences and their introduction to the *Metamorphoses*. Some would have discovered Ovid in school, certainly, but many would have first heard the name Philomela from some other source, perhaps from a play like *Titus Andronicus*, or a poem such as George Gascoigne's "The Fable of Philomela," or a broadside ballad, similar to the late seventeenth-century's "Cupid's tragedy."[20] Shakespeare himself, although he seems to have known Ovid's original Latin, was obviously very familiar with Arthur Golding's blunt, often clumsy, but extremely popular "englysshinge" of the *Metamorphoses* (1567) as well. As A. B. Taylor notes, "Repeatedly echoed, there are occasions when Golding seems to have become intertwined with the Latin text in [Shakespeare's] mind"; for *Titus Andronicus* in particular, Taylor observes that although Shakespeare "knew his main Ovidian source well enough to occasionally echo the Latin, there is clear evidence he had also been reading it in Golding."[21] Thus, at a minimum, Shakespeare's play engages in a palimpsestuous relationship with Golding's translation, which is itself a palimpsest of Ovid's poem, which is a palimpsest of earlier Greek narratives involving Philomela.

Early adaptation studies may have tried to trace specific lines of influence and appropriation among these texts, but I think recent work in Shakespearean adaptation studies might more usefully illuminate how and to what effect Ovid has been utilized by Shakespeare. These approaches acknowledge the shifting relationships and positions inherent in adaptation – as when one *hypertext* becomes the *hypotext* for a different text and, in some cases, even influences the reception and reproduction of the initial *hypotext* – and recognize the anachronistic cross-pollinization that occurs during adaptation. In the end, this means fewer critics placing Shakespeare in the central, privileged position of comparison and fewer discussions of modern adaptations that ridicule or dismiss the newer text because it is "not Shakespeare." Richard Burt proposes that longstanding obsessions over questions of authority, authenticity, or fidelity have been laid to rest in the subfield of Shakespearean adaptation so that "[n]ow the distinction between authentic and inauthentic Shakespeares is not even made consistently, much less policed. Few academic critics want to ask anymore how Shakespearean a given adaptation of a given play is" or even believe in the concept of an "authentic Shakespeare."[22] Similarly, a quest for authentic or inauthentic Ovids in Shakespeare's *Titus Andronicus* seems fruitless (and not very interesting). Instead, I would like to frame Shakespeare's adaptation of Ovid using current theories of Shakespearean adaptation in order to say something about what the play is, rather than lamenting what it is not.

At the time of this writing, the most influential theory of Shakespearean adaptation is Douglas Lanier's Shakespearean Rhizomatics, which co-opts Gilles Deleuze and Félix Guattari's conceptual rhizomes – sprawling, living networks that spread out horizontally, like crabgrass, and defy vertical hierarchies of origin and influence. Figuring Shakespeare as merely a part of a rhizomatic network removes the Shakespearean text from its position of centralized privilege and situates it and other related adaptations as equally important nodes within the larger structure. In such a model, Shakespeare is simply one more growth on the rhizome rather than the central trunk of the literary tree, part of what Lanier describes as a "vast web of adaptations, allusions, and (re)productions that comprises the ever-changing cultural phenomenon we call 'Shakespeare.'"[23] Just as importantly, a rhizomatic model frees the scholar from investigations concerning fidelity or authenticity and instead focuses the critical impulse on the constantly shifting cultural processes that make up "Shakespeare." Lanier suggests that

> [b]y emphasizing difference as essential to the cultural afterlife of "Shakespeare," and by refusing to treat the Shakespearean text as a

regulative standard or mystified icon of value, a rhizomatic approach
seeks to demonstrate how "Shakespeare" becomes ever-other-than-itself
precisely through the varied particularities of its manifestations, which
proliferate according to no preordained teleology.[24]

But as I have noted elsewhere,[25] while rhizomatics is particularly
valuable in dismantling hierarchical and evaluative paradigms of
relationships, it simultaneously obfuscates and even erases specific
lines of influence and appropriation. Deleuze and Guattari suggest
that "any point of a rhizome can be connected to anything other"
and quote Rémy Chauvin to explain how rhizomes comprise "the
aparallel evolution of two beings that have absolutely nothing to do
with each other."[26] Lanier emphasizes this point and insists that these
"elements in relation remain distinct – [Deleuze and Guattari] reject
the notion of a synthesis or symbiosis – yet through their relationship they move independently in the direction of each other."[27] Theo-
retically, this move is a useful way to map the interconnections of
related texts. Practically, however, it confuses the fact that one node
must be generated from another. In an abstract rhizomatic pattern,
this happens randomly and multidirectionally; but with adaptations,
this creation is purposive and unidirectional. Adaptations and the
Shakespearean plays from which they derive do not have "absolutely
nothing to do with each other" but, instead, clearly interact in some
intentional way.

Of course, for me, the provenance of Shakespearean adaptations matters less than what the new texts do with Shakespeare and
what that can reveal about the original text, the adaptation, and the
creator's own view regarding what is essential and defining about
the *hypotext*. For the last of these, I have expressed elsewhere my
belief that adaptations and other cultural outgrowths of Shakespeare
do not engage with the "real" plays or the "real" Shakespeare but
instead interact with plays ("*Titus Andronicus*" in this case) and a
"Shakespeare" that are themselves more akin to Jean Baudrillard's
"hyperreal (which is constructed of simulacra and simulation and
overwrites the 'real' world until the hyperreal becomes more real
than the real), mapping a 'Shakespearean' territory that itself is only
an *idea* of a territory."[28] This hyperreal Shakespeare is similar to Baudrillard's fourth stage of the image, which "bears no relation to any
reality whatever: it is its own pure simulacrum."[29] And like Umberto
Eco's "Absolute Fake,"[30] hyperreal "Shakespeare" bears no resemblance to the early modern playwright or his early modern plays.

Nonetheless, I find hyperreal Shakespeares incredibly useful because
they reveal what a culture or an adapting creator believes to be the

indispensable *qualia* of Shakespeare or his *hypotext*. The challenge, of course, is locating this fundamental "Shakespeare" in the text of the adaptation. Maurizio Calbi calls the traces of this "increasingly heterogenous and fragmentary *presence* of 'Shakespeare,'" which he finds in a variety of media and texts, "spectral Shakespeare," based on "Derrida's notion of spectrality – and the uncanny articulations of temporality and spatiality that this spectrality entails."[31] Locating the spectral and hyperreal Shakespeare in an adaptation and then comparing that ghostly not-Shakespeare to the Shakespearean *hypotext* can expose what an adapting artist believes to be essential to the text.

It seems to me that a similar approach can be taken with Shakespeare's use of Ovid in order to discover how the playwright may have interpreted particular themes and concerns from the *Metamorphoses*. David Cowart suggests that adaptation-connected texts exist in a relationship of "literary symbiosis" when the later text invites or provokes an artistic or "epistemic dialogue" with the original, renewing and transforming the *hypotext* in such a way that the meaning of the earlier work is affected by its invocation, adaptation, or continuation in the *hypertext*.[32] What did Ovid say to Shakespeare? What did Shakespeare say back? How do they speak to one another? For Jessica Lugo, Shakespeare's *Titus Andronicus* is "a blackly humorous interpretation of an already dark work" that takes "parodic delight in its roots in Ovid's version of the Philomela myth, transforming it into stage drama that both delights and sickens its audiences."[33] This point may be valid, but I find it hard to believe that a culture that was so close to everyday bloodshed and bodily harm would have found Lavinia's rape humorous or delighted in her mutilation. I am much more convinced by Lisa S. Starks-Estes' argument that "Shakespeare appropriates Ovid's myths and other legends to explore the erotics of cruelty at the heart of Roman literary tradition, the threats it poses to coherent selfhood, and the traumatic effects it produces."[34] Yes, the violence in *Titus Andronicus* is excessive, but I do not think Shakespeare is trying to mock Ovid; instead, I think he is trying to match him, even surpass him in horror, not humor.

The first scene where Shakespeare clearly out-Ovids Ovid is when Tamora is discovered in the "obscure plot" (II, ii, 77) of the forest by Bassianus and Lavinia. After Bassianus ironically imagines her as the chaste goddess Diana, Tamora expresses her desire to plant horns on the interloper's head – as Diana did with Actaeon when she transformed him into a deer – and have the hunting dogs "drive upon [his] new-transformèd limbs" (II, iii, 66) until Bassianus is torn apart. At first, it looks like she has no power to perform such deeds; but almost immediately after her wish, Tamora's sons enter. Chiron and Demetrius are later described by Titus as "[a] pair of cursed hell-hounds" (V, ii, 144) and, like the hounds in Ovid's story, they fall upon the young man whose great crime, as in the *Metamorphoses*, is seeing what he should not have seen. Like Actaeon, Bassianus is killed by these hounds and has his body transformed from life into death. As if that were not enough, however, Shakespeare then turns Bassianus's body into an object of sorrow and ill-omen; Martius describes the corpse to his brother Quintus as "the dismal'st object . . . / That ever eye with sight made heart lament" (II, iii, 204–5). Yet even this additional horror is not enough, as the Andronici brothers are then blamed for the murder and are beheaded even after Titus cuts off his own hand in exchange for their lives.

These moments of extreme violence in the play echo specific scenes and phrases from Ovid in order to emphasize how much more terrible they are in comparison to their counterparts in the Roman text. Immediately following Bassianus's death, for example, Shakespeare has Tamora's sons drag Lavinia off stage where she is raped and maimed in a manner explicitly reminiscent of Philomela's violation by Tereus in the *Metamorphoses*. But Shakespeare multiplies the horror of that maiming to include Lavinia's two hands and then proclaims the connection to Ovid by referencing not only Philomela's tale but also the fate of Actaeon when Demetrius taunts Lavinia with the words, "now go tell, an if thy tongue can speak, / Who 'twas that cut thy tongue and ravished thee" (II, iv, 1–2). These lines recall Diana's words to Actaeon, urging him to tell others that he saw her naked "if you can tell at all!"[35] ["*si poteris narrare, licet!*" (III, 193)]. As Taylor observes, in mocking Lavinia here, "the rapists are echoing Diana's ironic invitation to [Actaeon] as she deprives him of speech."[36] They too have read their Ovid, but rather than discovering *integer vitae* (the way to live with integrity) from their classical education, Chiron and Demetrius instead use the *Metamorphoses*, according to R. W. Maslen, "as a kind of rapists' instruction manual"[37] through which they learn to be craftier than Tereus by removing not only Lavinia's instrument of speech, but also the "sweet ornaments" (II, iv, 18) of her hands, which might have written their names or woven her story. As Bate suggests, what the Goth boys remember "is not *integer* but *Stuprum*, not integrity but rape. It is one of Shakespeare's darkest thoughts."[38]

In response to this darkness, Titus goes darker. When he captures Chiron and Demetrius, he tells them, "Worse than Philomel you used my daughter, / And worse than Progne I will be revenged" (V, ii, 193–4). The abundance of comparatives here and elsewhere in the play has led Leonard Barkan to remark, "*Craftier* than Tereus, *worse* than Philomel, *better* than Philomel, *worse* than Procne: this is mythology viewed in the competitive mode," with Shakespeare providing "[n]ot one rapist but two, not one murdered child but five, not one or two mutilated organs but six, not a one-course meal but a two."[39] In fact, *Titus Andronicus* features the reported deaths of Titus's twenty-one soldier-sons, the ritualized killing of Alarbus, the slaying of Mutius, the rape and mutilation of Lavinia, the murder of Bassianus, the maiming of Titus, the beheadings of Martius and Quintus, the stabbing of the Nurse, the hanging of the Clown, the cooking of Demetrius and Chiron, the honor killing of Lavinia, the triple murder of Tamora, Titus, and Saturninus, and the live burial of Aaron (not to mention the death of a fly).

Moments before he cuts the throats of Chiron and Demetrius, Titus says, "Come, come, be everyone officious / To make this banquet, which I wish may prove / More stern and bloody than the Centaurs' feast" (V, ii, 200–2). Initially, this allusion to the Centauromachy (the battle between the Centaurs and the Lapiths) and the attempted abduction of Pirithous's bride by Eurytus may call to mind Bassianus's early abduction of Lavinia – which Saturninus calls a "rape" (I, i, 401) – and Titus's reaction to it. But the association also links Titus to the rapists Tereus, Chiron, and Demetrius through the language that Ovid uses to describe the "stern and bloody" actions of the Centaurs. When the Centaur Eurytus sees Hippodame at her wedding feast, he is "fired by wine and by the sight / of that fair girl," and overcome by a drunkenness that has been "[d]oubled by lust"[40] ["*Euryte, quam vino pectus, tam virgine visa / ardet, et ebrietas geminata libidine regnat*" (XII, 220–1)]. The imagery of Eurytus's desire being "*ardet*" [aflame] is followed by the Centaur succumbing to his "*libidine*" [lust] and engaging in bestial, uncivilized behavior. Similarly, When Tereus encounters Philomela, we are told that "[t]he sight of her set Tereus' heart ablaze" and that "[h]er looks deserved his love; but inborn lust / Goaded him too, for men of that rough race / Are warm for wenching."[41] In *Titus Andronicus*, libidinous desire is also figured as fire or "burning lust" (V, i, 43), and that flame can be just as destructive as a Centaur's. This comparison is seen when Demetrius asks his mother, through metaphor, to delay killing Lavinia until after he and his brother have raped her: "First thresh the corn, and then after burn the straw" (II, iii, 123). Chiron adds that they can "make [Bassianus's] dead trunk pillow to [Chiron and Demetrius'] lust" (II, iii, 130). The concatenation of rapists to lust to fire to Centaurs to Titus creates a metaleptic correlation between the destructive cupidity of the Goth boys and Titus's own revenge upon them; by attempting to out-Centaur the Centaurs, Titus becomes as bestial and uncivilized as they are.

Like Philomela and Procne, Titus enacts his eventual revenge by committing the appalling act of killing, cooking, and feeding offspring to a parent. First, he binds Chiron and Demetrius and orders his attendants to "stop their mouths" (V, ii, 166), and then he stops their mother's mouth with a pie made of their blood and bones. In making Tamora "[l]ike to the earth swallow her own increase" (V, ii, 190) and then silencing her forever with a knife, Titus aligns her simultaneously with Tereus, who "swallows down / Flesh of his flesh,"[42] and with Lavinia, who swallows down her own words.

This violent gagging (in both senses of the word) holograms a theme that recurs in both Ovid and Shakespeare regarding actions that are literally unspeakable. In *Titus Andronicus*, for example, Marjorie Garber perceives Lavinia's speechlessness, which has been "forcibly imposed from without," as so effectively silencing her that it "signifies a living death."[43] But this living death has its roots in Philomela's experience in the *Metamorphoses* when Tereus takes his sister-in-law to a remote cabin, "And there pale, trembling, fearing everything, / Weeping and asking where her sister was, / He locked her, and revealed his own black heart / And ravished her, a virgin, all alone."[44] For the confessing of this horrible desire, Ovid uses the phrase "*fassusque nefas*" (VI, 524), which Sarah Annes Brown says has no equivalent in English, but may be glossed as Tereus speaking "that which may not be spoken."[45] This paradoxical construction captures both the horror of the act and the artistic (im)possibility of representing that act in poetry. Tereus may want to engage in "an act that is, literally, *ne-fas*, or 'unspeakable,'"[46] but this moment in the tale demonstrates what Elissa Marder identifies as "the convergence between speaking the crime and doing the deed. One cannot speak 'rape,' or speak about rape, merely in terms of a physical body. The sexual violation of the woman's body is itself embedded in discursive and symbolic structures."[47] And while those discursive and symbolic structures limit and restrict "unspeakable" acts, they also imbue them with dangerous, transgressive power whenever they do actually find voice. In this case, the performative speech-act allows Tereus to say the unspeakable in order to perform the unspeakable. Starks-Estes speculates that Shakespeare adapted this tale so he too could speak the unspeakable:

> In the context of Ovid's myth, *fassusque nefas* may suggest the unspeakable deed of sexual violence, the brutality that underlies the seemingly virtuous exterior, the aggression that cannot directly be voiced, the response to violence that is so fraught with pain that it cannot be uttered

directly. In my view, Shakespeare turns to Ovid for the means to articulate the unspeakable, to examine the erotics of aggression, and to investigate the tragic effects of violence – of trauma.[48]

For Shakespeare, the performance of the unspeakable takes on another dimension in the performance of the play. For just as there are acts that are unspeakable, there are acts that are unactable. In examining Lavinia's rape, Pascale Aebischer observes that, in contrast to the performance text (the play on stage), the playtext (the play on page) removes the rape from her body and (re)places it into the words of her male relatives; her suffering is thus subsumed by their grief. However, Lavinia's textual erasure is necessarily reversed by her very real physical presence on stage. In her body, the "unspeakable" is spoken, the "unrepresentable" represented. Thus, the actor's body in performance opens up the play in ways the playtext can only suggest. Aebischer notes that the stage direction for Lavinia's return after her rape and mutilation, "in its explicit display of the opened-up female body, borders on sadistic pornography."[49] The rape is both "ob-scene" and obscene. For her definition of "obscene," Aebischer borrows Lynda Nead's distinction between art and obscenity: "Art is being defined in terms of the containing of form within limits; obscenity, on the other hand, is defined in terms of excess, as form beyond limit, beyond the frame of representation."[50] Lavinia's rape is something that the early moderns would have considered obscene. Consequently, it occurred ob-scene.

Of course, Lavinia's rape is not exactly unspeakable in the play (Marcus will not shut up about it when he first discovers his niece), but it is the males in the play who speak rape and the female who must suffer in silence. The complex variation in that speech – from excitement to revulsion to mourning to revenge – demonstrates the contradictory and polyvalent attitudes of patriarchal culture toward such an act. By looking carefully at what may be said (and not said) and at what may be seen (and not seen) on stage, we may discover what was considered "beyond the frame of representation" for early modern England, and what was unspeakable and obscene for Shakespeare, especially in terms of the reification and regulation of gender norms.[51] For some, the play's violent expressions of gender may be tracked back to the treatment of the subject in the *Metamorphoses*. Cora Fox regards Ovid's mutable bodies as tied to immutable physical and political realities: "Ovidianism asserts the instability of all bodies . . . but insists that gender is linked in specific and politicized ways to biological sex."[52] This could be true, but I wonder about

Tiresias, who turns from a man to woman and back, or Caenis, who chooses to transform from a woman to a man, or the myriad characters in the *Metamorphoses* who subvert traditional gender roles and expectations.[53] In any case, I see the bodily changes in Ovid and Shakespeare as fundamentally different in their sources and causes. Whereas the sometimes capricious gods enact transformations in Ovid, only the sometimes vicious humans metamorphose bodies in Shakespeare.

Where the stories of Philomela and Lavinia intersect most is not in their transformations, but in their vengeful and sacrilegious reactions to the respective rapes. Like Lycaon, whose attempt to feed his son Nyctimus to Jupiter is alluded to toward the beginning of the *Metamorphoses*, Philomela and her sister perpetrate an act of shameful blasphemy when they kill Itys and feed him to his father; it is for this impious deed that they are turned into birds that bear the "marks of murder" and the "stamp of blood."[54] In this moment of impiety, the sisters perform an atrocity – an unspeakable spoken – of their own. If we return to Tereus's "*fassusque nefas*," then this ironic affiliation becomes even clearer, for the phrase signifies more than just "unspeakable": the *nefas* element of the word indicates a sin or a wrongness in Latin, but it also implies a violation of divine law through an impious act.

In *Titus Andronicus*, Titus and his daughter become just as impious as the Goths when they make a "feast" out of Chiron and Demetrius and then invite Tamora to the "banquet," where they arrange for her to "surfeit on" the flesh of her own children (V, ii, 191–2). The particulars of that purportedly Christian piety may seem different from the pagan devotion of Ovid's world, but the effect is the same. And despite Taylor's contention that Golding's "puritanical Calvinist" translation of Ovid represents an "unusually harsh version" of the "Christian tradition which had long superimposed its own values on the *Metamorphoses*,"[55] the characters in the play, drawn from both Golding's and Ovid's *hypotexts*, do not behave in an especially Christian manner. Not only do they claim vengeance as theirs instead of the Lord's, but they also begin the play with an overtly pagan, ritualized killing when Lucius demands an offering for the sake of his brothers' shades (I, i, 96–101). Tamora begs Titus to spare her son's life and emulate the compassionate "nature of the gods" by "being merciful," but Titus refuses, explaining that Alarbus must be sacrificed in order to appease the "groaning shadows" of the dead (I, i, 117–26). Heather James calls the ensuing ceremonial offering "a dubious act of piety,"[56] and Tamora herself refers to the Andronici's oblation as "cruel irreligious piety" (I, i, 130). Moreover, because of the strong etymological connection between pity and piety, the play seems to suggest that the various characters should all be read as impious because they consistently act without pity. When Lavinia is about to be raped, for instance, she pleads with Chiron and Demetrius to be "something pitiful" (II, iii, 156) toward her and begs Chiron to entreat his mother to "show a woman's pity" (II, iii, 147), but Tamora declares herself "pitiless" (II, iii, 162), specifically in response to Titus's own refusal to save her first-born son. Later, Lucius says of Tamora, "Her life was beastly, and devoid of pity, / And being dead, let birds on her take pity" (V, iii, 198–9). These are the final lines of the play, recalling the transformation into birds that concludes Ovid's tale and returning thematically to the consequences of revenge.

Modern audiences, familiar with the trope of revenge from countless blockbuster action films, may miss the pseudo-Christian ideology underlying Shakespeare's play. When viewed through the lens of the *Metamorphoses*, however, the principle becomes more obvious, even if the edict to avoid revenge is never stated. Revenge is damaging, a kind of inevitable "suicide" created through "'infinite' chains" of retribution, as R. L. Kesler suggests,[57] but the real damage is to the character of the person enacting the revenge. In Ovid, although Philomela and Procne are allowed "some measure of positive activity," Alison Sharrock calls attention to the fact that "in the process of taking action and communication into their own hands, they turn into monsters, like their enemy."[58] This transformation is perhaps the most painful part of the story. Some thoughts should not be spoken and the inability to self-silence "revenge" metamorphoses the sisters even before they change into birds. As sacrilegious killers, they become like Tereus, whom they despise, until they themselves become a danger to civilized society. Barkan observes that "all three characters have gone beyond the extremes of human experience; they have reached the endpoint of transformations, where all the distinctions that protect society, identity, and life itself have been destroyed."[59]

When Shakespeare appropriates the myth of Philomela for *Titus Andronicus*, he retains the destructive trajectory of this Ovidian trio, who, as Lugo explains, "have crossed the line and lost touch with civilization, [so] they must be transformed and contained away from spreading their savagery to others."[60] But unlike Ovid, Shakespeare ends on a hopeful note, with Marcus potentially teaching the "sad-faced men, people and sons of Rome" how to heal the state and "knit again / This scattered corn into one mutual sheaf, / These broken limbs again into one body" (V, iii, 66–71). Once again, this language parallels the tale of Philomela, with the reknitting of Roman history presented as an analogue to Philomela's cunning reweaving of her own "tragic tale" ["*carmen miserabile*" (VI, 582)]; in Ovid, there is a backwards echo here in the Latin, inverting the earlier "*fassusque nefas*," as the weaver herself is confused over "right and wrong" ["*fasque nefasque*" (VI, 585)] while plotting her revenge on Tereus.[61]

But I am much more interested in the choice of "*carmen*," the word Ovid uses for Philomela's tale itself. In Latin, the word *carmen* can be a "poem," or a "song," or an "oath," or an "incantation," or a "ritual," or a "prayer," or a "prophecy," or an "epitaph." All of these appear in both Ovid and Shakespeare and are relevant to the narratives of both the poem and the play. But *carmen* might also name the process of adaptation itself, with new poetic artifacts crafted from the material of old texts. In a way, Shakespeare weaves his own new *carmen* in the adaptation of Ovid: he takes the dismembered stories of *Metamorphoses* and reknits them into the tapestry of *Titus Andronicus*. The resulting re-membered play is poetry and prayer and epitaph and, most of all, a little bit of magic.

Notes

1. See especially Douglas Lanier's "Shakespearean Rhizomatics," Maurizio Calbi's *Spectral Shakespeares*, Daniel Fischlin's collection *Outerspeares*, and my collection *Shakespeare / Not Shakespeare*, with Christy Desmet and Natalie Loper.
2. Ovid, *Metamorphoses* (Melville), p. 55. All references to Ovid's *Metamorphoses* in English are from A. D. Melville's Oxford translation, with citations indicating the page number; Latin quotations are from the Loeb Classical Library *Metamorphoses*, with citations providing book and line numbers.
3. Ovid, *Metamorphoses* (Melville), p. 58.
4. Ibid. pp. 137–8.
5. All quotations of Shakespeare are from *The Norton Shakespeare*, edited by Greenblatt et al.
6. Bate, *Shakespeare and Ovid*, p. 13.
7. Gérard Genette defines *hypertextuality* as "any relationship uniting a text B (which I shall call the *hypertext*) to an earlier text A (I shall, of course, call it the *hypotext*), upon which it is grafted in a manner that is not that of commentary" (Genette, *Palimpsests*, p. 5).
8. Jameson, "Postmodernism and Consumer Society," p. 114.
9. Ibid. p. 116.
10. Bate, *Shakespeare and Ovid*, pp. 9–10.
11. Weber, "'Worse than Philomel,'" p. 710.

12. Ovid, *Metamorphoses* (Melville), p. 55.
13. Post-Ovidian authors generally do associate Philomela with the nightingale; for more on this rich allusive history, please see Starks-Estes's Coda to her *Violence, Trauma, and* Virtus, especially pp. 160–71.
14. Weber, "'Worse than Philomel,'" p. 711.
15. Ovid, *Metamorphoses* (Melville), p. 138.
16. Hutcheon, *A Theory of Adaptation*, p. 6; Hutcheon co-opts the term for adaptation theory, but Alexander's wonderfully evocative word first appears in Elizabeth Deeds Ermarth's application to the "Discursive Conditions" of individual identity (Ermarth, *Discursive Condition*, p. 56).
17. Hutcheon, *A Theory of Adaptation*, pp. 8–9.
18. Ibid. p. xv.
19. For more on Bannon's screenplay and his interest in *Titus Andronicus*, please see Weiner's "Titus in Space."
20. "The Fable of Philomela" first appeared as part of George Gascoigne's *The Steele Glas*, printed by Henrie Binneman for Richard Smith in 1576. The ballad "Cupids tragedy: eibng [*sic*] Corydon's courtship; or, Philomels exaltation" (ESTC: R227082) was published by P. Brooksby sometime between 1672 and 1696 and borrows the character's name for a contemporary affair, but it is possible that a ballad now lost recounted the classical Philomela's violation and transformation; the earlier ballad, "An excellent new Medly" (ESTC: R214082), probably published through Thomas Symcocke between 1619 and 1629, refers to Philomel only as the nightingale.
21. Taylor, "Introduction," pp. 2, 4.
22. Burt, "Shakespeare, 'Glo-cali-zation,'" p. 17.
23. Lanier, "Shakespearean Rhizomatics," p. 30.
24. Ibid. p. 31.
25. See especially Casey, "HypeRomeo & Juliet," p. 60, and "'I the matter will reword,'" pp. 74–5.
26. Deleuze and Guattari, *A Thousand Plateaus*, pp. 7, 10.
27. Lanier, "Shakespearean Rhizomatics," pp. 27–8.
28. Casey, "'I the matter will reword,'" p. 75; see also Casey, "HypeRomeo & Juliet," pp. 61–2.
29. Baudrillard, "Simulacra and Simulations," p. 173.
30. Eco, *Travels in HyperReality*, p. 35.
31. Calbi, *Spectral Shakespeares*, p. 2.
32. Cowart, *Literary Symbiosis*, p. 1.
33. Lugo, "Blood, Barbarism," pp. 401–2.
34. Starks-Estes, *Violence, Trauma, and* Virtus, p. 83.
35. Ovid, *Metamorphoses* (Melville), p. 56.
36. Taylor, "Animals in 'manly shape,'" p. 68.
37. Maslen, "Myths Exploited," p. 16.
38. Bate, *Shakespeare and Ovid*, pp. 107–8.
39. Barkan, *The Gods Made Flesh*, p. 244.
40. Ovid, *Metamorphoses* (Melville), p. 280.

41. Ibid. p. 135.
42. Ibid. p. 141.
43. Garber, *Shakespeare after All*, p. 79.
44. Ovid, *Metamorphoses* (Melville), p. 137.
45. Brown, "Philomela," p. 196.
46. Enterline, *The Rhetoric of the Body*, p. 3.
47. Marder, "Disarticulated Voices," p. 158.
48. Starks-Estes, *Violence, Trauma, and* Virtus, p. 2.
49. Aebischer, *Shakespeare's Violated Bodies*, p. 29; Cynthia Marshall also describes the portrayal of Lavinia here as "pornographic," with her wounded body rendered as "all vagina" (Marshall, *The Shattering of the Self*, p. 134); and Lisa S. Starks-Estes discusses the implications of the boy actor playing Lavina on the early modern stage (Starks-Estes, "Transforming Ovid," pp. 62–5).
50. Nead, *The Female Nude*, p. 20
51. Most of the recent critical exploration of gendered bodies in *Titus Andronicus* has focused on the violation of the female body in Lavinia; for a representative sample, please see (in addition to those essays discussed here), Green, "Interpreting 'Her martyr'd signs'" (1989); Marshall, "'I can interpret all her martyr'd signs'" (1991); Wynne-Davies, "'The Swallowing Womb'" (1995); Cunningham, "'Scars Can Witness'" (1995); Harris, "Sexuality as a Signifier for Power Relations" (1996); Eaton, "A Woman of Letters" (1996); Detmer-Goebel, "The Need for Lavinia's Voice" (2001); Sale, "Representing Lavinia" (2003); Romeo, "Engendering Silence" (2004); Solga, "Rape's Metatheatrical Return" (2006); Ritscher, *The Semiotics of Rape* (2009); Packard, "Lavinia as Coauthor" (2010); Lamb, "Physical Trauma" (2010); Bladen, "Pruning the Tree of Virtue" (2010); Lawrence, "Listening to Lavinia" (2010); King, "The Female Muselmann" (2012); Tronicke, "The Pain of Others" (2015); Billing, "'Though this be method'" (2016); Watkins, *After Lavinia* (2017); Routh, "'Enforced, Stained, and Deflowered'" (2017); Brockman, "Trauma and Abandoned Testimony" (2017). My essay on the violated male bodies in the play is one of the few examinations of masculine death and dismemberment; for more, please see Casey, "Hew His Limbs" (2012).
52. Fox, *Ovid and the Politics*, p. 9.
53. Ovid, *Metamorphoses* (Melville), pp. 60–1, 280.
54. Ibid. pp. 6, 141, 142.
55. Taylor, "Animals in 'manly shape,'" p. 71.
56. James, *Shakespeare's Troy*, p. 52.
57. Kesler, "Time and Causality," pp. 482–3.
58. Sharrock, "Gender and Sexuality," p. 101.
59. Barkan, *The Gods Made Flesh*, p. 63.
60. Lugo, "Blood, Barbarism," p. 404.
61. Ovid, *Metamorphoses* (Melville), p. 139.

Bibliography

Aebischer, Pascale, *Shakespeare's Violated Bodies: Stage and Screen Performance* (Cambridge: Cambridge University Press, 2004).

Barkan, Leonard, *The Gods Made Flesh: Metamorphosis and the Pursuit of Paganism* (New Haven: Yale University Press, 1986).

Bate, Jonathan, *Shakespeare and Ovid* (Oxford: Oxford University Press, 2001).

Baudrillard, Jean, "Simulacra and Simulations," in Mark Poster (ed.), *Jean Baudrillard: Selected Writings* (Stanford: Stanford University Press, 1988), pp. 166–84.

Billing, Christian M., "'Though this be method, yet there is madness in't': Cutting Ovid's Tongue in Recent Stage and Film Performances of *Titus Andronicus*," *Shakespeare Survey* 69, 2016, pp. 58–78.

Bladen, Victoria, "Pruning the Tree of Virtue in Shakespeare's *Titus Andronicus*," in Brett D. Hirsch and Christopher Wortham (eds), *"This earthly stage": World and Stage in Late Medieval and Early Modern England* (Turnhout, Belgium: Brepols, 2010), pp. 39–61.

Brockman, Sonya L., "Trauma and Abandoned Testimony in *Titus Andronicus* and *Rape of Lucrece*," *College Literature* 44.3, 2017, pp. 344–78.

Brown, Sarah Annes, "Philomela," *Translation and Literature* 13.2, 2004, pp. 194–206.

Burt, Richard, "Shakespeare, 'Glo-cali-zation,' Race, and the Small Screens of Post-Popular Culture," in Richard Burt and Lynda E. Boose (eds), *Shakespeare, the Movie II: Popularizing the Plays on Film, TV, Video, and DVD* (London: Routledge, 2003), pp. 14–36.

Calbi, Maurizio, *Spectral Shakespeares: Media Adaptations in the Twenty-First Century* (New York: Palgrave Macmillan, 2013).

Casey, Jim, "Hew His Limbs and Sacrifice His Flesh: The Destruction of the Male Body in *Titus Andronicus*," in Liberty Stanavage and Paxton Hehmeyer (eds), *Titus Out of Joint: Reading the Fragmented Titus Andronicus* (Newcastle upon Tyne: Cambridge Scholars Publishing, 2012), pp. 83–107.

Casey, Jim, "HypeRomeo & Juliet: Postmodern Adaptation and Shakespeare," in Christy Desmet, Natalie Loper, and Jim Casey (eds), *Shakespeare / Not Shakespeare* (New York: Palgrave Macmillan, 2017), pp. 59–75.

Casey, Jim, "'I the matter will reword': The Ghost of *Hamlet* in Translation," in Sonya Freeman Loftis, Allison Kellar, and Lisa Ulevich (eds), *Shakespeare's Hamlet in an Era of Textual Exhaustion* (New York: Palgrave Macmillan, 2018), pp. 73–86.

Cowart, David, *Literary Symbiosis: The Reconfigured Text in Twentieth-Century Writing* (Athens: University of Georgia Press, 1993).

Cunningham, Karen, "'Scars Can Witness': Trials by Ordeal and Lavinia's Body in *Titus Andronicus*," in Mark Rose (ed.), *Shakespeare's Early Tragedies: A Collection of Critical Essays* (Englewood Cliffs: Prentice Hall, 1995), pp. 65–78.

Deleuze, Gilles and Félix Guattari, *A Thousand Plateaus: Capitalism and Schizophrenia*, Brian Massumi (trans.) (Minneapolis and London: University of Minnesota Press, 1987).

Desmet, Christy, Natalie Loper, and Jim Casey (eds), *Shakespeare / Not Shakespeare* (New York: Palgrave Macmillan 2017).

Detmer-Goebel, Emily, "The Need for Lavinia's Voice: *Titus Andronicus* and the Telling of Rape," *Shakespeare Studies* 29, 2001, pp. 75–92.

Eaton, Sara, "A Woman of Letters: Lavinia in *Titus Andronicus*," in Shirley Nelson Garner and Madelon Sprengnether (eds), *Shakespearean Tragedy and Gender* (Bloomington: Indiana University Press, 1996), pp. 54–74.

Eco, Umberto, *Travels in HyperReality: Essays*, William Weaver (trans.) (San Diego: Harcourt Brace Jovanovich, 1986).

Enterline, Lynn, *The Rhetoric of the Body from Ovid to Shakespeare* (Cambridge: Cambridge University Press, 2000).

Ermarth, Elizabeth Deeds, *History in the Discursive Condition: Reconsidering the Tools of Thought*, 2nd edn (New York: Routledge, 2011).

Fischlin, Daniel (ed.), *Outerspeares: Shakespeare, Intermedia, and the Limits of Adaptation* (Toronto: University of Toronto Press, 2014).

Fox, Cora, *Ovid and the Politics of Emotion in Elizabethan England* (New York: Palgrave Macmillan, 2009).

Garber, Marjorie, *Shakespeare after All* (New York: Anchor, 2004).

Genette, Gérard, *Palimpsests: Literature in the Second Degree*, Channa Newman and Claude Doubinsky (trans.) (Lincoln: University of Nebraska Press, 1997).

Green, Douglas, "Interpreting 'Her martyr'd signs': Gender and Tragedy in *Titus Andronicus*," *Shakespeare Quarterly* 40.3, 1989, pp. 317–26.

Harris, Bernice, "Sexuality as a Signifier for Power Relations: Using Lavinia, of Shakespeare's *Titus Andronicus*," *Criticism* 38.3, 1996, pp. 383–406.

Hutcheon, Linda, with Siobhan O'Flynn, *A Theory of Adaptation*, 2nd edn (New York: Routledge, 2013).

James, Heather, *Shakespeare's Troy: Drama, Politics, and the Translation of Empire* (Cambridge: Cambridge University Press, 1997).

Jameson, Fredric, "Postmodernism and Consumer Society," in Hal Foster (ed.), *Postmodern Culture* (London: Pluto, 1983), pp. 111–25.

Kesler, R. L., "Time and Causality in Renaissance Revenge Tragedy," *University of Toronto Quarterly* 59.4, 1990, pp. 474–87.

King, Emily L., "The Female Muselmann: Desire, Violence, and Spectatorship in *Titus Andronicus*," in Liberty Stanavage and Paxton Hehmeyer (eds), *Titus Out of Joint: Reading the Fragmented Titus Andronicus* (Newcastle upon Tyne: Cambridge Scholars Publishing, 2012), pp. 125–39.

Lamb, Caroline, "Physical Trauma and (Adapt)ability in *Titus Andronicus*," *Critical Survey* 22.1, 2010, pp. 41–57.

Lanier, Douglas, "Shakespearean Rhizomatics: Adaptation, Ethics, Value," in Alexa Huang and Elizabeth Rivlin (eds), *Shakespeare and the Ethics of Appropriation* (New York: Palgrave Macmillan, 2014), pp. 21–40.

Lawrence, Sean, "Listening to Lavinia: Emmanuel Levinas's Saying and Said in *Titus Andronicus*," in Holly Faith Nelson, Lynn R. Szabo, and Jens Zimmermann (eds), *Through a Glass Darkly: Suffering, the Sacred, and the Sublime in Literature and Theory* (Waterloo, ON: Wilfrid Laurier University Press, 2010), pp. 57–69.

Lugo, Jessica, "Blood, Barbarism, and Belly Laughs: Shakespeare's Titus and Ovid's Philomela," *English Studies* 88.4, 2007, pp. 401–17.

Marder, Elissa, "Disarticulated Voices: Feminism and Philomela," *Hypatia* 7.2, 1992, pp. 148–66.

Marshall, Cynthia, "'I can interpret all her martyr'd signs': *Titus Andronicus*, Feminism, and the Limits of Interpretation," in Carole Levin and Karen Robertson (eds), *Sexuality and Politics in Renaissance Drama* (Lewiston, NY: Edwin Mellen Press, 1991), pp. 193–211.

Marshall, Cynthia, *The Shattering of the Self: Violence, Subjectivity, and Early Modern Texts* (Baltimore: Johns Hopkins University Press, 2002).

Maslen, R. W., "Myths Exploited: The *Metamorphoses* of Ovid in Early Elizabethan England," in A. B. Taylor (ed.), *Shakespeare's Ovid: The Metamorphoses in the Plays and Poems* (Cambridge: Cambridge University Press, 2000), pp. 15–30.

Nead, Lynda, *The Female Nude: Art, Obscenity, and Sexuality* (London: Routledge, 1992).

Ovid, *Metamorphoses*, Loeb Classical Library, 2 vols (Cambridge, MA: Harvard University Press, 1936).

Ovid, *Metamorphoses*, A. D. Melville (trans.) (Oxford: Oxford University Press, 2008).

Packard, Bethany, "Lavinia as Coauthor of Shakespeare's *Titus Andronicus*," *Studies in English Literature* 50.2, 2010, pp. 281–300.

Ritscher, Lee A., *The Semiotics of Rape in Renaissance English Literature* (New York: Peter Lang, 2009).

Romeo, Caterina, "Engendering Silence, Articulating Alternative Languages: Lavinia in *Titus Andronicus*, Philomela in *The Metamorphoses*, and Marianna in *La Lunga Vita di Marianna Urcrìa*," *Exit* 9.6, 2004, pp. 83–98.

Routh, Danielle, "'Enforced, Stained, and Deflowered': Considering the Reactions of Tamora and Lavinia to the Patriarchal System in *Titus Andronicus*," *Sigma Tau Delta Review* 14, 2017, pp. 99–106.

Sale, Carolyn, "Representing Lavinia: The (In)Significance of Women's Consent in Legal Discourses of Rape and Ravishment and Shakespeare's *Titus Andronicus*," in Linda Woodbridge and Sharon Beehler (eds), *Women, Violence, and English Renaissance Literature: Essays Honoring Paul Jorgensen* (Tempe: Arizona Center for Medieval and Renaissance Studies, 2003), pp. 1–27.

Shakespeare, William, *The Norton Shakespeare, Based on the Oxford Edition*, 1st edn, Stephen Greenblatt, Walter Cohen, Jean E. Howard, and Katharine Eisaman (eds), (New York: W. W. Norton, 1997).

Sharrock, Alison, "Gender and Sexuality," in Philip Hardie (ed.), *The Cambridge Companion to Ovid* (Cambridge: Cambridge University Press, 2002), pp. 95–107.

Solga, Kim, "Rape's Metatheatrical Return: Rehearsing Sexual Violence among the Early Moderns," *Theatre Journal* 58.1, 2006, pp. 53–72.

Starks-Estes, Lisa S. "Transforming Ovid: Images of Violence, Vulnerability, and Sexuality in Shakespeare's Titus Andronicus," in Deborah Uman and Sara Morrison (eds), *Staging the Blazon in Early Modern English Theater* (Farnham and Burlington: Ashgate, 2013), pp. 53–66.

Starks-Estes, Lisa S., *Violence, Trauma, and* Virtus *in Shakespeare's Roman Poems and Plays: Transforming Ovid* (Basingstoke: Palgrave Macmillan, 2014).

Taylor, A. B., "Animals in 'manly shape as too the outward showe': Moralizing and Metamorphosis in *Titus Andronicus*," in A. B. Taylor (ed.), *Shakespeare's Ovid: The Metamorphoses in the Plays and Poems* (Cambridge: Cambridge University Press, 2000), pp. 66–79.

Taylor, A. B., "Introduction," in A. B. Taylor (ed.), *Shakespeare's Ovid: The Metamorphoses in the Plays and Poems* (Cambridge: Cambridge University Press, 2000), pp. 1–12.

Tronicke, Marlena, "The Pain of Others: Silencing Lavinia in *Titus Andronicus*," *Shakespeare Seminar* 13, 2015, pp. 39–49.

Watkins, John, *After Lavinia: A Literary History of Premodern Marriage Diplomacy* (Ithaca: Cornell University Press, 2017).

Weber, William W., "'Worse than Philomel': Violence, Revenge, and Meta-Allusion in *Titus Andronicus*," *Studies in Philology* 112.4, 2015, pp. 698–717.

Weiner, Rex, "Titus in Space," *The Paris Review*, 29 November 2016, <https://www.theparisreview.org/blog/2016/11/29/titus-in-space/> (last accessed 10 August 2018).

Wynne-Davies, Marion, "'The Swallowing Womb': Consumed and Consuming Women in *Titus Andronicus*," in Valerie Wayne (ed.), *The Matter of Difference: Materialist Feminist Criticism of Shakespeare* (Ithaca: Cornell University Press, 1991), pp. 129–51.

Index